Population Management for Survival and Recovery

METHODS AND CASES IN CONSERVATION SCIENCE

MARY C. PEARL, EDITOR

Population Management for Survival and Recovery

Analytical Methods and Strategies in Small Population Conservation

J. D. Ballou
M. Gilpin and
T. J. Foose, editors

COLUMBIA UNIVERSITY PRESS   NEW YORK

Columbia University Press
New York   Chichester, West Sussex
Copyright © 1995 Smithsonian Institution
All rights reserved

Library of Congress Cataloging-in-Publication Data

Population management for survival and recovery / J. D. Ballou, M.
   Gilpin, and T. J. Foose, editors.
       p.   cm. — (Methods and cases in conservation science)
       Includes bibliographical references and index.
       ISBN 0–231–10176–7 (cloth : acid-free paper) : $65.00. — ISBN
   0–231–10177–5 (paper : acid-free paper) : $29.50
       1. Wildlife conservation—Methodology.   2. Population biology.
   I. Ballou, J. D. (Jonathan D.)   II. Gilpin, Michael E., 1943–   .
   III. Foose, Thomas J., 1945–   .   IV. Series.
   QL82.P67   1994
   639.9'3—dc20   94–25126
                                                                        CIP

⊗
Casebound editions of Columbia University Press books are printed on
permanent and durable acid-free paper.

Printed in the United States of America

c 10 9 8 7 6 5 4 3 2 1
p 10 9 8 7 6 5 4 3 2 1

Contents

PART TWO: GENETIC ANALYSES

PART THREE: MOLECULAR GENETICS

PART FOUR: CONSERVATION STRATEGIES

Contributors

STEVAN J. ARNOLD
Department of Ecology and Evolution
University of Chicago

JOHN C. AVISE
Department of Genetics
University of Georgia

JONATHAN D. BALLOU
Department of Zoological Research
National Zoological Park
Smithsonian Institution

JAY BARLOW
Southwest Fisheries Center
La Jolla Laboratory
National Marine Fisheries Service

WILLIAM CONWAY
New York Zoological Society

LEOBERT DE BOER
National Foundation for Zoological Research
Dutch Federation of Zoos

BENNETT DYKE
Genetics Department
Southwest Foundation for Biomedical Research

TORBJORN EBENHARD
Department of Zoology
Uppsala University
Uppsala, Sweden

THOMAS FOOSE
The Wilds

TIM GAGE
Department of Anthropology
State University of New York at Albany

CHARLES J. GEYER
School of Statistics
University of Minnesota

MICHAEL GILPIN
Department of Biology
University of California - San Diego

SUSAN HAIG
South Carolina Cooperative Wildlife Research Unit
Department of Aquaculture, Fisheries & Wildlife
Clemson University

KJETIL HINDAR
Norwegian Institute for Nature Research

ROBERT C. LACY
Department of Conservation Biology
Chicago Zoological Park

RUSSELL LANDE
Department of Biology
University of Oregon

MICHAEL LYNCH
Department of Biology
University of Oregon

PAUL MAMELKA
Genetics Department
Southwest Foundation for Biomedical Research

HENLEY QUADLING
Department of Computational and Applied Mathematics
University of the Witwatersrand

FRANK P. G. PRINCÉE
National Foundation for Zoological Research
Dutch Federation of Zoos

HENRY A. ROWLEY
Department of Ecology, Evolution, and Behavior
University of Minnesota

OLIVER A. RYDER
Research Department
San Diego Zoo

NILS RYMAN
Division of Genetics
University of Stockholm

ULYSSES S. SEAL
Captive Breeding Specialist Group

ANTHONY STARFIELD
Department of Ecology, Evolution, and Behavior
University of Minnesota

BARBARA TAYLOR
Southwest Fisheries Center
La Jolla Laboratory
National Marine Fisheries Service

ALUN THOMAS
School of Mathematical Sciences
Bath University

ELIZABETH A. THOMPSON
Department of Statistics
University of Washington

FRED UTTER
School of Fisheries
University of Washington

FOREWORD
Altered States: Population Viability Analysis, Planning, and Caring for Wildlife in Parks

:::

William Conway

The more swashbuckling ones of those who address themselves to the consequences of global climate change suggest that the next fifty years will produce temperatures in the eastern U.S. not seen since tapirs and peccaries roamed Pennsylvania and manatees browsed the grassy littoral of New Jersey shores and that conservation west of Washington is a waste of time. Nevertheless, I will avoid recounting the usual dreary litany of current environmental obscenities and impending extinctions and substitute one other suggestion: that we aim narrowly at finding ways to *assure* that tapirs, peccaries, and manatees will be available when their time comes to colonize the north. And I'd like to offer perhaps yet another suggestion, derived from the recent denigration of museums of art as "places where paintings and sculptures go to die": that we keep zoos and wildlife parks from earning a comparable distinction.

Of course, neither wholesale emigrations nor sneaky dispersals of large terrestrial wild creatures, north or south, are likely to happen. What is happening is an increasing loss of wild land, insularization of parks and refuges, and increasing alteration. And what is going to happen is more of the same, only faster.

Population viability analysis (PVA) can be directly translated into practical management strategies. It is the most promising generally applicable tool that conservation biology has offered conservation action so far. From its origins in recovery planning for endangered species and in the effort to secure the survival of small captive populations, PVA has developed to the point of being able to help guide the care of wildlife parks and remnants of wildlife. The essays in this volume focus primarily upon small captive populations in zoos, but they can have forceful implications for wildlife management in reserves.

FENCED IN

In 1987 Kenya's Nakuru National Park was fenced, and David Western and I flew down to see it. The park is small (about 184 sq.km), most of which is shallow salty Lake Nakuru, a renowned feeding place for hundreds of thousands of lesser and greater flamingos. The big mammal fauna is much reduced, and the lake is a dead end for its principal water source: a stinking stream draining runoff and sewage from the nearby town of Nakuru and its adjacent farms; its effects on the famous lake and its wildlife are yet to be seen.

From our Cessna the fences were easily seen; three meters high, electrified, and solar powered. Also visible were corrals, or bomas, for the new rhino reintroduction program and a growing herd of Rothschild's giraffes introduced some years ago. Overwhelming the lot and covering much of the lake like a vast pink blanket were more than half a million flamingos. On the ground, by truck, we spotted extraordinary numbers of warthogs, waterbuck, and impala and reviewed the park's state with resident ecologist Fred Waweru, one of Western's associates.

Recently, Western and I flew back to Nakuru. Rumors had reached us that the park's animals were multiplying excessively and beginning to have nutritional problems. The new fences prevent them from moving back and forth to historical mineral licks and from following the normal opportunities provided by changing nutritional values in annual vegetational sequences. Unharried by predators—there is only one lion and no hyenas in the park—the herbivore populations were growing apace, and, it was said, disease was beginning to affect the waterbuck and impala. Neither our short visit nor Fred Waweru's observations could confirm rumors of overgrazing or disease, but there were more animals than ever, and exploding populations seem likely. The rumors probably predict the future.

MEGAZOOS

Nakuru National Park has become a megazoo—a museum rather than a part of a larger more or less independently functioning ecosystem. From now on its animals will have to be managed ecologically, behaviorally, genetically, and demographically; they will have to be selectively culled and treated for disease. Their habitat will have to be just as carefully monitored and supervised; the health, regeneration, and distribution of its plants watched with as much care as that of its animals. The cost to Kenya of such sophisticated and responsive management will be much higher than the simple protection and benign neglect of the past—and this is only the beginning. Parks are growing smaller, and it is probable that the smaller the park and the smaller its key wildlife populations, the more intensive the necessary management and the higher the expense per unit.

At Nakuru, far-reaching decisions have been made without clearly thought-out, long-term objectives or supportive management programs. It is "early days" in megazoo management. Giraffes were introduced into Nakuru with little consideration of the nature of the wildlife community the park might one day be able to support. There is talk of hyenas now. The idea is to reintroduce species once seen there, although how resident some of these were is not always clear—and I doubt it matters. The Nakuru of today is not the Nakuru of yesterday. It is and will be in an altered state.

Planning, planning tools, responsive management, and continuity are what is important. Park-by-park masterplans and models are needed for resolving such questions as, What extant species should each protected area seek to house long-term? What should be reintroduced? What are the appropriate population sizes and compositions for ecologically high-impact species? How are these parameters to be met—and retained? PVA can play a critical role in finding the answers.

If elephants are to survive, the answers are deceptively straightforward: The number of elephants needed is at least the minimum viable population necessary to meet genetic and demographic requirements, distributed broadly enough to survive such chance events as natural disaster and disease, and within sufficient habitat to provide appropriate food, space, and water in suitable climatic and geographic zones on a sustainable basis. Those are the basics, then it gets complicated.

Where will these elephant zones be? Is the fact that there are "enough" elephants in Gabon sufficient for Kenya? Is a simple biologically calculated number an adequate replacement for the inspiring spectacle of great herds? What nations and communities will seek the honor and profits and expenses of caring for them, overseeing their protection, population control, and sustainable management? For how long?

Only continual monitoring can determine how Nakuru's megazoo species are affecting each other and their habitat, how introduced hyenas will shape the warthog and impala populations and if they are driving off the flamingos. Only a constantly updated management plan will provide for responsive supervision of these interrelationships, for the artificial dispersals needed for genetic interchange with other populations in other isolates, and for the avoidance of constantly recurring extinctions and irruptions of local populations. And such a plan can provide for interchange between and rescue by *ex situ* zoo populations secure from natural and social local catastrophes.

Major climatic change or not, refuge resources change over time, becoming less suitable for many original denizens. Indeed, I wonder if the effects of extinction in parks noted by Newmark and others may happen faster in reserves that are not only much smaller but located in tropical areas of potent change and vegetational growth. Nakuru is dependent on rains so inconstant that the lake can be expected to dry out every few years—but now only the birds will be able to move to traditional emergency habitats.

How will Kenya decide what to make of Nakuru? Will the Wildlife

Service determine that the park should sustain, for instance, its marginal population of colobus monkeys at the cost, I suspect, of expensive translocation, marking, monitoring, and vegetational manipulation? One way or the other, Nakuru will have to be cared for from now on. It is not alone.

Saiwa Park in Western Kenya is a 10 sq.km enclave of rare sitatungas surrounded by intensely cultivated farms. Lwambe Valley National Park, with its herds of roan antelope and Rothschild's giraffe, is in the same situation. Now the migratory wildebeest, kongoni, rhinos, and zebras of 140 sq.km Nairobi National Park, fenced in on three sides, are being cut off from their traditional wet season grazing ranges in the Athi Plains on the fourth side by the spread of agriculture. Even the fascinating Abedares National Park is gradually being fenced off from nearby farm lands.

These fences are being installed not to protect the animals but to keep them from depredating the crops. Cotton fields now border one side of Tanzania's great Serengeti, wheat lands confine the Mara, and the mountain gorilla's stronghold in the Virungas is encircled by some of the most intensely cultivated farms in the world. In Venezuela, cracids, primates, and tinamous are besieged in Henri Pittier and San Esteban National Parks, jaguars and cracids in the 25,000 ha Yacambu, and the 40,000 ha Terepama. Elephants, gaur, three species of deer, and two of gibbons are surrounded in Thailand's 200,000 ha Khao Yai National Park. Whatever the spaces, the numbers of most large species within them are small in terms of the intrinsic requirements of genetics and demography and more vulnerable still in the extrinsic ones of ecology. Yet, the concepts discussed in this volume are not even on the agendas of most of those charged with refuge management and preservation in the developing world, where the wildlife is.

COLONIAL SPECIES

In December 1988, while visiting Wildlife Conservation International (WCI) projects in Latin America's "Southern Cone," I examined the status of the rare Andean and James flamingos at several nesting sites in the Chilean altiplano following similar explorations in Argentina in previous years. In Chile many former nesting areas are abandoned, and we do not always know why. In Argentina flocks of the more common South American flamingo can still be seen throughout the country, but of eight colonies known a few years ago, only two seem active now. I also evaluated WCI-Chilean attempts to understand and protect one of the pitiful remnants of the great Humboldt penguin colonies that dotted South America's Pacific seaboard from Peru to Tierra del Fuego twenty-five years ago.

Thus far, PVAs have mostly focused on mom-and-pop (noncolonial) species. The problems of the "huddled masses" of colonial birds and herd mammals, individually numerous but extraordinarily vulnerable at their reproductive sites, are different. I am not at all convinced that it is more difficult to preserve the great megavertebrates *in situ* than the modest-sized colonial species. For the most part, we do not know the lower limits of successful colony size, the necessary interchange within the metapopulations, nor the minimum numbers of colonies. With these creatures, colony viability and species viability are interdependent. Once focused, PVA is bound to contribute new insights to the task of dealing with such species as penguins and cormorants, terns, seals and sea lions, geladas, flamingos, and such spectacular phenomena as the migrations of wildebeest and kob and those of caribou, saiga, and shorebirds. Their study will enlarge the framework of PVA.

Flamingos, penguins, and many seabirds are big, long-lived creatures and can afford to miss a breeding season or two. Besides, they usually nest in such inhospitable places, so far out of people's way, that they ought not to be in trouble. But they are. It turns out that the vast colonies of seabirds along Chile's coast I visited in 1960 are mostly gone without a trace. For great colonial birds, the prime symptom of trouble is not the number of individuals but the number of those superbirds we call colonies.

NEEDED: TOOLS AND TESTS

Tomorrow's conservation biologist/reserve manager will come equipped with a fully calibrated Multiprobe Leopoldian Sampler. Inserting it carefully under Nakuru's tongue, or someplace, he or she will take a rich variety of measurements, such as soil chemistry, species-by-species vegetational breakdowns by cover and condition, animal species by demographic status and heterozygosity, inter- and intraspecies ethograms, and then download this information, along with that of the Infallible Weatherometer, to a Conservation Biology Viabilaputer—and read out the resulting management actions necessary to maintain the approved park model.

Pending the perfection of the Viabilaputer, wildlife managers need new and practical tools, and, alas, the big biological questions, the least flexible parameters of *in situ* conservation, will be those of ecology not genetics. Nor is building SST (Super Sonic Transport) capacity to run on tricycle capability much help. But PVA has already been effective in focusing action on otherwise too-little-too-late situations: those of the Florida panther, the red wolf, the black-footed ferret, the Puerto Rican parrot—not one with a contiguous natural population of even fifty individuals. It is surely time to apply the principles of PVA beyond zoos and crises to parks and refuges, to populations of wildlife where intervention can make a larger difference—and where wildlife is not so well off as its protectors have led themselves to believe.

PVA profits from an underlying political understandability of its concepts that is not common in science. And this, especially, can win fast acceptance and inspire involvement in advancing collaborative management of wildlife across national boundaries between zoos and reserves, *ex situ* and *in situ*. But what we do with it and the other conservation biology tools we develop will depend upon what "conservation" we *think* we want.

What is it that we want? Much of what conservation biology must do is confused by notions of animal "wildness," and "freedom," and even by the belief of a few that when a species' historical home is altered, that species is no longer worthy of interest. Are not some creatures so marvelous and so important to our concept of Earth that they should be preserved even when all traces of their evolutionary homes are gone? If not, what are we doing here? After all, tomorrow's wildlife can only be maintained in an altered state.

Introduction

■■

As William Conway so eloquently states in the foreword, populations of conservation interest will increasingly need to be monitored and managed to ensure their long-term survival. This is obviously the case for populations of endangered or threatened species kept in zoos or more naturalistic nature parks, and it has long been recognized that both the daily and long-term (evolutionary) needs of these species require management intervention. The need for management of small, wild populations has not been acknowledged as readily. But this is likely to change as more "wild" populations approach a status similar to that, say, of the black rhinoceros (*Diceros bicornis*), mountain gorilla (*Gorilla gorilla berengei*), Florida panther (*Felis concolor coryi*), or Puerto Rican parrot (*Amazona villata*), where every individual (and its pedigree) is known and day-to-day survival requires constant monitoring (e.g., game wardens with rifles) for protection against poachers, diseases, etc. The same is likely to be true for reintroduced populations, such as the Arabian oryx (*Oryx leucoryx*), golden lion tamarin (*Leontopithecus rosalia*), black-footed ferret (*Mustela nigripes*) and red wolf (*Canis rufus*), all of which are managed at the individual level. The management demands of these "wild" populations will in many ways not be fundamentally different from those of captive populations.

This volume is evidence of the converging disciplines of wildlife management and captive management (zoo biology), placed in the context of the developing field of population (and habitat) viability analysis (PVA). The basic premise of PVA, and of this volume, is that species conservation management strategies are best developed through a process of scientific analyses of population trends. This is as true for wild as it is for captive populations. Within this framework, this volume is intended to advance the science of genetic and demographic management of small populations, both in zoos and the wild, by presenting a series of essays addressing in detail specific issues fundamental to this field. The essays combine development of theoretical topics with basic and practical analysis techniques for scientific management of populations. The reader will notice a theme common to many of these papers: the data available for the kinds of analyses required is often extremely limited. Management decisions and analyses, however, need to proceed in spite of missing or poor data. Thus, the methods presented aim to simplify analyses and management, apply to analysis of small data sets, or deal with problems associated with missing data.

Management for survival and recovery of both captive and wild populations requires three processes: defining management objectives and concerns, monitoring and analyzing population trends, and formulating and implementing management actions. This volume addresses all three processes, focusing primarily, but not exclusively, on methods for demographic and genetic analyses and management. The volume is divided into four sections, reflecting the areas of analysis emphasized by the contributions. This should not be interpreted as an attempt to separate issues in conservation conceptually, e.g., genetic versus demographic issues. In fact, it should be clear from these contributions that issues of genetics, demographics, and conservation goals are inseparable, and analytical methods in one area often rely on data from another.

The first section of the volume deals with a problem confronting those needing to analyze the demographic characteristics of populations based on small or incomplete data sets. Traditional methods for estimating population growth rates (r or λ for discrete processes) are based on stable population theory. Unless fertility and mortality estimates are measured accurately, however, error is incorporated into estimates of r and generation length (T). Gage (first essay) presents an indirect method of computing r and T based on nonstable population theory, which does not require prior estimation of mortality rates. Taylor and Barlow (essay 2) also address the issue of incomplete demographic data, but they examine the case where estimates of mortality rates are desirable. They present the step-wise Siler method (a type of bathtub function, named after its shape) for estimating mortality rates in these situations. This method uses a predefined standard mortality model (perhaps based on extensive data from another species) as a basis for developing a specific model for the species and data observed. The efficacy of this approach when used on partial or small data sets is tested using subsampled data from the captive population of Przewalski's horse (*Equus przewalskii*). Taylor et al. (essay 3) then compare the step-wise Siler method to various other methods currently being used by population managers to estimate mortality rates in mammalian populations. The methods illustrated in these papers can be applied to both captive and wild populations.

The second section deals with genetic management and concentrates on pedigree analyses and pedigree management techniques. Here, because of the nature of the data, the focus is more naturally on (but not limited to) management of captive populations. Lacy et al. (essay 4) provide a review of the strategies and analytical tools for genetic management. The most common goal of genetic management of captive populations is to maintain genetic diversity (expected heterozygosity and number of alleles) under selective neutrality. Lacy et al. contend that this is best achieved by using pedigree analysis as a management tool. This depends on: (1) the intended intensity of management, (2) the completeness of genealogical knowledge of all individuals in the population, and (3) knowledge of the species' population biology. Pedigree analysis methods and management vary with each of these three factors. For example, when knowledge of the pedigree is complete and intensive management is feasible, precise pairings can be recommended to achieve genetic objectives. Ballou and Lacy (essay 5) present and evaluate through computer simulation several methods that use pedigree analysis techniques to identify genetically important individuals for breeding priority (even when some pedigree data may be lacking). The concept of genetic importance is expanded in Thompson's article (essay

6) to include groups of individuals that are at risk of not contributing genes to future generations. She also argues that strategies to conserve genomes should take into consideration gene linkage rather than only single, independent, Mendelian loci.

These techniques require, for the most part, intensive genetic management based on analyzing pedigree data and achieved through manipulating individual breedings. Intensive management, however, may not be appropriate, necessary, or even possible for some captive populations (i.e., herds of nonendangered species) and most wild populations. Princée (essay 7) shows that some level of genetic management can still be accomplished by managing natural social groups (herds), in which animals are not individually identified, if levels of migration between herds are carefully regulated. Computer simulations are used to evaluate the effect of this low-intensity management on the maintenance of genetic diversity.

Taking genetic management one step further, Starfield et al. (essay 8) show that genetic management and pedigree analysis need not apply to captive populations alone. The authors describe a stochastic model that simulates the social and territorial behavior of a wild lion (*Panthera leo*) population in a fenced park and tracks gene flow through the pedigrees created by these simulations. This article stresses the concept of risk and evaluates the effect of different management strategies and social behavior on gene flow and population extinction.

The application of molecular genetics to population analysis and management is the subject of the third section. Avise et al. (essay 9) present an extensive review of the application of molecular genetic studies to conservation problems. The first part of the essay reviews molecular and cytological techniques while the second part shows how they can be applied to population management issues. This is followed by two essays providing examples of the integration of pedigree analysis methods with molecular data methods to address specific conservation issues. Geyer and Thompson (essay 10) describe the approach they used to infer relationships among founders of the California condor (*Gymnogyps californianus*) captive population using DNA fingerprinting data. They applied a maximum-likelihood approach to analyzing similarity of band patterns while adjusting for the differing population frequencies of bands and the different number of bands expected in differentially inbred individuals. Thomas (essay 11) considers the opposite situation and reviews a method for inferring genotype from pedigree information. He shows that a simulation technique commonly used in the field of image processing, called the Gibbs Sampler, can be applied to the problem of estimating missing genomic data in pedigrees. The method is demonstrated on a partially incomplete set of genotypic information for nine diallelic allozyme markers for a recent subset of the Przewalski's horse pedigree.

The last section of this volume addresses issues of integrating captive breeding conservation strategies with conservation of wild (or reintroduced) populations. Foose et al. (essay 12) discuss the role of population and habitat viability analyses (PHVA) as a tool for defining and developing conservation objectives for single-species conservation programs. In this article the authors define the role of captive breeding programs within the context of more comprehensive species and habitat conservation programs. Arnold (essay 13) discusses another important concern relating to the goals of captive breeding programs: maintenance of genetic variation, in particular, quantitative genetic variation. His paper outlines methods and strategies for assessing levels of quantitative genetic variation in captive populations in order to determine whether the population could respond to selection if and when returned to nature and to determine whether genetic variation should be supplemented by importation of additional wild animals.

Clearly, the level and type of genetic diversity to be maintained is an important consideration in developing captive breeding objectives. Currently, captive breeding programs base population size objectives on the number of individuals needed to maintain a specified level of selectively neutral genetic variation (e.g., 90% of original) for some specified amount of time (e.g., 100 years). Lande (essay 14) observes that this approach ignores the potentially significant contributions of mutation, immigration, and selection to levels of quantitative genetic variation. His paper discusses the effect of these factors on levels of quantitative variation in populations and their impact on the population sizes necessary to maintain desired levels of variation. The last essay, by Ryman et al. (essay 15), addresses the important issue of genetic introgression between captive and wild gene pools, using data from releases of salmon bred in captivity into the natural environment. Concerns about the effects of captivity on the fitness of released individuals and the effects of gene flow from the released animals to wild populations are discussed.

Much of the material presented in this volume has been developed within the context of applications for captive management. However, to reiterate the statement in the foreword, the management of small populations, wild or captive, shares common goals, problems, and analytical methods. While it is not the intent of this volume to provide a broad overview of the field of management of small populations, it is hoped that the material will introduce the reader to the diverse disciplines and analytical methods required to formulate conservation strategies and that it will also serve as a stimulus to encourage further development in this field.

The papers presented in this volume are the result of a workshop entitled "Analytical Methods for Population Viability Analyses" held in Front Royal, Virginia, in October of 1989. The papers were written following the workshop and are based on perceived areas of concern and need identified during the workshop. The workshop was hosted by the Smithsonian Institution's National Zoological Park and sponsored by the National Zoological Park; the American Association of Zoological Parks and Aquariums; the University of California, San Diego; the Institute for Museum Services; and the Chicago Zoological Society.

We wish to express our gratitude to all the contributors for their patience as well as to Laurie Bingaman and Beate Rettberg-Beck for their superb organizational assistance during the workshop. Special thanks are due to both Laurie Bingaman and Jane Mansour, who contributed their editorial skills, time, and support during the preparation of this volume.

PART ONE

Demographic Analyses

1

A Robust Estimator of the Intrinsic Rate of Increase and Generation Length

■■

Timothy B. Gage

Accurate estimates of the intrinsic rate of increase and the generation length are vital for designing the demographic and genetic management components of a species survival plan. The intrinsic rate of increase represents the long-term, sustainable growth potential a population can achieve, and in conjunction with mortality it determines the stable age-sex structure of a population. The generation length is the time required for a population to increase by the net reproductive rate, where the net reproductive rate is the number of female offspring expected to be born to a female just born. Estimates of the intrinsic rate of increase and age structure are useful for evaluating diverse management practices and predicting the future size and maintenance requirements of the population. Both the intrinsic rate of increase and the generation length are linked to the rate of accumulation of inbreeding within a population.

Inbreeding is important because it can detrimentally affect the reproductive performance of a population and hence the future growth rates
of the population. A difficulty with respect to designing species survival
plans is that neither the intrinsic rate of increase nor the generation
length are simple parameters that can be estimated accurately from data
on small, closely managed populations.

Typically, the intrinsic rate of increase is estimated from the Euler
equation:

$$\int_{x=0}^{\infty} l_x m_x e^{-rx} dx = 1 \tag{1.1}$$

where r is the intrinsic rate of increase, l_x is the proportion of a cohort
surviving to age x, and m_x is the age-specific fecundity of the population
(Coale 1972). As is conventional in biology, the term fecundity will be
used in this study to refer to achieved reproductive performance, that is,
age-specific birth rates, while fertility is defined as the capacity to reproduce, whether or not births actually occur. (Human demographers traditionally reverse these definitions.) A problem with Euler's equation is
that the net maternity function, that is, $l_x m_x$ (usually designated NMF),
requires prior estimates of both age-specific mortality and fecundity.
Any errors in estimating either of these vital rates will be reflected in the
reliability of r. Additionally, the generation length (T) is defined as
the ratio of the natural log of the net reproductive rate (R_0, which is the
integral of NMF) to the intrinsic rate of increase (Keyfitz and Fleiger
1971). In formal terms,

$$T = \frac{\ln \int_{x=0}^{\infty} l_x m_x dx}{r} \tag{1.2}$$

Any error in estimating either NMF or r will be compounded in T. An
alternative method of estimating NMF and subsequently r and T that
does not rely on prior estimation of mortality and fecundity could substantially improve the accuracy of estimates of these parameters from
small population data. A possible substitute is provided by the extension of stable population theory to nonstable conditions and the derivation from this theory of several indirect estimation procedures collec-

tively referred to as variable-r methods (Preston and Coale 1982). The variable-r method of estimating NMF is

$$NMF_x = v_x e^{\int_{a=0}^{x} r_a da} \tag{1.3}$$

where v_x is the probability density function of fecundity, that is, the shape of the age-specific fecundity curve, and the r_a are age-specific rates of increase, which can easily be estimated from an enumeration of the population at two different points in time (Preston and Coale 1982). The relative simplicity of v_x and the r_x, compared to l_x and m_x, suggests that equation (1.3) represents a more robust method of computing NMF than the traditional approach proposed by Euler (Preston and Coale 1982; Gage et al. 1984; Gage 1985). The purpose of this essay is to demonstrate how the nonstable theory can be applied to the estimation of the intrinsic rate of increase and generation length of a closely managed species, Przewalski's horse (*Equus przewalskii*). The specific aims are: (a) to examine the shape of the age-specific fecundity distribution for Przewalski's horse; (b) estimate the NMF from equation (1.3); and (c) compute the intrinsic rate of increase and generation length from the NMF using conventional demographic methods and programs.

METHODS AND MATERIALS

The demographic data for this analysis consist of two censuses enumerating the living population of Przewalski's horses by single years of age on January 1, 1975, and January 1, 1985, respectively, and the age-specific fecundity rates by single year of age estimated from longitudinal data over the same ten-year period (table 1.1). The censuses are for the female population only (figure 1.1), which corresponds with the normal demographic practice of estimating the net maternity function for the female population alone. On the other hand, fecundity rates were computed from both male and female births, under the assumption that the sex ratio at birth is independent of the mother's age. Combining the sexes tends to maximize the sample of births and hence reduce any stochastic error in the estimates of the age-specific fecundity distribution. The use of both sexes is permissible since only the probability den-

Table 1.1 The 1975 and 1985 censuses and age-specific fecundity rates (m) of the captive population of Przewalski's horse

AGE	1975	1985	m_{obs}	m_{smo}
0	18	54	0.000	0.0000
1	15	30	0.000	0.0508
2	13	28	0.118	0.1726
3	13	34	0.363	0.2754
4	8	18	0.406	0.3604
5	5	27	0.486	0.4288
6	7	26	0.434	0.4815
7	7	22	0.456	0.5198
8	6	11	0.608	0.5449
9	6	13	0.533	0.5577
10	5	12	0.627	0.5596
11	6	10	0.505	0.5516
12	5	12	0.643	0.5348
13	5	7	0.353	0.5103
14	5	6	0.474	0.4794
15	3	4	0.525	0.4432
16	3	5	0.328	0.4027
17	1	3	0.259	0.3591
18	2	3	0.295	0.3136
19	1	4	0.308	0.2672
20	1	1	0.197	0.2212
21	0	3	0.228	0.1766
22	3	2	0.324	0.1346
23	0	3	0.000	0.0963
24+	1	8		

obs = observed fecundity distribution
smo = smoothed fecundity distribution

sity function of fecundity is used in equation (1.3). The censuses and fecundity rates were computed from the Przewalski's horse studbook (Volf 1988) using the program LifeTabl (Dyke and Mamelka 1989).

The intrinsic rate of increase and the generation length are sensitive to the moments of the net maternity function (Keyfitz 1972). Consequently, the estimates of these parameters based on raw fecundity data might be adversely influenced by stochastic variation due to small sample sizes. To test this, the observed fecundity rates were smoothed by fitting a third degree polynomial originally developed for this purpose by Brass (1975). This assumes that Przewalski's horse has a fecundity schedule similar in shape to those characteristic of human populations. Brass's polynomial, modified here for use on populations with varying life spans and life histories, is

$$m_x = c(x - s)(s + w - x)^2 \qquad 1.4$$

over the range $x \geq s$ and $x \leq (s + w)$ where s is the expected age at first reproduction, w is the expected length of the fecund period, and c is a coefficient representing the overall level of fecundity. The age range is constrained to avoid biologically meaningless values of fecundity, that is, negative fecundities, which would occur if m_x were computed from equation (1.4) outside the fecund ages. Equation (1.4) is a nonlinear function and is fitted using the nonlinear regression routine MODFIT

Figure 1.1 The number of female Przewalski's horses alive on January 1, 1975 and 1985.

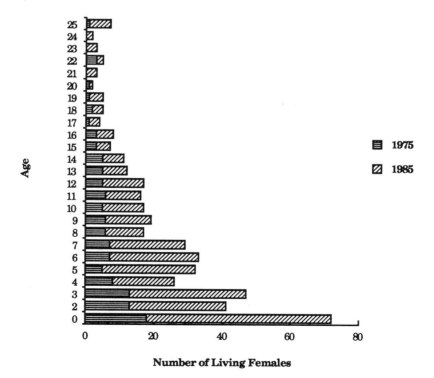

Number of Living Females

(McIntosh and McIntosh 1980) by least squares. Subsequent analyses have been conducted on both the observed $(m_{x,obs})$ and smoothed $(m_{x,smo})$ age-specific fecundity distributions (table 1.1).

The probability density function of fecundity by single years of age, v_x, is estimated from the age-specific fecundity distribution as

$$v_x = \frac{m_x}{\sum\limits_{x=0}^{\infty} m_x} \quad (1.5)$$

The age-specific rates of increase, r_x, are estimated for one-year age groups, although the method is not restrictd to one-year age groups, as

$$r_x = \frac{\ln \dfrac{n_{x,t+z}}{n_{x,t}}}{z} \quad (1.6)$$

where z is the period of time between the censuses, $n_{x,t}$ is the number of females age x alive at time t, and $n_{x,t+z}$ is the number of females age x alive at time $t + z$ (Preston 1983; Gage et al. 1984). The r_x may take positive or negative values depending upon the relative size of $n_{x,t}$ and $n_{x,t+z}$. A problem does arise, however, if either n is equal to 0.0, in which case r_x is undefined. This can be avoided by combining age categories and/or by truncating the age categories so that no zero values occur. The integral of r_x from age 0 to x in equation (1.3) is estimated simply as $r_0 + \ldots + r_{x-1}$. The NMF is then calculated from equation (1.3), and analyzed using conventional demographic programs, in this case ZEROS (Keyfitz and Fleiger 1971), modified for one-year age categories. This program was employed because it uses the Leslie matrix method of solving for the intrinsic rate of increase. It provides an estimate of λ, the dominant real root of the Leslie matrix, where $r = \ln(\lambda)$, as well as estimates of the complex roots of the matrix. The complex roots describe the periodicities and half-lives of transient waves that occur in a population's age structure if the age structure is perturbed from its stable state (Keyfitz 1972).

The analyses of the age-specific fecundity distribution uses all of the ages presented in table 1.1. The analysis of NMF, on the other hand, has been truncated at age 20, because there are few animals alive at older ages (particularly in the 1975 census when there were no animals alive at age 21), and because the observed fecundity rates above age 20 are

based on the experience of only a small number of animals and are likely
to be unreliable (table 1.1, figure 1.1).

RESULTS

The third degree polynomial appears to fit and to smooth the general
shape of the fecundity distribution reasonably well (figure 1.2). This is
particularly true at older ages where large stochastic variation in fecundity rates is apparent in the observed data as a result of the small sample
sizes. On the other hand, the predicted age of sexual maturation is
0.625 (S.D. 0.438) years, and the predicted reproductive span is 27.1
(S.D. 1.35) years, while the earliest age of observed reproduction is significantly later, at 2 years of age, and the oldest observed age of repro-

Figure 1.2 The observed and smoothed age-specific fecundity distributions of Przewalski's horse. Smoothing was conducted with a third-
degree polynomial (equation 1.4).

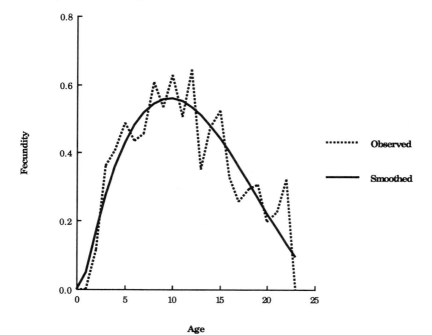

Table 1.2 Details of the Calculations

AGE	r	v_{obs}	NMF_{obs}	v_{com}	NMF_{com}
0	0.1099	0.0000	0.0000	0.0000	0.0000
1	0.0693	0.0000	0.0000	0.0000	0.0000
2	0.0767	0.0149	0.0178	0.0216	0.0259
3	0.0961	0.0458	0.0592	0.0345	0.0446
4	0.0811	0.0513	0.0729	0.0451	0.0642
5	0.1686	0.0614	0.0947	0.0537	0.0828
6	0.1312	0.0548	0.1001	0.0603	0.1101
7	0.1145	0.0576	0.1199	0.0651	0.1355
8	0.0606	0.0768	0.1792	0.0682	0.1593
9	0.0773	0.0673	0.1669	0.0699	0.1732
10	0.0875	0.0792	0.2121	0.0701	0.1878
11	0.0511	0.0638	0.1865	0.0691	0.2020
12	0.0875	0.0812	0.2499	0.0670	0.2061
13	0.0336	0.0446	0.1497	0.0639	0.2147
14	0.0182	0.0599	0.2080	0.0601	0.2086
15	0.0288	0.0663	0.2346	0.0555	0.1964
16	0.0511	0.0414	0.1508	0.0504	0.1836
17	0.1099	0.0327	0.1253	0.0450	0.1723
18	0.0405	0.0373	0.1593	0.0393	0.1680
19	0.1386	0.0389	0.1732	0.0335	0.1491
20	0.0000	0.0249	0.1273	0.0277	0.1417

obs = observed distribution
com = composite distribution

duction is significantly earlier, at 23 years of age (table 1.1). As a result of these findings, two potential fecundity schedules (v_x) have been used in the subsequent analyses of population dynamics: first, the observed rates to age 20, and second, a composite of the observed rates to age 2 and the fitted rates from age 2 to 20 (table 1.2). This latter fecundity schedule thus uses the observed age of maturation, for which there is considerable confidence, and the smoothed fecundity rates at older ages where sample sizes are small and the underlying fecundity distribution is not well determined by the observed data. Results based on the observed fecundity distribution are subscripted as obs, while those based on the composite fecundity distribution are subscripted com.

The net reproductive rate indicates that the Przewalski's horse population was expanding at a rapid rate during the period under consideration. The R_0 are 2.79_{obs} and 2.80_{com}, suggesting that a female just born will contribute almost three female offspring to the next generation. The details of these calculations are presented in table 1.2, along with the estimates of NMF both *obs* and *com*. A graph of NMF_{com} is presented in figure 1.3.

Estimates of the real and first and second complex roots of the characteristic equation derived from NMF_{obs} and NMF_{com} are presented in table 1.3. The roots in table 1.3 are the λ, while r is computed as the natural logarithm of the real dominant λ. The r_{obs} is estimated at 0.103, while r_{com} is estimated as 0.102. The complex roots presented in table 1.3, which occur in pairs, describe the periodicities and half-lives of

Figure 1.3 The estimated composite net maternity function (NMF_{com}) for Przewalski's horse.

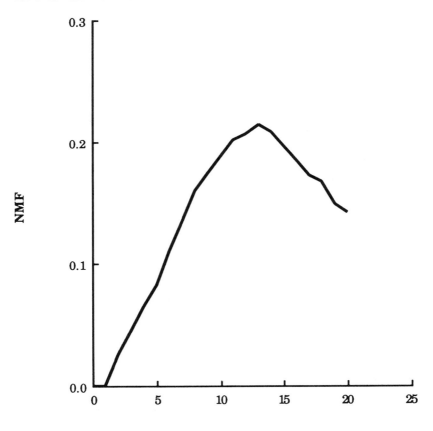

Table 1.3 Roots of *NMF*

	Root (λ)		ln(Root)*			
	Real	Complex	Real	Complex	Wavelength	Half-life
Roots of NMF_{obs}						
1	1.1085	0.0000	.1031	0.0000	0.0000	0.0000
2	.8358	−.4047	−.0741	−.4509	−13.9270	9.3531
3	.8358	.4047	−.0741	.4509	13.9270	9.3531
Roots of the NMF_{com}						
1	1.1076	0.0000	.1022	0.0000	0.0000	0.0000
2	.8437	−.4061	−.0658	−.4486	−13.9984	10.5347
3	.8437	.4061	−.0658	.4486	13.9984	10.5347

* $\ln(\text{Root}_1) = r$
obs = observed distribution
com = composite distribution

waves in the age structure. The periodicity or wavelength is the length of time for the peak of the disturbance to travel from the youngest age category through the age structure and to reappear in the youngest age category again. The half-life is the length of time necessary for the amplitude of the disturbance to be reduced by one half of its current amplitude. These complex roots describe the dominant wave resulting from a disturbance in the age structure (Keyfitz 1972). The estimated periodicity of this wave is 13.9_{obs} and 14.0_{com} years and the half-life is 9.35_{obs} and 10.5_{com} years. There is a root for each age category used in the analysis, although only the first three roots are shown in table 1.3. The remaining roots represent additional waves in the age structure, which have shorter periodicities and half-lives than the dominant wave and have smaller effects.

Finally, the estimates of the generation length are: $T_{obs} = 9.9$ years and $T_{com} = 10.2$ years.

DISCUSSION

The shapes of the fecundity and net maternity functions are known to influence the dynamics of a population (Keyfitz 1972) and are important for estimating population dynamics in general. There are, however, inherent limitations to our understanding of the fecundity and *NMF* distributions among small populations due to the samples available for analysis. In this analysis, a statistical model was adopted from human demography to smooth the estimated distribution. There are, however, alternative solutions. In humans, fecundity rises rapidly to a peak shortly after the age of sexual maturity is reached and then declines gradually to the end of reproductive life, resulting in a positively skewed distribution. This distribution is so consistent across noncontracepting human populations that Preston and Coale (1982) suggest that the v_x might profitably be taken from a model fecundity schedule, such as that developed by Coale and Trussell (1974), rather than estimated for the population under study. The fecundity distribution observed for Przewalski's horse conforms qualitatively to the human pattern (figure 1.1) and can be fitted to the same empirical models used to fit human populations, although certain details of the fit are not completely reliable, particularly the estimated age at sexual maturity. Whether most mammalian or animal fecundity distributions decline at the older ages and are positively skewed remains to be determined. If the shapes of animal fecundity distributions are as consistent as those for humans, it might be profitable to develop a set of model fecundity distributions for use with closely managed species.

A second problem involving the shape of the fecundity and net maternity distributions is the question of how to handle the end of reproductive life. In humans, the fecundity distribution and consequently the *NMF* declines to zero at menopause. In nonhuman populations, however, the end of reproductive life may coincide more often with the end of the life span. If this is true, then the tail of the fecundity distribution and the *NMF* will always be difficult to measure precisely because sample sizes in the tail will invariably be small. One possible solution to this problem would be to find an appropriate parametric distribution for the *NMF* and then extend the observed *NMF* out to zero. A normal distribution is considered to fit the *NMF* of humans adequately (Keyfitz and Fleiger 1971). Inspection of figure 1.3 indicates that a normal distribution might approximate the *NMF* of Przewalski's horse. Yet even if this were appropriate, the possibility remains that the true *NMF* of Przewalski's horse is a truncated normal distribution as a result of mortality. As mentioned above, the truncation point will be difficult to estimate precisely due to small sample sizes at these ages. This problem was solved in the analyses above by arbitrarily truncating the data at age 20 and accepting a slight underestimate of r and T. More information is needed concerning reproductivity at older ages in Przewalski's horse and in mammalian populations in general if very precise estimates of r and T are required. These limitations concerning our knowledge of the distribution of the net maternity function apply equally to the traditional and variable-r methods of estimating a species' population dynamics.

The estimates of Przewalski's horse population dynamics presented above indicate a population expanding at a rapid rate between 1975 and 1985. The estimates of R_0 and intrinsic rate of increase suggest that the population will almost triple in each generation and increase by about 10.2% per year once it attains a stable age distribution. In fact, these are underestimates of the maximum sustainable rates of increase for this species resulting from truncating the NMF at age 20. The results presented in table 1.2 indicate that the reproductive capacity of individuals at age 20 is still as high as that of animals at age 7 or 8. Nevertheless, the estimates of r, observed and composite, both exceed the observed yearly rate of growth of the population between 1975 and 1985, which was only 8.9% per year. The low observed rate of growth is a result of the very young age structure in 1975. Most of the observed population growth is due to the contributions of animals younger than the age of peak reproductivity, which occurs at about age 13 (table 1.2). As the population continues to age and approaches the stable age distribution, the observed rate of increase can be expected to accelerate by at least 1% (and perhaps more) provided that mortality and fecundity rates remain constant.

These results suggest that simply smoothing the fecundity distribution may not improve estimates for populations as large as that of Przewalski's horse. The estimates based on the observed and composite fecundity distributions differ by only 0.4%, 1.0%, and 3.0% for the R_0, r, and T respectively. The differences between the two analyses, however, become increasingly disparate in the higher order complex roots. Since these roots describe the dynamics of waves in the age structure and the rate of approach to the stable age distribution, they might be of interest to population managers if the age structure of the founding population is not stable. However, the waves described by the higher order roots will generally have short half-lives and disappear rapidly from the age structure. Unless extremely precise results are required, or the fecundity distribution is severely distorted, as might occur with populations smaller than that of Przewalski's horse, smoothing may not be necessary.

One particularly interesting and unusual feature of the analyses (for a human demographer interested in the details of population dynamics) is that the dynamics of this species differ qualitatively as well as quantitatively from human population dynamics. In particular, the generation length for Przewalski's horse is less than the age of peak reproductivity and significantly shorter than the periodicity of the dominant wave. In human populations, the generation length is invariably longer than the age of peak reproductivity, and the periodicity of the dominant wave is very close to the generation length (Keyfitz 1972). In fact, the periodicity of the dominant wave is frequently used as an estimate of the generation length by human demographers. These differences between the dynamics of humans and Przewalski's horses are due to the comparatively low age of first reproduction of Przewalski's horses (Coale 1972). Given the unusually long developmental period of humans, the Przewalski's horse pattern of population dynamics is likely to be more representative of mammals in general than the human pattern, although additional analyses of other species are warranted.

The analysis of the population dynamics of Przewalski's horse using the variable-r method is likely to be the best estimate available until a clearer understanding of the NMF of this species, particularly at older ages, is available. The variable-r estimates are likely to be more dependable because the demographic parameters required are more accurately assessed with defective and/or small population data. For example, the v_x require only a reliable evaluation of the shape of the fecundity distribution, while the m_x depend on precise estimates of both the shape and level of the fecundity distribution. Additionally, the r_x can be easily obtained from two accurate censuses taken at two points in time, while the evaluation of l_x requires a complete enumeration of deaths as well as an accounting of years at risk of death, which is usually approximated from a census or from longitudinal records (Taylor and Barlow, essay 2 of this volume). Stochastic error in either component of the l_x and m_x will be compounded in the final result. Briefly stated, reliable estimates of mortality and fecundity require greater data quality and quantity than do reliable assessments of the probability density function of births and the age-specific rates of increase. This feature of the variable-r

method may also prove advantageous in situations where the demographic data are likely to be poor or scarce, such as in the management of small or free-ranging populations.

CONCLUSIONS

The analyses of the Przewalski's horse population dynamics using variable-r methods indicate several characteristics that may be of general importance to animal management:

1. The fecundity distribution for Przewalski's horse appears to be a positively skewed distribution that increases rapidly to a peak after the first age of reproduction and then declines gradually in later life. Whether this distribution, particularly the decline in fecundity in later life, is characteristic of the fecundity of mammals in general will require additional research.

2. The tail of the fecundity distribution and hence the tail of the NMF is not well defined due to small numbers of animals surviving to the upper ages. It is possible that NMF in animals only goes to zero at the end of the life span and will never be well defined since few animals will survive to these ages. Special methods may need to be developed to handle this problem.

3. Due to the comparatively early age of sexual maturity, the population dynamics of Przewalski's horse differ qualitatively from the population dynamics of human populations. The Przewalski's horse pattern is likely to be characteristic of most mammalian populations.

4. The variable-r method of computing NMF and hence the r and T is likely to be a convenient method for studying the population dynamics of small and/or wild populations because the necessary parameters (v_x and r_x) can be more robustly estimated than the parameters required for the traditional approach.

Acknowledgments
This research was supported by NIH grant HD25346, which is gratefully acknowledged.

REFERENCES
Brass, W. 1975. *Methods for Estimating Fertility and Mortality from Limited and Defective Data.* Chapel Hill: The Carolina Population Center.

Coale, A. J. 1972. *The Growth and Structure of Human Populations*. Princeton: Princeton University Press.

Coale, A. J. and J. T. Trussell. 1974. Model fertility schedules: Variations in the age structure of childbearing in human populations. *Population Index* 40 (2): 185–258.

Dyke, B. and P. M. Mamelka. 1989. *Animal Colony Management Package: User Guide*. San Antonio: Southwest Foundation for Biomedical Research.

Gage, T. B. 1985. Demographic estimation from anthropological data: A review of the nonstable methods. *Current Anthropology* 26:644–47.

Gage, T. B., B. Dyke, and P. G. Riviere. 1984. Estimating fertility and population dynamics from two censuses: An application to the Trio of Surinam. *Human Biology* 56 (4): 691–701.

Keyfitz, N. 1972. Population Waves. In T. N. E. Greville, ed., *Population Dynamics*, pp. 1–38. New York: Academic Press.

Keyfitz, N. and W. Fleiger. 1971. *Population*. San Francisco: Freeman.

McIntosh, J. E. A. and R. P. McIntosh. 1980. *Mathematical Modeling and Computers in Endocrinology*. Berlin: Springer-Verlag.

Preston, S. H. 1983. An integrated system for demographic estimation from two age distributions. *Demography* 20 (2): 213–26.

Preston, S. H. and A. J. Coale. 1982. Age structure, growth, attrition and accession: A new synthesis. *Population Index* 48:217–59.

Volf, J. 1988. *Pedigree Book for Przewalski's horse*. Prague: The Zoological Garden of Prague.

2

The Step-wise Fit: A New Model for Estimating Mammalian Mortality from Incomplete Data Sets

■■

Barbara L. Taylor and Jay Barlow

Using traditional demographic techniques for nonhuman populations is difficult because of the quantity and quality of the data available. Demographic models are useful for predicting possible ranges of population growth rate. As the number of endangered species continues to grow and as more populations require active management, the need for such information about population growth increases. Unfortunately, the rate at which such data are acquired can be maddeningly slow. For many endangered species, age-specific mortality data can be obtained only through years of following the history of individuals whose age is known. Management programs for captive populations are faced with similar data inadequacies: most of the known-aged population is still living, and because most research and captive breeding programs have begun recently sample sizes decrease with age. The object of this essay is to develop and analyze a new method of estimating age-specific mortality that specifically addresses these types of incomplete data.

The data in table 2.1 illustrate the problem. These data are from two captive species: the Przewalski's horse (*Equus przewalskii*) (Volf 1959), which has been bred in captivity for more than eighty years, and the red ruffed lemur (*Varecia variegata rubra*) (Brockman 1986), for which the oldest individual whose age was known was 16 years old in 1985. Examination of the lemur data reveals two major problems: (1) small sample size and (2) a likely lack of any data for the older age categories. This particular example illustrates the need for age-specific mortality information for the management of captive populations. The lemur population is growing very rapidly and will probably reach a level at which managers would like to limit the growth before there are sufficient data to accurately estimate age-specific mortality using traditional demographic methods. Managers may wish to both limit the growth rate and maximize the generation time so as to slow genetic drift (Soulé et al. 1986). Mortality schedules are used for both captive and wild populations to determine the likely range of population growth rates and to detect trends in juvenile mortality, among other things. An accurate mortality schedule will reduce errors.

Standard methods of estimating mortality rates can use a variety of data. There are two common methods. Cohort analysis estimates mortality by recording the mortality for a group of animals all born at the same time throughout the lifetime of all individuals. Longitudinal analysis estimates mortality by using the current age structure as a representation of the survivorship schedule. This assumes that the population is not growing and is in a stable age distribution (details in Caughley 1977). Both are usually inappropriate for small populations of captive animals. The data for such populations typically consist of known histories of individuals. Two statistics are known for each individual: the number of years an animal has been at risk of mortality and whether that animal was living or dead at the end of the time it was monitored. Mortality models have been developed to smooth mortality rates based on biological criteria that fit the mammalian life history pattern. Although we can use these demographic models, we must consider the special problems caused by both small sample size and a possible lack of data for the later age categories. As we will show, estimating mortality

Table 2.1 At-risk data, survival rate (p_x), and survivorship (l_x) for Przewalski's horses through 1988 and red ruffed lemurs through 1985.

	PRZEWALSKI'S HORSES				RED RUFFED LEMURS			
AGE CLASS	# AT RISK	# DEAD	p_x	l_x	# AT RISK	# DEAD	p_x	l_x
1	1245	272	0.782	0.782	116	35	0.698	0.698
2	877	74	0.916	0.716	58	3	0.948	0.662
3	738	38	0.949	0.679	39	1	0.974	0.645
4	645	22	0.966	0.656	33	0	1.000	0.645
5	572	24	0.958	0.628	24	2	0.917	0.591
6	508	15	0.970	0.609	16	0	1.000	0.591
7	443	20	0.955	0.582	10	0	1.000	0.591
8	387	11	0.972	0.566	8	0	1.000	0.591
9	347	11	0.968	0.548	7	0	1.000	0.591
10	316	9	0.972	0.533	5	0	1.000	0.591
11	280	7	0.975	0.520	3	0	1.000	0.591
12	253	13	0.949	0.493	1	0	1.000	0.591
13	224	10	0.955	0.471	1	0	1.000	0.591
14	194	7	0.964	0.454	1	0	1.000	0.591
15	176	9	0.949	0.431	1	0	1.000	0.591
16	153	9	0.941	0.406	1	1	0.000	0.000
17	139	14	0.899	0.365				
18	115	5	0.957	0.349				
19	106	10	0.906	0.316				
20	93	10	0.892	0.282				
21	80	4	0.950	0.268				
22	74	8	0.892	0.239				
23	60	4	0.933	0.223				
24	53	2	0.962	0.214				
25	45	8	0.822	0.176				
26	34	8	0.765	0.135				
27	25	6	0.760	0.102				
28	17	2	0.882	0.090				
29	15	3	0.800	0.072				
30	12	1	0.917	0.066				
31	10	5	0.500	0.033				
32	5	2	0.600	0.020				
33	3	2	0.333	0.007				

Note: Data is for known-aged (zoo-born) individuals (Volf 1959; Brockman 1986).

parameters directly with a characteristic mammalian mortality model, the Siler model (Siler 1979), can lead to serious biases when used on incomplete data sets; this can be remedied by using a new method we call the step-wise Siler method. This method (proposed by Barlow and Boveng 1991) begins the parameter estimating procedure using parameters from a chosen standard species, which we will refer to as the standard model. Parameters are estimated in a step-wise fashion until the data no longer justify adding additional parameters. The result is a hybrid model between the standard model and the observed data. We will first show in detail how mortality data should be coded for populations of animals whose age is known. This is followed by an introduction to the Siler equation and the method of step-wise fitting. The step-wise Siler method is then examined for errors and bias introduced when estimating longevity and choosing a standard model. The results of the step-wise fits are compared to those of full Siler fits by examining the resulting estimates for the intrinsic rate of increase (r, Caswell [1989]) and the error sum of squares (SS) between the known and estimated age-specific survivorship values.

OBTAINING RAW MORTALITY RATES

Because we usually obtain data from known-aged populations in which most individuals are extant, it behooves us to use a method that allows us to use data on living animals. For example, an animal that is now living at age ten has successfully completed the first ten age classes, i.e., it was at risk for ten years. Because we are using at-risk data, an uncommon practice in animal demography, we will first explain how these data are correctly classified into age-specific numbers of animals at risk and numbers of animals dead. Care must be taken in deciding which data are included and which data are excluded in order to avoid bias. For any given age category, the statistics needed are the number of animals that were at risk for that entire age category and the number that died during that period. In order to be classified as at risk, an animal must have been observed for the entire time period so we can be certain that its status at the end of the period is noted. Table 2.2 details the classification of some sample data. When we excluded data for a sample case, we did so because we did not have the opportunity to observe the

Table 2.2 Example of classification of at-risk data for an observation period ending 01/01/90. Some data for animals B through E (all in cases C and D) were excluded because we did not have the opportunity to fully observe their last year.

ANIMAL	BIRTH DATE	DEATH DATE	AGE	NUMBER OF YEARS AT RISK	DEAD IN YEAR	DATA EXCLUDED
A	06/01/82	10/01/85	3.33	4	4	No
B	06/01/83	–	6.50	6	-	Yes
C	09/01/89	–	0.25	-	-	Yes
D	08/01/89	11/01/89	0.25	-	-	Yes
E	02/01/80	09/01/89	9.50	9	-	Yes
F	10/01/80	04/01/89	8.50	9	9	No

entire time period (in this case a one-year-long age class). Perhaps the most difficult case to understand is represented by animal E in table 2.2. Although the death date of the animal is known, we did not have the opportunity to observe the entirety of its last year. Its next birthday (02/01/90) is after the date we were making the assessment (01/01/90). For animals that did not die, such as animal B, this last partial year would have been excluded because they may have died before that year of life was concluded. It would, therefore, introduce bias if only animals that died in their last partial year were included in the at-risk analysis.

There are methods for using data from partial years, but all are based on the assumption that mortality rates are constant for the entire age category, a year in our case. This is certainly not the case for the first year, the year that would have the largest proportion of partial-year data. The small amount of data gained does not compensate for the probable bias introduced.

THE SILER EQUATION

Mammalian mortality schedules have a common pattern: an initially high but declining juvenile mortality, a relatively constant adult mortality, and an increasing senescent mortality (Caughley 1966; Spinage 1972; Siler 1979). Siler (1979) combined these competing risks in to a single five-parameter model. Survivorship ($l(x)$) from birth to age x is given by:

$$l(x) = l_j(x)l_c(x)l_s(x) \qquad (2.1),$$

where:

$$l_j(x) = \exp[(-a_1/b_1)\{1 - \exp(-b_1x/\Omega)\}] \qquad (2.2),$$

$$l_c(x) = \exp(-a_2x/\Omega) \qquad (2.3),$$

$$l_s(x) = \exp[(a_3/b_3)\{1 - \exp(b_3x/\Omega)\}] \qquad (2.4).$$

x = age,
$l(x)$ = survivorship to age x,
l_j = juvenile component of mortality risk (an exponentially decreasing function),
l_c = the adult (constant) component of mortality rate, and
l_s = the senescent component of mortality risk (an exponentially increasing function).

The above equations are the Siler model as modified by Barlow and Boveng (1991) so that age is normalized by dividing by longevity (Ω). Thus, standard models can be used for species with different longevities. To estimate the five parameters (a_1, a_2, a_3, b_1, and b_3) and thus fit the model to actual data, we use maximum likelihood methods by finding the values that maximize

$$L = \sum_{x=1}^{\Omega} (s_x\log(p_x) + (d_x\log(1 - p_x))) \qquad (2.5)$$

where L is the log likelihood, Ω is longevity, s_x is the observed number that survived age class x (calculated as the number at risk minus the number dead), d_x is the number dead in age class x, and p_x is the estimated survival rate for age class x from the model fit. Fitting the five parameters of the Siler equation when there are no data for the later years may not be justified and may introduce errors into the mortality estimation. Although it is likely that a full Siler fit to an incomplete life table will result in error, the effect of this error on, for example, estimating the growth rate, is unclear. One can readily see the danger of over-parameterizing by examining the lemur data in table 2.1. A full Siler fit to these data would, in effect, smooth out the noise due to sample size but would also fit the data for the oldest individual, which happened (by chance) to have died. The best fit will, therefore, be a survivorship that plummets precipitously at this point (though there are few data to extrapolate this to the population). More typically, the case is that the oldest animal is extant, which causes the best-fit adult and senescent survivorship to remain constant (see figure 3.1 in Taylor et al., essay 3 of this volume). Because there is no senescence, the result is a survivorship curve that frequently has rather high values even at maximum longevity (the estimated maximum age): another highly improbable scenario. We should be able to improve our mortality model by using our prior knowledge about the species and about mammal mortality schedules.

There are two sources of information that could improve the estimation of the mortality schedule. First, we probably have some idea of what longevity is likely to be, either from similar species or, in the case of captive animals, from the number of years wild-caught individuals have been held in captivity. Second, because mammals have a common shape to their survivorship curve, we can choose a species we feel would be similar and use the shape of its survivorship curve to "fill in" the poorly defined sections of the survivorship curve under consideration. Our step-wise fit procedure utilizes both of these sources of information. First, we introduce the details of the step-wise procedure. We then evaluate how the choice of longevity and standard model affect error in estimating age-specific mortality with the step-wise Siler model. The evaluation will be based on subsamples of increasing sample sizes from Przewalski's horse data (described later) and will be contrasted to the full Siler fit.

THE STEP-WISE FIT

As mentioned, this method produces a hybrid model based on observed data and a standard survivorship curve. The approach begins with the five Siler parameters of the standard model normalized to the estimated longevity for the species being considered. Parameters in equations (2.2) through (2.4) are fit in the following order: b_1, a_1, a_2, a_3, b_3. The order for parameters was determined first by estimating the parameters describing juvenile mortality (the ages at which the sample size is typically large). Within the juvenile phase (equation 2.2), the parameter order was decided by examining the coefficient of variation for each parameter using the parameters from the four species serving as standard models in this study (Old World monkeys, Siberian tigers, Northern fur seals, and human females, see below). Parameters with the highest coefficients of variation were fit first because they were most likely to vary among species. The same procedure was used for the senescent phase (equation 2.4). The simplex fitting algorithm (Press et al. 1988) was used to find the best fit possible by adjusting only the first parameter. A Kolmogorov-Smirnov test (Zar 1984) is then used to find the probability that the observed data could have been a random sample taken from a population with a survivorship curve that was based on the one fitted parameter and the four parameters from the standard model. The decision as to whether the fit adequately represents the data was based on the choice of a critical probability value. A probability of $\alpha = 0.50$ would mean that the observed data could have been taken from a population with the estimated mortality in 50% of all random samples. Critical probability values were investigated empirically from $\alpha = 0.50$ to $\alpha = 0.95$ in increments of 0.05. The sum of squared errors and the estimates of r were used to judge goodness of fit. In cases where the survivorship curve of the standard model deviated strongly from that of the Przewalski's horse population, error was high. It was impossible to obtain α higher than 0.95 for many cases with low sample size. An α value of 0.95 means that the step-wise fit conforms very closely to the observed data.

EVALUATING THE MODEL FITS:
CREATING INCOMPLETE DATA SETS

The probability a given mortality schedule could have generated the observed data does not tell us how close the schedule is to the actual mortality schedule for that species nor does it tell us whether there might be biases. We are interested in how well the step-wise method performs with incomplete data sets. We created incomplete data sets from a known mortality schedule by subsampling a complete data set (that set is considered to be the population). In subsampling these data we wish to duplicate the problems expected in real incomplete data sets. To subsample the Przewalski's horse data with a sample size of 50, 50 individuals were randomly drawn (with replacement) from the total (1245 horses) data set. It took 22 years for the first 50 horses to be born in captivity. To be realistic, years at risk cannot exceed the duration of the study. For example, horses born in the first year of captive breeding could be 22 years old when the fiftieth horse was born in captivity. Therefore, if a random horse was drawn that had lived 26 years, it would be counted as extant and at risk for 22 years. Similarly, horses

Figure 2.1 Fits for 100 subsamples of sample size 50. The oldest possible individual could have been 22 years old. Figure 2.1a represents the fits from all five Siler parameters. Figure 2.1b represents the fits for the same data but using the step-wise fitting procedure. Statistics for these fits can be seen in figures 2.5 and 2.6 for *r* and *SS* respectively where the sample size is 50.

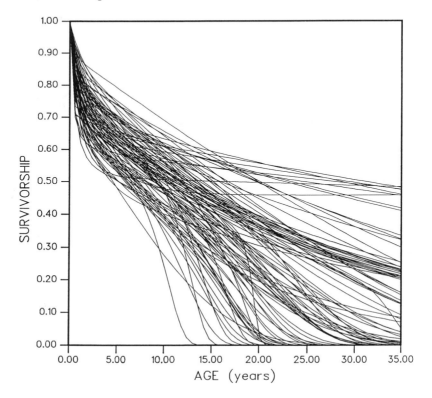

born in the twentieth year of captive breeding could be at most 2 years old at the end of the 22 years. Any individual that was younger than the maximum possible age was recorded as it was classified (e.g., at-risk six years, dead in year six). One hundred subsamples were taken at sample sizes of 50, 100, 200, and 1200, which correspond to the following years of captive breeding: 22, 33, 52, and 75. These are the same subsamples used in Taylor et al. (essay 3 of this volume).

EVALUATING THE MODEL FITS: GOODNESS OF FIT

We still need a measure for how well our fits of the subsamples represent the actual population of 1245 horses. Goodness-of-fit measures

Figure 2.1b

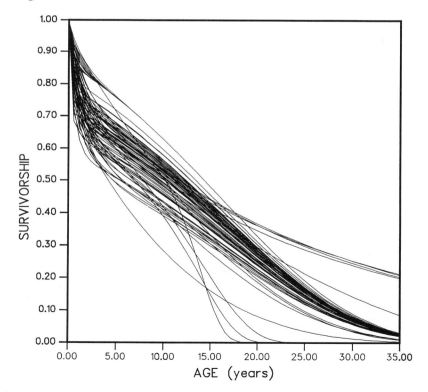

should measure error in the quantity that interests us. In some cases, we may be interested in the age-specific mortality itself. In this case a measure that weights the error in each age equally, such as the sum of squared errors (*SS*) is appropriate:

$$SS = \sum_{x=1}^{\Omega} (l_x - \hat{l}_x)^2 \qquad (2.6)$$

where Ω is the estimated longevity, l_x is the survivorship for age x from the entire data set, and $\hat{l}_x$ is the estimated survivorship from the subsample. If, however, we are actually interested in estimating the growth rate, errors in the early ages have a much stronger effect on error in the intrinsic growth rate (r) than do errors later in the life table. For this reason, we present statistics on both *SS* and r. The intrinsic rate of increase (r) is calculated using the discrete version of Lotka's equation (equation 5.16 in Caswell [1989]) and the raw fecundity schedule for the horses. Figure 2.1 illustrates how differently the full Siler method and the step-wise Siler method (using the Old World monkey standard) fit the same data. Figure 2.1a is the full fit for the 100 subsamples with a sample size of 50 horses. The step-wise fits for the same data are shown in figure 2.1b. Clearly, the step-wise method constrains the possible shapes of the survivorship curve more than the full Siler method. The effects on r and *SS* are discussed below in our evaluation of different standard models.

EVALUATING THE CHOICE OF LONGEVITY

Longevity has had a series of definitions that are reviewed in Barlow and Boveng (1991). Most of these definitions require far more data than will be available for the incomplete data sets treated in this study. Because the use of a standard model requires prior estimation of longevity, it is worth considering whether the error introduced by this estimation defeats any gain in accuracy over the full Siler fit. We considered that one should be able to estimate longevity within ± 33%. We thus found r and *SS* for each of the 100 horse subsamples at each sample size starting with longevity estimates of 25, 30, 35, 40, and 45 years. The fitting was allowed to modify the longevity estimate in two ways: (1) if the maximum age of an individual in a sample was greater than the estimated longevity, then the maximum known age became the longevity, and (2) if the maximum known age at a given sample size changes by less than 5 years from the maximum of the next smaller sample size, then the maximum age becomes the longevity. The latter rule was invoked to allow for the case where longevity was overestimated, which was made obvious by the fact that for many years, the maximum observed age was relatively stable and well below the estimated longevity.

The results are shown in figures 2.2 and 2.3. Overestimation of longevity produces less bias in r than an equivalent underestimation. This is because underestimation produces a shortening of the survivorship curve that makes the step-wise fits more similar to the full Siler fits (which for this species also produced negatively biased estimates of r). Overestimation makes the hybrid step-wise fit more like the standard.

Figure 2.2 Mean intrinsic rate of growth (r) assuming different longevities and at different sample sizes. The growth rate for the full horse data set is depicted by the horizontal line at 0.0405. Error bars indicate ± one standard error. Lines between the means are for visual continuity.

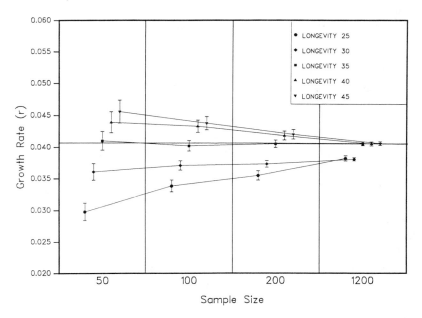

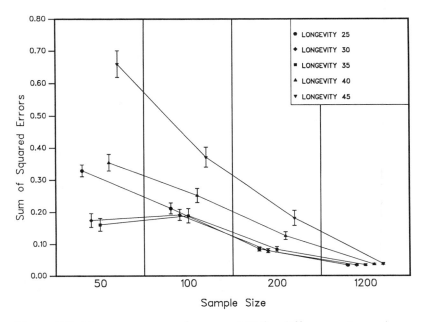

Figure 2.3 Mean error sum of squares (*SS*) for different estimated longevities and different sample sizes. Error bars indicate ± one standard error. Lines between the means are for visual continuity.

This is also revealed in the general patterns in *SS:* the values are lower for the underestimated longevity, i.e., the model conforms more closely to the observed data.

EVALUATION OF THE CHOICE OF STANDARD MODELS

Four different standard models were evaluated: the standard for Old World monkeys (Gage and Dyke 1988), the full Siler fit to captive Siberian tigers (*Panthera tigris*) (fit using ISIS tiger data), wild Northern fur seals (*Callorhinus ursinus*) (Barlow and Boveng 1991), and human (*Homo sapiens*) females born circa 1900 (Barlow and Boveng 1991). The parameters for the Siler equation are given in table 2.3. The fits for these species (figure 2.4) span much of the expected ranges for mammals. The choice of standard models affects the estimated growth rates and the overall fit of the survivorship rates. Figure 2.5 shows *r* and fig-

Table 2.3 Estimates of survival rate parameters for northern fur seals, Old World monkeys, human females, Siberian tigers, and Przewalski's horses based on the Siler model (equations 2.1–2.4).

SPECIES	a_1	a_2	a_3	b_1	b_3
Northern fur seal females	14.343	0.1710	0.0121	10.259	6.6878
Old World monkeys	30.430	0.0000	0.7276	206.720	2.3188
Human females	40.409	0.4772	0.0047	310.360	8.0290
Siberian tigers	12.082	1.1464	0.0392	38.268	6.5131
Przewalski's horses	12.558	1.0304	0.0414	42.850	6.1544

Figure 2.4 Survivorship curves for the four species used as standard models plus that for the complete horse data set. Ages have been normalized by dividing by longevity. Longevities used are seals—18, monkeys—34, humans—81, tigers—24, horses—34.

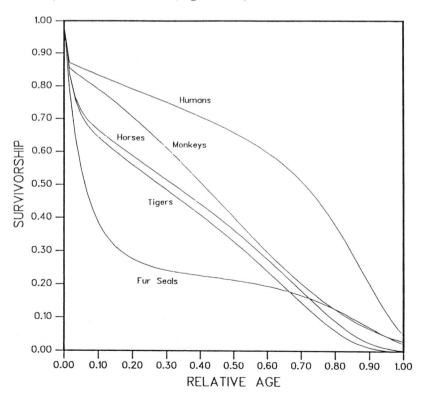

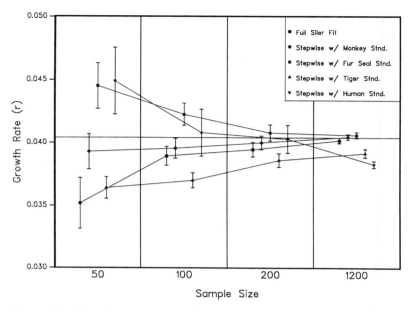

Figure 2.5 Mean intrinsic rate of growth (r) for the full Siler fit plus the step-wise fits using four different standard models. The growth rate for the full horse data set is depicted by the horizontal line at 0.0405. Error bars indicate ± one standard deviation. Lines between the means are for visual continuity.

ure 2.6 shows SS for the different sample sizes and for the four different standard models plus the full Siler fit.

The sum of squared errors indicates the absolute difference between the estimated and the "real" survivorship curves. As can be seen in figure 2.6, the two captive species' standards (monkeys and tigers) provide better fits than does the full Siler fit. It is also evident, however, that the choice of an inappropriate standard, such as humans or fur seals, can lead to higher errors. The interpretation of figure 2.5, showing bias and precision in estimating r, is more complex. Because SS is an absolute measure, we do not know whether there is a consistent bias or whether certain age classes might be consistently biased. We are also weighting the error in each age class equally. As mentioned previously, in many demographic applications it may be more desirable to have a goodness-of-fit measure that gives more weight to age classes in which errors will be more costly to management. Generally speaking, errors made in the early years will have more profound consequences. The intrinsic rate of increase (r) is both directly useful to management and weights errors in the early years more heavily. In addition, SS is not a value that lends itself to an intuitive grasp: the magnitude of error is displayed, but it is difficult to judge the importance of the error. On the other hand, figure 2.5 immediately tells us that, given a correct guess on longevity, the errors in estimating r are around one half of a percent even for a sample size of only fifty. It is also clear that models are prone to consistent biases, which is not obvious from an examination of SS or the survivorship curve of the standard. For example, the tiger standard, which gives a low SS, appears most similar to that of horses in figure 2.4 and yet yields a consistent negative bias in r.

Figure 2.6 Mean sum of squares error (SS) for the full Siler fit plus the step-wise fits using four different standard models. Error bars indicate ± one standard error. Lines between the means are for visual continuity.

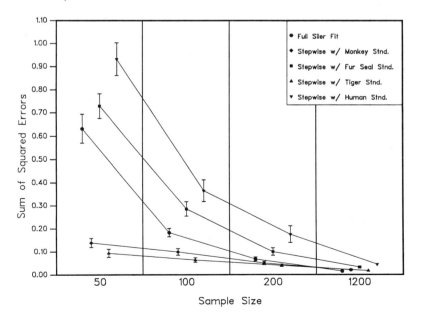

DISCUSSION AND CONCLUSIONS

The problem of how to best estimate the underlying mortality schedule given only small amounts of data that cover only part of the life span will become more important as more species require active management. Figure 2.1a reveals that the use of standard demographic models, like the Siler model, can estimate mortality schedules well for complete data sets but are rather unstable with incomplete data sets. For Przewalski's horses, acquisition of mortality data for 50 individuals took 22 years. Data sets from wild populations are usually from studies of shorter duration. Figure 2.5 shows that at this sample size, the full Siler fit is negatively biased by one half percent on average. It would be interesting to investigate whether this is a general property of fitting the full Siler model to incomplete data sets regardless of life history strategy. It is worth commenting that estimates of r are actually rather good considering the small amount of data. An error of one percent is quite reasonable for most management purposes. One must remember, however, that this estimate of r was made as a goodness-of-fit measure and assumes only sampling error in the fecundity schedule and no errors in the mortality data.

Although we have cast doubt on the use of the full Siler model, have we improved the estimation of mortality schedules with the step-wise Siler approach? Yes and no. The usefulness of the step-wise approach is dependent on the estimation of longevity and the choice of standard models. At a low sample size, misestimation of longevity caused relatively large errors in estimating r and, considering that only the monkey standard was used, large SS. While the SS was lower when longevity was underestimated, underestimation resulted in a curious downward bias in r (figure 2.2) even when the sample size was very large. Thus, the first consideration in assessing whether the step-wise approach would be better than the full Siler fit is a judgment as to how accurately longevity can be estimated. For many animals, particularly those that have been harvested and can be aged, quite accurate estimates can be made. In captive situations, longevity data may exist from wild-caught individuals and from closely related species. Finally, empirical relationships between certain physical measurements (body size, brain size, cardiac cycle, etc.) and longevity could be used (Lindstedt and Calder 1981; Calder 1983).

The choice of a standard model is likely to be more difficult and has a strong effect on the accuracy of the step-wise model. Even so, the magnitude of error is again surprisingly low. The standard model is a prior mortality schedule used as a default when observed data are lacking. On what should we base the choice of the standard model? It is tempting to base our choice on biological criteria: wild or captive animals, taxonomic relationship, similar life history strategies (relative age at first reproduction, litter size, longevity), etc. Correlations have been found between age-specific mortality shapes and other life history measures, such as reproductive effort and life expectancy (Dobson and Lyles 1989; Emlen 1970; Calder 1983; Gunderson and Dygert 1988). It is not clear, however, how these biological criteria relate to how well a standard will perform in the step-wise approach.

To get a more intuitive feel for this problem, we examine the different standards used in this study. The Old World monkey standard was originally chosen because among limited choices it was both from captive animals and based on data that had been checked for accuracy. It turned out to be a good model by both goodness-of-fit measures. The tiger model was a second choice because it had a very large sample size and concerned a captive species. It probably includes a few spurious data points for old individuals but is quite accurate for most of the life span. Figure 2.4 shows that the survivorship curve for tigers is most similar to that of horses. The *SS* shown in figure 2.6 is consistently small. In contrast, the goodness-of-fit measure for *r* shows the tiger standard to be rather poor. It was never an improvement on the full Siler fit. Because the survivorship curves are so similar, the tiger survivorship curve was judged not statistically different and was accepted as the true horse survivorship curve. This resulted in the negative bias seen in figure 2.5. Although biased, even the smallest sample size has a mean difference in *r* of less than 0.004. A comparison of the fur seal and horse survivorship curves reveals the largest difference in mortality to be in the juvenile years. Higher mortality rates throughout life are to be expected for wild populations. The parameters for juvenile mortality (equation 2.2) are estimated first in the step-wise Siler method. Because the juvenile survivorship values are so different, the fur seal parameters will be rejected even though we have very little data on the horses. The resulting range of possible shapes for survivorship curves when parameters a_1 and b_1 are allowed to take any value is not intuitive.

Thus, although the Siler equation is biologically interpretable because it represents known competing risks of mortality, the parameters themselves are not biologically meaningful. For this reason, a good standard will not necessarily have a similar shape to the survivorship curve to be estimated. Because the choice of a standard determines whether the step-wise Siler method is a better estimator of mortality than the full Siler method, more comparative work needs to be done using standards from different mortality patterns.

The step-wise Siler method offers the prospect of improving age-specific mortality estimation in the absence of data for the entire life span. This lack of data is the norm for most wild populations and for many species that have recently been taken into captivity. The Przewalski's horse example shows that dramatic improvement can be made (compare the full Siler to the step-wise Siler using the Old World monkey standard at the sample size of 50) when evaluated by either SS or r. For many species, estimation of longevity can be made with relative accuracy. The choice of standards, however, remains a difficult problem. After data are acquired for the full life span, the full Siler is the safest choice of models. Before that point is reached, the step-wise Siler method may be more accurate and is at least comparable to the full Siler method. All estimates, regardless of model or standard, were biased when the data were incomplete. Both bias and standard error are reduced rapidly as the sample size increases, emphasizing that mortality estimates should be updated frequently.

Acknowledgments

We would like to thank Michael Gilpin for suggesting demographic analyses of captive mortality and for providing the initial data. Oliver Ryder provided the studbook for the Przewalski's horses and helped in completing missing records. The study was improved through interactions with participants at the workshop entitled "Analytical Methods for Population Viability Analysis" hosted by the National Zoological Park and organized by Jon Ballou, Michael Gilpin, and Thomas Foose. Thoughtful reviews were given by Daniel Goodman, Doug DeMaster, Michael Gilpin, Ted Case, and Jon Ballou. B. Taylor was supported by a National Institute of Health, Genetics Training Grant to the Department of Biology.

REFERENCES

Barlow, J. and P. Boveng. 1991. Modeling age-specific mortality for marine mammal populations. *Marine Mammal Science* 7:50–66.

Brockman, D. K. 1986. *International Studbook of the Ruffed Lemur.* San Diego: San Diego Zoological Society.

Calder, W. A. III. 1983. Body size, mortality, and longevity. *Journal of Theoretical Biology* 102:135–44.

Caswell, H. 1989. *Matrix Population Models: Construction, Analysis, and Interpretation.* Sunderland, Mass.: Sinauer.

Caughley, G. 1966. Mortality patterns in mammals. *Ecology* 47:906–18.

Caughley, G. 1977. *Analysis of Vertebrate Populations.* Chichester: Wiley.

Dobson, A. P. and A. M. Lyles. 1989. The population dynamics and conservation of primate populations. *Conservation Biology* 3:362–80.

Emlen, J. M. 1970. Age specificity and ecological theory. *Ecology* 51:588–601.

Gage, T. B. and B. Dyke. 1988. Model life tables for the larger Old World monkeys. *American Journal of Primatology* 16:305–20.

Gunderson, D. R. and P. H. Dygert. 1988. Reproductive effort as a predictor of natural mortality rate. *Journal du Conseil International Pour L'Exploration de la Mer* 44:200–9.

Lindstedt, S. L. and W. A. Calder III. 1981. Body size, physiological time, and longevity of homeothermic animals. *Quarterly Review of Biology* 56:1–16.

Press, W. H., B. P. Flannery, S. A. Teulkolsky, and W. T. Vetterling. 1988. *Numerical Recipes: The Art of Scientific Computing.* Cambridge: Cambridge University Press.

Siler, W. 1979. A competing-risk model for animal mortality. *Ecology* 60:750–57.

Soulé, M., M. Gilpin, W. Conway, and T. Foose. 1986. The millennium ark: How long a voyage, how many staterooms, how many passengers? *Zoo Biology* 5:101–13.

Spinage, C. A. 1972. African ungulate life tables. *Ecology* 53:645–52.

Volf, J. 1959 et seq. *Pedigree Book of the Przewalski Horse.* Prague, Czechoslovakia: Prague Zoological Garden.

Zar, J. H. 1984. *Biostatistical Analysis.* Englewood Cliffs, N.J.: Prentice-Hall.

3

Mortality Models for Numerically Small Populations of Mammals

::

Barbara L. Taylor, Timothy B. Gage, Jay Barlow,
Paul Mamelka, and Bennett Dyke

Demographic techniques were largely developed for human populations, for which there commonly exist large quantities of high-quality
data covering the entire life span. With populations of many species
dwindling and thus requiring intense management either in the wild or
in captivity, knowledge of demographic parameters becomes very useful. Estimating demographic parameters, however, is problematic for
small populations. This essay focuses on evaluating methods that have
been proposed for use in estimating age-specific mortality rates from
data sets based on samples that are small and decrease even more with
age to the point that there are often no data for the older age categories.
Our evaluation will be based on subsampling one of the most complete
sets of nonhuman demographic data: that of the captive Przewalski's
horse (*Equus przewalskii*) (Volf 1959).

Most studies of mortality for small populations are either very short or have been started in the relatively recent past. This study focuses on the type of data obtained from a history of known-aged individuals. In the wild, this consists primarily of mark/recapture or sight/resight data. In captivity, the age-specific data are from zoo-born individuals. This means necessarily that sample size decreases with age. This problem is magnified if the population is growing, as is the case with many captive populations. For example, the first red ruffed lemur, *Varecia variegata rubra,* was born in captivity in 1968 (Brockman 1986). In 1985 there were 164 individuals that had lived through their first year, 25 that had lived to age 8, but only 2 that lived to age 20, and the same 2 individuals were still living at age 28. Given such data, it is not clear how to estimate age-specific mortality rates accurately.

DEMOGRAPHIC METHODS FOR IMPROVING MORTALITY ESTIMATES

We explore two families of approaches that have been employed to improve estimates when the raw mortality rate data have noise due to small sample size. The first family is model-free smoothing, such as running means, polynomial regression, splines, etc. This approach assumes no expected mathematical form and simply makes the form smoother by using various nonbiological criteria. We examine two methods employed by managers of captive animals. The first method uses the observed mortality for the first age, a mean of the second and third age classes for the smoothed value of the second age, and running means of three thereafter. This method is used by SPARKS (Single Population Animal Record Keeping System; ISIS 1991), the most commonly used software for captive population management in zoos (Ballou, personal communication). The second method uses repeated smoothing with a series of three medians followed by an additional smoothing using weighted averages (Tukey 1977). It is implemented in a demography program used by zoo managers (DEMOG; Bingaman and Ballou 1993) and will be referred to as the DEMOG smoothing method.

The second family of approaches uses mathematical models of the underlying processes (such as Gompertz 1825; Makeham 1860; Siler 1979). In this case, we are interested in whether there is an underlying pattern of age-specific mortality that is common to many species. Such a form is apparent in large mammals: mortality is high but decreasing in early life, constant through most of adulthood, and increasing in later life (Caughley 1966; Spinage 1972; Siler 1979). These life phases can be thought of as presenting competing risks during life and are represented in an equation due to Siler (1979) and modified by Barlow and Boveng (1991). Survivorship, or the probability of survival from birth to age x, is given by:

$$l(x) = l_j(x)l_c(x)l_s(x) \qquad (3.1),$$

where

$$l_j(x) = \exp[(-a_1/b_1)\{1 - \exp(-b_1 x/\Omega)\}] \qquad (3.2),$$

$$l_c(x) = \exp(-a_2 x/\Omega) \qquad (3.3),$$

$$l_s(x) = \exp[(a_3/b_3)\{1 - \exp(b_3 x/\Omega)\}] \qquad (3.4).$$

The equations partition mortality risks into the juvenile (3.2), adult (3.3), and senescent (3.4) phases of life. The ages (x) are standardized by dividing by longevity (Ω) to facilitate comparison with other species, which may have different longevities. This equation and its interpretation are explained at length by Gage and Dyke (1988), Barlow and Boveng (1991), and Taylor and Barlow (essay 2 of this volume).

There are a priori reasons to believe there may be advantages to the latter model-based approach, because it allows us to fill gaps in our knowledge about a particular species with more complete knowledge from other species. This study compares three different mathematical models. The first model-based approach uses the full Siler equation. Parameters (excluding Ω) are estimated using a maximum likelihood approach that essentially weights each age according to the number of animals at risk in that age. Problems arise when data are not available for the older age classes. The model will maximize the likelihood that the observed data are explained by the estimated parameters (see Taylor and Barlow, essay 2 of this volume). It seems of dubious value to estimate the parameters from the data for senescence (equation 3.4) when there are no data for that part of life. Figure 3.1 shows two hypothetical cases, one in which the oldest observed animal is still living, and one in which this animal died in the last year of observation. The actual data used are for red ruffed lemurs (*Varecia variegata rubra*) as presented in table 2.1 in Taylor and Barlow (essay 2 of this volume). The only difference between the two data sets is whether the last individual is living or dead. Neither of these fits accurately portrays the underlying mortality schedule, but both closely conform to the observed data. In this case, the

Figure 3.1 Full Siler fits to two at-risk data sets that differ by only one individual. For the steep curve the oldest individual was the only animal at-risk at age 16 and died in that year. The other fit used the same data except that last individual was changed to be extant at the end of its sixteenth year. The data, presented in table 2.1 of Taylor and Barlow's study in this volume, is for known-aged red ruffed lemurs in 1985. At that time, there were wild-caught individuals that had been in captivity for 28 years.

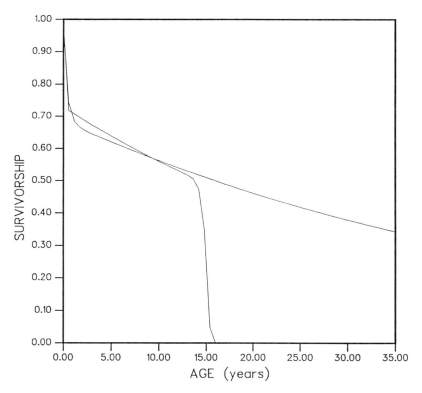

five parameters of the Siler equation allow for more flexibility in getting a good fit than is desirable. Clearly, there is a danger of overparameterization when fitting the full Siler model to an incomplete data set.

In many cases, we have prior knowledge allowing us to better estimate what the survivorship curve should look like. More importantly, we probably have an estimate of longevity either from wild-caught animals (with years in captivity as a minimum age) or from similar species. The step-wise Siler fit uses this knowledge. The model begins with parameters from another species judged to be most similar, in this case we chose to use the standard developed by Gage and Dyke (1988) for Old World monkeys. This standard was developed for captive animals and seemed the most appropriate choice. Siler parameters are fit in order of data available for estimation. Longevity must be estimated independently. Details for the method are in Taylor and Barlow (essay 2 of this volume). In essence, the curve is fit to empirical data where those are available (commonly just the juvenile and early adult ages for small data sets covering a short period) and uses the data from the "substitute" species in all other cases.

Another method is the logit or relational model life-table technique developed originally for smoothing human life tables by Brass (1971). This method is based on the observation that the logit transform of the survivorship column of human life tables is close to a linear function of age. Whether this is true of most animals remains to be determined, although Gage and Dyke (1988) have found that the logit of Old World monkey life tables is approximately linear. In any event, if the logit transform successfully linearizes age-specific survivorship, then ordinary linear regression can be used to "relate" a standard tabular life table with an observed life table.

Specifically, the logit of the standard life table is regressed on the logit of the observed life table. The constant or intercept of the regression represents the difference in the level of mortality (life expectancy) between the observed and standard life tables. If the constant is negative, the observed mortality is lower than that of the standard; if the constant is positive, the observed mortality is higher than the standard. Similarly, the slope of the regression adjusts the shape of the life table. If the slope is less than 1.0, the standard life table will have lower infant mortality and higher adult mortality than the observed life table. If the slope is greater than 1.0, the observed table has lower infant mortality.

Once the coefficients of the regression equation have been estimated, a fitted survivorship distribution that matches the observed survival distribution can be derived from the standard life table and the coefficients and the complete life table can be computed from the fitted survivorship column. Because the regression coefficients adjust the level and shape of the standard life table, a single standard can often be used to fit a wide range of observed life tables. Nevertheless, the quality of the results ultimately depends on the use of an appropriate standard life table for a particular population. Standard life tables may need to be developed for different species and/or genera, or even for the same species existing in a variety of habitats. A number of standard model life tables have been developed for human populations (Brass 1971; Gage 1990). Gage and Dyke (1988) have developed a standard model life table for the larger Old World monkeys under captive and provisioned conditions. Barlow and Boveng (1991) have developed a standard model for wild fur seals.

EVALUATING METHODS

We wish to evaluate how well each of these methods (the SPARKS smooth, the DEMOG smooth, the full Siler model, the step-wise Siler, and logit models using the Old World monkey standard) performs with data sets of increasing completeness. The different methods for estimating mortality rates will be compared for subsamples of the Przewalski's horse data where age-specific mortality rates from the fit to the full 1245 individuals are assumed to be the actual mortality rates. We use two approaches to judge performance. We measure how close an estimated mortality schedule matches the actual mortality schedule using the error sum of squares (SS) in equation (3.5):

$$SS = \sum_{i=1}^{\Omega} (l_i - \hat{l}_i)^2 \qquad (3.5)$$

where Ω is the estimated longevity, l_i is the survivorship (the probability of surviving from birth to age i) for age i from the entire data set, and $\hat{l}_i$ is the estimated survivorship from the fit.

The second approach gives a weighting to the error. If one is interested in manipulating the intrinsic rate of increase for the purposes of maximizing generation time, thereby minimizing genetic drift, errors in estimating survival rates for young ages will be more crucial than those for older ages. This is because the reproductive value generally declines with age after sexual maturity is reached. Thus, one may be more concerned with how the estimated mortality rates affect the estimation of the intrinsic rate of increase (r). In estimating r for all cases, the same definition of crude age-specific fecundity rate was used: number of females born that reached age 1 per adult female aged x. We calculate r using Lotka's equation with the estimated survivorship ($\hat{l}_i$) and aforementioned fecundity rates (equation 5.16 in Caswell [1989]).

CREATING THE BOOTSTRAP SUBSAMPLES

We use two pieces of data from each individual in the original data set: the number of years at risk, and the current status (extant or dead) (see Taylor and Barlow, essay 2 of this volume for details on determining years at risk). The goal of this analysis is to compare different demographic methods as the amount of data increases. Repeated subsampling from the complete data set at a given sample size, say fifty horses, allows us to compare the performance of each method. In order to better simulate the situation common to most real data, i.e., a paucity or absence of data for older animals in the early phases of data gathering, the data was subsampled "historically." One would not expect to have data on older individuals during the early years of data accumulation. For example, the smallest sample size used here (50) corresponds to the point when the horses had been breeding in captivity for 22 years. Thus the oldest animal could be 22 years old. The bootstrap data sets were created by sampling n times with replacement. For animals exceeding the maximum age (in this example, 22 years) years at risk were truncated to the maximum age. In all, 100 bootstrap data sets were created for sample sizes of 50, 100, 200, and 1200. These numbers approximate the exponential acquisition of data that actually occurred with the horse population. These sample sizes actually correspond to 22, 33, 51, and 75 years in captivity. These are the same data sets used in the study by Taylor and Barlow in this volume (essay 2) to evaluate the step-wise Siler method.

RESULTS AND DISCUSSION

Results are given in figures 3.2 and 3.3 for estimates of growth rate (r) and SS respectively. The evaluation of the performance of the different approaches depends on the intended use of the mortality estimates as shown by our two goodness-of-fit measures. Recall that SS is simply a measure of how divergent the estimated survivorship values are from the true survivorship values. Each age receives equal weight, and it makes no difference if errors are positive or negative. The intrinsic rate

Figure 3.2 Mean intrinsic rates of growth (r) as calculated from fixed m_x rates and from l_x values determined by the different smoothing and model-based methods. For each sample size, 100 bootstrap subsamples were generated, which were then fit by each of the methods listed in the key. The growth rate for the full population of 1245 horses is depicted as the horizontal line at $r = 0.0405$. Error bars indicate $\pm$ one standard error. Sample size categories are represented on the abscissa with methods displaced for visual clarity. Lines between the means are for visual continuity.

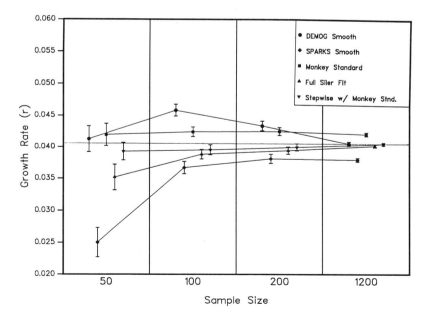

of growth (r), on the other hand, essentially weights the error by reproductive value. Further, negative and positive biases are revealed. It is interesting to note that the SPARKS smooth method is roughly equivalent to the full Siler and logit methods in SS but is consistently the worst method for estimating r and is negatively biased even at very large sample sizes. The DEMOG smooth method is the worst in terms of SS but performs better at estimating r and appears not to be biased at large sample sizes. The logit method appears to be quite similar to the full Siler in terms of SS but is remarkably stable and positively biased in estimating r. The step-wise Siler method appears to be best by both measures, but this is due in large part to the choice of standards (further discussion in Taylor and Barlow, essay 2 of this volume).

The mathematical models do as well as or better than the model-free

Figure 3.3 Mean error sum of squares for the methods listed in the key. Error bars indicate ± one standard error. Sample size categories are represented on the abscissa with methods displaced for visual clarity. Lines between the means are for visual continuity.

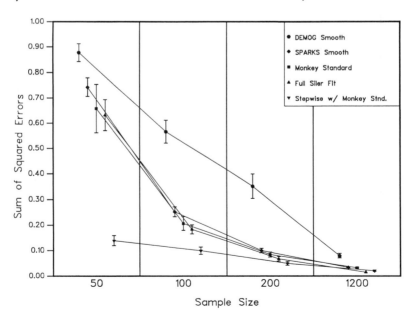

smoothing method and provide more reliable estimates of r. All three mathematical approaches provide remarkably good estimates of r even with very low sample sizes. Techniques using age-frequency data are often not even attempted at sample sizes less than about ninety (Spinage 1972), and yet we can see that for the mathematical models, estimates of r are generally within $\pm 1\%$ even for a sample size of 50 horses of which none were older than 22 years. It is likely, however, that this degree of accuracy at this sample size cannot be generalized to species with much higher reproductive rates, like the red ruffed lemur mentioned previously. Faster reproduction results in a younger distribution of animals. Thus, a sample size of 50 will probably be reached when a lower proportion of the total life span is represented. Further exploration of these models with different life history strategies would be useful. For management of captive animal populations, it is most likely that slow-growing populations will be allowed to grow at their maximum rate for sufficient time to gather data for most or all of the life span. Lemurlike species, on the other hand, are more likely to require active management at the early stages of data acquisition. Further analyses need to be done for captive mammals with high growth rates. The problem may need to be approached on a theoretical level.

Known-aged data for wild populations will, at least for most species, be acquired much more slowly. Although known-aged data will be accumulated primarily for early ages, the relative constancy of mortality for the adult ages of long-lived mammals may prompt a new technique that allows known-aged data to be combined with a constant adult estimate from sight/resight animals known to be adults but whose exact age is unknown. Evaluation of models, as was done for captive mammals in this study, using the types and quantities of data obtainable from wild populations would be useful to give a "most likely" mortality rate scenario. Upper and lower bounds for growth rates can be estimated using the techniques described in Barlow and Boveng (1991).

Acknowledgments
We would like to thank Michael Gilpin for suggesting demographic analyses of captive mortality and for providing the initial data. The study was improved through interactions with participants at the workshop entitled "Analytical Methods for Population Viability Analysis" hosted by the National Zoo and organized by Jon Ballou, Michael Gilpin, and Thomas Foose. Thoughtful reviews were given by Daniel Goodman, Doug DeMaster,

Michael Gilpin, Ted Case, and Jon Ballou. B. Taylor was supported by a National Institute of Health, Genetics Training grant to the Department of Biology. B. Dyke is supported by NIH Grant RR02229.

REFERENCES

Barlow, J. and P. Boveng. 1991. Modeling age-specific mortality for marine mammal populations. *Marine Mammal Science* 7:50–66.

Bingaman, L. and J. D. Ballou. 1993. *DEMOG (Version 4.1): Demographic Modeling Software.* Washington, D.C.: National Zoological Park.

Brass, W. 1971. On the scale of mortality. In W. Brass, ed., *Biological Aspects of Demography,* pp. 60–110. Symposia of the Society for the Study of Human Biology, vol. 10. London: Taylor and Francis.

Brockman, D. K. 1986. *International Studbook of the Ruffed Lemur.* San Diego: San Diego Zoological Society.

Caswell, H. 1989. *Matrix Population Models: Construction, Analysis, and Interpretation.* Sunderland, Mass.: Sinauer.

Caughley, G. 1966. Mortality patterns in mammals. *Ecology* 47:906–18.

Gage, T. B. 1990. Variation and classification of human age patterns of mortality: Analysis using competing hazards models. *Human Biology* 62:589–617.

Gage, T. B. and B. Dyke. 1988. Model life tables for the larger Old World monkeys. *American Journal of Primatology* 16:305–20.

Gompertz, B. 1825. On the nature of function expressive of the law of human mortality. *Philosophical Transactions of the Royal Society of London* 36:573–85.

ISIS. 1991. *Single Population Animal Records Keeping System (SPARKS).* Apple Valley, Minn.: International Species Information System.

Makeham, W. M. 1860. On the law of mortality. *Journal of the Institute of Actuaries* 13:325–58.

Siler, W. 1979. A competing-risk model for animal mortality. *Ecology* 60:750–57.

Spinage, C. A. 1972. African ungulate life tables. *Ecology* 53:645–52.

Tukey, J. W. 1977. *Exploratory Data Analysis.* Reading: Addison-Wesley.

Volf, J. 1959 et seq. *Pedigree Book of the Przewalski Horse.* Prague, Czechoslovakia: Prague Zoological Garden.

PART TWO

Genetic Analyses

4

Pedigree Analysis for Population Management

::

Robert C. Lacy, Jonathan D. Ballou, Frank Princée,
Anthony Starfield, and Elizabeth A. Thompson

The long-term survival of a population depends on the maintenance of sufficient genetic variation for individual fitness and population adaptability. Inbreeding depression, the reduction of fecundity and viability in progeny of matings between close genetic relatives, has been extensively documented in domesticated livestock (Darwin 1868; Wright 1977; Falconer 1981), captive populations of wild animals (Ralls et al. 1988; Lacy et al. 1993), and in many, but not all, wild populations (Wildt et al. 1987; Thornhill 1993). The loss of individual heterozygosity that occurs with inbreeding results in the expression of deleterious recessive genes and the loss of heterotic effects at overdominant loci (both components of the "genetic load" of a normally outbreeding population). Even if an inbred population is viable in its present environment, a lack of allelic diversity due to fixation of alleles by genetic drift would preclude an adaptive response to natural selection when the environment changes (Robertson 1960; Selander 1983; Allendorf 1986).

One component of population viability analysis (PVA) is the assessment of the genetic health of a population (Gilpin 1989). At the most general level, genetic analysis and management could consist of the application of the 50/500 rule for a minimum population size (Franklin 1980) or perhaps of an estimation of the fraction of the census population contributing to the genetically effective population size (N_e), and substitution of N_e into a standard equation for the loss of genetic variation (Lande and Barrowclough 1987). Unfortunately, this is as far as genetic analysis has been taken for many recovery programs for endangered species. The specific status of a particular population must be determined and its genetic vulnerability assessed before an effective management program for its preservation and recovery can be designed (e.g., Haig et al. 1993). This more intensive population management requires analyses tailored to the population's history, present status, and management needs. This approach requires an understanding of general processes, with focus on their impact on the specific case; this is the essence of population viability analysis.

Pedigree analysis, broadly defined as the genetic study of a particular multigenerational population with ancestral linkages that are known, knowable, or can be reasonably assumed or modeled, encompasses this class of case-specific analyses of genetic change. The emphasis is on examining the genetic structure imparted to the population by its pedigree relationships and evaluating the consequences of that structure on the long-term conservation of the population. The purpose of this study is to review the application of specific pedigree analysis techniques to the conservation of small populations and to discuss how genetic management is affected by the quality and quantity of the information available.

THE ASSUMPTION OF NEUTRALITY

Although the concern of genetic management for maintaining the viability of a population is to prevent its decimation caused by rapid selective removal of inbred animals and to allow for continued adaptive evolution via natural selection, pedigree analyses usually begin with an assumption of selective neutrality of the genetic variation under study. Because of the regularity of Mendelian inheritance, the transmission of a neutral genetic variant follows simple probabilistic rules. Results obtained for neutral variants at one genetic locus are applicable to all unlinked, neutral loci. The effect of selection on the maintenance of genetic variation is much more complex and is unpredictable when the agents of selection are not well understood. Natural selection can take on any of a number of forms (directional selection against an allele, balancing heterozygote superiority, disruptive homozygote superiority, frequency-dependent selection, epistatic dependence between loci), can fall anywhere along the spectrum of no selection to lethal alleles, and is dependent on the environment.

Because of the simplicity of the transmission of neutral alleles, because neutral variation represents the limiting case of weak selection, and because much existing genetic variation in natural populations is likely neutral or near neutral under existing conditions (Kimura 1983), models of change in neutral variation serve as very useful baselines for studying genetic change in pedigreed populations. Even the genetic variation necessary for adaptation to future environments is probably not under selection most of the time, for example, when populations bred in benevolent captive environments are to be used for releases into natural habitats. Thus, analysis of the fate of presently neutral variation may, in fact, accurately model the changes in the genetic variation that will be critical for a population's long-term viability. The use of pedigree analysis in population viability analysis will presumably be restricted to relatively small populations of up to several thousand individuals. The viability of larger populations would be affected minimally by stochastic changes in gene frequencies, and the use of pedigree analysis on a larger scale is difficult even when accurate data are available. Neutral models of genetic change in pedigree analysis will thus be inappropriate only for those genes under selection sufficiently strong to control genetic dynamics in the face of random genetic drift in small populations. Clearly, some traits do come under such strong selection during intensive management, and other methods of analysis should be used to consider the likely effects of modified natural or inadvertent artificial selection (see Arnold, essay 13 of this volume).

TOOLS FOR PEDIGREE ANALYSIS

The methods described in the following essays build upon earlier work by these authors and others. Previously available methods fall into three general classes: (1) the analytical calculation of genotype probabilities in completely known pedigrees, (2) the simulation of possible pedigrees resulting from known aspects of a population's structure, and (3) the determination of equations that broadly describe population genetic processes (table 4.1).

Analytical Calculation of Genotypes and Pedigree Relationships

The most complete and fundamental pedigree analysis (short of the empirical measurement of the state of each gene in every individual) is the specification of exact genetic relationships between every pair of individuals in a population. Measures of genetic relatedness (coefficient of kinship or consanguinity, coefficient of relationship) and the related concept of the inbreeding coefficient (which is a measure of the relatedness of the maternally inherited haploid genome of an individual to the paternally inherited haploid complement) were developed by Wright (1921, 1922), Malécot (1948), and others. Techniques for calculating genetic relatedness between every pair of individuals and the inbreeding coefficient of each individual are provided by Wright (1969) and Crow and Kimura (1970). The additive matrix method (Ballou 1983; Boyce 1983) provides an efficient means of calculating all pairwise kinships for even large populations. If the pedigree is known and if management calls for and allows precise control over each pairing, or accurate monitoring of the effects of inbreeding, the additive matrix should be calculated. This matrix also provides substantial information on the distribution of alleles descended from each founder (see below).

Every pedigree analysis must assume a starting population (the founders) among which there are no known genetic relationships. These founders are assumed to be unrelated and all subsequent calculations of genetic relatedness trace common ancestries only as far back as this founder stock. If two initial members of the population are thought to be related, ancestors of these animals, perhaps never directly observed, would be considered the genetic founders of the population, thereby preserving the condition that no two founders share a known common ancestor. Except for mutations, no closed population can ever have more genetic variation than did the founder stock, and several authors have suggested guidelines for the minimum numbers of founders needed for maintaining viable populations for conservation (e.g., Denniston

Table 4.1 Tools for Pedigree Analysis

METHOD	USE	REFERENCES*
I) Calculations of genotype or relationship probabilities from pedigrees:		
Path analysis	Kinships, inbreeding coefficients, causal basis for inherited traits	Wright 1921; Wright 1969; Ballou 1983; Lacy 1994*
Additive matrix	Kinships, inbreeding coefficients	Boyce 1983; Ballou 1983; Lacy 1994*
Mean kinship	Identification of genetically important individuals	Ballou and Lacy, essay 5, this vol.; Lacy 1994*
Founder analysis	Determination of gene diversity retained from founder stock and identification of under-represented lineages	Lacy 1989; Ballou and Foose in press; Lacy 1994*
Joint probabilities ("peeling")	Inference of ancestry of rare alleles; probability of survival of founder alleles	Thompson et al. 1978; Thompson 1983; 1986; Thomas 1986; Geyer and Thompson 1988; Thompson, essay 6, this vol.; Thomas 1991*
Trimming	Reduction of pedigree complexity to simplify calculations	Geyer et al. 1989; Thomas 1991*
II) Simulation of genotype or pedigree relationships:		
Gene drop	Simulation of gene transmission; determination of gene diversity and allelic loss, genetic relationships	MacCluer et al. 1986; Princée 1988; Lacy 1994*
Pedigree simulation	Elucidation of likely pedigree structure and genetic consequences from social biology	Harris et al. 1986; Seal and Lacy 1989; Princée, essay 7, this vol.; Starfield et al., essay 8, this vol.; Lacy 1993*
Gibbs sampler	Estimation of missing genotypes within a pedigree	Sheehan 1990; Thomas, essay. 11, this vol.
III) Equations for describing genetic consequences of pedigree structure:		
Effective population size	Calculation of expected rate of loss of gene diversity	Wright 1931; Wright 1969; Crow and Kimura 1970; Chesser 1983; Lande and Barrowclough 1987; Harris and Allendorf 1989
Calculated loss of alleles	Probability of allele loss	Crow and Kimura 1970; Allendorf 1986; Denniston 1977

* Computer software

1977; Foose 1983; Foose et al. 1986; Soulé et al. 1986; Lacy 1989). Because each generation is a genetic sampling from the previous one, some of the variation present in the founders will be lost in each generation by random drift. The goal of maintaining genetic diversity is equivalent to selecting pairings that maximize the retention of the founders' diversity.

For this reason, much of the present genetic management of captive populations focuses on the genetic representation of each founder in the descendant population (Foose et al. 1986). The expected representation of each founder's genes in each descendant can be determined simply as the genetic relatedness between the founder and each descendant. (A founder, by definition, can have no relatives in the pedigree other than direct descendants.) The total contribution of each founder to the population is simply the summed relationships to the living descendants.

Each founder's contributions can also be obtained from computer simulation (MacCluer et al. 1986; Princée 1988) of the stochastic process of Mendelian transmission through the pedigree. Simulations provide not only the mean number of copies of a founder's genome present in the descendant population but also the probability distribution for the number of extant copies of each founder allele. Lacy (1988; 1989) presented metrics for summarizing the retention of the founders' variation. Ballou and Foose (in press) presented measures for assessing the genetic importance of each descendant for the maintenance of genetic diversity, based on the rareness of the founder alleles that constitute the descendants' genomes. Haig et al. (1990) compared the utility of these metrics in identifying a maximally diverse set of Guam rails (*Rallus owstoni*) from a captive population to be reintroduced to the wild. In essay 5 of this volume Ballou and Lacy present additional such metrics and evaluate their effectiveness in managing hypothetical populations modeled by computer simulation. Tonkyn (1993) described the use of mathematical optimization techniques to extend metrics that identify genetically valuable individuals to the identification of genetically optimal sets of animals for breeding or release.

Thomas and Thompson (1984) and Thompson (1986) provided an exact method for calculating the probability of each possible distribution of founder alleles in the descendant population. Although the requirements for computer memory and computational time currently prohibit the use of this technique on highly complex pedigrees, methods developed to reduce a pedigree to just the information essential to an analysis of the living population allow calculations to be performed on most managed pedigrees ("peeling" methodology: Cannings et al. 1978; Thompson et al. 1978; "likelihood factorization": Thomas 1986; Thompson 1986, and "trimming": Geyer et al. 1989). An example of the use of these exact methods on a complex pedigree that could be reduced to a manageable analysis has been given for the Przewalski's horse (*Equus przewalskii*) (Geyer and Thompson 1988; Geyer et al. 1989). A survey comparing this method with the simulation method is described by Thomas (1990).

In essay 6 of this volume, Thompson develops further the use of exact techniques to identify individuals and groups of individuals containing unique genetic information that is at risk of being lost from the population. Thomas (essay 11 of this volume) uses a simulation technique from the field of image processing to estimate missing genomic information in a pedigree with partial information about the genotype of some individuals. This allows the simulation of genotypes in a pedigree subject to constraints of known phenotypes.

General Guidelines from Population Genetics Theory

The exact computation of relationships within known pedigrees as described above is necessary for intensive management of populations, where optimal matings are to be chosen for each generation. At a less specific level, population genetic theorists have provided analytical formulas describing the expected fate of alleles within generalized populations under varying assumptions about breeding structure, selection, and mutation (Wright 1969; Crow and Kimura 1970; Falconer 1981). While this large body of population genetic theory provides insights into the genetic processes of populations and forms the basis for most of our understanding of microevolutionary dynamics, it is both too general and too simplified to provide a complete guide to the selection of breeders in an intensive management program. Although theoretical formulas could be derived for the specific population structure of each population managed, such a case-by-case development of theory is not always practical; population genetics theory is appropriately focused on the elucidation of general principles.

Nevertheless, this theory can be, and has been, applied to the development of guidelines for population management. Chesser (1983) used inbreeding theory and several formulations of effective population size to examine the genetic consequences of a range of dispersal rates and mating structures and provided some general suggestions for the development of breeding programs for conservation. Another such derivation of a general guideline is provided by Thompson (essay 6 of this volume). Thompson shows that with the typical number of linkage groups in vertebrate genomes derived from the arrangement of genes along chromosomes, twelve progeny would be sufficient to obtain the entire genome of a progenitor with 99% certainty. The presence of linkage among genes is ignored in most analyses of gene transmission through pedigrees, but Thompson provides methods for utilizing the linkage information in deriving rules for effective genome conservation. Using general analytical formulas of the dynamics of additive genetic variance in quantitative traits, Lande (essay 14 of this volume) provides guidelines for the size of populations necessary to maintain particular levels of quantitative genetic variation. These results build on the earlier work of Franklin (1980) and Soulé et al. (1986), discussing the impact of population size on the conservation of genetic diversity.

Simulating Pedigrees

Simulation methods can be valuable for examining populations whose structure and dynamics are at least partially known (e.g., numbers of animals, sex ratio, social structure, fecundity and mortality rates, migration rates), even though individuals may not be identifiable, and therefore the existing pedigree cannot be reconstructed. These methods usually generate multiple simulated pedigrees from what is known about the dynamics of the population. These multiple pedigrees are then analyzed by one or more of the pedigree analysis techniques described above for general trends. Computer models of idealized populations thought to be representative of typical managed populations have been used to provide general guidelines for management, without addressing a particular pedigree structure or even the biological parameters of any specific population (e.g., Allendorf 1986; Lacy 1987; Ballou and Lacy, essay 5 of this volume).

Population viability analyses have made extensive use of pedigree simulation to examine the genetic consequences of the range of pedigree relationships possible given the constraints of known biological parameters. These analyses of genetic effects can be incorporated into overall assessments of the interacting genetic, demographic, and environmental risks faced by small populations and can then be used in developing conservation strategies (e.g., Mace 1990; Haig et al. 1993). The Captive Breeding Specialist Group (CBSG) of the International Union for the Conservation of Nature (e.g., Seal and Lacy 1989) and others have been using simulations to examine the likely retention of genetic variability and the consequent impact on a population's survival based on knowledge of basic population parameters (age-specific birth and death schedules, population numbers and age distribution, current and projected habitat availability). For example, Foose et al. (1991) used a computer simulation of a subdivided population structure to examine the loss of genetic diversity likely to occur subsequent to the fragmentation and isolation of black rhinoceros (*Diceros bicornis*) populations into small parks and preserves in Kenya. This assessment provided indications of the minimal size of a reserve capable of sustaining a population of rhinos and of the amount of managed migration necessary to prevent severe loss of diversity within the isolates. Harris et al. (1986) and Lacy (1993) have provided flexible and comprehensive simulation packages for these types of population projections.

The above studies used simulated pedigrees to examine likely genetic changes across a population and then to make recommendations as to the numbers of animals having to be maintained in the population or its subdivisions. Each assumed random mating (at least within local isolates), thus explicitly ignoring the pedigree structure that arises from nonrandom breeding systems. Yet, the social structure as well as the geographical structure of a population delineates the range of pedigrees possible as well as their genetic consequences. In Princée's study in this volume (essay 7) pedigree simulations that incorporate the breeding structure of a population are used to help guide the selection of specific breeding designs for captive populations. Starfield et al. (essay 8 of this volume) uses a similar approach to develop management techniques for African lions (*Panthera leo leo*) that utilize manipulation of the social structure in free-ranging populations. Information on social behavior allows a considerable refinement of analyses of genetic change; the manipulation of a population's social structure allows further opportunity for genetic management.

Selection of Appropriate Methods for Pedigree Management

The methods described above were developed to provide insight into the maintenance of genetic variability in small populations subject to stochastic genetic drift, and all are used to guide management programs designed to minimize losses of genetic variation. Although focused on the same overall management objective, the methods require different sorts and amounts of data as input, provide different kinds of information at varying levels of precision, and attend to different management subgoals (e.g., preservation of a particular genetic variant, assurance of no allelic losses, or management without identification of individuals within the population). Accordingly, the methods most appropriate for a management program will depend on available or attainable information, intended intensity of management, and specific needs of the population or population manager.

Data used in pedigree analysis can be broadly categorized as information on the population biology of the species (e.g., mating system, litter size, period of dependency on parental care, timing and distance of dispersal, group size, and sex ratio) and information on each individual (e.g., parentage, membership in kinship groups, and genotype as determined by molecular genetic analysis). At one extreme are those populations managed as social groups, such as herd-living ungulates, colonial birds or bats, or schooling fish, in which the identification of individuals may be difficult and the assignment of parentage may not be possible without extensive and expensive genetic testing. While information on individuals may be lacking, the degree of polygamy, monopolization of mating opportunities, fecundity and mortality schedules, and other biological parameters of the population may be well enough known to allow genetic modeling. Models that simulate pedigrees may be accurate enough to provide guidelines for the management of the genetics of these populations.

At the other extreme of information about individual and population biology are populations such as captive okapis (*Okapia johnstoni*),

Sumatran rhinos (*Dicerorhinus sumatrensis*), and Puerto Rican crested toads (*Peltophryne lemur*). For each of these species, all animals in captivity are well known, pairings are arranged deliberately with little possibility of confusion of parentage, records are kept on each captive individual in a studbook, and, consequently, the ancestry of each animal can be traced back to the original wild-caught founders. Unfortunately, relatively little is known of the population biology of these species in their natural habitats. The management of captive populations can (and does) include intensive discussion of appropriate pairings, but we would not know what to expect demographically, socially, or genetically if the animals were kept more or less free-ranging, in loosely managed environments.

The amount and type of information available limit, therefore, the methods of analysis that can be applied and define the intensity of genetic management that is possible. Figure 4.1 crudely represents the constraint of information available about individual and population biology (the horizontal axes) on the scope of genetic management possible (the vertical axis). If we had complete information on both the population biology of the species and the individuals within the population under study (the back upper corner of the surface in figure 4.1; labeled as area I) we could apply any of the available analytical methods discussed earlier (although some might have little value in the case of complete information, because they are tools for estimating missing information based on partial knowledge). Inbreeding coefficients, genetic relatedness, and genotype probabilities could be calculated precisely, pairings could be made that would optimize the retention of genetic variation (either mean heterozygosity or number of allelic variants, but perhaps not both simultaneously), and a mating scheme could be designed that approximates the natural social behavior of the species.

If some individual information is absent but data on the population biology are excellent, analytical methods can be used to solve some of the problems associated with missing individual data, and intensive genetic management can still be practiced (figure 4.1, area II). For example, when the mating system is well known, various scenarios for missing parentage can be modeled using some of the techniques discussed earlier. A "most likely" complete pedigree can then be used to calculate the needed genetic relationships. Generally, as less individual information is known about the pedigree structure, more information on the population biology will be needed to design management programs that adequately address the genetic requirements for population viability.

If individual information is complete (and animals are amenable to all desired manipulations), then population biological information is not essential to the design of intensive genetic management plans that optimize various genetic criteria (figure 4.1, area III). At least among sexually reproducing diploid organisms, Mendelian inheritance is near-

Figure 4.1 Possible intensity of population management (vertical axis) constrained by the amount of information available on individuals within the population (*x*-axis) and on the population biology parameters of the species (*y*-axis). Roman numerals indicate regions of information availability and intended management intensity as described in the text.

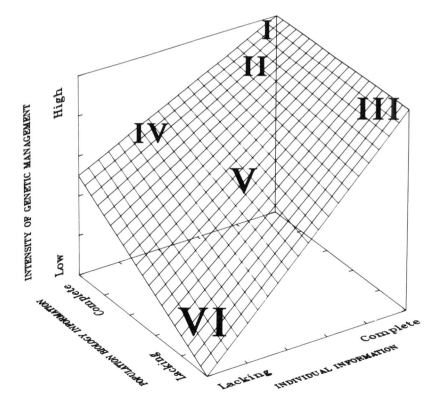

ly universal and the stochastic effects of genetic drift are definable in terms of probability distributions if the complete pedigree structure is known. (Obviously, the management of diets, behaviors, epidemiology, and virtually all nongenetic aspects of biology does require more knowledge of the population.)

If less complete individual and population biology information is available, the methods of pedigree analysis possible are restricted and, consequently, the possible intensity of genetic management is reduced (figure 4.1, areas IV and V). Exact genetic relationships cannot be determined for any animals lacking a complete record of ancestry. It would, therefore, not be possible to determine the matings that would absolutely minimize inbreeding and maximize gene diversity. Willis (1993) assessed the possible costs in terms of lost gene diversity of incorporating or omitting individuals with unknown parentage in breeding programs. Pedigree and population simulation models that generate a range of possible pedigrees based on whatever individual and population biology data are available will be necessary to formulate more generalized recommendations for genetic management.

Molecular genetic analyses of DNA similarity can be used to fill in the gaps of incomplete pedigrees or to estimate relationships among animals when pedigree records are missing (Avise et al., essay 9 of this volume). Morin and Ryder (1991) used mitochondrial DNA and DNA fingerprint analyses to generate sufficient information on relationships in a colony of lion-tailed macaques (*Macaca silenus*) to allow the animals to be incorporated into a population being managed via pedigree analyses. Haig et al. (1994) used the similarity of DNA profiles to examine hypotheses regarding the relationships among the founders of the captive population of Guam rails. They also tested the usefulness of DNA similarity profiles as a substitute for mean kinships (Ballou and Lacy, essay 5 of this volume) in identifying genetically important individuals when information about the pedigree is missing.

When little or no information is available on either the population biology or individual identities of the population (figure 4.1, area VI), guidelines for genetic management must be based on generalized population genetics theory without reference to specific details of the managed population. Management then can only be of very low intensity and is likely to be insufficient for the long-term conservation of genetic diversity in small populations.

The option of precise and intensive management may not necessarily always be desirable or even appropriate. Tragically, the number of endangered species grows daily, and monetary, facility, and human resources for the management of endangered species are limited. Thus, just as managers of endangered captive populations often strive to maintain no more than the minimum number of animals required for population viability in order not to exclude other needy taxa (Conway 1986; Soulé et al. 1986), efficient use of limited resources would employ the least intensive management required to achieve success for each population. For example, if group management with minimal control of breeding can be shown to achieve adequate long-term demographic and genetic stability (see Princée, essay 7 of this volume), intensive efforts can be directed elsewhere.

Figure 4.1 can also be used to identify the approximate information and management intensity space addressed by the methods described in the following studies. The tools presented by Ballou and Lacy (essay 5 of this volume) and Thompson (essay 6 of this volume) for identifying genetically important individuals can be very powerful and precise, leading to optimal solutions to management goals. To be fully utilized, these approaches require that the ancestry of all animals can be fully traced back to the founder stock, but no knowledge of the population's biology is used in these analyses (figure 4.1, regions I to III). Ballou and Lacy also present the modifications to their techniques necessary to omit from consideration portions of pedigrees that are unknown. Thompson's (essay 6 of this volume) calculation of the probability that entire founder genomes have survived among progeny requires an accurate count of the founder's progeny but does not (yet) use information about descendants in later generations. This method can be applied to situations described by areas I, II, III, and perhaps V. The technique of genotype estimation presented by Thomas (essay 11 of this volume) applies to area II: it requires considerable information about each individual (the pedigree structure and some data on genotypes), makes use of additional information on genotype frequencies in the population, and provides access to additional individual information (the likely genotypes of unobserved individuals). Princée (essay 7 of this volume) utilizes information on the managed social structure of a population to simulate genetic dynamics and thereby assess the impact of the group structure on the goals of genetic management. Thus, modest information on the population biology (the likely breeding outcomes resulting from a managed group structure) is used to determine whether the resulting pedigree would be adequate (area V). Starfield et al. (essay 8 of this volume) demonstrate computer modeling of the natural social system in a wild population of lions (thereby using considerable population biological information) to examine the genetic consequences of the resulting simulated pedigrees (area IV). Modifications of the social system are possible in order to achieve some genetic management but only within the constraints of the natural behaviors of free-ranging lions.

DIRECTIONS FOR THE FUTURE

The methods of pedigree analysis available in the literature and presented in the following studies leave many gaps on figure 4.1. For many populations we will have considerable information about individuals and the population as a whole, but the available information may not be sufficient to utilize fully the desired techniques. A single gap in a pedigree can confound an analysis of genetically important individuals; an uncertain migration rate can shift a simulation of population structure from a useful exploration to meaningless guesswork. Analysis can be restricted to those parts of pedigrees that are completely known (Ballou and Lacy, essay 5 of this volume) or to those populations with well-understood structure and dynamics, but gaps in data will then cause individuals or populations to be omitted from management plans. Often, assumptions can be made (about probable fathers or likely migration rates, for example) that allow an analysis of uncertain data to still be useful. If several equally likely possibilities exist, each can be assumed and the consequences can be assessed in turn, and then the impact of the missing data on management decisions can be examined (e.g., Willis 1993). Alternatively, a less demanding and less precise analytical method can be used that does not require information beyond what is available. Managers will need guidance as to when to stretch the reliability of the data to use powerful tools and when to fall back on simple tools that require fewer data.

Often multiple methods could be applied, independently or interactively, to increase the precision of results. A general simulation might indicate how much could be achieved with minimal management;

complete calculations of kinships and losses of diversity may indicate whether the additional gains from intensive management would be worth the effort. A simulation program may be developed to provide a sampling of possible relationships needed to fill in a gap in an otherwise complete pedigree, somewhat analogous to Thomas' use of partial information to estimate missing genotypic data (essay 11 of this volume). Molecular genetic analyses can be used to infer the most probable ancestries in an incomplete pedigree (e.g., Morin and Ryder 1991; Avise et al., essay 9 of this volume). It should be possible to use all the individual information available in an incomplete data set together with simulations that utilize population biology information to generate many possible resolutions—or even an enumeration of all possible resolutions—of uncertainties in order to maximize genetic criteria based on the available information.

Finally, we need to continue to develop, expand, refine, and evaluate techniques for genetic management. The genetic management of populations for conservation (as opposed to management of domesticated stocks for rapid improvement in production characteristics) is a very new field, but it can advance rapidly by adapting the analytical methods of fields such as human genetics and animal sciences. Methods used in other fields may have valuable applications to genetic management not yet recognized by wildlife managers having little familiarity with these approaches. The continued development and application of techniques for pedigree analysis will depend on continued feedback between those developing methods and those requiring them for population management.

Acknowledgments

Many of the workshop participants made comments and suggestions that helped to clarify our thinking and the presentation of the material. We thank Alun Thomas especially for insights during the workshop and comments on a draft of this chapter.

REFERENCES

Allendorf, F. W. 1986. Genetic drift and the loss of alleles versus heterozygosity. *Zoo Biology* 5:181–90.

Ballou, J. D. 1983. Calculating inbreeding coefficients from pedigrees. In C. M. Schonewald-Cox, S. M. Chambers, B. MacBryde, and W. L. Thomas, eds., *Genetics and Conservation: A Reference for Managing Wild Animal and Plant Populations,* pp. 509–20. Menlo Park: Benjamin/Cummings.

Ballou, J. D. and T. J. Foose. In press. Demographic and genetic management of captive populations. In D. G. Kleiman, S. Lumpkin, M. Allen, H. Harris, and K. Thompson, eds., *Wild Mammals in Captivity*. Chicago: University of Chicago Press.

Boyce, A. J. 1983. Computation of inbreeding and kinship coefficients on extended pedigrees. *Journal of Heredity* 74:400–94.

Cannings, C., E. A. Thompson, and M. H. Skolnick. 1978. Probability functions on complex pedigrees. *Advances in Applied Probability* 10:26–61.

Chesser, R. K. 1983. Isolation by distance: Relationship to the management of genetic resources. In C. M. Schonewald-Cox, S. M. Chambers, B. MacBryde, and W. L. Thomas, eds., *Genetics and Conservation: A Reference for Managing Wild Animal and Plant Populations*, pp. 66–77. Menlo Park: Benjamin/Cummings.

Conway, W. G. 1986. The practical difficulties and financial implications of endangered species breeding programmes. *International Zoo Yearbook* 24/25:210–19.

Crow, J. F. and M. Kimura. 1970. *An Introduction to Population Genetics Theory.* New York: Harper and Row.

Darwin, C. 1868. *The Variation of Animals and Plants Under Domestication.* London: John Murray.

Denniston, C. 1977. Small population size and genetic diversity: Implications for endangered species. In S. A. Temple, ed., *Endangered Birds: Management Techniques for Preserving Threatened Species*, pp. 281–89. Madison: University of Wisconsin Press.

Falconer, D. S. 1981. *Introduction to Quantitative Genetics.* 2d ed. New York: Longman.

Foose, T. J. 1983. The relevance of captive populations to the conservation of biotic diversity. In C. M. Schonewald-Cox, S. M. Chambers, B. MacBryde, and W. L. Thomas, eds., *Genetics and Conservation: A Reference for Managing Wild Animal and Plant Populations*, pp. 374–401. Menlo Park: Benjamin/Cummings.

Foose, T. J., R. Lande, N. R. Flesness, G. Rabb, and B. Read. 1986. Propagation plans. *Zoo Biology* 5:139–46.

Foose, T. J., R. C. Lacy, R. Brett, and U. S. Seal. 1991. *Kenya Black Rhinoceros Metapopulation Workshop Report.* Apple Valley, Minn.: IUCN SSC Captive Breeding Specialist Group.

Franklin, I. 1980. Evolutionary change in small populations. In M. E. Soulé and B. Wilcox, eds., *Conservation Biology: An Evolutionary Ecological Perspective*, pp. 135–49. Sunderland, Mass.: Sinauer.

Geyer, C. J. and E. A. Thompson. 1988. Gene survival in the Asian wild horse (*Equus przewalskii*), I: Dependence of gene survival in the Calgary Breeding Group pedigree. *Zoo Biology* 7:313–27.

Geyer, C. J., E. A. Thompson, and O. A. Ryder. 1989. Gene survival in the Asian wild horse (*Equus przewalskii*), II: Gene survival in the whole population, in subgroups, and through history. *Zoo Biology* 8:313–29.

Gilpin, M. 1989. Population viability analysis. *Endangered Species Update* 6 (10): 15–18.

Haig, S. M., J. D. Ballou, and S. R. Derrickson. 1990. Management options for preserving genetic diversity: Reintroduction of Guam rails to the wild. *Conservation Biology* 4:290–300.

Haig, S. M., J. R. Belthoff, and D. H. Allen. 1993. Population viability analysis for a small population of red-cockaded woodpeckers and an evaluation of enhancement strategies. *Conservation Biology* 7:289–301.

Haig, S. M., J. D. Ballou, and N. J. Casna. 1994. Identification of kin structure among Guam rail founders: A comparison of pedigrees and DNA profiles. *Molecular Ecology* 3:109–19.

Harris, R. B. and F. W. Allendorf. 1989. Genetically effective population size of large mammals: An assessment of estimators. *Conservation Biology* 3:181–91.

Harris, R. B., L. H. Metzgar, and C. D. Bevins. 1986. *GAPPS (Generalized Animal Population Projection System) User's Manual.* Missoula, Montana: Montana Cooperative Wildlife Research Unit, University of Montana.

Kimura, M. 1983. *The Neutral Theory of Molecular Evolution.* Cambridge: Cambridge University Press.

Lacy, R. C. 1987. Loss of genetic diversity from managed populations: Interacting effects of drift, mutation, immigration, selection, and population subdivision. *Conservation Biology* 1:143–58.

Lacy, R. C. 1988. Genetic variability in captive stocks: Assessing past loss, present status, and future outlook. *AAZPA 1988 Annual Proceedings:* 113–21.

Lacy, R. C. 1989. Analysis of founder representation in pedigrees: Founder equivalents and founder genome equivalents. *Zoo Biology* 8:111–24.

Lacy, R. C. 1993. VORTEX: A computer simulation model for Population Viability Analysis. *Wildlife Research* 20:45–65.

Lacy, R. C. 1994. *GENES: A computer program for pedigree analysis and genetic management.* Chicago: Chicago Zoological Society.

Lacy, R. C., A. M. Petric, and M. Warneke. 1993. Inbreeding and outbreeding depression in captive populations of wild species. In N. W. Thornhill, ed., *The Natural History of Inbreeding and Outbreeding,* pp. 352–74. Chicago: University of Chicago Press.

Lande, R. and G. F. Barrowclough. 1987. Effective population size, genetic variation, and their use in population management. In M. E. Soulé, ed., *Viable Populations for Conservation,* pp. 87–123. Cambridge: Cambridge University Press.

MacCluer, J. W., J. L. VandeBerg, B. Read, and O. A. Ryder. 1986. Pedigree analysis by computer simulation. *Zoo Biology* 5:147–60.

Mace, G. 1990. Effect of immigration and inbreeding on addax populations. In U. S. Seal, K. Sausman, and J. Mikolai, eds., *CBSG Aridland Antelope Workshop,* pp. 175–82. San Antonio, Texas: Captive Breeding Specialist Group, International Union for the Conservation of Nature and Natural Resources.

Malécot, G. 1948. *Les mathématiques de l'hérédité.* Paris: Masson.

Morin, P. A. and O. A. Ryder. 1991. Founder contribution and pedigree inference in a captive breeding colony of lion-tailed macaques, using mitochondrial DNA and DNA fingerprint analyses. *Zoo Biology* 10:341–52.

Princée, F. P. G. 1988. Genetic variation in the zoo population of the red panda subspecies *Ailurus fulgens fulgens. Zoo Biology* 7:219–31.

Ralls, K., J. D. Ballou, and A. Templeton. 1988. Estimates of lethal equivalents and the cost of inbreeding in mammals. *Conservation Biology* 2:185–93.

Robertson, A. 1960. A theory of limits in artificial selection. *Proceedings of the Royal Society of London* 153B:234–49.

Seal, U. S. and R. C. Lacy. 1989. *Florida Panther Population Viability Analysis.* Report to the U.S. Fish and Wildlife Service. Apple Valley, Minnesota: Captive Breeding Specialist Group, Species Survival Commission, IUCN.

Selander, R. K. 1983. Evolutionary consequences of inbreeding. In C. M. Schonewald-Cox, S. M. Chambers, B. MacBryde, and W. L. Thomas, eds., *Genetics and Conservation: A Reference for Managing Wild Animal and Plant Populations,* pp. 201–15. Menlo Park: Benjamin/Cummings.

Sheehan, N. A. 1990. Genetic reconstruction on complex pedigrees. Ph.D. diss., University of Washington, Seattle.

Soulé, M., M. Gilpin, W. Conway, and T. Foose. 1986. The millennium ark: How long a voyage, how many staterooms, how many passengers? *Zoo Biology* 5:101–13.

Thomas, A. 1986. Approximate computation of probability functions for pedigree analysis. *IMA Journal of Mathematics Applied in Medicine and Biology* 3:157–66.

Thomas, A. 1990. A comparison of an exact and a simulation method for calculating gene extinction probabilities in pedigrees. *Zoo Biology* 9:259–74.

Thomas, A. 1991. *PEDPACK.* Bath, U.K.: School of Mathematical Sciences, University of Bath.

Thomas, A. and E. A. Thompson. 1984. Gene survival in an isolated population: The number of distinct genes on Tristan da Cunha. *Annals of Human Biology* 11:101–12.

Thompson, E. A. 1983. A recursive algorithm for inferring gene origins. *Annals of Human Genetics* 47:143–52.

Thompson, E. A. 1986. Ancestry of alleles and extinction of genes in populations with defined pedigrees. *Zoo Biology* 5:161–70.

Thompson, E. A., C. Cannings, and M. H. Skolnick. 1978. Ancestral inference. I: The problem and the method. *Annals of Human Genetics* 42:95–108.

Thornhill, N. W., ed. 1993. *The Natural History of Inbreeding and Outbreeding.* Chicago: University of Chicago Press.

Tonkyn, D. W. 1993. Optimization techniques for the genetic management of endangered species. *Endangered Species Update* 10:1–4, 9.

Wildt, D. E., M. Bush, K. L. Goodrowe, C. Packer, A. E. Pusey, J. L. Brown, P. Joslin, and S. J. O'Brien. 1987. Reproductive and genetic consequences of founding isolated lion populations. *Nature* 329:328–31.

Willis, K. 1993. Use of animals with unknown ancestries in scientifically managed breeding programs. *Zoo Biology* 12:161–72.

Wright, S. 1921. Systems of mating. *Genetics* 6:111–78.

Wright, S. 1922. Coefficients of inbreeding and relationship. *American Naturalist* 56:330–38.

Wright, S. 1931. Evolution in Mendelian populations. *Genetics* 16:97–159.

Wright, S. 1969. *Evolution and the Genetics of Populations. Vol. 2. The Theory of Gene Frequencies.* Chicago: University of Chicago Press.

Wright, S. 1977. *Evolution and the Genetics of Populations. Vol. 3. Experimental Results and Evolutionary Deductions.* Chicago: University of Chicago Press.

5

Identifying Genetically Important Individuals for Management of Genetic Variation in Pedigreed Populations

Jonathan D. Ballou and Robert C. Lacy

Captive populations are a valuable contribution to the conservation of threatened and endangered species (Foose 1983; Foose et al., essay 12 of this volume). Captive populations, by nature, however, are small, fragmented, and often dispersed among many zoos distributed over a wide geographic range. The capacity of any single institution to hold a large number of individuals of any one species is limited. Cooperative breeding programs are needed to ensure that zoo collections are managed jointly under the goal of the species' long-term conservation. Ideally, these programs should be part of a comprehensive and integrated conservation strategy that includes protection and management of wild populations and habitat as well as the captive component (Jones 1990).

The primary role of the captive population in such an integrated program is, if necessary, to provide animals for reinforcing or reestablishing wild populations.

The principal objective for cooperative breeding programs is to establish demographically secure and self-sustaining populations capable of maintaining high levels of genetic variation (Foose 1983). The genetic challenges that confront small populations in the zoo environment are extensive. Loss of genetic variation through genetic drift (Nei et al. 1975), inbreeding depression (Ralls et al. 1988; Lacy et al. 1993), and selection for the captive environment (Arnold, essay 13 of this volume) all affect the species' short- and long-term fitness. Genetic management attempts to mitigate these problems by implementing breeding strategies that retain genetic variation. This approach minimizes changes in the population's gene pool and thereby retains, as much as possible, the genetic characteristics of the original founders of the population. Genetic management is most effectively accomplished under conditions that allow intensive management and in populations with completely known pedigrees. This permits explicit decisions to be made about who breeds, how often, with whom, and when.

This study addresses the issue of how breeding recommendations are made. In particular, it discusses several analytical methods, based on pedigree analyses, for identifying genetically "important" animals— those individuals whose reproduction is most critical for the retention of genetic diversity. These individuals are then given the highest breeding priority. We present the concept of genetic importance as defined by mean kinship and kinship value, and present the results of computer models that evaluate how well various breeding strategies based on different measures of genetic importance maintain genetic diversity in a variety of pedigrees. Methods to calculate these measures when pedigree data are only partially known are also presented.

GENETIC CHARACTERISTICS OF CAPTIVE POPULATIONS

One basis for developing genetic management recommendations is to minimize the loss of genetic variation through maximizing a population's effective size (N_e). The concept of an effective size of a population was originally introduced by Wright (1931) as the number of individuals that, if there were random union of gametes, would lose hetero-zygosity at the rate observed in the real population. However, loss of heterozygosity is just one consequence of genetic drift. The concept of effective size has also been applied to the number of individuals in a population with random union of gametes that would drift at the rate of the studied population, with the rate of genetic drift being measured as the sampling variance of gene frequencies from parental to offspring generations (the "variance effective number") instead of the rate of change of heterozygosity or inbreeding (the "inbreeding effective num-ber"). In a randomly breeding population of constant size, the inbreed-ing and variance effective sizes will be the same, but in a population that is changing in size, the consequences of genetic drift (loss of hetero-zygosity and variance in allele frequencies) can occur at somewhat dif-ferent times. The inbreeding effective size depends primarily on the size of the parental generation, while the variance effective size is more de-pendent on the number of offspring (Crow and Kimura 1970). Hetero-zygosity is retained through maximizing the inbreeding effective size, while allelic diversity is retained through maximizing the variance effec-tive size. Both effective numbers are functions of sex ratio, number of breeders, and the mean and variance in numbers of offspring they pro-duce (Harris and Allendorf 1989; Lande and Barrowclough 1987; Crow and Kimura 1970). A general strategy for maintaining genetic di-versity would be to maximize the number of breeders, equalize family size, equalize the sex ratio of breeders, and reduce fluctuations in popu-lation size over time (Foose et al. 1986).

Maximizing N_e, however, might not be the most effective strategy for maintaining genetic diversity in populations with known pedigrees. Pedigree analysis should allow the population manager to target indi-viduals and lineages for preferential breeding. Quite possibly, a strategy that utilizes all the information contained within a pedigree could pre-serve genetic variation better than one that is based on maximization of N_e but ignores the ancestry of each individual. Two factors make this an interesting and difficult problem. The first is that there has been no strong theoretical development of the concepts of breeding strategies based on pedigree analyses, and the second is that pedigrees of captive populations are often extremely complex.

Captive populations are generally characterized by a small number of founders and relatively small population sizes (Hutchins et al. 1991).

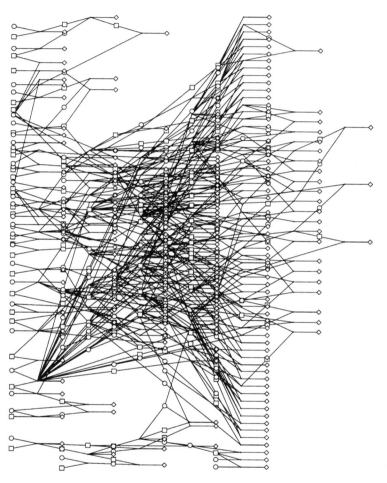

Figure 5.1 Marriage node pedigree of the 1990 golden lion tamarin (*Leontopithecus rosalia*) captive population (Ballou 1989). Pedigree drawn using PEDPACK (Thomas 1991).

Few captive populations have had the benefit of genetic management throughout their history. In unmanaged populations, reproduction is often highly skewed in favor of tractable, easily handled animals. Because of this, the genetic contribution of the founders to the extant gene pool is often highly skewed, with a large proportion of the gene pool having descended from only a small proportion of the founders. Furthermore, a large proportion of the founders' alleles may have already been lost due to genetic drift, and inbreeding levels may also be high. Preferential breeding has usually resulted in a high variance of family size and the likelihood of strong selection for the captive environment. In addition, sex ratios of breeders are highly skewed in many species managed as herds with a single breeding male. These characteristics combine to result in populations with historically small effective sizes and extremely complex pedigrees (figure 5.1).

The genetics of the population may be further complicated by population subdivision. Populations in zoos in different regions are likely to be founded by unrelated individuals. When migration between regions is limited or nonexistent (due to either logistic difficulties or lack of management), separate lineages are established and perpetuated, resulting in highly inbred lines descended from different founder stocks.

When genetic management is applied to a population, the population manager must attempt not only to compensate for these past management deficiencies but also to minimize further loss of genetic variation. Simply applying a general strategy to maximize the effective population size may not be the most appropriate approach. Compensation will require preferential breeding of some individuals rather than breeding to equalize family size. Formulating genetic management recommendations, therefore, is a process of identifying through pedigree analyses the genetically most important animals in the population.

GENETIC MANAGEMENT AT THE POPULATION LEVEL

The goal of genetic management is the preservation of the genetic variation of the population from which the founders were drawn (Lacy 1994). Since the source population's genetic variation is represented by the gene pool of the founders, genetic management therefore strives to minimize the loss of the founders' genetic variation.

The status of the founders' genetic variation in the extant population can be described by using two concepts. The first is the genetic contribution of the founders to the extant gene pool. In accord with the rules of Mendelian segregation, the "founder contribution" ($p_{i.}$) is the expected proportion of the population's gene pool that has descended from founder i (Lacy 1989). The second is the loss of founder alleles due to genetic drift (Thompson 1986). Allele "retention" (r_i) is defined as the expected proportion of founder i's alleles that have survived to the extant population (Lacy 1989). Information on founder contribution and retention can be combined and summarized by "founder genome equivalents" (f_g, Lacy 1989). Founder genome equivalent is the theoretically expected number of founders that would be required to provide the level of genetic diversity observed in the living population if the founders were all equally represented and had lost no alleles (100% retention) (Lacy 1989). The value of f_g can be estimated by:

$$f_g = \frac{1}{\displaystyle\sum_{j=1}^{N_f} (p_{j.}^2/r_j)} \tag{5.1}$$

in which N_f is the number of founders. Both skewed founder contribution and low retention result in a decrease in founder genome equivalents.

As pointed out by Lacy (1989), founder genome equivalent is directly related to loss of gene diversity (GD, the heterozygosity expected if the population were in Hardy-Weinberg equilibrium: $GD = 1 - \Sigma[q_i^2]$, in which q_i is the frequency of allele i). The gene diversity of the descendants of a randomly mating population, as a proportion of the gene diversity of the population from which the founders were randomly sampled, is $1 - 1/[2f_g]$. Therefore, genetic management strategies that maximize founder genome equivalents also maximize gene diversity. As can be noted from equation (5.1), this is not simply a matter of equalizing the founder contributions ($p_{i.} = p_{j.}$). The upper limit to founder genome equivalents for any population is the retention totaled over all founders (Σr_i), a value Lacy (1989) terms the number of founder genomes surviving (f_s). It can be seen by substitution in equation (5.1) that f_g is maximized when

$$p_{j.} = \frac{r_j}{f_s} \qquad (5.2)$$

Thus, to maximize founder genome equivalents, and hence gene diversity, each founder's contribution should be proportional to its contribution to the number of founder genomes surviving. This is defined as the "target founder contribution" (Ballou and Foose 1994). Management for maintaining genetic diversity within the population could therefore strive to adjust the observed founder contributions to match the target founder contributions by preferentially breeding individuals descended from founders whose contributions currently fall below their targets. This achieves equalization, not of the proportion of the gene pool contributed by each founder, but of the frequencies of those founder alleles that are still retained within the population.

MEASURES OF GENETIC IMPORTANCE

While the target founder contribution can provide goals for genetic management, identifying individuals that achieve this result is problematic. Pedigree analyses provide data on the founder contribution, the allele probability distributions, and the level of inbreeding for each individual in the population. In large populations with many founders the amount of information to consider can be formidable. In addition, complex pedigrees result in genetically complex individuals, many descended from numerous founders. For example, individuals that are descendants of "underrepresented" founders may also carry alleles from "overrepresented" founders. These complexities have led to the development of a number of strategies to identify, or rank, animals by their genetic importance. These are described below.

Founder Importance Coefficient (fic)

The first measure of genetic importance used in captive breeding programs was based on the goal of equalizing the genetic contribution of founders to the gene pool (Foose 1983), ignoring the complications (above) of the loss of some founder alleles. Equal representation of founders assures that the genetic variation present in each founder is not excluded from the gene pool, while also ensuring that the gene pool is not dominated by genes from a few founders. Under this strategy, genetic importance is assigned to descendants of underrepresented founders; they are given breeding preference.

The degree to which an individual (i) is descended from under- or overrepresented founders can be summarized by its *founder importance coefficient* (fic_i):

$$fic_i = \sum_{j=1}^{N_f} (p_{j.} \times p_{ji}) \tag{5.3}$$

in which $p_{j.}$ is the founder contribution of founder j to the population's gene pool; p_{ji} is the contribution of founder j to individual i; and N_f is the number of founders contributing descendants to the population (Ballou and Foose 1994). The value of *fic* is the weighted average of the founder contribution in that individual with each founders' contribution to the total population acting as the weights. Individuals with high *fic* values are descended from overrepresented founders. Generally, *fic* values range from a low of $\min(p_{j.})$ (the $p_{j.}$ of the most underrepresented founder if it is still alive) to $\max(p_{j.})$ if the most overrepresented founder is alive. Ranking individuals by their *fic* provides a simple method of identifying genetically important animals as defined by founder contribution.

The problem is, however, that *fic* does not consider any loss of founder alleles. Equalizing the founder contribution will not maximize gene diversity because it results in overrepresentation of alleles from founders that have low allelic retention. For this reason, it is no longer used for population management. It was, however, used for the Species Survival Plan (SSP) program of the American Association of Zoological Parks and Aquariums (AAZPA) to identify genetically important animals during the late 1980s before other measures of genetic importance were developed (see below).

Genome Uniqueness (gu)

Genome uniqueness provides another method for measuring genetic importance. The genome uniqueness of an individual is the probability that an allele chosen at random from that individual is unique within the living population (i.e., the selected allele is identical by descent to no alleles in any other living animal). Under the assumption that loci are independent, genome uniqueness, by extension, is the proportion of an individual's genome that is unique in the population. Genome uniqueness is used to identify individuals carrying alleles at high risk of being lost (not passed on to the next generation; MacCluer et al. 1986).

While genome uniqueness can be calculated exactly (i.e., using peeling algorithms, Cannings et al. 1978; Thomas 1991), the methods are computationally intensive, even for moderate-sized pedigrees. An alternative is to use a "gene-drop" analysis, which simulates the transmission of founder alleles (each founder is assigned two uniquely identifiable alleles) through the pedigree to the living population (MacCluer et al 1986; Lacy et al., essay 4 of this volume). The frequency and distribution of alleles in the living population is inferred from multiple simulations. Genome uniqueness is calculated as the proportion of simulations in which an individual receives the only copy of a founder allele:

$$gu_i = \frac{\sum_{j=1}^{NSIM} a_j}{2 \times NSIM} \tag{5.4}$$

in which a_j is the number of individual i's alleles at a given locus that are present in no other living animal in simulation j (a_j = 0, 1, or 2) and $NSIM$ is the number of simulations. Individuals with high gu should be given breeding priority in order to ensure that their unique alleles are maintained in the population.

The primary problem with genome uniqueness is that it measures only alleles that are unique and does not consider other alleles that are at high risk of being lost, for example, alleles that have only two copies in the population. While genome uniqueness as discussed here refers to the uniqueness of an individual's genome, the concept has been extended to the uniqueness of the gene pool of predefined groups of individuals (e.g., families or animals within a geographic region; Geyer et al. 1989; Thompson, essay 6 of this volume).

Mean Kinship (*mk*)

We propose a third method of identifying genetically important individuals, based on the concept of kinship. Genetic importance can be defined using the average relationship of each individual to the population as a whole. Conceptually, genetic importance is related to the number and degree of relatives an individual has in the population. Individuals with many living, close relatives carry alleles that are more common in the population and therefore are less important than individuals with few relatives. This can be quantified by mean kinship (*mk*).

The relationship between a pair of individuals can be measured with the kinship coefficient (f_{ij}), which is defined as the probability that alleles drawn randomly from each of two individuals (*i* and *j*) are identical by descent (Falconer 1981). The *mean kinship* of individual *i* (mk_i) is then defined as the average of the kinship coefficients between that individual and all living individuals (including itself):

$$mk_i = \frac{\sum\limits_{j=1}^{N} f_{ij}}{N} \qquad (5.5)$$

in which N is the number of living animals in the population. Individuals with low mean kinship values represent genetically important animals.

Mean kinship is an intuitively appealing method for ranking individuals in terms of their genetic importance. It also relates directly to maximizing founder genome equivalents and gene diversity. The mean kinship of an animal is the expected (in the statistical sense) inbreeding coefficient of progeny of this individual if it were mated at random in the population (regardless of the age or sex of itself or its mate and including possibly mating with itself). By extension, the average mean kinship ($\overline{mk}$) of the population is the expected mean inbreeding coefficient of all progeny if mating were at random. It is therefore equal to the proportional loss of gene diversity of the descendant population. The relationship between average mean kinship, founder genome equivalents, and proportional gene diversity of the descendants (GD) is given by:

$$\overline{mk} = \frac{1}{2f_g} = 1 - GD \qquad (5.6)$$

A strategy that minimizes average mk therefore maximizes gene diversity. Mean kinship is easily calculated using the additive relationship matrix (Ballou 1983).

Relationship between Mean Kinship and Genome Uniqueness

Managing by mean kinship maximizes gene diversity, while management by genome uniqueness aims for retention of allelic diversity. Both allelic and gene diversity are important for a population's fitness (Allen-

Figure 5.2 Frequency of golden lion tamarin #1142's alleles in the living golden lion tamarin population. Mean kinship is a function of the mean of this distribution, while genome uniqueness is a function of its lower tail.

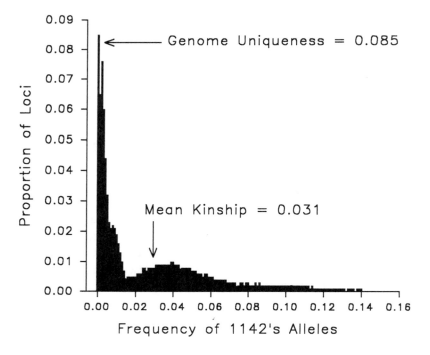

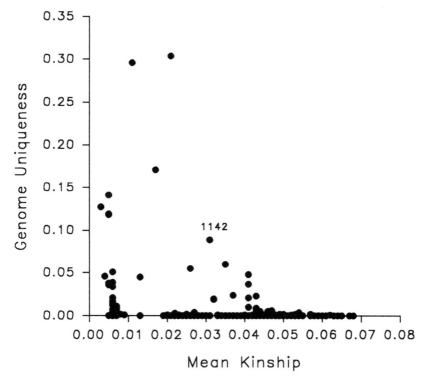

Figure 5.3 Genome uniqueness plotted against mean kinship for the 1991 captive population of golden lion tamarins (Ballou 1990). The values for GLT 1142 are shown.

dorf 1986), and, in general, strategies to retain gene diversity will also retain allelic diversity (Allendorf 1986; Lacy et al., essay 4 of this volume). This is also true for management strategies based on *mk* and *gu* because both are measures of the "rareness" of an individual's alleles. In fact, both are functions of the frequency distribution of an individual's alleles in the population. Such a frequency distribution can be calculated as the proportion of simulations (i.e., loci) in a gene drop analysis in which the individual's alleles were present at different frequencies in the population's gene pool. Figure 5.2 shows such an allele frequency distribution for the golden lion tamarin (GLT) studbook # 1142 (Ballou 1991a). Mean kinship is a function of the mean of this distribution, while genome uniqueness is a function of its lower limit: it is the probability that the individual's alleles have a frequency of zero (figure 5.2). As an individual's alleles become more frequent, the distribution shifts to the right, increasing *mk* and decreasing *gu*. For example, about 1% of 1142's alleles have a frequency of .04 in the population.

Genome uniqueness and mean kinship are therefore expected to be negatively correlated, as is seen when mean kinship is plotted against *gu* (figure 5.3). Individuals that are ranked highly by genome uniqueness often have low mean kinship values. It is possible, however, for an animal to have many relatives (resulting in moderately high mean kinship), but still to carry unique alleles. This can occur, for example, in an animal who has one parent descended from a common lineage and the other descended from a rare lineage (e.g., GLT 1142 in figure 5.3). The resulting offspring has a combination of both rare and common alleles; its allele frequency distribution will be bimodal. Likewise, animals with low mean kinship values may not have any unique genes (figure 5.3). For example, if both parents of any animal are alive, that individual will have no unique alleles, regardless of how few other relatives it may have.

Mean Kinship Under Demographic Constraints:
Kinship Value (*kv*)

Mean kinship is blind to the age-structure of the population. It is calculated relative to the total gene pool. This may include postreproductive animals, who can make no further genetic contribution to future generations. Including these animals when calculating mean kinship may underestimate an individual's genetic importance to the future genetic variation of the population. At the extreme, an individual whose relatives consist only of postreproductive animals might have a moderate mean kinship value and therefore not be recognized as genetically important, even though it is the only individual in the population with the ability to perpetuate the genes it carries. The utility of mean kinship (as well as genome uniqueness or any genetic metric that ignores the potential of individuals for future reproduction) is constrained by the demographic properties of an age-structured population.

This problem can be dealt with by taking into consideration the future reproductive potential of animals when calculating mean kinships. We define the *kinship value* of an individual (kv_i) as a weighted mean of the kinship coefficients between individual i and all members of the population (including itself):

$$kv_i = \frac{\displaystyle\sum_{j=1}^{N} f_{ij} V_{xj}}{\displaystyle\sum_{j=1}^{N} V_{xj}} \qquad (5.7)$$

in which the weight (V_{xj}) is the reproductive value (Fisher 1930) for the age class (x) of which individual j is a member. The reproductive value is a measure of the extent to which an individual of age x contributes to the ancestry of future generations (Crow and Kimura 1970). It is defined as:

$$V_x = \frac{\displaystyle\sum_{y=x}^{\infty} e^{-ry} l_y m_y}{e^{-rx} l_x} \qquad (5.8)$$

in which r is the intrinsic rate of increase, and l_y and m_y are the age–specific survival and fecundity rates (Caughley 1977).

Kinship values will be lower than mean kinships (suggesting greater genetic value of that animal) if most of the kin of an animal are post-reproductive or nearly so. Kinship values will be greater (worse) than mean kinships if most of the kin are at a good breeding age. The kinship value of an individual is the expected inbreeding coefficient of progeny if it were mated at random and reproduced according to the V_x of its mate. Whereas the average mean kinship is the genetic diversity of the descendant population if all individuals in the population were to be randomly bred, the average kinship value is the expected gene diversity of the descendant population if the current population is paired at random but reproduces according to its life-table expectations.

Note that when calculating kv, the genetic importance of individuals will not be obscured by their own reproductive limitations. The reproductive value of the individual under consideration acts *only* as a weight, as do the reproductive values of the other members of the population. A postreproductive individual can, in fact, have a nonzero kv. Consequently, a genetically important animal just entering reproductive senescence can still be identified as important and can be considered as a candidate for exceptional treatment (e.g., reproductive stimulation or surgical harvest of gametes).

Kinship value allows us to calculate genetic importance on the basis of the future expected genetic characteristics of the population, not solely on the basis of the current population's genetic status (as with mk). The implications of managing on the basis of the current population's genetic status can be easily seen in species with extremely short generation times. If genetic importance were determined relative to the current population, the importance could be heavily weighted by animals who would soon be dead. The problems associated with genetic importance based on current versus future population structure are mitigated in species with longer generation lengths when the degree to which the population turns over in each breeding cycle is reduced. Long generation times are more typical of the populations now being managed. In such cases mean kinship and kinship value will be similar.

COMPARISON OF GENETIC MANAGEMENT STRATEGIES

Each of the measures of genetic importance defined above have been or currently are being used to develop breeding strategies for endangered species. The strategies differ in how they define genetic importance and could have different effects on the maintenance of genetic diversity.

This concern was addressed by developing computer simulation models to compare how well different breeding strategies maintained genetic variation in complex pedigrees. Breeding strategies based on fic, mk, and gu were compared to strategies based on maximum avoidance of inbreeding (MAI; Lasley 1978) and random breeding. The MAI strategy was used to represent a strategy that maximized the inbreeding effective population size. The formula for mk was used rather than that for kv because the model lacked age-structure (see below). Each of the strategies was used to select breeding animals in five simulated populations with different genetic characteristics. These populations were "managed" under each strategy for 20 generations and the strategies were evaluated on how well they maintained alleles and gene diversity. The model is an extension of the one presented by Ballou (1991b).

The Model

The characteristics of the model were as follows:

1. The model considered a population of 30 sexually reproducing individuals (all reproductively capable) in nonoverlapping generations. Population sizes were maintained at 30. Sexes were assigned randomly to individuals at the beginning of each generation; a 50/50 sex ratio was maintained.

2. The model was provided with 5 "seed" populations that had already undergone several generations (two to four, depending on the population) of unmanaged breeding. These populations had fairly complex pedigrees, with different characteristics (see below).

3. Each of the breeding strategies was used to "manage" the seed populations for 20 generations by selecting in each generation the parents to produce the 30 offspring in the next generation. For the *fic, mk,* and *gu* strategies, parents were selected using the following iterative approach:

(a) the genetic importance values (*fic, mk,* or *gu*) of the 30 parents in the last generation were calculated;

(b) the male and female with highest genetic importance were selected;

(c) an offspring from this pair was added to the next generation;

(d) the genetic importance values of all parents were recalculated *relative to only the gene pool of the offspring generation;*

(e) the highest ranking male and female breeders were again selected to produce the next offspring, which was then added to the next generation. In the case of a tie (equal genetic value), the animal having produced the fewest number of offspring was selected;

(f) steps (d) and (e) were repeated until 30 offspring were produced.

Since the genetic importance of the parental generation changed as offspring were produced, this iterative approach allowed genetically valuable individuals to continue to be selected as breeders until their declining genetic importance values caused them to be replaced at the top of the list.

Founder contributions and mean kinship were calculated using an additive relationship matrix (Ballou 1983). Genome uniqueness was calculated using Monte Carlo simulations of 100 independent loci. Each founder was given 2 uniquely identifiable alleles (numbered from 1 to $2N = 60$) per locus and alleles were transmitted from parents to offspring by randomly selecting one allele each from the mother and father for each locus. Genome uniqueness for an individual was defined as the total number of unique alleles held by that individual (summed across all 100 loci) divided by 200.

For the *MAI* strategy, the approach was somewhat different since calculations of genetic importance were not used. This strategy utilizes a recursive mating strategy that assigns equal genetic value to all individuals (Lasley 1978; Flesness 1977; Senner 1980; Princée, essay 7 of this volume). Individuals in the first generation to be managed were sorted randomly and each assigned a number between 1 and 30; odd numbers were given to males, even ones to females. Female x was paired with male x - 1 to produce male $x/2$ and female $15 + (x/2)$ in the next generation. Thus, each pair produced two offspring and all pairs bred, maximizing the population's inbreeding effective size.

Under the random breeding strategy, the process of selecting a male and female randomly, with replacement, to produce one offspring was repeated until 30 offspring were "born."

4. The five breeding strategies being tested were each evaluated based on their ability to: (a) retain gene diversity; (b) retain allelic diversity; and (c) minimize inbreeding. Proportional gene diversity is defined as the percent of the original population's expected heterozygosity retained and can be calculated as $1 - \overline{mk}$. Allelic diversity is defined as the average number of founder alleles surviving in each generation. It is calculated here as the number of different founder alleles per locus in the population averaged across the 100 loci.

5. Each complete simulation, starting with the complex pedigree provided and selecting breeders (according to the genetic importance measure being tested) until the 20th generation, was

repeated 50 times. The breeding strategies were evaluated by averaging the results over the 50 simulations.

The Five "Seed" Pedigrees

The five populations used to seed the model were created to resemble populations that had already undergone several (two to four) genera-

Figure 5.4 (A) Allelic diversity (number of surviving founder alleles) versus gene diversity in the last generation of the five "seed" pedigrees used in the computer simulation model, and (B) the variance in mean kinship and allelic diversity (number of surviving founder alleles) among individuals in the last generation of the five "seed" pedigrees.

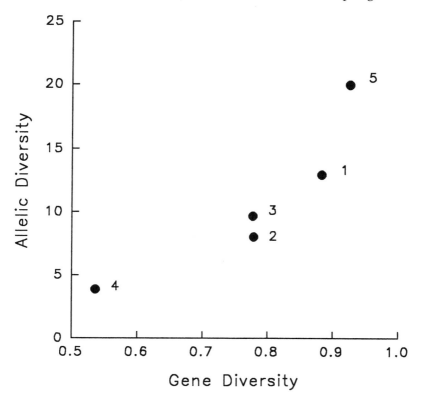

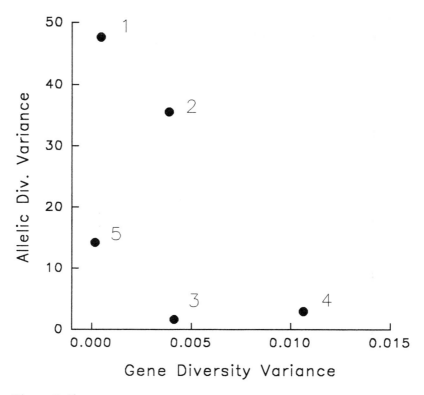

Figure 5.4b

tions of unmanaged breeding and therefore represented a variety of genetic characteristics typical of captive populations. The overall genetic
diversity of the pedigreed population can be described in terms of gene
and allelic diversity. However, it is also useful to consider individual
differences within these pedigrees. Regardless of the level of genetic diversity present in the population, if all individuals are of similar genetic
value, then the problem of selecting the ones to breed is irrelevant. The
complexity and need for guidance increase when there are significant
differences in genetic value among individuals. Figure 5.4a shows the
level of gene diversity versus allelic diversity in the test pedigrees, while
figure 5.4b shows the variation of these measures at the individual level.
The five pedigrees span a range of population levels of genetic diversity
as well as a range of interindividual variances in genetic diversity.

Model Simulation Results and Discussion

The genetic diversity retained after 20 generations in each of the five test pedigrees using the different breeding strategies is given in table 5.1. Figures 5.5 and 5.6 show the changes in genetic diversity over the 20 generations for two of the test pedigrees: pedigree 1, which started with one of the highest overall levels of genetic diversity, and pedigree 4, which started with the lowest.

The mean kinship strategy retained the highest levels of gene and allelic diversity in all five pedigrees. It did not always minimize inbreeding. This is not unexpected since the strategy, as used by the model, does not preclude mating among sibs. Often the two individuals with the lowest mean kinships are related (e.g., full sibs). In practice, the mean kinship strategy can be constrained to preclude mating among highly related individuals.

While three of four breeding strategies performed substantially better than simple random breeding, the strategy to equalize founder contribution using fic performed the least well compared to the other strategies, and in some cases it was worse than random breeding. This is because the fic strategy cannot discriminate between individuals with the same founder contributions (e.g., siblings). Thus, changes in genetic importance will be highly correlated among individuals from the same sibship or lineage, often leading to pairings between individuals descended from a common set of founders. Depending on the starting pedigree configuration, this can lead to population subdivision and linebreeding, resulting in a rapid loss of gene diversity and high inbreeding. This occurred in test population 1 (figures 5.5a and 5.5b), in which levels of gene and allelic diversity dropped rapidly as the population was subdivided. Average allelic diversity converges toward the preservation of only 2.6 alleles as alleles become fixed within the population subdivisions.

The mk and gu strategies can increase gene diversity (figure 5.6a), because they adjust for past mismanagement or lack of management. These strategies preferentially breed individuals who are carriers of rare genotypes, while the MAI and random strategies can only decrease gene diversity at rates dependent on the effective population size.

Figures 5.5 and 5.6 also show that after a few generations of manage-

Table 5.1 Levels of gene diversity retained in the 5 "seed" pedigrees after 20 generations of breeding under the 5 breeding strategies. Means and standard errors (SEM) are calculated over 50 simulations.

PEDIGREE 1

BREEDING STRATEGY	GENE DIVERSITY		# FOUNDER ALLELES		INBREEDING	
	MEAN	SEM	MEAN	SEM	MEAN	SEM
mk	0.784	0.001	7.397	0.169	0.219	0.014
GU	0.759	0.002	7.042	0.123	0.223	0.008
MAI	0.770	0.002	7.007	0.122	0.211	0.015
FIC	0.606	0.022	3.604	0.334	0.376	0.017
RANDOM	0.679	0.012	5.091	0.195	0.298	0.013

PEDIGREE 2

BREEDING STRATEGY	GENE DIVERSITY		# FOUNDER ALLELES		INBREEDING	
	MEAN	SEM	MEAN	SEM	MEAN	SEM
mk	0.729	0.001	5.818	0.121	0.275	0.011
GU	0.697	0.003	5.547	0.102	0.287	0.007
MAI	0.679	0.001	5.230	0.101	0.305	0.011
FIC	0.652	0.012	4.324	0.190	0.453	0.037
RANDOM	0.598	0.018	4.181	0.201	0.383	0.020

PEDIGREE 3

BREEDING STRATEGY	GENE DIVERSITY		# FOUNDER ALLELES		INBREEDING	
	MEAN	SEM	MEAN	SEM	MEAN	SEM
mk	0.760	0.003	6.494	0.111	0.244	0.014
GU	0.728	0.003	6.184	0.102	0.255	0.007
MAI	0.667	0.002	4.965	0.114	0.322	0.019
FIC	0.726	0.010	5.362	0.211	0.550	0.058
RANDOM	0.580	0.026	3.840	0.252	0.400	0.028

(continued)

Table 5.1 (*Continued*)

PEDIGREE 4

BREEDING STRATEGY	GENE DIVERSITY		# FOUNDER ALLELES		INBREEDING	
	MEAN	SEM	MEAN	SEM	MEAN	SEM
mk	0.545	0.005	3.266	0.058	0.458	0.011
GU	0.505	0.007	3.195	0.067	0.482	0.008
MAI	0.468	0.001	2.893	0.075	0.525	0.015
FIC	0.455	0.008	2.614	0.082	0.528	0.009
RANDOM	0.411	0.019	2.544	0.106	0.575	0.020

PEDIGREE 5

BREEDING STRATEGY	GENE DIVERSITY		# FOUNDER ALLELES		INBREEDING	
	MEAN	SEM	MEAN	SEM	MEAN	SEM
mk	0.814	0.001	8.600	0.129	0.193	0.017
GU	0.796	0.002	8.234	0.148	0.187	0.008
MAI	0.808	0.002	8.356	0.156	0.175	0.016
FIC	0.789	0.012	6.556	0.308	0.651	0.068
RANDOM	0.709	0.013	5.711	0.238	0.267	0.015

ment the rate of loss of genetic diversity is often similar under the *MAI*, *mk*, and *gu* breeding strategies. It does not take long for these breeding strategies to compensate for the initial complexities of pedigrees. Once this happens, all individuals have equal genetic importance, and each breeding strategy results in each animal producing two offspring.

Over the long term, gene diversity declined slightly more rapidly under the *gu* strategy than under *mk* and *MAI*, but this was because of sampling error in the simulation model. The probability of an allele being unique is based on a sample of 100 loci, which will have a sampling error large enough to affect the results when estimating small probabilities. Small nonzero probabilities of allele uniqueness are usually estimated as zero probabilities, giving incorrect breeding priority and increasing the variance in family size (in accord with the sampling

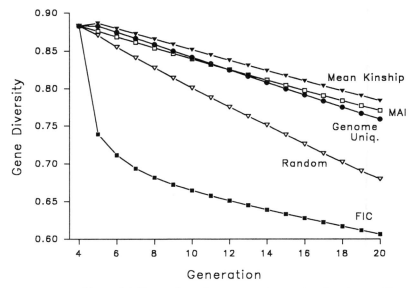

Figure 5.5 Effect of different breeding strategies on levels of gene diversity (A), allelic diversity (B), and inbreeding (C) in population 1 over 20 generations.

variance of the simulation). When the number of loci is increased to 200, the rate of gene diversity loss more closely approximates that of the *mk* and *MAI* strategies. In practice, estimates of genome uniqueness should be based on many thousands of simulations so that sampling problems do not measurably affect the results (Thomas 1990).

Despite its name, the *MAI* strategy does not always minimize inbreeding (table 5.1; figures 5.5c and 5.6c). This is because it does not take into consideration the pedigree of the initial population, but simply breeds animals according to the recursive *MAI* strategy. By chance, some initially related animals will be paired. *MAI* does minimize inbreeding (Crow and Kimura 1970) when applied to a population of initially unrelated individuals (e.g., founders).

In summary, mean kinship performed significantly better than all other strategies for all pedigrees provided. Both *MAI* and *gu* did fairly well, in general outperforming both *fic* and random breeding. Management to equalize founder contribution using *fic*s is not recommended. Strategies that minimize the loss of gene diversity (expected heterozygosity) generally also minimize the loss of allelic diversity.

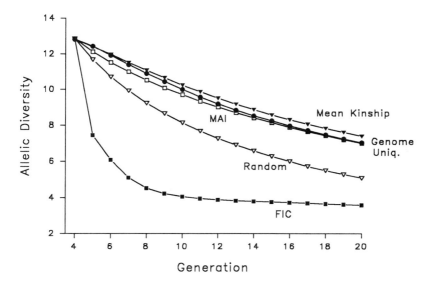

Figure 5.5 b

Figure 5.5 c

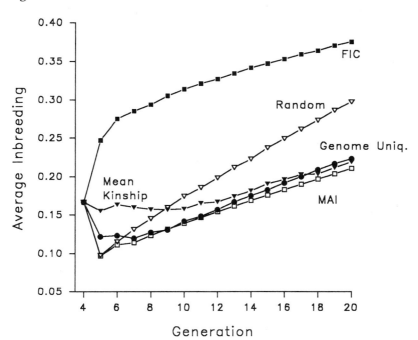

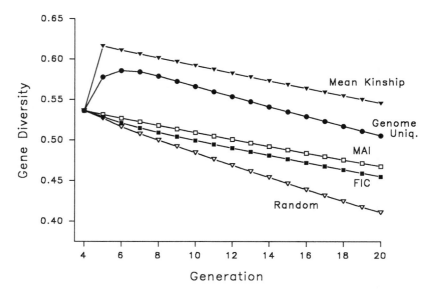

Figure 5.6 Effect of different breeding strategies on levels of gene diversity (A), allelic diversity (B), and inbreeding (C) in population 4 over 20 generations.

Figure 5.6 b

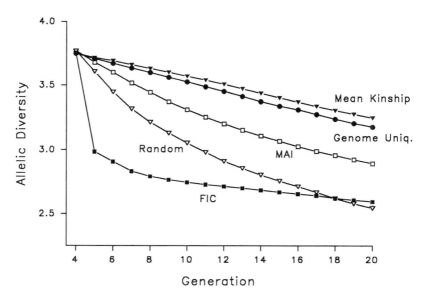

EFFECT OF UNKNOWN PARENTAGE ON MEASURES
OF GENETIC IMPORTANCE

Calculations of kinships, inbreeding coefficients, and the survival of founder alleles are critically dependent on complete knowledge of the pedigree. Unfortunately, however, many pedigrees of interest have some individuals with one or both parents unknown. Molecular genetic information can resolve some of these uncertainties (Morin and Ryder 1991; Haig et al. 1994; Avise et al., essay 9 of this volume), or alternative methods of population analysis and management can be applied (Lacy et al., essay 4 of this volume). Traditionally, such gaps in the pedigree have been bypassed in pedigree analysis by assuming that animals with unknown parents are founders, unrelated to all nondescendant an-

Figure 5.6c

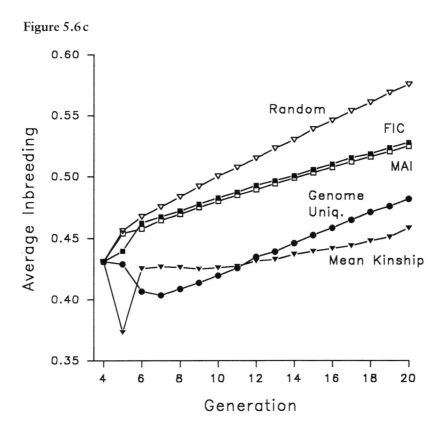

imals within the pedigree. Minimum estimates of kinships, inbreeding, and rates of loss of genetic diversity can then be obtained. In cases in which the unknown parents are likely to be unrelated to other animals in the pedigree (for example, when unknowns came from zoos on another continent), this optimistic assumption may be appropriate. In other cases, however, it may be known that the unknown parents are within the pedigree, such as when paternity cannot be assigned with certainty to any one of several males in a multimale, multifemale social group. In such cases, the assignment of founder status to unknown parents can lead to substantial errors in estimating genetic parameters, often assigning high genetic importance to those animals descended from the unknown "founders."

One approach to the problem is to exclude individuals with unknown ancestry from the breeding program. This is likely to reduce levels of genetic diversity (Willis 1993). An alternative is to consider only the known part of these individuals' genomes. Unbiased estimates of kinships and inbreeding coefficients for the known proportion of the genome would omit from consideration those parts of genomes that descend from unknown parents. In a gene drop analysis, the exclusion of genes that cannot be traced to properly classified founders is accomplished simply: statistics on genetic variation within the population and on sharing of genes among individuals can be calculated after exclusion of any "founder" alleles derived from unknown animals that had been treated as founders. The gene drop analysis within the program GENES (Lacy 1994) calculates all parameters with and without any such unknown alleles.

Precise calculations of kinships (and therefore mean kinship and kinship values) and inbreeding coefficients can also be made from partially known pedigree data after exclusion of those parts of genomes that cannot be traced to the pedigree founders. Conceptually, the task is to estimate the probability that two alleles drawn randomly from two individuals are identical by descent under the condition that those alleles have traceable ancestries. To derive the appropriate equations, let k_i be the proportion of the genome of animal i that can be traced to known founders. Thus, k_i will be 1 for animals with completely known ancestry, $1/2$ for animals with one unknown parent, and 0 for those with two unknown parents. For any other animal, $k_i = (k_m + k_p)/2$, the mean of the proportions known of the parents (m and p). Let f'_{ij} be the kinship between animals i and j relative only to those parts of the genomes that are traceable to known founders. Let F' be the inbreeding coefficient of an individual defined as the probability of identity by descent of a maternal allele and a paternal allele drawn at random from among those that are traceable. As in the case of a completely known pedigree, $F' = f'_{mp}$, in which m and p are the parents.

The kinship, f'_{ij}, between two individuals will be the probability that an allele sampled from the traceable (known) genome in j is identical by descent to an allele sampled from among the known maternal alleles in i, multiplied by the probability that a known allele sampled from i is maternally derived, plus the probability that the allele sampled from j is identical by descent to an allele sampled from among the paternal alleles in i multiplied by the probability that an (known) allele sampled from i is paternally derived. Thus,

$$f'_{ij} = f'_{mj} \times k_m / (k_m + k_p) + f'_{pj} \times k_p / (k_m + k_p) \quad (5.9)$$
$$= (f'_{mj} \times k_m + f'_{pj} \times k_p) / (2 \times k_i)$$

in which: the subscripts m and p refer to the parents of i; i is not an ancestor of j; $f'_{ij} = 0$ when i and j are founders; and $k = 1$ for founders. Using the above formula, f'_{ij} can be calculated for all i,j combinations provided i is not a founder (simply reverse i and j in this case to allow the calculation to proceed using the above formula) and provided that values for ancestors are calculated before their descendants. The kinship is undefined if an animal's ancestry is unknown ($k_i = 0$). This formula is particularly apropos for calculating f'_{ij} using a modified additive relationship matrix approach.

The kinship of an animal to itself, f'_{ii}, will be the probability that when two alleles are drawn at random from the known portion of the genome, the first allele drawn is resampled (both alleles are the maternally derived allele or both are the paternal allele) or that the allele is not resampled (one paternal allele sampled, one maternal allele sampled) but that the two alleles are identical by descent nonetheless. The probability that the maternal allele is sampled twice is $[k_m/(k_m + k_p)]^2$, and analogously for the probability that the paternal allele is sampled twice. The probability that one maternal allele and one paternal allele are sampled is $2 \times [k_m / (k_m + k_p)] \times [k_p / (k_m + k_p)]$. The probability that they are identical by descent is, by definition, f'_{mp}. Hence,

$$f'_{ii} = [k_m/(k_m + k_p)]^2 + [k_p/(k_m + k_p)]^2$$
$$+ 2 \times f'_{mp} \times [k_m/(k_m + k_p)] \times [k_p/(k_m + k_p)]$$
$$= [k_m^2 + k_p^2 + 2 \times k_m \times k_p \times f'_{mp}]/(4 * k_i^2). \qquad (5.10)$$

Figure 5.7 shows a simple pedigree in which one animal is unknown. Table 5.2 shows the matrix of kinships of those animals when unknown genes are omitted as described in equations (5.9) and (5.10). Omitting unknown genes, $f'_{BD} = 1/2$, because all genes known in D come from B, but only half of the genes in B were transmitted to D. Note that $f'_{DD} = 1$, because only the maternal genes in D are known. (D is haploid with respect to known genes.) The inbreeding coefficient of E is $1/4$ (= f'_{CD}), when unknown genes are omitted.

The kinship and inbreeding coefficients calculated without unknown genes may be less than or greater than the values that would be calculated if the pedigree were fully known. In the above example, if the unknown animal is unrelated to A and to B, then animal E is the product of a half-sib mating and has an inbreeding coefficient of $1/8$. If the

Figure 5.7 Hypothetical pedigree containing one unknown parent.

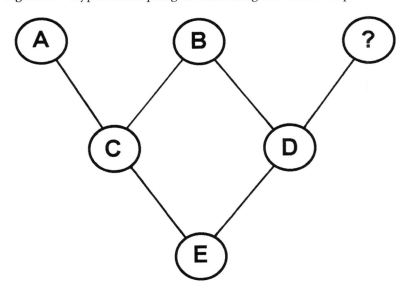

Table 5.2 Matrix of kinships among animals in the pedigree shown in figure 5.7 calculated by excluding the unknown portions of individuals' genomes.

	A	B	C	D	E
A	1/2	0	1/4	0	1/6
B	0	1/2	1/4	1/2	1/3
C	1/4	1/4	1/2	1/4	5/12
D	0	1/2	1/4	1	1/2
E	1/6	1/3	5/12	1/2	2/3

unknown is the same animal as A, then E is the product of a full-sib mating and has an inbreeding coefficient of 1/4. If the unknown is the same as animal C, then E is the product of two generations of parent-offspring matings and has an inbreeding coefficient of 3/8. The inbreeding coefficient calculated after omitting the unknown genes (1/4) is intermediate to the extreme possibilities.

Mean Kinships When Unknown Genes Are Excluded

Mean kinship can be calculated from the above statistics when pedigrees contain unknown animals. This can give an unbiased estimate of the gene diversity when excluding the portion of the gene pool that has descended from unknown animals. The mean kinship of individual i should be a weighted average of f'_{ij}'s, with the weights being the probability that individual j's alleles are chosen from the gene pool. Because some animals' pedigrees are only partly known ($k < 1$) and therefore contribute only partially to the gene pool, the probability that j's known alleles are chosen when the gene pool is sampled randomly will be proportional to k_j. Thus,

$$mk'_i = \frac{\sum_{j=1}^{N} (k_j \times f'_{ij})}{\sum_{j=1}^{N} k_j} \tag{5.11}$$

For the population, the average mean kinship (the expected loss of gene diversity in the descendants if all animals were mated at random) must be weighted by the probability that alleles from each pair of animals are selected from the gene pool. Thus,

$$\overline{mk}' = \frac{\sum\limits_{i=1}^{N} \sum\limits_{j=1}^{N} (k_i \times k_j \times f'_{ij})}{\sum\limits_{i=1}^{N} \sum\limits_{j=1}^{N} (k_j \times k_i)} \tag{5.12}$$

The accuracy of these methods for correcting mean kinship (and, therefore, estimates of losses of gene diversity) when there are unknown parents within a pedigree has been confirmed by comparing gene diversities calculated by equation (5.12) to those generated by a gene drop simulation (in which unknown alleles were excluded from the calculations).

When a large proportion of the pedigree is unknown, detailed pedigree analyses are not appropriate; estimates of mk based on the procedures outlined above will apply only to a small part of the gene pool. However, the results from the MAI breeding strategy in the computer modeling discussed earlier have interesting implications for managing populations with unknown pedigrees. Despite lack of pedigree information, high levels of genetic variation can be maintained using a strategy of maximum avoidance of inbreeding that does not rely on (nor make use of) prior pedigree information; thus, populations with unknown pedigrees need not be excluded from genetic management (e.g., barasinga, *Cervus duvaceli duvaceli*; Killmar 1991). The cost of not knowing the pedigree, however, is the potential for high levels of inbreeding (and the deleterious consequences of inbreeding depression) early in the breeding program resulting from unknowingly pairing closely related animals. The use of MAI strategies in these cases is discussed further by Princée (essay 7 of this volume).

CONCLUSIONS AND RECOMMENDATIONS

Both theory and model results support the conclusion that management by mean kinship provides an efficient and relatively easy strategy for maintenance of both expected heterozygosity and alleles in populations with complex pedigrees. In the Guam rail (*Rallus owstoni*), Haig et al. (1990) also found that a mate selection based on maximizing founder genome equivalents performed better than strategies based on prior reproductive success, allozyme data, equalizing founder representation, or simple random selection. As has been shown here, a breeding strategy that minimizes mean kinship is equivalent to strategies that maximize founder genome equivalents and gene diversity and relates directly to the previously recommended strategy of managing by target founder contributions.

In practice, we recommend that both kinship value and mean kinship be used to identify genetically important individuals. It is not recommended that kinship value be used alone since the reproductive values used in its calculation are based on life-table statistics summarizing average population trends. As is often the case for small captive populations, these may be based on poor data, particularly in the older age classes (see Taylor and Barlow, essay 2 of this volume). Expert knowledge of the reproductive potential of specific individuals is obscured. Examining both mean kinship and kinship value rankings provides a dual approach to identifying genetic importance both with and without demographic constraints. We recommend also that genome uniqueness be calculated as a secondary measure of genetic importance to assure that individuals with high levels of genome uniqueness are provided with breeding opportunities. As was discussed above, it is possible for individuals with moderate levels of mean kinship to have high levels of genome uniqueness, and ranking by mk alone may not identify these individuals.

One approach to developing breeding recommendations is to select pairs from the top of sorted lists of mean kinship, kinship value, or genome uniqueness, excluding combinations involving highly related mates. The definition of "highly related" will be relative to the overall level of inbreeding in the population. Therefore, a useful rule of thumb is to select as mates animals whose kinships do not greatly exceed the average mean kinship (Ballou and Foose 1994). This will keep inbreeding coefficients near or below the mean expected if the population were randomly bred in that generation. In avoiding breeding related animals, attempts should be made to pair mates with similar levels of mk. Mating a low mk to a high mk animal will result in mixing rare and common alleles, as in GLT 1142 (figure 5.2); thereafter, the number of copies of the rare alleles cannot be increased without also increasing that of the overrepresented alleles.

A second approach to developing breeding recommendations is to select breeding pairs by iteratively recalculating the *mk* rankings as breeding pairs are selected (as was done in the computer model). Each pair, once selected, is assumed to produce one offspring (or several offspring, depending on the life history of the species), which is added to the population. Then *mk* and *kv* are recalculated to provide a revised ranking of individuals based on pairs already selected to breed (but recalculating *gu* is problematic since it requires a time-consuming gene drop analysis). With this method it is possible to determine the set of matings and the number of offspring from each that will maximize a population's gene diversity.

The efficiency of any breeding strategy based on theory is limited by demographic constraints that are imposed by a population's life history and management considerations. Breeding strategies must recognize these constraints. One obvious constraint is that there is a limit to the number of young any one pair (or individual) can produce over its lifetime. The maximum number of young desired from a pair for genetic management may exceed their reproductive limits. In this case, optimal genetic management may not be possible.

Application of the mean kinship concept can be applied to problems other than mate selection. Calculating *mk* values of animals in one population relative to another population allows one to weigh the genetic effects of transferring animals between populations. Both the effect of removing individuals from one population and adding them to another can be determined. This approach can easily be used to manage subdivided populations, and it can, and has been, applied in such diverse cases as selecting animals for reintroduction (in the California condor, *Gymnogyps californianus* and golden lion tamarin) and for identifying males to donate sperm to a genome resource bank (Johnston and Lacy in press). Haig et al. (1994) also applied the mean kinship concept to an analysis of DNA fingerprinting data in Guam rails. They were able to show that mean DNA profile similarity (calculated as the average profile similarity between an individual and the rest of the population) correlated significantly with mean kinship. A large variance in the data precluded accurate predictions of genetic importance at the individual level strictly from the band sharing data.

The concept is easily extended to the value of groups of individuals and can be applied to identify groups of priority breeders, groups (e.g., families) for reintroduction (Tonkyn 1993), or differences in genetic value of population subdivisions (Geyer et al. 1989; Thompson, essay 6 of this volume).

Computer software is available for calculating inbreeding coefficients, mean kinship, genome uniqueness, and kinship value from pedigrees. The Single Population Animal Record Keeping System (SPARKS; ISIS 1991), an IBM-compatible software system for population management, is distributed with the genetic analysis program GENES (Lacy 1994) and the demographic analysis program DEMOG (Bingaman and Ballou 1986) to provide an integrated system combining the demographic and genetic calculations discussed above. This software may be obtained from ISIS, 12101 Johnny Cake Ridge Road, Apple Valley, MN 55124, USA.

Acknowledgments

We thank Richard Frankham, Kevin Willis, Jane Mansour, and David Tonkyn for their helpful comments on earlier drafts of the manuscript.

REFERENCES

Allendorf, F. 1986. Genetic drift and the loss of alleles versus heterozygosity. *Zoo Biology* 5:181–90.

Ballou, J. D. 1983. Calculating inbreeding coefficients from pedigrees. In C. M. Schonewald-Cox, S. M. Chambers, B. MacBryde, and L. Thomas, eds., *Genetics and Conservation: A Reference for Managing Wild Animal and Plant Populations,* pp. 509–20. Menlo Park: Benjamin/Cummings.

Ballou, J. D. 1991a. *1990 International Golden Lion Tamarin Studbook.* Washington, D.C.: National Zoological Park.

Ballou, J. D. 1991b. Management of genetic variation in captive populations. In E. C. Dudley, ed., *The Unity of Evolutionary Biology,* pp. 602–10. Portland, Oregon: Dioscorides Press.

Ballou, J. D. and T. J. Foose. In press. Demographic and genetic management of captive populations. In D. G. Kleiman, S. Lumpkin, M. Allen, H. Harris, and K. Thompson, eds., *Wild Mammals in Captivity.* Chicago: University of Chicago Press.

Bingaman, L. and J. D. Ballou. 1986. *DEMOGPHY: Lotus 1–2–3 Spreadsheet Demographic Model.* Washington, D.C.: National Zoological Park.

Cannings, C., E. S. Thompson, and M. H. Skolnick. 1978. Probability functions on complex pedigrees. *Advances in Applied Probability* 10:26–61.

Caughley, G. 1977. *Analysis of Vertebrate Populations*. New York: Wiley.

Crow, J. F. and M. Kimura. 1970. *An Introduction to Population Genetic Theory*. New York: Harper and Row.

Falconer, D. S. 1981. *Introduction to Quantitative Genetics*. New York: Longman.

Fisher, R. A. 1930. *The Genetical Theory of Natural Selection*. Oxford: Clarendon Press.

Flesness, N. 1977. Gene pool conservation and computer analysis. *International Zoo Yearbook* 17:77–81.

Foose, T. J. 1983. The relevance of captive populations to the conservation of biotic diversity. In C. M. Schonewald-Cox, S. M. Chambers, B. MacBryde, and W. L. Thomas, eds., *Genetics and Conservation: A Reference for Managing Wild Animal and Plant Populations*, pp. 374–401. Menlo Park: Benjamin/Cummings.

Foose, T. J., R. Lande, N. R. Flesness, G. Rabb, and B. Read. 1986. Propagation plans. *Zoo Biology* 5:139–46.

Geyer, C. J., E. A. Thompson, and O. A. Ryder. 1989. Gene survival in the Asian Wild Horse (*Equus przewalskii*), II: Gene survival in the whole population, in subgroups, and through history. *Zoo Biology* 8:313–29.

Haig, S. M., J. D. Ballou, and S. R. Derrickson. 1990. Management options for preserving genetic diversity: Reintroduction of Guam rails to the wild. *Conservation Biology* 4:290–300.

Haig, S. M., J. D. Ballou, and N. J. Casna. 1994. Identification of kin structure among Guam rail founders: A comparison of pedigrees and DNA profiles. *Molecular Ecology* 3:109–19.

Harris, R. B. and F. W. Allendorf. 1989. Genetically effective population size of large mammals: An assessment of estimators. *Conservation Biology* 3:181–91.

Hutchins, M., R. J. Wiese, K. Willis, and S. Becker. 1991. *AAZPA Annual Report on Conservation and Science, 1990–1991*. Bethesda, Maryland: American Association of Zoological Parks and Aquariums.

ISIS. 1991. *SPARKS* (Single Population Animal Record Keeping System). Apple Valley, Minn.: International Species Information System.

Johnston, L. A. and R. C. Lacy. In press. Genome resource banking for species conservation: Selection of sperm donors. *Cryobiology*.

Jones, S. R., ed. 1990. Captive propagation and reintroduction: A strategy for preserving endangered species? *Endangered Species Update*, vol. 8.

Killmar, L. 1991. Barasinga (*Cervus duvaceli duvaceli*). In M. Hutchins, R. J. Wiese, K. Willis, and S. Becker, eds., *AAZPA Annual Report on Conservation and Science, 1990–91*, pp. 109–10. Bethesda, MD: American Association of Zoological Parks and Aquariums.

Lacy, R. C. 1989. Analysis of founder representation in pedigrees: Founder equivalents and founder genome equivalents. *Zoo Biology* 8:111–23.

Lacy, R. C. 1994. *GENES: A computer program for the analysis of pedigrees and genetic management*. Brookfield, Ill.: Chicago Zoological Society.

Lacy, R. C. 1994. Managing genetic diversity in captive populations of animals. In M. L. Bowles and C. J. Whelan, eds., *Restoration of Endangered Species*, pp. 63–89. Cambridge: Cambridge University Press.

Lacy, R. C., A. Petric, and M. Warneke. 1993. Inbreeding and outbreeding in captive populations of wild animal species. In N. W. Thornhill, ed., *The Natural History of Inbreeding and Outbreeding,* pp. 352–374. Chicago: University of Chicago Press.

Lande, R. and G. F. Barrowclough. 1987. Effective population size, genetic variation, and their use in population management. In M. E. Soulé, ed., *Viable Populations for Conservation,* pp. 87–123. Cambridge: Cambridge University Press.

Lasley, J. F. 1978. *Genetics of Livestock Improvement.* Englewood Cliffs, N.J.: Prentice-Hall.

MacCluer, J. W., J. L. VandeBerg, B. Read, and O. A. Ryder. 1986. Pedigree analysis by computer simulation. *Zoo Biology* 5:147–60.

Morin, P. A. and O. A. Ryder. 1991. Founder contribution and pedigree inference in a captive breeding colony of lion-tailed macaques, using mitochondrial DNA and DNA fingerprint analyses. *Zoo Biology* 10:341–52.

Nei, M., T. Maruyama, and R. Chakraborty. 1975. The bottleneck effect and genetic variability in populations. *Evolution* 29:1–10.

Ralls, K., J. D. Ballou, and A. R. Templeton. 1988. Estimates of lethal equivalents and the cost of inbreeding in mammals. *Conservation Biology* 2:185–93.

Senner, J. 1980. Inbreeding depression and the survival of zoo populations. In M. E. Soulé and B. A. Wilcox, eds., *Conservation Biology,* pp. 209–24. Sunderland, Mass.: Sinauer.

Thomas, A. 1990. Comparison of an exact and a simulation method for calculating gene extinction probabilities in pedigrees. *Zoo Biology* 9:259–74.

Thomas, A. 1991. *PEDPACK.* Bath, U.K.: School of Mathematical Sciences, University of Bath.

Thompson, E. A. 1986. Ancestry of alleles and extinction of genes in populations with defined pedigrees. *Zoo Biology* 5:161–70.

Tonkyn, D. W. 1993. Optimization techniques for the genetic management of endangered species. *Endangered Species Update* 10:1–9.

Willis, K. 1993. Use of animals with unknown ancestries in scientifically managed breeding programs. *Zoo Biology* 12:161–72.

Wright, S. 1931. Evolution in Mendelian populations. *Genetics* 16:97–159.

6

Genetic Importance and Genomic Descent

∷

Elizabeth A. Thompson

Preservation of the genetic variability of a species entails the preservation of its gene pool to the maximal extent possible by avoiding loss of surviving founder genes. Analyses of founder contributions and simulation analyses of gene extinction (MacCluer et al. 1986) have provided useful information on expected numbers of surviving genes in different segments of a small population whose pedigree is known. Two types of dependence, however, limit the usefulness of analyses that focus upon expectations. The first is the dependence between individuals and the second is the dependence between gene loci. Aspects of each of these are discussed in this study.

The dependence between individuals in the survival of genes itself has two aspects. The first, discussed by Geyer and Thompson (1988), is the dependence between founders, within and between founder lineages, in the survival of their genes. If the genes from one founder or ancestral group survive in the population, or in any specified subset of the population, others are less likely to survive also. In the case of the Przewalski's horse (*Equus przewalskii*) pedigree (Volf 1959 et seq.), this leads to a variance of the number of distinct surviving founder genes that is only about two thirds of the variance obtained on an assumption of independence. Over independent Mendelian loci the variability in the number of distinct surviving founder genes is significantly less than is suggested by an analysis of survival probabilities of each founder gene separately.

In this study, however, the focus is on a different aspect of dependence between individuals. The objective of retaining currently surviving genes has led to the development of the idea of *genetic importance* (see also Ballou and Lacy, essay 5 of this volume). We define the genetic importance of an individual as the measure of the probability that it carries founder genes that are currently at risk of being lost (MacCluer et al. 1986). More precisely, it can be defined, for a given individual and a single Mendelian locus, as the expected number of distinct founder genes carried that are not present elsewhere in the population (i.e., genome uniqueness; Ballou and Lacy, essay 5 of this volume). Such genes will be lost with the death of the individual unless they are transmitted to offspring. Due to genealogical structure, a founder gene may be limited to a small segment of the population, although it may be present in several copies within that subgroup. Because of this dependence between related individuals, it is necessary to extend the idea of genetic importance to groups of individuals whose collective loss may deplete the pool of surviving founder genes. For example, a founder gene that does not appear to be at risk may be limited to a single zoo collection. Even major subdivisions of a population may be at risk of collective loss from the management of the species, due to policy or politics. The Przewalski's horse pedigree provides two examples of subdivision, where the genetic importance of large groups of individuals may be the key to developing a global management plan. This is the question addressed in the first section of this essay.

Previous approaches to and analyses of the study of gene survival in small populations have considered independently segregating Mendelian loci (Lacy et al., essay 4 of this volume; Ballou and Lacy, essay 5 of this volume). There has been, moreover, a tendency to interpret a gene survival probability, p, as survival of a proportion p of the genome. An average over independent realizations is converted, explicitly or implicitly, to an average over the genome of an individual. As an expectation over genomes among individuals of identical ancestry, this interpretation cannot be faulted, though it provides a misleading picture of the distribution of the amount of the original founder genome surviving in an individual or group of individuals. The genome is not a collection of independently segregating genes. All organisms have chromosomes; many have at least some large chromosomes. Failure to consider the genomic continuum may lead to misleading perceptions of gene identity and survival. Those endangered species for which detailed pedigree information is available typically survive in small populations, and significant gene loss may occur over even a few generations. For such population sizes and time scales the dependencies and disequilibria between closely linked genes will be substantial. Fisher (1949) introduced his *theory of junctions* as the first attempt to "move from a point theory to a strand theory" of population genetics. This theory provides a framework for the study of the segregation of chromosome segments in a pedigree. The second objective of this study is to present preliminary ideas on this topic as it relates to preservation of the gene pool.

GENETIC IMPORTANCE OF POPULATION SUBDIVISIONS

In order to evaluate the genetic importance of individuals or subgroups of a population of known pedigree, methods for computing probabilities of patterns of gene survival in large and complex pedigrees are required. These methods have been described elsewhere (Thompson 1983) and have been applied principally to the Przewalski's horse pedigree (Volf 1959 et seq.). Geyer et al. (1989) analyzed gene survival in population subgroups and through history in this large and complex pedigree. Additionally, they addressed questions of genetic importance and extended the idea of genetic importance to pairs and small groups of individuals who collectively carry founder genes not present outside the group. Here we use the computations of Geyer et al. (1989) to consider a still wider view of genetic importance—the genetic importance of the major subdivisions of the world population of Przewalski's horses.

Historically, in the management of the Przewalski's horse, there have been two ways of dividing the world population. The first is geographic. While there has been a North American management plan for some years (Ryder 1991), it was only in 1990 that there was agreement on a global management plan, and the logistics of global management remain complex. In advocating global management, one issue was the genetic importance of those animals outside the population managed by the North American Species Survival Plan (SSP). Numerically, non-SSP animals are the majority of the world population, but it was not clear how many distinct original founder genes could be lost by failure to manage the population outside of North America.

The second subdivision, which cuts across the geographic one, relates to the known domestic horse ancestry in many members of the species. The management policy considers separately animals having some descent from the known Mongolian domestic mare (DOM), and those that do not (non-DOM). The original policy dictated that DOM mares were to breed only with non-DOM stallions; DOM stallions were not to be bred. This would have led to the eventual extinction of all of the founder genes currently present only in DOM-descended individuals. The genetic importance of the DOM-descended horses measures the cost in terms of the Przewalski's horse genes that would be lost through such a management policy. These considerations have provided input for the development of a global management plan.

Part A of table 6.1 shows the expected numbers of founder genes surviving in these four major world subdivisions. In these computations the DOM genes are accounted for separately; genetic importance is assessed with respect to the "desirable" non-DOM genes, whether in non-DOM or in DOM-descended animals. From part B of table 6.1, we see that the world population carries some genes not present in the North American population; 1.24 of the total 9.91 surviving non-DOM founder genes would be lost if only the North American population were to survive. Among the non-DOM descended horses, the population outside of North America contributes 0.76 genes of the total 7.30 expected distinct surviving founder genes. More than 10% of surviving distinct original founder genes exist only outside the North American population; this is the extent of the genetic importance of the population outside of North America.

The genetic importance of the DOM-descended horses, however, is substantially greater. From part C of table 6.1, we see that both within

Table 6.1 Expected number of surviving founder genes within, and consequent *genetic importance*[1] of, some subgroups of the Przewalski's horse world population.

A: EXPECTED SURVIVING GENES

	WORLD POPULATION		NORTH AMERICAN POPULATION	
	TOTAL	NON-DOM[2]	TOTAL	NON-DOM[2]
DOM genes	0.57	0.00	0.45	0.00
Non-DOM[3] genes	9.91	7.30	8.67	6.64
Total genes	10.48	7.30	9.13	6.64

B: GENETIC IMPORTANCE OF NON-NORTH AMERICAN HORSES

	ALL HORSES	NON-DOM[2] Horses
DOM genes	0.11	0.00
Non-DOM[3] genes	1.24	0.76
Total genes	1.36	0.76

C: GENETIC IMPORTANCE OF DOM-DESCENDED HORSES

	WORLD	NORTH AMERICA
DOM genes	0.57	0.45
Other Old-Prague genes	1.55	1.27
Other founder genes	1.06	0.77
Total genes	3.18	2.49

1. Genetic importance is the expected number for surviving non-DOM genes present only within the specified subgroup of the population.
2. Non-DOM horses are animals who do not have descent from DOM, the Mongolian domestic mare.
3. Non-DOM genes are genes that are not identical by descent to the genes in DOM.

North America and within the total world population about 25% of the distinct founder non-DOM genes are present only in DOM-descended horses. The DOM-descended horses are genetically important for these non-DOM genes. The non-DOM genes for which the DOM-descended horses are genetically important are principally genes from the Old Prague founder lineage (two Przewalski's horse founders and DOM). This is not surprising; through the original mating of DOM and the subsequent population bottleneck, the DOM and Old Prague genes are completely confounded. On the other hand, note that there is a substantial number of non-Old Prague genes for which the DOM-descended horses are genetically important. Due to matings early in the pedigree, this population subgroup received genes of other founders that did not also segregate into the non-DOM descended segment of the population.

DEPENDENCE BETWEEN LOCI: A MODEL FOR CHROMOSOME SEGMENTS

The above analyses have considered only single Mendelian loci. We turn now to the effects of recombination and linkage on questions of gene descent and gene survival. The simplest model of the recombination process is that crossovers occur as a Poisson process at some rate λ. This model gives rise to independently exponentially distributed intervals (mean $1/\lambda$) between crossovers. The model does not allow for interference and does not explicitly recognize the heterogeneity of recombination along the chromosome. If chromosome lengths are measured in units of recombination distance, however, any such heterogeneity is implicitly subsumed. This model (proposed by Fisher 1949) is a useful approximation to the process; it is a good model on the larger scale but not on the small scale of intragenic processes. For the sake of simplicity, we don't consider here the potentially different recombination rates in males and females, although this type of heterogeneity could be modeled. If chromosomal distances are measured in Morgans (Haldane 1919), the rate of the Poisson process is 1 (that is, $\lambda = 1$).

In this first analysis of genome inheritance under this model, we consider just two results, each of which typifies broader questions. The first is a question of shared genomes between relatives. The single-locus gene identity-by-descent probabilities for relatives provide, of course, the expected proportions of shared genomes, but the proportion is a random variable whose distribution is a function of the pedigree and the recombination process. Secondly, there are questions of the surviving proportions of the genome. Again, the single-locus computations provide the expected proportion, but the distribution is more complex.

One of the simplest relationships between a pair of individuals involves the segregation from a single parent to two offspring. Due to the structure of small subpopulations of many species, this half-sib relationship is often of interest in conservation genetics. Maternal half-sibs arise as seedlings from a single maternal plant. Paternal half-sibs are cohort members in species where each group has a single breeding male. It is well known that at each locus, the offspring of a common mother share their maternal gene with a probability of 1/2; the expected proportion of shared maternal genome is 1/2. However, we wish to consider the distribution of this proportion and, in particular, its variance.

Consider first a single chromosome length of L Morgans. In the segregation to each offspring, the recombination process provides a maternal chromosome, which is a sequence of segments deriving alternately from the maternal and paternal chromosomes within the mother. The *junctions* between these segments arise as a Poisson process of rate 1. Comparing the two realizations of this process (figure 6.1), we find alternating chromosome segments that are identical by descent and nonidentical by descent between the two half-sib offspring. The points of interchange are the combined set of junctions in the two segregations and thus form a Poisson process of rate 2 (figure 6.1). The total number of interchanges, N, is Poisson, with mean $2L$. The number of identical-by-descent segments, K, is $(N + 1)/2$ if N is odd, and is $N/2$ or $(N + 2)/2$, each with probability 1/2 if N is even.

Conditional on N, the locations of interchanges are the order statistic of a sample of size N from a uniform distribution on an interval length L. Standard theory thus provides a beta distribution for the proportion, Q, of shared genome; $Be\ (K, N + 1 - K)$. In this simple case, therefore, the exact distribution of length, QL, of shared chromosome is easily found. For an organism with k chromosomes, of lengths L_1, . . . , L_k, the result is a sum of independent random variables, Q_iL_i, where Q_i has, conditional on N_i, the appropriate beta distribution. For the sake of simplicity, we consider here only the mean and variance of this distribution.

For a single chromosome length L, conditional on N, the mean proportion of chromosome shared is 1/2 and the variance $\dfrac{1}{4(N+2)}$ if N is odd. If N is even, we have mean either $\dfrac{N}{2(N+1)}$ or $\dfrac{N+2}{2(N+1)}$ and variance (in either case) $\dfrac{N}{4(N+1)^2}$. Combining these gives mean 1/2 and variance $\dfrac{1}{4(N+1)}$. The unconditional variance is thus difficult to obtain exactly, but it is approximately $\dfrac{1}{4}E\left(\dfrac{1}{N+1}\right)$ where N is Poisson with mean $2L$; i.e., $\dfrac{(1-e^{-2L})}{8L}$. This expression reduces to the single-locus Binomial variance 1/4 when L is small, and is approximately $1/8L$ for long chromosomes. Summing over independently segregating chromosomes, the length of shared genome has mean $\sum\limits_{i}\dfrac{L_i}{2}$ and variance $\sum\limits_{i} L_i(1-e^{-2L_i})/8$.

It is of interest to compare this result with that obtained for a set of independently segregating unlinked loci. For m independent loci, the number of maternal genes shared by a pair of half sibs has a binomial distribution, $Bi(m,\tfrac{1}{2})$. The mean proportion of the loci shared is 1/2,

Figure 6.1 Segregation of chromosomes to two offspring.

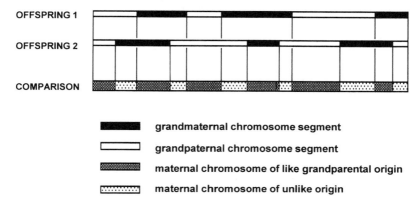

OFFSPRING 1

OFFSPRING 2

COMPARISON

    grandmaternal chromosome segment

    grandpaternal chromosome segment

    maternal chromosome of like grandparental origin

    maternal chromosome of unlike origin

and the variance of this proportion is $1/4m$. In terms of the mean, one Morgan translates to one locus, but in terms of variance, in a long chromosome, the "rate of exchange" is two Morgans/locus. The exact "rate of exchange" depends on the individual chromosome lengths as well as on the total length of the genome. There is thus no simple way to convert a continuous genome into an "equivalent" number of independently segregating loci.

As an example of analysis of the survival of genomes, rather than single genes, we consider the probability that the entire genome of an individual is present among its offspring. It will seldom be possible to preserve the entire genomes of individuals over multiple generations; some proportion of a founder's genome will be lost. It remains, nonetheless, an interesting question as to how many offspring are required in order to have a reasonable chance of preserving the entire genome of an individual at least to the offspring generation. The answer, of course, depends on the length of the genome in question and on its subdivision into chromosomes; as above, very small chromosomes will behave much like independently segregating genes.

The number of offspring required to have a high probability of retaining entire genomes does have some practical relevance. A new founder may enter a highly inbred established population, as the founder 231 entered into the Przewalski's horse pedigree in the 1950s. It may be a reasonable goal to attempt to preserve as much of such a founder's genome as possible; for example, if ten offspring are required, this may be realistic for one animal, even though not all members of the population can be permitted to be so prolific. A second application lies in frozen embryos; there, the limitation of the habitat for living animals does not apply. To ask how many embryos should be stored is a reasonable question, to which a practical answer can be given.

The required formula was given by Donnelly (1983); the probability that the whole of a chromosome-pair length L is preserved among the k offspring is approximately $exp(-kL/2^{k-1})$. Again, it is of interest to compare this result with that for a set of unlinked loci. The probability that both parental homologous alleles survive at any given locus is $q = 1 - 2^{-k+1}$, and thus this is also the expected proportion of the total haploid genome at which both parental homologues survive. The probability that both alleles survive at all of m independently segregating loci is thus q^m or approximately $exp(-m/2^{k-1})$. Note that the dependence on the number of offspring k is different in these two expressions; there is no number of independently segregating loci that can be considered "equivalent" for all k to a chromosome of length L. Donnelly (1983) also gave a more exact formula: $exp(-(k(k - 3)L + J(k - 1))/(k - 2)2^{k-1})$ for a set of J pairs of autosomes of total length L. When k is not small, this is effectively equal to $exp(-(kL + J)/2^{k-1})$, which, in the limit for small L, gives the independent loci result, whereas for a small number of large chromosomes gives the previous approximation $exp(-kL/2^{k-1})$. Note that although the number of chromosome pairs (J) and the total length (L) have some effect on these probabilities, the relative lengths of chromosome enters only as a higher order correction. Donnelly (1983) verified that any correction due to different relative lengths of chromosome is indeed slight.

Table 6.2 gives some numerical results for varying sizes of genomes and numbers of offspring. (The human genome is approximated by the middle combination; about twenty pairs of autosomes and a total length of about 30 Morgans.) Except for small numbers of offspring, the dependence of the number of autosome pairs is slight; the major factor in the probability of passing on one's entire genome is the total length, measured in Morgans. With only four offspring there is little chance of passing on the whole of even the smallest genome in the example, consisting of ten pairs of autosomes of a total length of 10 Morgans. With sixteen offspring, there is a high probability of passing on the whole of even a very large genome, consisting of thirty pairs of autosomes of a total length of 60 Morgans. Of greater significance is that for eight offspring the probabilities remain low, but are very substantially higher for twelve offspring. For the question of preserving an entire parental genome, this is the critical range of offspring numbers. If one requires a high probability of passing on an entire genome, at least twelve offspring are necessary. For many species this is not a practical proposition, even for a few key individuals.

The question of the survival of entire genomes to offspring can, of course, be extended. What is the chance of preserving at least $x\%$ of the genome if there are k offspring? What is the chance of preserving genomes among grandoffspring? Blossey (1993) has found that whereas impractically large numbers of offspring may be required to retain

Table 6.2 Probability that all of an individual's genome survives among its offspring.

J = NUMBER OF AUTOSOME PAIRS	L = LENGTH OF GENOME (MORGANS)	NUMBER OF OFFSPRING			
		4	8	12	16
10	10	0.0126	0.5423	0.9436	0.9952
	30	0.0001	0.1913	0.8491	0.9862
	60	0.0000	0.0401	0.7249	0.9728
20	10	0.0019	0.4950	0.9385	0.9948
	30	0.0000	0.1747	0.8446	0.9858
	60	0.0000	0.0366	0.7210	0.9725
30	10	0.0003	0.4519	0.9334	0.9945
	30	0.0000	0.1595	0.8400	0.9855
	60	0.0000	0.0334	0.7171	0.9722

whole genomes, a substantially smaller number, such as four or five, is required for high probabilities of preserving at least 90% of the parental genome.

DISCUSSION

In analyses of founder gene survival, the idea of genetic importance was first developed as a measure of individual animals, relating to single Mendelian loci (MacCluer et al. 1986). In this study, two extensions of this idea are reviewed briefly. The first develops genetic importance as a characteristic of groups of individuals, or of major subsets of the population, as well as of single individuals. It is the survival of genes in the collective population that is of primary interest in preserving potential genetic variability. It is the collective loss of all genes that are currently represented only in individuals who may not breed that causes loss of variability.

The second direction of extension of analyses of gene survival is from measures relating to single loci to measures relating to the continuous genome of DNA strands. In conserving the genetic variation in a population, we need to think in terms of conservation of genomes, not just of individual genes. In this study, we considered only two preliminary questions: the distribution of the amount of genome shared by maternal half sibs, and the probability that the entire genome of an individual survives among its offspring. One important general point emerges: there is no "equivalent Mendelian gene number" for genomes. The correspondence between genome length and loci numbers depends on the number of pairs of chromosomes, on the total chromosome length, and on the relative lengths. Moreover, the answer depends on the question: mean survival, variance of survival, and probabilities of total survival each provides a different "rate of exchange."

Acknowledgment

This research was supported in part by NSF grant BSR–8921839. I am grateful to Charles Geyer for the computations for table 6.1 and for many helpful discussions.

REFERENCES

Blossey, H. 1993. The Poisson clumping heuristic and survival of a genome continuum. Ph.D. diss., Department of Statistics, University of Washington, Seattle.

Donnelly, K. P. 1983. The probability that related individuals share some section of the genome identical by descent. *Theoretical Population Biology* 23:34–63.

Fisher, R. A. 1949. *The Theory of Inbreeding.* New York: Academic Press.

Geyer, C. J. and E. A. Thompson. 1988. Gene survival in the Asian Wild Horse (*Equus przewalskii*), I: Dependence in gene survival in the Calgary Breeding Group pedigree. *Zoo Biology* 7:313–27.

Geyer, C. J., E. A. Thompson, and O. A. Ryder. 1989. Gene survival in the Asian Wild Horse (*Equus przewalskii*), II: Gene survival in the whole population, in subgroups, and through history. *Zoo Biology* 8:313–29.

Haldane, J. B. S. 1919. The combination of linkage values and the calculation of distances between the loci of linked factors. *Journal of Genetics* 8:299–309.

MacCluer, J. W., J. L. VandeBerg, B. Read, and O. A. Ryder. 1986. Pedigree analysis by computer simulation. *Zoo Biology* 5:147–60.

Ryder, O. A. 1991. Asian wild horse (*Equus przewalskii*). In M. Hutchins, R. J. Wiese, K. Willis, and S. Becker, eds., *AAZPA Annual Report on Conservation and Science,* pp. 132–33. Bethesda, Maryland: American Association of Zoological Parks and Aquariums.

Thompson, E. A. 1983. Gene extinction and allelic origins in complex genealogies. *Proceedings of the Royal Society of London* B219:241–51.

Volf, J. 1959 (et seq.). *International Studbook of Przewalski's horse.* Prague Zoo, Prague.

7

Overcoming the Constraints of Social Structure and Incomplete Pedigree Data Through Low-intensity Genetic Management

■■

Frank P. G. Princée

Genetic management of wild animal species in captivity and wildlife reserves has become increasingly important in breeding programs. The maintenance of sufficient levels of genetic variation and the avoidance of inbreeding are now considered vital prerequisites for the survival of small populations (Soulé et al. 1986).

Knowledge about the genetics of small populations has evolved rapidly during the last decade to meet the needs of zoos and other institutions involved in breeding endangered wild animal species. New techniques of pedigree analyses have been developed. Computer simulation models such as "gene drop" (MacCluer et al. 1986), GENES (Lacy 1994), and GENEFLOW (Princée 1988) have proven to be useful for genetic management. These models allow detailed studies of genetic processes within complex pedigrees (e.g., Speke's gazelle, *Gazella spekii*; Przewalski's horse, *Equus przewalskii* [MacCluer et al. 1986]; and red panda, *Ailurus fulgens* [Princée 1988, 1989]). However, the application of models in population genetic theory and the use of simulation models for pedigree analyses are limited by the quality of pedigree data. It is obvious that results of these analyses can be unreliable in cases where many data on ancestries are missing and assumptions with respect to parentages have been made (Lacy et al., essay 4 of this volume).

Poor and missing pedigree data are not uncommon. Historical data on individuals of many species in zoo collections may not be available. Different societal attitudes in the past with respect to wild animals and the relatively late implementation of population genetics in breeding management account for the inconsistencies found in zoos' records of animal ancestry. It is likely that in cases where historical data are available, these data are restricted to a few zoo collections and/or high-profile species.

Although computerized in-house registration of zoo collections has increased the quality and quantity of pedigree data tremendously at a global level (Flesness and Mace 1988), poor and missing pedigree data in a number of species will always occur. This refers especially to species that live and necessarily are maintained in groups with complex mating structures. Identification of every individual's parentage is not always possible. For example, captive animals may not reproduce or raise their young properly if the breeding group does not reflect the natural, species-specific social structure (e.g., Rijksen 1981; Erwin 1986; Tilson 1986). Raising young in breeding groups that resemble natural compositions may also be a prerequisite for the successful reintroduction of species into the wild. In addition, the educational role of modern zoos goes beyond showing specimens of various species. Visitors get more involved in the protection of species and their natural habitat when they can watch natural behavior than when they can only gaze at some external features of the exhibited species (van Hooff 1986). Moreover, a changing attitude toward animals is also reflected in studies on animal welfare. Guidelines for housing primates in zoos and other related institutions in countries of the European Community recommend a group composition that resembles natural social units (Griede 1989).

Propagation of animal species also stretches beyond captive breeding programs in zoos. Wild populations become more isolated from each other as wild habitat becomes more fragmented. This means that genetic management of these populations is required (e.g., migration, see preface to this volume; Foose et al., essay 12 of this volume), and this also applies to populations that are reestablished in wild habitat. Here, social structure is a natural factor that needs to be considered in population management viability analysis as discussed by Soulé (1987).

Lack of pedigree data due to historical neglect, current management practices, or the difficulty in obtaining information about wild populations, as well as the need to incorporate natural social structure in breeding programs limit the extent to which some populations can be intensively genetically managed. In these cases, development of low-intensity management techniques is essential. The purpose of this essay is to present and evaluate the concept of low-intensity genetic management as a possible alternative to intensive genetic management in populations lacking complete data or under husbandry constraints that prohibit intense management strategies. Such techniques would necessarily be based on a limited use of pedigree data and incorporate into genetic management biological information, such as social organization, mating system, dispersal patterns, estrus cycles, and age of sexual maturity.

Development of low-intensity management techniques for nonendangered species will also reduce the time and resources required to manage large captive populations. Intensive genetic management, through manipulating individual breeding combinations, consumes time and energy, therefore limiting the number of species that can be managed. Obviously, we should be careful in selecting species to which intensive management is applied. This should not mean, however, that other species are not managed at all or that management stops once relatively large populations have been established. The status of nonendangered species can deteriorate very rapidly in a time when the destruction of natural habitat still continues. These species can greatly benefit from a lower level of genetic management.

GENETIC MANAGEMENT

The main objective of genetic management is to preserve sufficient levels of natural genetic variation (both heterozygosity and allelic diversity) to enable populations to adapt to both short- and long-term changes in the environment. Soulé et al. (1986) have recommended that captive breeding programs strive to maintain 90% of the wild population's genetic diversity for 200 years. This issue is discussed by several authors in this volume (Lacy et al., essay 4; Lande, essay 14). Therefore, only some short comments on processes endangering this objective in the context of management of social groups will be presented here.

Three processes can result in loss of genetic diversity: (1) genetic drift; (2) consanguineous matings; and (3) selection. Genetic drift (or random loss of alleles) is directly related to the effective population size (N_e). Effective size is determined by the number of breeding males and females and the distribution of progeny over breeding combinations. Social organizations that have hierarchical mating systems may affect (i.e, reduce) effective population size (and, therefore, have higher rates of genetic drift). This issue will be discussed in later sections.

Consanguineous matings (often referred to as inbreeding or incest) decrease the proportion of loci that are heterozygous. However, loss of alleles in subdivided populations under continuous inbreeding will be lower than under random mating among the subpopulations (e.g., Lacy 1987). Thus, our definition of genetic variation determines whether inbreeding directly results in genetic loss. Inbreeding can have at least an indirect effect on the loss of alleles. Increased homozygosity can affect the average fitness of individuals due to the expression of deleterious alleles. This effect, called inbreeding depression, has an enormous impact on genetic variation in small populations. The loss of individuals due to inbreeding depression means the loss of entire genomes.

Inbreeding depression is a result of selection against deleterious alleles. Thus, it actually shows the impact of selection on genetic variation. However, the effects of selection on genetic variation are extremely complex and will not be discussed in this essay. First, it is not feasible to qualify and quantify all selection pressures in captive and natural environments (Arnold, essay 13 of this volume). Second, the level of acceptance of selection will differ between management of captive populations and management of wild populations. The general guideline is to avoid selection by either the manager or the environment in captive populations (Frankham et al. 1986; Arnold, essay 13 of this volume). In general, all individuals in a captive population should have an equal chance to reproduce. However, selection in wild populations is generally accepted as a desirable phenomenon.

Genetic management of zoo populations is based on pedigree data of each individual in the population. Calculation of exact inbreeding coefficients, founder representation, or mean kinship will be impossible in the absence of such data (but see Ballou and Lacy, essay 5 of this volume). As mentioned in the introduction, pedigree data is often not available for individuals living in social groups. In these cases, information on mating systems of the species involved can be used to reconstruct pedigree data or at least to provide some meaningful assumptions with respect to parentages. Unfortunately, information on mating systems is lacking for a large number of (endangered) species. For example, Ewer's paper "Why study small mammals?" (1975) may still reflect our limited knowledge on various groups of species.

The minimum information needed for genetic management is group composition, i.e., sex ratio and size. To obtain these data, (comparative) studies on foraging behaviors or rearing systems, for example, may be helpful. Although the mating system may remain unknown, information on group composition may allow us to determine upper and lower ranges of effective size (and thus genetic loss).

AVOIDANCE OF INBREEDING

Avoidance of inbreeding has often been considered as a synonym for genetic management. This is not surprising since inbreeding depression may occur within a few generations, as has been observed in many zoo populations (Ralls and Ballou 1983; Templeton and Read 1983) and in some wild populations (e.g., van Noordwijk and Scharloo 1981; Gibbs and Grant 1989; Bouwmeester et al. 1989).

The maintenance of sufficient levels of genetic variation, however, is the main objective of genetic management (Lacy et al., essay 4 of this volume). It addresses all factors that reduce genetic loss. Theoretically, fragmenting populations into subpopulations (and thus increasing the rate of inbreeding) would aid in accomplishing this objective as it reduces the overall loss of alleles (Lacy 1987). However, a management strategy that tolerates certain levels of inbreeding incorporates a risk: the cost of inbreeding depression, in terms of increased possibility of population extinction and loss of entire genomes, may override the benefit of inbreeding. This risk is difficult to estimate as it requires information on numbers and frequencies of deleterious alleles in natural populations. Furthermore, tolerance for inbreeding varies with the species or even the population (Shields 1987; Ralls et al. 1988).

Sex-biased natural dispersal of subadult or younger individuals has been observed in several primate species (Pusey and Packer 1987; Smuts et al. 1987, appendix A-1). These data suggest that, at least in several different families of primates, inbreeding is avoided. Eisenberg (1981) and Templeton (1987) assume that avoidance of inbreeding occurs in most mammalian species. It must be stated, however, that sex-biased dispersal itself is not necessarily a mechanism to avoid inbreeding but may be caused by other factors (e.g., social status, ecological factors).

Given the cases of inbreeding depression in zoo populations and data on natural dispersal patterns, one would tend to consider avoidance of inbreeding as a basic guideline in genetic management. Future studies should reveal whether cases of (extreme) inbreeding in natural populations, as for instance in the pika (*Ochotona princeps,* Smith 1987; Chepko-Sade et al. 1987), are exceptions or more common features. The issue of dispersal and avoidance of inbreeding is discussed more intensively in Chepko-Sade and Halpin (1987) and Thornhill (1993).

MAXIMAL AVOIDANCE OF INBREEDING

Breeding schemes to avoid inbreeding for as long as possible and to slow down the process of inbreeding in cases where avoidance is no longer possible have long been developed for use in domestic and lab animal sciences and, more recently, have been recommended for conservation applications (Flesness 1977; Princée 1986). Flesness (1977) and Princée (1986) present figures that illustrate the maximum avoidance of inbreeding (*MAI*) scheme. In general, the *MAI* scheme requires all individuals to be clearly identified, pedigrees to be kept, and reproductive success to be tightly controlled.

One would expect, then, that *MAI* schemes can only be applied through intensive genetic management and only if detailed pedigree data are available. However, inbreeding can be managed in populations kept in natural social groups even when pedigree data are limited or nonexistent. This is accomplished by applying the *MAI* scheme to groups of individuals rather than to individuals directly. This section describes the concept of *MAI* schemes under such conditions, using as an example a population that consists of eight breeding groups.

GUIDELINES FOR *MAI* SCHEMES ARE:

1. The number of breeding groups in the population should be a power of two. In this example: 8 groups = 2^3.
2. Breeding groups are identified by location (e.g., zoo or wildlife preserve) and assigned a number (1–8 in this example).
3. The population starts with unrelated animals (founders). They are defined as generation zero.
4. Offspring in breeding groups are considered full sibs, regardless of the breeding combinations in that group. Pedigree data within groups is not necessary. Bloodlines (e.g., **A, B, C, D**) are assigned to maternal and paternal lines in each initial group. Group 1 consists of lines **A** and **B**, group 2 of lines **C** and **D**, etc. (figure 7.1).
5. Offspring inherit the maternal and paternal bloodlines, e.g., offspring of group 1 have bloodlines **AB**.
6. Each generation offspring of one sex (males in this example) are moved to another group. In this way, natural dispersal patterns could be followed. The breeding group to which an offspring is moved is determined as follows:

$$Target = Source + 2^{[(G-1)\,modulus\,log_2(N_G)]}$$
$$for\ Target \leq N_G \tag{7.1}$$

and

$$Target = Source + 2^{[(G-1)\,modulus\,log_2(N_G)]} - N_G$$
$$for\ Target > N_G \tag{7.2}$$

where *Source* is the number of the natal group; *Target* is the number of the breeding group that receives offspring from the *Source* group; G is the number of generations since the population was started; and N_G is the number of breeding groups in the population.

Figures 7.1 and 7.2 present this *MAI* model for generations one and two, respectively. The *MAI* model will be illustrated by "following" breeding group 1. This group starts with lines **A** and **B**. Male offspring of the first generation (bloodlines **AB**) are moved, according to equation (7.1), to group 2. Male offspring of group 8 (bloodlines **OP**) are transferred to and mated with female offspring of group 1. Male offspring of the second generation in group 1 (lines **ABOP**) cannot be combined with female offspring in group 2 (lines **ABCD**) as they are cousins. According to *MAI* equation (7.1), males of group 1 will be combined with females of group 3 (lines **CDEF**). Inbreeding can be avoided in

Figure 7.1 Maximal Avoidance of Inbreeding scheme for a population composed of eight breeding groups in the first generation. Maternal and paternal lineages are indicated with characters **A** to **P**. Boxes represent breeding groups. Arrows indicate transfers of males from natal to host groups. Bloodlines of male offspring are shown near the arrows.

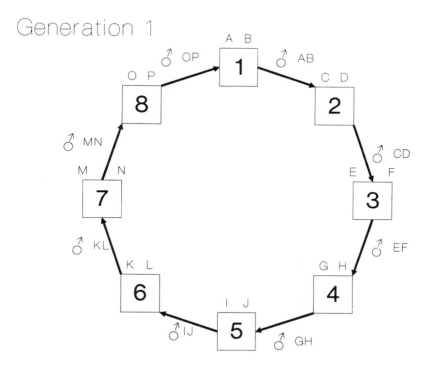

the third generation by bidirectional breeding combinations between groups 1 and 5, 2 and 6, 3 and 7, and 4 and 8.

Inbreeding can no longer be avoided after the third generation. All offspring in the fourth generation have bloodlines **ABCDEFGHI-JKLMNOP**. Exchanges of offspring in the fourth generation are according to the schemes for the first generation. The same cycle of steps between groups (i.e, transfer by steps 1, 2, and 4 for generation one, two, and three, respectively) is repeated continuously. Inbreeding coefficients will increase gradually and equally for all offspring after the fourth generation.

The power of 2 is a keyword in the *MAI* model. The *MAI* model presented cannot be applied properly for populations that consist of numbers of breeding groups that are unequal to powers of 2. The number of

Figure 7.2 Maximal Avoidance of Inbreeding scheme for a population composed of eight breeding units in the second generation.

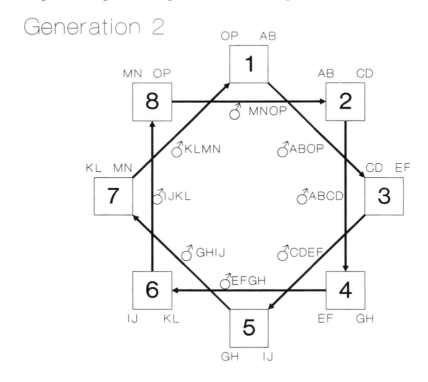

generations during which inbreeding can be avoided can be calculated by solving the following equation:

$$2^{\text{Generations}} = N_G \qquad (7.3)$$

or,

$$\text{Generations} = \log_2 (N_G). \qquad (7.4)$$

Thus, for example, inbreeding can be avoided for five generations in a population that is composed of 32 breeding units. I would like to call these exchange steps between generations the *MAI* cycle. Maximal avoidance can be seen as a sequence of *MAI* cycles (*MAI* sequence).

Variation in *MAI* Models

The *MAI* model just described is a simple, low-intensity genetic management model that allows one to calculate exchange schemes for groups in each generation. Detailed data on breeding within groups is not required. It basically uses a cycle of steps that represent powers of 2 in ascending order (i.e., 1, 2, 4). This cycle is repeated continuously. Note that *MAI* can be started using different cycles of exchange steps e.g., 4, 2, 1 or 2, 1, 4. The following rules have to be taken in account:

1. Each step must represent a power of 2.
2. A step cannot be larger than $2^{(MAI\ cycle-1)}$ (see equation [7.3]).
3. All steps between 1 and the maximum step must occur in the *MAI* cycle.
4. Each step may occur only once during a *MAI* cycle.
5. The *MAI* cycle can not be changed in midcycle. Variations in the *MAI* cycle may be required to adapt this model to management that has already started with avoidance of inbreeding schemes that differ from the cycle calculated from equations (7.1) and (7.2).

Maximal avoidance of inbreeding models have to be considered as guidelines for genetic management rather than as rules. Histories of populations, the number of breeding groups, and the reproductive success in individual groups determine the extent to which *MAI* can be applied. Population managers' creativity will always be essential for further application of this model.

MAI Models for Subpopulations

The *MAI* model can also be applied to populations that are divided into subpopulations, e.g., regional breeding programs. Figure 7.3 shows the *MAI* management of a population composed of four subpopulations (I through IV). Each subpopulation is composed of four breeding groups (1 through 4). Inbreeding in this population of sixteen breeding groups can be avoided for four generations (equation [7.3]).

According to the "normal" *MAI* model, exchanges between groups in different subpopulations would take place during each generation. Logistic considerations, such as coordination or costs of transport,

Figure 7.3 Combination of Maximal Avoidance of Inbreeding schemes that act between subpopulations (numbered I to IV) and breeding units (1 to 4) within the subpopulation.

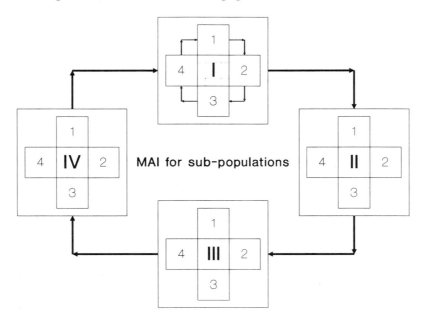

might require that exchanges between subpopulations be limited and that they be managed collectively. These requirements can be achieved by nesting different *MAI* schemes with each acting on a different level. The first level acts between units in a subpopulation; the second between subpopulations. The basic guideline of such management is to start *MAI* cycles of a next level at moments that *MAI* cycles of previous levels have been completed. In our example we would start a *MAI* cycle between units within subpopulations. This cycle would be complete after the second generation. Offspring of the third generation would then migrate between subpopulations to the equivalent group in the appropriate subpopulation, e.g., I-1 to II-1, II-2 to III-2 etc. (figure 7.3). Exchanges between subpopulations I to IV occur during generations three and four. The *MAI* cycle in subpopulations then begins again.

Male Groups

Genetic management of harem groups involves replacement of male breeders and removal of male offspring. Since generally only one male per group can be placed in another group, a surplus of young males will exist. In this context, surplus refers to available space and not to genetic importance. To increase effective population size, each individual in small populations should have the opportunity to breed. A solution can be found in establishing male groups.

Figure 7.4 shows a *MAI* model for harem groups that includes a male group. In each generation the male breeder of a harem group is replaced by another male according to the *MAI* guidelines as described previously. The surplus male offspring are moved to the male group. Once the male breeder has produced offspring, he is replaced by a male sib from the male group. This means that animals in male groups need to be identified on the individual or on the natal group level.

Male groups can also be established in the management of colonies. For instance, females and female descendants of ring-tailed lemurs (*Lemur catta*) form the core of a social group, while males transfer frequently (Richard 1987). Young males can be removed from the colony as soon as they are sexually mature. They are either immediately introduced to new colonies or to male groups. In contrast to the management of harem groups, not only one but all males are replaced. Implementa-

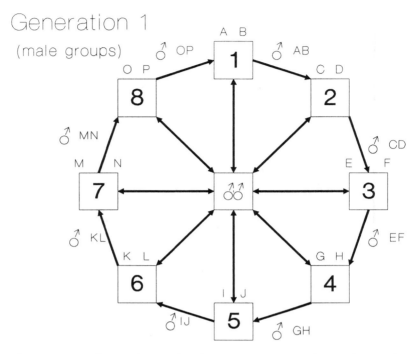

Figure 7.4 Implementation of male group in Maximal Avoidance of Inbreeding scheme for a population composed of eight breeding units in the first generation. Maternal and paternal lineages are indicated with characters **A** to **P**. Arrows indicate transfer of newborn males.

tion of male groups in genetic management largely depends on the species-specific social structure and practical conditions. While housing male groups may not be feasible under zoo conditions, semireserves and (larger) safari-parks may provide the required facilities.

Group Composition

The *MAI* model is based on discrete generations, i.e., the offspring of two groups will form the new breeding generation. This suggests that not only the offspring of one sex but also the parental group is removed in each generation. However, sex ratio, age structure, and family relationships of breeding groups can influence reproductive success. For example, Rijksen (1981) observed extreme infanticide in a captive group of Hamadryas baboons (*Papio hamadryas*) that had been established with juveniles. The natural social organization, a colony composed of several harems, did not evolve in this captive group. Effects of removing the remaining specific age/sex groups from the breeding groups need to be understood.

MAINTENANCE OF GENETIC VARIATION IN "BLACK-BOX" POPULATIONS

While *MAI* schemes delay and reduce the rate of inbreeding in populations, they are not necessarily the best breeding strategy to accomplish the primary goal of genetic management, namely, the maintenance of genetic variation. As is the case for minimizing inbreeding, maximizing the retention of genetic variation is best achieved through management based on completely known pedigrees (Ballou and Lacy, essay 5 of this volume). As mentioned earlier, however, this level of detailed, intensive genetic management may not be possible in populations for which such pedigree information is lacking because it has been impossible to identify individuals or assign parentage. Given the importance of genetic variation for the long-term survival of populations, methods and guidelines have to be developed for less intensive genetic management of these "black-box" populations. These strategies are based on the concept of managing the effective size of a population and are discussed in the following sections.

Effective Population Size

The rate of genetic loss due to genetic drift depends on a population's effective size (Wright 1931). The larger the effective size, the smaller the rate of loss. In ideal populations (i.e., populations that follow the Hardy-Weinberg model) the effective size equals the population size. Mating structures in real populations, however, can deviate significantly from the Hardy-Weinberg model. Unequal sex ratio (e.g., harem groups) and individual reproductive success reduce a population's effective size, while dispersal between population subdivisions and increasing the number of animals participating in breeding causes it to increase. Manipulating these factors within the context of maintaining the desired social groupings thus provides the population manager with the ability to manage, within constraints, a population's effective size.

Several formulas have been developed for estimating effective population size in nonideal populations (Kimura and Crow 1963; Crow and Kimura 1970; Felsenstein 1971; Lande and Barrowclough 1987). The method described by Lande and Barrowclough is based on detailed demographic data (i.e., age-specific fecundity and mortality tables) and information on variance in reproductive success. Like pedigree data, however, these data may also be extremely difficult to obtain in many populations, and estimating a population's effective size using these approaches, even for a captive population, is problematic at best.

Social Rank and Reproductive Success

Behavioral data can be used to assist in estimating effective population size. Nozawa (1972) used information on the sexual activities of males to estimate effective troop size in Japanese macaques (*Macaca fuscata*). Mating activities of males and social dominance, however, may be a poor indicator of reproductive success. For example, subordinate males of brown-tufted capuchins (*Cebus apella*) copulate with females at the end of estrus. Janson (1984) suggests these are infertile matings since ovulation probably takes place in the middle of estrus. Curie-Cohen et al. (1983) studied a troop of rhesus macaques (*Macaca mulatta*) over an eight-year period. Although second-rank males participated less in observed copulations than dominant males, they sired more offspring.

Blood protein analysis and, more recently, DNA fingerprinting have been used to study social rank and reproductive success in various species of macaques (*Macaca*) (e.g., Smith 1981; Curie-Cohen et al. 1983; Stern and Smith 1984, de Ruiter et al. 1992). Ideally, the results from such studies could be used to estimate effective size of multimale/female groups that have not been monitored. However, the history and environmental conditions of the group(s) that have been studied should be carefully evaluated. The conditions of captivity may influence the reproductive success of dominant males (de Ruiter et al. 1992). Depending on the species' life span, studies on reproductive success should last for several years.

Difficulties in estimating effective population sizes are certainly not restricted to species with complex hierarchic social systems. Studies on species that are considered monogamous breeders and nest in colonies revealed that promiscuity or extra-pair fertilization may occur more frequently than is generally assumed (e.g., Quinn et al. 1987; Morton et al. 1990; McKilligan 1990).

Risks in Genetic Management

Difficulties in estimating effective size and, thus, loss of genetic variation, have been described in the previous section. Accurate estimates of N_e may be extremely difficult to obtain for most "black-box" populations. However, are extremely accurate estimates necessary for the practical breeding management of populations? Approximations based on existing models may be sufficient for populations appropriate for low-intensity genetic management. Risks associated with the use of approximations may be acceptable in these situations: an increasing number of species that need preservation and/or conservation management and the benefits of managing a larger number of species under low-intensity management may outweigh the genetic risks.

High-intensity management, based on known pedigree data and manipulation of individual breeding combinations, also incorporates aspects of risks. It is based on predictions with respect to the expected genetic loss per generation. However, Mendelian segregation is a stochastic process. Thus, the actual genetic variation in intensively managed populations can differ from the expected genetic variation. This is clearly illustrated by results of individual iterations in simulation models (Starfield et al., essay 8 of this volume; Lacy 1987). Furthermore, monitoring actual genetic loss by such means as allozyme studies on at least thirty to forty polymorphic loci is rarely carried out for captive populations. Thus, the issue of "risk" is not an unknown aspect in breeding management.

The management of "black-box" populations a priori involves aspects of risk. Underestimates of effective sizes can result in establishing and maintaining populations that are larger than would be required to meet the goal of preserving specific levels of genetic variation (Soulé et al. 1986; Lande, essay 14 of this volume). This will reduce the number of species that can be managed under captive conditions. Overestimates can result in losing populations due to inbreeding depression, thus limiting the number of successfully managed species. It is obvious that risks should be evaluated in low-intensity management. The effect of population size, composition, and size of breeding units on minimal and maximal genetic losses in "black-box" populations should be evaluated. The following sections will present some guidelines for the management of such populations based on simulation experiments.

Simulation Models

Pedigree analyses based on computer simulations have proven to be valuable for genetic studies of populations (Lacy et al., essay 4 of this volume; Starfield et al., essay 8 of this volume; Ballou and Lacy, essay 5 of this volume). These tools allow one to study trends in genetic processes that occur in nonideal populations. The model GSPED (described below) is used to create pedigrees of populations that are composed of several breeding groups. Dispersal according to *MAI* models can be included in this model. The model GENEFLOW (Princée 1988) is then used to estimate loss of genetic variation using Monte Carlo simulations in populations created by GSPED.

Pedigree Simulation. The following parameters can be set in the GSPED model:

1. The number of founders.
2. The number of breeding groups. The number of breeding groups should equal a power of 2 to make the use of *MAI* dispersal strategies possible (see section "Maximal Avoidance of Inbreeding").
3. The type of social system: pair, harem, multimale/female group.
4. The number of females in harem groups and the number of males and females in multimale/female groups.
5. The number of offspring per breeding group. Each breeding

group will produce the same number of offspring. Sex ratio in offspring will match the parental sex ratio.

6. The reproductive success of individuals in breeding groups. The distribution of offspring over males and females and breeding combinations can be: (1) random (generated using Monte Carlo methods); (2) uniform (involves equal numbers of offspring per individual with as many mating combinations as possible); or (3) a user-defined distribution.

7. The number of generations. Generations do not overlap, i.e., the parental group is removed from the breeding unit before offspring become parents.

8. The dispersal of male offspring between breeding units according to *MAI* schemes can be selected.

Nine populations ([A] to [I]) have been simulated with the GSPED model. These populations will be used in the following sections to illustrate trends in the loss of genetic variation that occur in populations with different numbers, sizes, and composition of breeding groups. Each population starts with 64 founders and is simulated for 10 generations. No population growth is assumed in these simulation experiments. Specific characteristics of these populations are presented in table 7.1. Effective sizes have been calculated for breeding units and populations according to the method of Lande and Barrowclough (1987).

Pedigree Analysis. The version of GENEFLOW used here is an extended version of that described by Princée (1988). New extensions and characteristics of this model relevant for the simulation experiments in this study are described in this section. GENEFLOW supposes a source population of infinite size with a maximum of 40 independent autosomal loci. Each locus can have up to five allelic variants with user-defined frequencies in the source population. For each iteration, Monte Carlo methods are used to draw random genotypes for founders and random genotypes, based upon Mendelian segregation of parental alleles, for their descendants. Neither selection nor mutation is assumed in this simulation model. Averages of observed heterozygosities and gene diversities (expected heterozygosity) over all loci are estimated for each generation after each iteration. Finally, averages of these measures over all iterations and variances within iterations are calculated.

Table 7.1 Characteristics of populations created with the GSPED simulation model.

POPULATION	No. GROUPS	GROUP SEX RATIO N_m	GROUP SEX RATIO N_f	REPRODUCTIVE SUCCESS	GROUP N_e	MAI[1]	POPULATION N_e
A	16	1	3	females equal	3.35	+	71.93
B	8	1	7	females equal	3.85	+	34.75
C	4	1	15	females equal	3.97	–	16.67
D	4	1	15	females equal	3.97	+	16.67
E	4	4	12	equal	17.07	+	71.93
F	4	8	8	1 male, females equal	3.33	+	15.32
G	4	8	8	unequal[2]	10.50	+	47.07
H	4	8	8	equal for 4 males and 4 females	9.13	+	41.12
I	4	8	8	equal	30.00	+	126.00

Notes: Nm = number of males, Nf = number of females, N_e = effective size according to Lande and Barrowclough (1987).

[1] "+" indicates that dispersal between groups according to Maximal Avoidance of Inbreeding schemes has been simulated; "–" indicates no dispersal.

[2] Distribution of progeny is presented in table 7.3.

Table 7.2 Results of GENEFLOW simulation
experiment for population [H] and individual
breeding units after ten generations (table 7.1)
(averages over 50 simulations).

GROUP	H_e (variance)	H_o (variance)
1	0.726 (0.0001)	0.780 (0.0003)
2	0.726 (0.0001)	0.784 (0.0004)
3	0.724 (0.0001)	0.783 (0.0004)
4	0.728 (0.0001)	0.786 (0.0003)
Population	0.763 (0.0000)	0.783 (0.0001)

Notes: Variance among the 50 simulations is also shown. H_e = average
expected heterozygosity gene diversity; H_o = average observed
heterozygosity.

Nei and RoyChoudury (1974) showed that the number of loci
screened in isozyme studies is more important for obtaining reliable estimates of genetic variation than the number of individuals. This also
applies for simulation experiments with GENEFLOW (i.e., the number
of loci is more important than the number of iterations). Simulation experiments were carried out with all 40 loci using five allelic variants
with equal frequencies. A total of 50 simulations were run. Thus, gene
diversity and observed heterozygosity were both 0.800 in the source
population and 0.794 (99.19% of the "source") in the founder generation, respectively. This is in accordance with expected genetic variation
in a random sample of 64 individuals from an ideal population (Frankel
and Soulé 1981).

An example of the results of one simulation experiment is presented
in table 7.2. This table shows the gene diversity and observed heterozygosity in a population composed of four breeding units (population
[H], table 7.1). Note that heterozygosity in small groups is more subject
to variation within iterations than gene diversity. Still, the variance is in
an acceptable range. Gene diversity in the entire population is larger
than the arithmetic mean over individual breeding units. This is because
genetic drift and inbreeding in subpopulations can lead to fixation of
different alleles in different subpopulations. As allele frequencies drift
toward fixation, both heterozygosity and gene diversity decline within
subpopulations. However, gene diversity in the total population is high-

er than the mean of gene diversity within subpopulations. In the extreme case of complete fixation of different alleles in subpopulations, all individuals are homozygous for all loci (thus, heterozygosity in both population and subpopulations is zero), but gene diversity in the total population is still high.

Results of the simulation experiments are presented in figures 7.5 to 7.10. They are discussed in the following section. Values for genetic variation are presented as percentages of genetic variation in the "source" population.

Effect of Social Structure on Genetic Loss

Dispersal. The effect(s) of dispersal through *MAI* management on genetic variation is illustrated in figures 7.5 to 7.7. Levels of observed heterozygosity and gene diversity in population [C], composed of four harem groups (table 7.1), are presented in figure 7.5. In each generation

Figure 7.5 Effect of *MAI* schemes on gene diversity and observed heterozygosity in a population of 64 individuals composed of four harem groups (population [C], table 7.1).

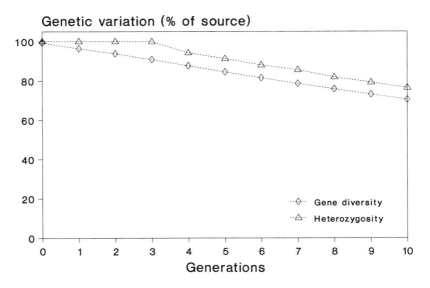

newborn males in this population are moved between breeding groups according to the *MAI* schemes.

Gene diversity decreases in each generation. Observed heterozygosity starts to decline after three generations as the first *MAI* cycle has been completed (and inbreeding can no longer be avoided). The delay of loss in heterozygosity depends not only on the number of breeding groups but also on the numbers of allelic variants and their frequencies. Levels of genetic variation in the simulation experiments are extremely high compared with levels found in various animal species (Nevo 1978). Therefore, the effects of *MAI* on stabilizing heterozygosity in the first generations will be limited in real populations. Further simulation experiments based on empirical data from allozyme studies are required to study this feature.

Figures 7.6 and 7.7 illustrate the effects of *MAI* management versus intentional inbreeding on genetic variation. The levels of genetic variation in population [C] are compared with those in population [D]. Dispersal does not occur between harem groups in population [D]. This will result in continuous full-sib and half-sib matings in these groups. The observed heterozygosity in population [D] declines much faster than in population [C], where *MAI* is applied (figure 7.6). However, the decrease in gene diversity under inbreeding conditions is slower than under *MAI* conditions (figure 7.7). These differences are caused by fixation of different alleles within isolated breeding groups. These effects have also been described by Lacy (1987).

Variances in reproductive success do not differ between populations [C] and [D]. Therefore, the effective population size is the same for both populations (N_e = 16.67; table 7.1). Still, loss in gene diversity differs between these populations. This discrepancy can be explained by the fact that the methods used here to calculate effective population size are not sensitive to nonrandom partner choice.

Sex Ratio in Breeding Groups. Effects of sex ratio in breeding groups on genetic loss are presented in figure 7.8. Each of the three populations in this experiment is composed of four breeding groups. These populations differ, however, in the composition of breeding groups: a harem group (population [C]), a multimale/female group with unequal sex ratio (population [E]), and a multimale/female group with equal sex ratio (population [I]; table 7.1).

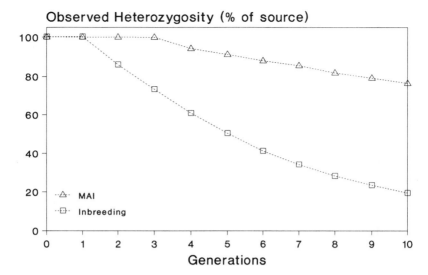

Figure 7.6 Effect of *MAI* and inbreeding schemes on observed hetero-zygosity in a population of 64 individuals composed of four harem groups (populations [C] and [D] in table 7.1, respectively).

Figure 7.7 Effect of *MAI* and inbreeding schemes on gene diversity in a population of 64 individuals composed of four harem groups (populations [C] and [D] in table 7.1, respectively). These data are compared with the expected loss of genetic diversity for a N_e of 16.67 (table 7.1).

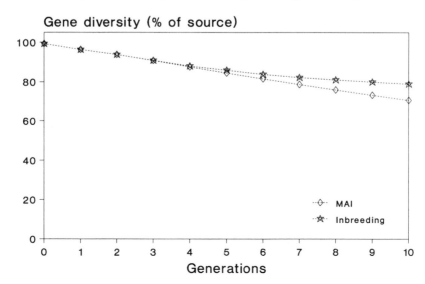

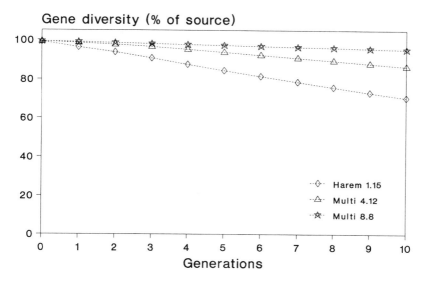

Figure 7.8 Effect of different sex ratios on gene diversity in a population of 64 individuals. Harem 1.15 (1 male, 15 females) refers to population [C]; multi 4.12 and multi 8.8 refer to population [E] and population [I], respectively (table 7.1).

Populations composed of harem units are especially vulnerable to genetic loss. This effect is illustrated by the genetic loss in population [C]. Even a luxury of 64 founders and optimal breeding conditions (i.e., equal reproductive success for all individuals) does not prevent a rapid decline in gene diversity. Gene diversity in this population drops below the 90% level (recommended by Soulé et al. 1986) within five generations. The genetic loss in population [E] can also be considered high. Sex ratios in the multimale/female breeding groups of this population are still not optimal. The gene diversity in population [E] drops below 90% after seven generations. Population [I] represents an optimal genetic situation. Equal sex ratio and equal reproductive success limit genetic loss to 0.044 percent per generation.

Size of Breeding Units. Effects of group size on genetic variation are demonstrated in figure 7.9. Populations [A] through [C], composed of harem groups, have been used in this simulation experiment. While these populations are of the same size, the size of the harem groups in-

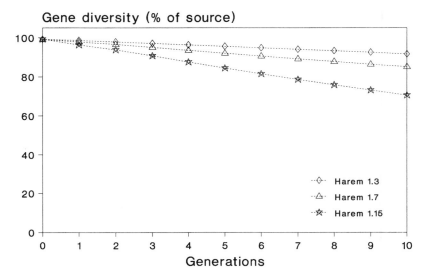

Figure 7.9 Effect of different sizes of harem groups on gene diversity in a population of 64 individuals. Harem 1.3 (1 male, 3 females), harem 1.7 and harem 1.15 refer to populations [A] to [C] in table 7.1, respectively.

creases from population [A] to [C]. Genetic loss decreases as the population is subdivided into smaller harem groups because more animals participate in breeding and the total effective size is larger.

Reproductive Success. Effects of differences in reproductive success in a population composed of four breeding groups with equal sex ratios are illustrated in figure 7.10. The populations used for these experiments are [F] through [I] in table 7.1. Male reproductive success in the breeding groups of population [F] is limited to dominant males. Unequal distribution of offspring in both males and females is assumed in the breeding groups of population [G]. Breeding combinations in these breeding groups are presented in table 7.3. Equal reproductive success for half the number of breeding animals is assumed for the breeding groups of population [H]. Population [I] has an optimal mating system: all animals produce equal numbers of offspring.

The levels of genetic variation in populations [F] through [I] are com-

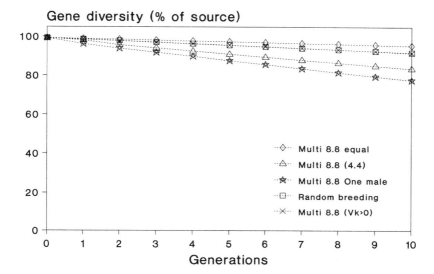

Figure 7.10 Effect of different distributions of progeny in a population of 64 individuals composed of four multi-male/female groups (populations [F]–[G] in table 7.1). The random breeding model refers to a Poisson distribution of progeny in a population of 64 individuals.

Table 7.3 Number of offspring per breeding combination in individual groups of population [G] (table 7.1)

Male Number	FEMALE NUMBER								
	1	2	3	4	5	6	7	8	Total
1	4	2	1	—	—	—	—	—	7
2	—	2	—	2	—	—	—	—	4
3	—	—	—	—	1	1	—	—	2
4	—	—	—	—	—	—	—	—	0
5	—	—	—	—	—	—	1	—	1
6	—	—	—	—	1	—	—	—	1
7	—	—	—	—	—	—	—	1	1
8	—	—	—	—	—	—	—	—	0
Total	4	4	1	2	2	1	1	1	16

pared with the expected levels of genetic variation in a random breeding population of the same size. Gene diversities differ significantly between breeding systems. By the tenth generation gene diversities in populations [F] and [H] are 18% and 10% lower than expected under random breeding. The gene diversity in population [G] is almost as expected by the random breeding model, while that in population [I] (equal distribution of progeny) is greater than expected.

RECOMMENDATIONS AND CONCLUSIONS

Genetic management of species living in social groups and for which detailed pedigree data are lacking (in captivity and the wild) can be achieved through low-intensity management techniques that incorporate the species' natural social structure into genetic management strategies. These techniques are based on the concepts of avoiding inbreeding and maximizing effective population size.

Avoidance of inbreeding in species where intensive genetic management is not possible or desirable can be achieved by implementing *MAI* schemes in breeding management. These schemes are independent of the size or composition of the breeding groups, i.e., they can be applied to pairs, harem groups, or colonies, and permit natural social systems to be maintained within breeding groups. Given the large number of data on inbreeding depression in (zoo) populations, strategies that avoid inbreeding are often recommended as a preventive guideline. Information on natural dispersal patterns can be used to determine the age and sex of individuals that are moved between breeding groups.

Loss of genetic diversity in populations that are managed in social groups will often be higher than for those managed in breeding pairs or under intense management strategies. This is caused by unequal sex ratio (e.g., harem groups) and unequal reproductive success (e.g., related to social rank). In cases where genetic loss is considered too high to preserve significant levels of variation, measures need to be taken. A simple measure is to increase the effective population size by extending the number of breeding groups. This may be feasible for the management of (semi-) wild populations, but it has its limitations for the management of captive populations. Given the large number of species that need propagation, the amount of zoo space available for each species is limited. In captivity, the effective size can be increased by optimizing the reproductive success of each individual. Subdivision into small breeding groups generally increases the total effective size by allowing more animals to participate in breeding (see, for example, population [A] through [C] in table 7.1). Additionally, male groups could be established to maintain "surplus" animals of species that live in harem groups. However, dispersal (migration) needs to be managed (e.g., using a *MAI* scheme) to avoid high levels of inbreeding within small groups. Information on the minimum size and composition of breeding groups under natural conditions can be used as guidelines to meet behavioral (and educational) requirements.

The application of low-intensity management does not exclude high-intensity management. Especially in cases where genetic variation is expected to drop below acceptable levels, blood protein analysis and DNA fingerprinting techniques may be applied to determine ancestries and to study reproductive patterns in social groups (Avise et al., essay 9 of this volume).

Acknowledgments
I would like to acknowledge Leobert de Boer, Tine Griede (National Foundation for Research in Zoological Gardens, Amsterdam), and Angela Glatston (The Royal Rotterdam Zoological and Botanical Gardens) for their various suggestions and comments on this manuscript.

R E F E R E N C E S
Bouwmeester, J., J. L. Mulder, and P. J. H. van Bree. 1989. High incidence of malocclusion in an isolated population of the red fox (*Vulpes vulpes*) in the Netherlands. *Journal of Zoology* (London) 219:123–36.

Chepko-Sade, B. D. and Z. T. Halpin, eds. 1987. *Mammalian Dispersal Patterns: The Effects of Social Structure on Population Genetics*. Chicago: University of Chicago Press.

Chepko-Sade, B. D., W. M. Shields, J. Berger, Z. T. Halpin, W. T. Jones, L. L. Rogers, J. R. Rood, and A. T. Smith. 1987. The effects of dispersal and social structure on effective population size. In B. D. Chepko-Sade and Z. T. Halpin, eds., *Mammalian Dispersal Patterns: The Effects of Social Structure on Population Genetics*, pp. 287–321. Chicago: University of Chicago Press.

Crow, J. F. and M. Kimura. 1970. *An Introduction to Population Genetics Theory*. Minneapolis: Burgess.

Curie-Cohen, M., D. Yoshihara, L. Lutrell, K. Benforado, J. W. MacCluer, and W. H. Stone. 1983. The effects of dominance on mating behavior and paternity in a captive troop of rhesus monkeys (*Macaca mulatta*). *American Journal of Primatology* 5:127–38.

Eisenberg, J. F. 1981. *The Mammalian Radiations: An Analysis of Trends in Evolution, Adaptation, and Behavior.* Chicago: University of Chicago Press.

Erwin, J. 1986. Environments for captive propagation of primates: Interaction of social and physical factors. In K. Benirschke, ed., *The Road to Self-Sustaining Populations,* pp. 297–305. New York: Springer Verlag.

Ewer, R. F. 1975. Why study small mammals? *International Zoo Yearbook* 15:1–3.

Felsenstein, J. 1971. Inbreeding and variance effective number in populations with overlapping generations. *Genetics* 68:581–97.

Flesness, N. R. 1977. Gene pool conservation and computer analysis. *International Zoo Yearbook* 17:77–81.

Flesness, N. R. and G. M. Mace. 1988. Population databases and zoological conservation. *International Zoo Yearbook* 27:42–49.

Frankel, O. H. and M. E. Soulé. 1981. *Conservation and Evolution.* Cambridge: Cambridge University Press.

Frankham, R., H. Hemmer, O. A. Ryder, E. G. Cothran, M. E. Soulé, N. D. Murray, and M. Snyder. 1986. Selection in captive populations. *Zoo Biology* 5:127–38.

Gibbs, H. L. and P. R. Grant. 1989. Inbreeding in Darwin's medium ground finches (*Geospiza fortis*). *Evolution* 43 (6): 1273–84.

Griede, T. 1989. *Guidelines for Adequate Housing and Care of Non-Human Primates in Zoos.* Amsterdam: E.E.C./C.I.T.E.S. Department, Bruxelles and Stichting Nationaal Onderziek Dierentuinen.

Hooff, J. A. R. A. M. van. 1986. Behavior requirements for self-sustaining primate populations: Some theoretical considerations and a closer look at social behavior. In K. Benirschke, ed., *The Road to Self-Sustaining Populations,* pp. 307–19. New York: Springer Verlag.

Janson, C. H. 1984. Female choice and mating system of the brown capuchin monkey (*Cebus apella*) (Primates: *Cebidae*). *Zeitschrift für Tierpsychologie* 65:177–200.

Kimura, M. and J. M. Crow. 1963. The measurement of effective population number. *Evolution* 17:279–88.

Lacy, R. C. 1987. Loss of genetic diversity from managed populations: Interacting effects of drift, mutation, immigration, selection, and population subdivision. *Conservation Biology* 1:143–57.

Lacy, R. C. 1994. *GENES:* A computer program for pedigree analysis and population management. Chicago: Chicago Zoological Society.

Lande, R. L. and G. F. Barrowclough. 1987. Effective population size and genetic variation. In M. E. Soulé, ed., *Viable Populations for Conservation,* pp. 87–123. Cambridge: Cambridge University Press.

MacCluer, J. W., J. L. VandeBerg, B. Read, and O. A. Ryder. 1986. Pedigree analysis by computer simulation. *Zoo Biology* 5:147–60.

McKilligan, N. G. 1990. Promiscuity in the cattle egret (*Bulbulcus ibis*). *The Auk* 107:334–41.

Morton, E. S., L. Forman, and M. Braun. 1990. Extra-pair fertilizations and the evolution of colonial breeding in purple martins. *The Auk* 107:275–83.

Nei, M. and A. K. RoyChoudury. 1974. Sampling variances of heterozygosity and genetic distance. *Genetics* 76:379–90.

Nevo, E. 1978. Genetic variation in natural populations: Patterns and theory. *Theoretical Population Biology* 13:121–77.

Noordwijk, A. J. van and W. Scharloo. 1981. Inbreeding in an island population of the great tit. *Genetica* 55:221–32.

Nozawa, K. 1972. Population genetics of Japanese monkeys: I. Estimation of the effective troop size. *Primates* 13 (4): 381–93.

Princée, F. P. G. 1986. Het behoud van genetische variatie in zeldzame huisdierrassen. *Zeldzaam Huisdier* 11 (1): 8–12.

Princée, F. P. G. 1988. Genetic variation in the zoo population of the red panda subspecies *Ailurus fulgens fulgens*. *Zoo Biology* 7:219–31.

Princée, F. P. G. 1989. Preservation of genetic variation in the red panda population. In A. R. Glatston, ed., *Red Panda Biology*, pp. 171–82. The Hague: SPB Academic Publishing.

Pusey, A. E. and C. Packer. 1987. Dispersal and philopatry. In B. B. Smuts, D. L. Cheney, R. M. Seyfarth, R. W. Wrangham, and T. T. Struhsaker, eds., *Primate Societies*, pp. 250–66. Chicago: University of Chicago Press.

Quinn, T. W., J. S. Quinn, F. Cooke, and B. N. White. 1987. DNA marker analysis detects multiple maternity and paternity in single broods of the lesser snow goose. *Nature* 326:392–94.

Ralls, K. and J. D. Ballou. 1983. Extinction: Lessons from zoos. In C. M. Schonewald-Cox, S. M. Chambers, B. MacBryde, and W. L. Thomas, eds., *Genetics and Conservation: A Reference for Managing Wild Animal and Plant Populations*, pp. 164–84. Menlo Park: Benjamin/Cummings.

Ralls, K., J. D. Ballou, and A. R. Templeton. 1988. Estimates of lethal equivalents and the cost of inbreeding in mammals. *Conservation Biology* 2:185–93.

Richard, A. F. 1987. Malagasy Prosimians: Female dominance. In B. B. Smuts, D. L. Cheney, R. M. Seyfarth, R. W. Wrangham, and T. T. Struhsaker, eds., *Primate Societies*, pp. 25–33. Chicago: University of Chicago Press.

Rijksen, H. D. 1981. Infantkilling: A possible consequence of a disputed leader role. *Behaviour* 78:138–68.

Ruiter, J. R. de, W. Scheffrahn, G. J. J. M. Trommelen, A. G. Uitterlinden, R. D. Martin, and J. A. R. A. M. van Hooff. 1992. Male social rank and reproductive success in wild long-tailed macaques: Paternity exclusions by blood protein analysis and DNA fingerprinting. In R. D. Martin, A. F. Dixson, and E. J. Wickings, eds., *Paternity in Primates: Genetic Tests and Theories*, pp. 175–91. Basel: Karger.

Shields, W. M. 1987. Dispersal and mating systems: Investigating their causal connections. In B. D. Chepko-Sade and Z. T. Halpin, eds., *Mammalian Dispersal Patterns: The Effects of Social Structure on Population Genetics*, pp. 3–24. Chicago: University of Chicago Press.

Smith, A. T. 1987. Population structure of pikas: Dispersal versus philopatry. In B. D. Chepko-Sade and Z. T. Halpin, eds., *Mammalian Dispersal Patterns: The Effects of Social Structure on Population Genetics*, pp. 128–42. Chicago: University of Chicago Press.

Smith, D. G. 1981. The association between rank and reproductive success of male rhesus monkeys. *American Journal of Primatology* 1:83–90.

Smuts, B. B., D. L. Cheney, R. M. Seyfarth, R. W. Wrangham, and T. T. Struhsaker.

1987. Taxonomy and organization of living primates. In B. B. Smuts, D. L. Cheney, R. M. Seyfarth, R. W. Wrangham, and T. T. Struhsaker, eds., *Primate Societies,* pp. 501–5. Chicago: University of Chicago Press.

Soulé, M. E. 1987. Introduction. In: M. E. Soulé, ed., *Viable Populations for Conservation,* pp. 1–10. Cambridge: Cambridge University Press.

Soulé, M. E., M. Gilpin, W. Conway, and T. Foose. 1986. The millennium ark: How long a voyage, how many staterooms, how many passengers? *Zoo Biology* 5:101–13.

Stern, B. R. and D. G. Smith. 1984. Sexual behavior and paternity in three captive groups of rhesus monkeys (*Macaca mulatta*). *Animal Behaviour* 32:23–32.

Templeton, A. R. 1987. Inferences on natural population structure from genetic studies on captive mammalian populations. In B. D. Chepko-Sade and Z. T. Halpin, eds., *Mammalian Dispersal Patterns: The Effects of Social Structure on Population Genetics,* pp. 257–72. Chicago: University of Chicago Press.

Templeton, A. R. and B. Read. 1983. The elimination of inbreeding depression in a captive herd of Speke's gazelle. In C. M. Schonewald-Cox, S. M. Chambers, B. MacBryde, and W. L. Thomas, eds., *Genetics and Conservation: A Reference for Managing Wild Animal and Plant Populations,* pp. 241–61. Menlo Park: Benjamin/Cummings.

Thornhill, N. W., ed. 1993. *The Natural History of Inbreeding and Outbreeding.* Chicago: University of Chicago Press.

Tilson, R. L. 1986. Primate mating systems and their consequences for captive management. In K. Benirschke, ed., *The Road to Self-Sustaining Populations,* pp. 361–73. New York: Springer Verlag.

Wright, S. 1931. Evolution in Mendelian populations. *Genetics* 16:97–159.

8

Genetic Risk Analysis of a Small Wild Lion Population

⚏

Anthony M. Starfield, Henry A. Rowley,
Henley Quadling, and Thomas J. Foose

Lacy et al. (essay. 4 of this volume) describe a spectrum of problems in conservation biology where one might want to estimate genetic drift. At one end of the spectrum a small, endangered population may consist of captive individuals of known pedigree. At the other end there may be a small number of individuals in the wild. In between there are a number of possible scenarios, including captive populations with an incomplete pedigree, a wild population with some pedigree information, or a population that is partly captive and partly wild.

Lacy et al. also describe the various methods available for assessing genetic drift in small captive populations of known pedigree. In this study we conduct a computer experiment to explore what we can do in a similar vein for a small, wild population where virtually nothing may be known about individual animals, let alone their pedigrees. We chose to analyze a lion (*Panthera leo*) population, not because lions are an endangered species, but because they have been extensively studied in the wild. The experimental scenario is based on an actual situation.

In 1958 a lone male lion appeared in the Umfolozi and Hluhluwe Game Reserve Complex in South Africa. Lions had been eradicated prior to the establishment of the reserves, and their reintroduction was not intended. In 1965, however, two adult females and two cubs were surreptitiously introduced. The present population (of over one hundred lions in seven or eight prides) is descended from these demographic founders (Anderson 1980). The population has been extensively managed (to prevent the slaughter of cattle by dispersing subadults), and the present study was motivated by questions relating to the effect of management on the genetics of the population. Attempting to answer these questions raised more fundamental methodological considerations: How does one analyze a wild population? How much does one need to know about the social and territorial behavior of the species? What information would be useful to have about the population? and so on. This essay explores these questions, particularly the one of how to represent and cope with the large degree of uncertainty characterizing this kind of problem.

THE MODEL

The model is a stochastic version of that described by Starfield et al. (1981) and Starfield and Bleloch (1991, ch. 4). It assigns all pride lions to one of eight territories, configured as in figure 8.1. The model keeps track of individual lions and their status (cubs in a pride, subadult lionesses in a pride, pride lionesses, cohorts of nomadic lions, or a coalition of pride males). The model performs the following operations each year:

Survival: A survival rate is specified for lions of different ages and status, and a random number generator is used to decide whether each lion lives or dies.

Births: Pride lionesses produce a litter of between one and five cubs (chosen from a distribution by a random number generator) every two years, unless they have lost all their cubs from the previous litter, in which case they breed the following year.

Recruitment and expulsion: If the number of adult lionesses in a pride is less than a prescribed pride size, there is an assigned probability that female cubs aged three will be recruited into the pride. All other three-year-olds in a pride are expelled and form a nomadic cohort.

Dispersion: Nomadic cohorts do not breed but wander from one territory to another according to prescribed rules. The nomads will form a pride if they find a vacant territory, and nomadic females may (with an assigned probability) be recruited to breed with pride males in a territory short of both adult and subadult lionesses. Nomadic cohorts may also wander outside the boundaries of the reserves, in which case there is a probability that individuals will be killed.

Challenge and takeover: As they pass through occupied territories, the nomadic males test the resident pride lions and, if evenly

Figure 8.1 The configuration of the eight territories. The lines indicate direct access. The founding pride occupied the shaded territory.

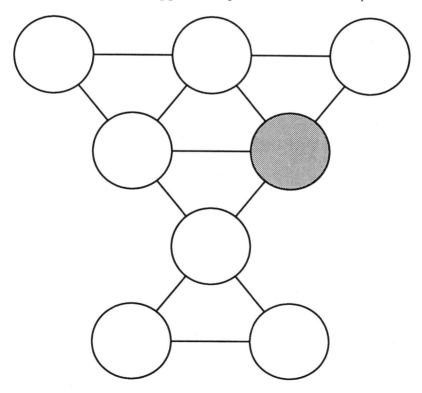

matched, challenge them. If the pride males win, the nomads may suffer mortality. If the nomads win, the pride males are killed, and the nomadic males take over the pride. Their first act is to kill (with a certain probability) the young cubs.

The above is an overview of the population dynamics of the model. The parameter estimates are presented in Starfield et al. (1981). The details of the model reflect what is known of lion behavior. For example, the survival rates reflect the hardships of a nomadic life. Nomads move preferentially to neighboring territories that are either vacant or occupied only by lionesses and cubs (implying the use of cues such as roaring and marking). Cubs may survive even if their mothers die by nursing from other lionesses in the pride. All males in a coalition have an equal opportunity of fathering cubs (they tend to have equal access to the females), and if there are no adult males in a pride, sires will be chosen from one of the neighboring coalitions.

Choosing a sire for each litter was the first step in adding genetics to the population dynamics. Computationally there were then two choices for following the loss of genetic diversity. The first was to compute a pedigree that could then be input into a gene drop program (MacCluer et al. 1986; Lacy 1989; 1994). The second was to add a record of, say, 100 loci to each individual and to calculate the alleles at each locus at birth from the parent alleles using simple Mendelian segregation. The former was, at first, more attractive because it interfaced with available software (Lacy 1994). We adopted, however, the latter for the following reasons.

Gene drop programs start with a single, known pedigree and perform a large number of repeated genetic simulations to follow the transmission of alleles in the pedigree. Their output reflects the means and variances of those replicates. In our case, the pedigree is itself the outcome of a stochastic process; we also have to repeat the demographic simulation a large number of times. Computational considerations favor the second approach; storing a hundred or more pedigrees for each problem is clumsy. A more important consideration, however, is that the second approach leads to results that are easier to interpret. Each simulation is a plausible *demographic and genetic* outcome. As will be seen, this leads to different ways of looking at and presenting the results of the simulations.

THE STARTING CONDITIONS

The simulations start with five lions: the adult male, two adult females, and two cubs (we assume one cub is male, the other female). These are the demographic founders of the population, but they are not the genetic founders; in order to assign and track alleles we need to make assumptions about the parentage of the cubs and about the degree of relatedness of the two lionesses.

Figure 8.2 illustrates the arbitrary assumptions we made: the adult lionesses are half sisters, each has a cub, and the fathers of the cubs are unrelated males. These assumptions are not easy to defend. For example, the fathers of the cubs are likely to be members of the same coalition and are probably related. Figure 8.2 thus serves two purposes: first, to demonstrate the difficulties in establishing the genetic founders even in a relatively simple case, and second, to underscore that even before the simulation begins, there is a large degree of uncertainty in the starting conditions.

Having said this, we accept figure 8.2 as our starting condition for all the results in this study. We thus have six genetic founders of which only one (the 1958 adult male) is present at the start of the simulation. To each of the genetic founders we assign 100 loci, each with two distinct alleles (in other words, there are 12 distinct founder alleles at each lo-

Figure 8.2 Showing the five demographic founders (all living adults and cubs) and the assumed genetic founders (shaded).

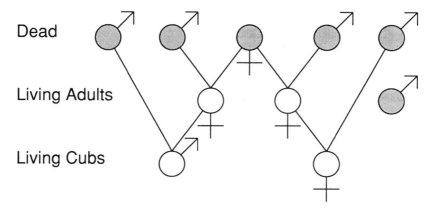

cus). We then simulate for 100 years, and, with the same starting conditions, repeat the simulations 100 times.

PRELIMINARY RESULTS

Demographic Results

How should the results from 100 simulations, each different, and each over a period of 100 years, be presented? Figure 8.3 shows alternative ways of summarizing what happens to the lion population. First, in figure 8.3a, we plot the mean population versus time, but even calculating means is not as simple as one might think. Suppose in one simulation the

Figure 8.3 Different ways of representing the growth of the lion population: (a) The mean population versus time. Line A includes all simulations where the population went extinct, while line B excludes those runs; (b) Population histograms at (A) 10 years, (B) 30 years, and, (C) 100 years; (c) The probability that the population will be less than a given size after (A) 10 years, (B) 30 years, and (C) 100 years.

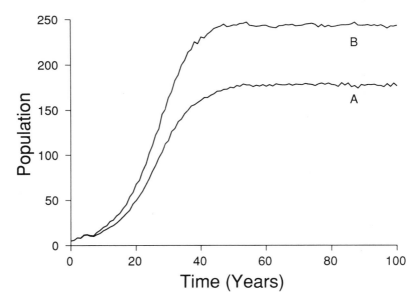

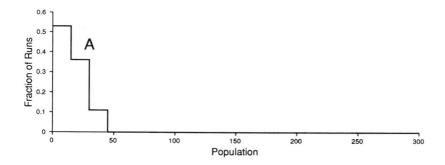

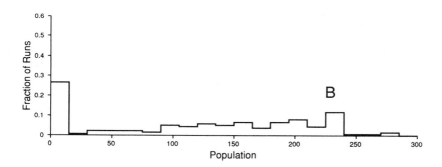

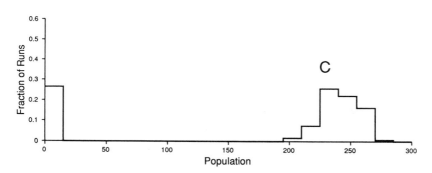

Figure 8.3 b

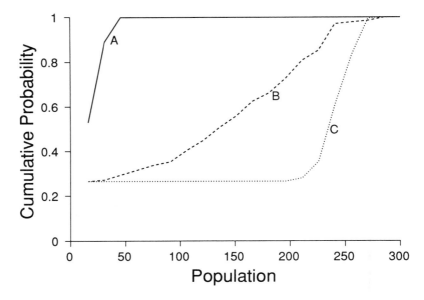

Figure 8.3 c

lions become extinct in year 8. Do we include that simulation (recording the population as zero from year 9 on) or do we discard it? Figure 8.3a shows both methods of computation. From a statistician's viewpoint, the lower graph (where we include all extinctions) might seem more logical, but, as we shall see, the upper graph is more meaningful.

Figure 8.3b presents the same data in a different way. Here we answer questions such as "After 30 years, in how many of the hundred different runs was the total population less than 5 lions, or between 150 and 155, or 155 and 160 lions?" The result is a series of histograms, each at a different time. The histograms tell us about *variance* as well as average population sizes. They show, for example, a very wide spread of potential outcomes after 30 years, while after 100 years it is evident that all those populations that did not become extinct have grown to somewhere between 200 and 270 lions. Looking back at figure 8.3a, we see that the upper graph, which ignores extinction, reflects this better than the lower graph.

Figure 8.3c is yet another representation of the same data. Here we answer questions such as "What is the probability that after 30 years the population will be less than, say, 100 lions?" The answer is approximately 0.40. The figure also shows the probability of extinction; the left-most data points (the probability that the population will be less than 5) converge to a value of 0.28. This representation is useful to a manager or decision maker because a probability can be interpreted directly as the *risk* (see Ginzburg et al. 1982; Burgman et al. 1993) associated with a specific choice or action. Figure 8.3c tells a manager that reintroducing only 5 lions leads to a 28% risk of extinction and a 40% risk that there will be less than 100 lions after 30 years. These risks could be compared to the risks associated with other scenarios.

Retention of Founder Alleles

We started with six genetic founders, each with 100 loci and two alleles at each locus. Figure 8.4 illustrates the proportion of those original 1200 founder alleles that are retained in the breeding population as time progresses. Here, again, there are a number of different ways of presenting the results. Figure 8.4a, for example, shows the average (over the 100 runs) proportion of alleles retained in the breeding population. More than half the founder alleles are lost before the simulations begin. This is an example of what is called a genetic founder effect. The increase in retention after a few years is due to one or both of the starting cubs entering the breeding population. Thereafter, the loss of alleles is due to genetic drift. After 100 years just under a third of the founding alleles remain.

Theoretically, the rate at which a small population increases has a marked effect on genetic drift (Lande and Barrowclough 1987). Figure 8.3b shows that in some runs the lion population did not increase substantially during the first 10 years, in others, there were 40 or more lions after 10 years. This suggests a computer experiment that categorizes the simulations by how fast the population grew during the crucial first 10 years. Figure 8.4b illustrates the results of that experiment. We noted from figure 8.4a that after 100 years the average fraction of alleles retained was just under one third. Figure 8.4b shows that slowly growing populations (less than 10 lions after 10 years) on average retained less than a quarter of the founder alleles, while populations that thrived during the first 10 years (more than 20 lions) retained, on average, about 35% of the founder alleles.

Figures 8.4a and 8.4b depict average values only; neither shows how

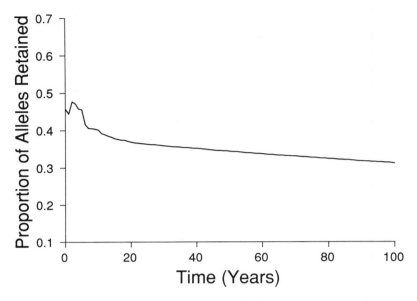

Figure 8.4 Different representations of the loss of founder alleles in the breeding population: (a) Mean retention versus time; (b) Mean retention versus time, grouping those simulations where the population after the first 10 years was (A) less than or equal to 10 lions, (B) between 11 and 20, and (C) over 20 lions; (c) Distributions (or histograms) after 100 years, for groups (A) and (C); (d) The probability that less than a certain proportion of alleles will be present in the population after 100 years, for each of the three groups.

the results may vary from one run to the next. In figure 8.4c we show a histogram that reflects the variance in retention (after 100 years) in those populations that grew very slowly and also in those that thrived during the first 10 years. Histograms are not easily overlapped or compared on one diagram; that is why we only show two of the three categories in figure 8.4c. The data for figure 8.4b can, however, be reworked and presented in terms of cumulative probabilities, as shown in figure 8.4d. This is a much richer representation than either the one in figure 8.4b or that in figure 8.4c. It shows, for example, that the risk of retaining less than one fifth of the founder alleles after 100 years is nearly 40% in the case of a slowly growing population but is negligible if the population grows quickly during the first 10 years.

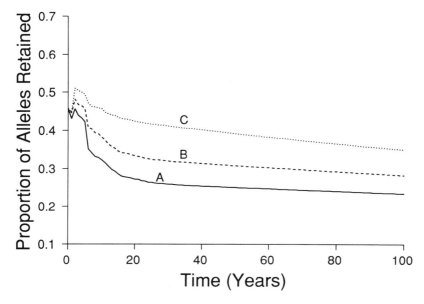

Figure 8.4b

Figure 8.4c

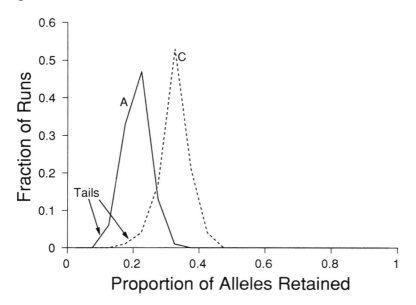

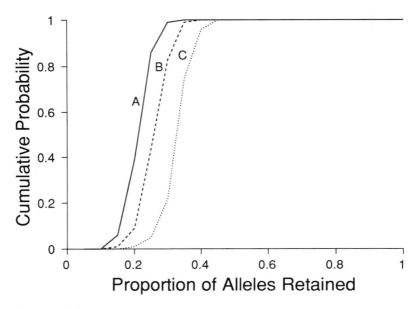

Figure 8.4 d

Loss of Heterozygosity

There are a number of different ways of defining heterozygosity (Lacy 1994). Crow and Kimura (1970) define the heterozygosity of a population as the *expected* heterozygosity, calculated from gene frequencies and an assumption of random future matings. In this study we will always refer to the *actual* heterozygosity, defined as the fraction of loci in the breeding population that are heterozygous. (All of the founding loci are assumed to be heterozygous.) Figure 8.5a shows the actual heterozygosity as an average (over the 100 runs) versus time. Here, too, we have categorized the runs by how fast the population grew during the first 10 years.

Figure 8.5b presents the same data in terms of cumulative probabilities. It shows, for example, that the risk of losing more than half the original heterozygosity is substantial (more than 80%) in a population that grows slowly during the first 10 years. If the population grows to more than 20 lions in those first 10 years, the risk is reduced to less than 10%.

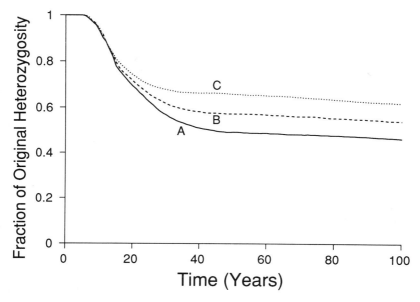

Figure 8.5 The fraction of heterozygous loci in the breeding population: (a) As a function of time for the three cases where the population after 10 years was (A) less than or equal to 10, (B) between 11 and 20, and (C) greater than 20 lions; (b) The probability that less than a certain fraction of loci will be heterozygous after 100 years, for all three cases.

A MANAGEMENT EXPERIMENT: REMOVAL OF SUBADULTS

In the description of the model, we mentioned that dispersing nomads may wander out of the reserve and either return or be killed. This effect is represented by two probabilities in the model: the first indicates the likelihood that a nomadic group will move outside instead of to a neighboring territory; the second is the probability that an individual in a group will be killed outside the reserve.

In practice, subadult lions were regularly sought and destroyed in the Umfolozi-Hluhluwe Complex to prevent them from causing havoc outside the complex. We can simulate this by varying the two probabilities mentioned in the previous paragraph and so explore how management

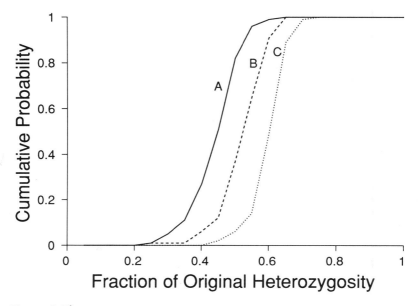

Figure 8.5 b

actions might influence the genetics of the lion population. The expectation is that vigorous removal of subadults will lead to fewer successful challenges of pride males, longer tenure on their part, and thus a much higher probability that they will breed with their own daughters.

Figure 8.6a shows the number of successful challenges that occurred on average each year. During the first 20 years there are very few challenges (the subadults are dispersing into new territories). During the last 50 years of the simulations, the number of challenges does not change significantly with time. As anticipated, however, management action can result in considerably fewer challenges.

Figure 8.6b shows the effect this has on the tenure of pride males. Here we plot the probability that tenure will be less than *x* years. Without either control or loss of subadults outside the reserve, only half the pride males have a tenure of more than 3.5 years. Vigorous removal of subadults results in half the pride males having a tenure of more than 5 years.

So far the results confirm our intuition. Figure 8.6c depicts the effect of this increased tenure on heterozygosity. Consider a population that increases slowly during the first 10 years. The risk of losing more than

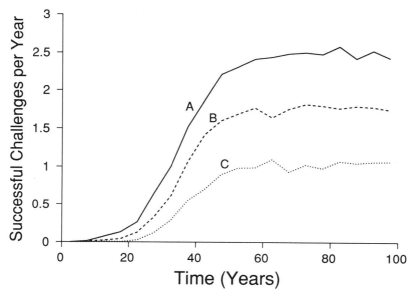

Figure 8.6 Showing the effect of the dispersion or removal of sub-adults on: (a) The number of successful challenges in a year; (b) The probability that a male coalition's tenure will be less than a certain number of years; (c) The probability that less than a certain fraction of loci in the breeding population will be heterozygous after 100 years, depending on whether the population grew quickly (A, B, and C) or slowly (D, E, and F) during the first 10 years. (Lines A and D represent no removal or dispersal, B and E represent the dispersal probabilities used throughout this study, while C and F represent a drastic removal of nomadic cohorts.)

half the original heterozygosity in 100 years is 60% if there is no removal of subadults; the risk increases to about 85% if the subadults are vigorously controlled.

A BEHAVIORAL EXPERIMENT

Until recently it was thought that all males in a pride coalition had equal access to the pride lionesses. Our model makes this assumption. Packer et al. (1991) have shown, however, that in coalitions of three or more

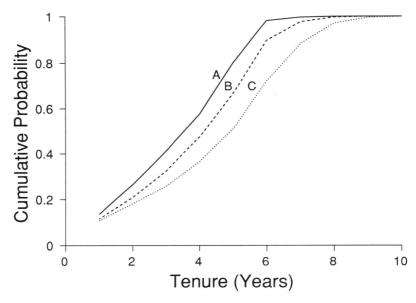

Figure 8.6 b

Figure 8.6 c

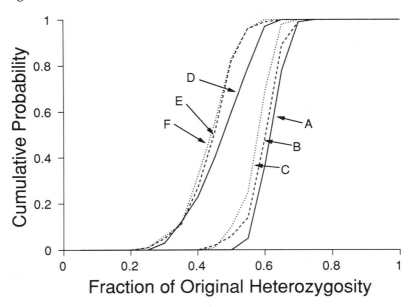

males, two of the lions are likely to father a disproportionate share of the cubs. This suggests a computer experiment requiring only slight modifications to our model. Consider two scenarios: either one dominant male in each coalition breeds with the lionesses, or, in effect, all adult males (nomads as well as pride males) wander around and father cubs at random.

Figure 8.7 shows the results obtained for the above two scenarios as well as the original "equal access in a coalition" model. The cumulative probability is shown for the retention of founder alleles in figure 8.7a and for heterozygosity in figure 8.7b, both after 100 years. The effect of different lion behaviors is noticeable. It should be stressed that these scenarios lead to runs that are identical demographically; only the im-

Figure 8.7 The effect of alternative models of male access to females on: (a) The risk of losing alleles (after 100 years); (b) The probability that less than a certain fraction of the original heterozygosity will be maintained after 100 years. Line A assumes that only the dominant male in each coalition breeds, in B all males in a coalition have equal access to lionesses in their pride (the standard model), while in C all adult males (including nomads) have equal access to all lionesses.

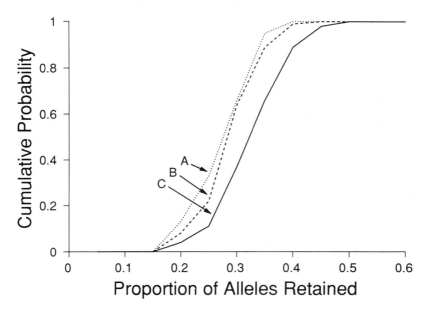

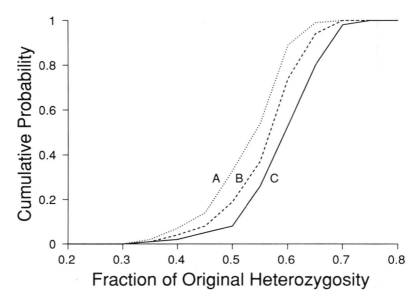

Figure 8.7b

plicit pedigrees are different. These experiments thus demonstrate how social behavior *alone* can influence genetic drift.

FRAGMENTED HABITATS

A standard problem in conservation biology is that of fragmented habitats and subpopulations that have little or no contact with each other. The eight lion territories in the Zululand game reserves are separated by an area that, though partly cultivated, acts nevertheless as a corridor for the movement of lions and other animals. As a final computer experiment, we decided to investigate what difference it would have made if that corridor had been closed.

We therefore split our eight territories into two groups of four as shown in figure 8.8. We started our simulations with one pride of five lions in each of the two halves (i.e., in this experiment we have twice as many founders) and then considered the following three scenarios:

1. Easy (unrestricted) access between the two groups of territories

2. No access until year 50; thereafter two nomadic cohorts are interchanged every five years (the cohorts are chosen at random but must each include at least four lions)

3. No access at all

Allendorf (1986) and Lacy (1987) suggest what we should observe from these experiments. They expect that separating the two subpopulations completely (case 3) will lead to an accelerated loss of heterozygosity as compared to case 1. The rule of thumb is that about one effective migrant per generation will restore the lost heterozygosity. In the field, one does not know whether an interchange of cohorts will lead to successful breeding, but in the model we can keep track, in case 2, of when the migrants breed successfully. On average, they closely approximated the rule of thumb.

The model results are shown in figure 8.9. Figure 8.9a confirms the expected effects on heterozygosity. Figure 8.9b suggests that there may be a cost to restoring heterozygosity; it shows a very slight increase in the loss of founder alleles for case 2. Both figure 8.9a and figure 8.9b show average *results*. Figure 8.9c superimposes on figure 8.9a the actual loss in heterozygosity from *one* of the hundred simulations. The con-

Figure 8.8 The territorial configuration of two subpopulations, each containing four territories. Solid lines depict direct access, dotted lines depict controlled access. The founding prides were introduced in the shaded territories.

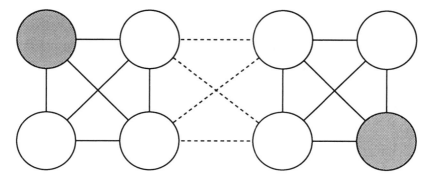

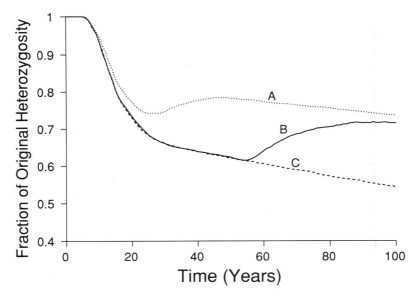

Figure 8.9 Interactions between two subpopulations: (a) The fraction of heterozygous loci in the metapopulation. In A there was uncontrolled access between the two subpopulations. In B there were controlled interchanges of nomadic cohorts (every five years) but only after the first 50 years. In C there was no access whatsoever between the two subpopulations; (b) Uncontrolled access (A) leads to a slightly faster rate of loss of founder alleles; (c) The effect of controlled interchange of nomadic cohorts in a specific instance (the dashed line) may be significantly different from the average of a large number of similar computer experiments.

trast between mean results and individual runs reconfirms the results of Lacy (1987). Figure 8.9c is a fitting final figure because it underscores how difficult it might be to discover or validate these effects in the field. That in itself is a major motivation for computer experiments of this kind.

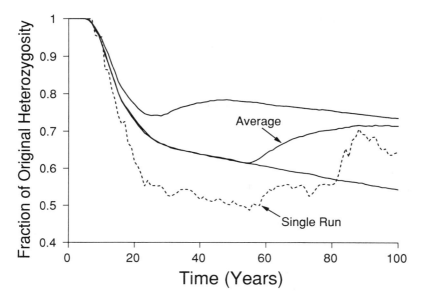

Figure 8.9 b

Figure 8.9 c

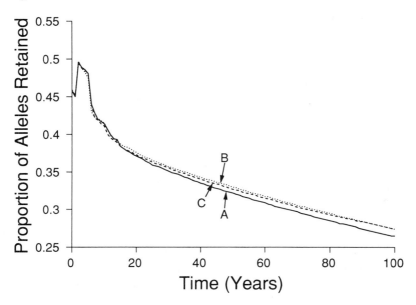

DISCUSSION

It is useful to think of the simulation results presented in this essay as a computational experiment. Was it necessary, in hindsight, to perform the experiments, and what have we learned from it?

First, we have developed our experimental technique. We have chosen to compute genetic drift by providing each individual lion with a genetic record of 100 loci computed from the records of its parents at birth. We prefer this to the alternative of generating a pedigree for each of our simulations and feeding that pedigree into standard software.

Second, we posed the question of how to present the results. The answer seems to be "in as many different ways as possible." For example, separating results according to how fast the population grew in the early years is illuminating. So too are the cumulative probability plots (such as figures 8.3c, 8.4d, 8.5b, 8.6b, 8.6c, 7.7a, and 7.7b) in that they lead directly to interpretations in terms of *risk*.

Theoretically, the rate of loss of heterozygosity and alleles depends on the effective population size (Lande and Barrowclough 1987). How best to calculate the effective population size in specific cases, however, continues to be unclear (Harris and Allendorf 1989). We know that we started with a breeding population of three (one male and two females). Since there are only eight territories, it is unlikely that we will ever have more than five or six breeding animals per territory. We should be able to estimate the loss rates from rough figures such as these; however, arguments at this level of resolution cannot discriminate, for example, between the effects of different management actions toward removal of subadults (figure 8.6) nor do they lend themselves to interpretation in terms of risk.

Third, the results are characterized by a large amount of variance. This is not "experimental error," but rather a reflection of the variance one should expect to find in the real world. From both a scientific and a management perspective, we need to learn to cope with this variance. Obviously, presenting results in terms of probabilities and interpreting them in terms of risk is essential, but this has several implications.

The "tail" ends of distributions (see figure 8.4d, for example) may be especially significant. Two different management actions may have little effect on the median or mean loss of alleles or heterozygosity but may lead to significantly different risks of reducing retention or heterozygosity below certain prespecified limits. Cumulative probability plots, such as figure 8.6b, help to highlight these effects.

It follows that certain management actions could be especially damaging precisely in those cases where a population is already at risk. It will then be inappropriate to make decisions on the basis of mean or average outcomes. The proper criterion is "minimum regret"— decisions should be made so as to minimize the probability of being "sorry" in the long run.

The "tails" of distributions can also be sensitive to details in the sociobiology of a species that the more general results in population viability analysis do not yet adequately consider (Captive Breeding Specialist Group 1989a, 1989b, 1990). Figure 8.7 illustrates this. This does not imply that *all* details are important but rather that we need to learn what is and is not important. This study poses, rather than answers, that question.

It follows that there is a need to test the sensitivity of models not only to parameter values but also to the underlying assumptions of the model. For example, we discovered at a late stage in this exercise that we were probably underestimating the amount of infanticide occurring when a new male coalition takes over a pride. We had visions of having to recompute all our results, but one or two simulations convinced us that our results were insensitive to this.

Statisticians deal with high variance by looking at a larger number of replicates or measurements. Conservation biologists may not have that luxury; the population they are managing or investigating may be the only replicate. In the first place, this makes it that much harder (perhaps impossible) to validate models, such as the one described here; the real population may fit anywhere in a wide range of possibilities. This is where results such as those presented in figure 8.6 become important. We can think of the number of challenges to pride tenure as an "indicator" that can perhaps be measured in a population and may help to develop a pattern of data that fits one set of circumstances rather than another.

In the same vein, it becomes crucial to look for information (molecular genetic, demographic, social, or behavioral) that may narrow the variance. For example, figure 8.4b shows how useful it is to know how fast the population grew during the first 10 years. In fact, the real strength of the modeling approach described in this study will be to help answer the question "What data do we need to collect in the field?" The primary objective of collecting field data on wild populations will be to reduce variance.

Fourth, the attitudes and approaches we develop to deal with the inherent variance in simulating genetic drift in small, wild populations are likely to serve us well in analyzing incomplete pedigrees for captive populations. They suggest the following algorithm: simulate the missing data (within the constraints of what is known about a captive population) and interpret the results in terms of risk.

We began this essay by referring to a spectrum of problems, from complete pedigrees to wild populations where very little is known about the founders (as in this study). The previous paragraph suggests that it is the complete pedigree, rather than the wild population, that is the anomaly in that spectrum; all other problems are likely to yield to the approach described here.

Finally, the approach developed in this study lends itself to an obvious extension: if we can speculate how, for example, loss of heterozygosity might affect reproductive success, then the model could easily incorporate feedback from genetics into the population dynamics.

Acknowledgments

This work was supported by a Grant-in-Aid from the Graduate School, University of Minnesota. The authors would like to thank Franck Rellier for his work on an early version of the model, Bob Lacy, Nate Flesness, and Randy Rockwell for their help and advice, and Joe Venter of the Natal Parks Board for his enthusiastic assistance.

REFERENCES

Allendorf, F. W. 1986. Genetic drift and the loss of alleles versus heterozygosity. *Zoo Biology* 5:181–90.

Anderson, J. 1980. The re-establishment and management of a lion *Panthera leo* population in Zululand. *Biological Conservation* 19:107–17.

Burgman, M. A., S. Ferson, and H. R. Akcakaya. 1993. *Risk Assessment in Conservation Biology*. New York: Chapman & Hall.

Captive Breeding Specialist Group. 1989a. *Javan Rhinoceros Population Viability Analysis and Recommendations*. Apple Valley, Minn.: Captive Breeding Specialist Group.

Captive Breeding Specialist Group. 1989b. *Florida Panther Viability Analysis and Species Survival Plan*. Apple Valley, Minn.: Captive Breeding Specialist Group.

Captive Breeding Specialist Group. 1990. *Leontopithecus: Population Viability Workshop*. Apple Valley, Minn.: Captive Breeding Specialist Group.

Crow, J. F. and M. Kimura. 1970. *An Introduction to Population Genetics Theory.* New York: Harper and Row.

Ginzburg, L., L. B. Slobodkin, K. Johnson, and A. G. Bindman. 1982. Quasiextinction probabilities as a measure of impact on population growth. *Risk Analysis* 2:171–81.

Harris, R. D. and F. W. Allendorf. 1989. Genetically effective population size of large mammals: An assessment of estimators. *Conservation Biology* 3:181–91.

Lacy, R. C. 1987. Loss of genetic diversity from managed populations: Interacting effects of drift, mutation, immigration, selection, and population subdivision. *Conservation Biology* 1:143–58.

Lacy, R. C. 1989. Analysis of founder representation in pedigrees: Founder equivalents and founder genome equivalents. *Zoo Biology* 8:111–24.

Lacy, R. C. 1994. *GENES:* Computer program for pedigree analysis and genetic management. Chicago: Chicago Zoological Society.

Lande, R. and G. F. Barrowclough. 1987. Effective population size, genetic variation, and their use in population management. In M. E. Soulé, ed., *Viable Populations for Conservation,* pp. 87–123. Cambridge: Cambridge University Press.

MacCluer, J. W., J. L. VandeBerg, B. Read, and O. A. Ryder. 1986. Pedigree analysis by computer simulation. *Zoo Biology* 8:111–24.

Packer, C., D. A. Gilbert, A. E. Pusey, and S. J. O'Brien. 1991. A molecular genetic analysis of kinship and cooperation in African lions. *Nature* 351:562–65.

Starfield, A. M. and A. L. Bleloch. 1991. *Building Models for Conservation and Wildlife Management.* 2d ed. Edina: The Bellwether Press.

Starfield, A. M., P. R. Furniss, and G. L. Smuts. 1981. A model of lion population dynamics as a function of social behaviour. In C. W. Fowler and T. D. Smith, eds., *Dynamics of Large Mammal Populations,* pp. 121–34. New York: Wiley.

PART THREE

Molecular Genetics

9

Descriptive Genetic Studies: Applications in Population Management and Conservation Biology

■■

John C. Avise, Susan M. Haig, Oliver A. Ryder,
Michael Lynch, and Charles J. Geyer

Results from descriptive genetic analyses can play an important role in the development of Species Survival Plans (Hutchins and Wiese 1991), Endangered Species Recovery Plans, and Population Viability Analyses (Foose et al., essay 12 in this volume; Haig et al. 1993a). There are a wide variety of molecular and cytogenetic methods for revealing genetic markers, as well as a large pool of biological applications for such markers. This review adopts the precept that most management applications of genetic data can be viewed as attempts to elucidate phylogenetic relationships at one or another hierarchical level of biological divergence. It is assumed that results from genetic analyses are then put in perspective through consideration of numerous other critical factors such as demographics, habitat availability, economics, and political implications of any actions.

Phylogenetic assessment may entail estimation of genetic relationships at any level ranging from micropedigrees to macroevolutionary trees with applications in such areas as: (1) forensics (including genetic identity versus nonidentity); (2) parentage (maternity and paternity assessment); (3) relatedness (kinship within a population pedigree); (4) population structure within a species (including subspecies descriptions); and (5) phylogenetic relationships of species and higher taxa. Combined with empirical experience and theoretical considerations, the data provided by each molecular technique offer a circumscribed window of resolution along this phylogenetic hierarchy.

This essay is divided into two sections: (1) a brief description of the most widely employed molecular methods used in conservation of small populations and of the nature of the genetic data provided by each; and (2) examples of applications of these methods to conservation issues arising in the phylogenetic hierarchy described above (summarized in table 9.1). This minireview is intended to be a primer and quick reference guide for those with limited familiarity of genetic methods in population management. A greatly extended treatment may be found in Avise (1994).

DESCRIPTIVE GENETIC TECHNIQUES RELEVANT TO POPULATION MANAGEMENT

Karyotype Analysis

Karyotypes can be highly informative with regard to the extent of reproductive isolation and gene flow between populations. They may also be an indication of environmental insults to a population. For example, Norwegian reindeer (*Rangifer tarandus*) calves exposed to fallout from the 1986 Chernobyl nuclear accident are now showing chromosomal aberrations (Roed et al. 1991). Chromosomal differences between isolated populations can often be potent inhibitors of gene flow—the chromosomal basis of hybrid sterility is well documented in a variety of species of plants and animals. When populations differ in karyotypic features, such as chromosome number, inversions, or translocations, it is very likely that the populations are reproductively isolated and that gene flow between them has been diminished or absent for some time. Although chromosomal polymorphisms in mammals are common—especially numerical polymorphisms involving fission-fusion rearrangements (Robertsonian translocations)—it is generally believed that such chromosomal polymorphism is a transient phenomenon.

The reproductive consequences of chromosomal difference suggest that karyotype information should be gathered whenever possible, for example, prior to the merging of separate populations and whenever the introduction of individuals to captive breeding programs or to indigenous populations is contemplated. The rate of chromosomal evolution is higher in mammals than in most vertebrate taxa. Consequently, these recommendations may apply particularly to mammals. However, only approximately one-half of all mammalian species have been karyotyped and usually only a small number of individuals; some mammalian groups remain grossly underrepresented in chromosomal studies.

Nature of the data. Raw data in karyotypic studies consist of enlarged photos of chromosomes. Chromosomes are counted and identified as homologous sets by placing the largest chromosomes first in the karyotype and the smallest last. Variation in karyotype can be numerical or structural. Thus, chromosomes are classified by their length and the location of the centromere. A species is considered to be monomorphic in karyotype if all individuals studied possess the same diploid $(2n)$ chromosome number and sets of homologous chromosomes that appear to be identical (Shields 1987).

Key references. Laboratory techniques: Cram et al. 1983. *Overviews:* Hsu and Benirschke 1967–77; Shields 1982, 1987; Benirschke and Kumamoto 1991.

Protein Analyses

Protein electrophoresis. Multilocus protein electrophoresis was among the first of molecular methods successfully applied to problems in population biology (Hubby and Lewontin 1966), and it continues to be a widely used and extremely valuable source of markers for the nuclear genome. Major advantages of the method are its technical simplicity, low cost, and the large number of samples that can be examined. A disadvantage is that only a tiny fraction of genome variation is revealed, because only protein-coding loci are assayed, and most nucleotide changes at these loci do not result in amino acid substitutions detectable by this method. A paucity of protein electrophoretic variation may be an especially serious limitation in providing markers for small or endangered populations (but see Leberg 1992). This limitation becomes more of a concern if small populations are managed based on the presence of specific electrophoretic loci in some individuals (Haig et al. 1990). Screening for additional enzymes (e.g., thirty or forty) for forty or more individuals per population may improve the usefulness of protein electrophoresis in population studies.

This method takes advantage of the fact that proteins with different net charges migrate at different rates through a starch or acrylamide gel matrix to which an electric current is applied. An extract of water-soluble proteins from a particular tissue (e.g., liver, heart, blood, skeletal muscle, feather pulp) is prepared by homogenization and centrifugation. Such extracts from perhaps twenty to thirty individuals per population are placed in different lanes in a gel and electrophoresed for several hours. Positions in the gel to which a particular enzymatic protein (such as lactate dehydrogenase) has migrated are then revealed by applying a histochemical stain specific for that enzyme. Differences in band mobility arise from nucleotide changes in the DNA that cause amino acid substitutions, which in turn alter the net protein charge.

Typically, a multilocus protein electrophoretic survey may involve separate assay of ten or more enzymes and provide data for perhaps twenty to forty (usually unlinked) nuclear genes (many enzyme classes are encoded by two or three loci, often with tissue-specific expression). In many large, outbreeding species, 30% or more of the assayed genes are polymorphic, and a typical individual is detectably heterozygous at 5–15% of its assayed loci.

Nature of the data. Banding patterns on gels can usually be interpreted in terms of alleles and genotypes at each of the genes encoding the assayed proteins. Thus, the single-locus, Mendelian basis of particular polymorphisms may be inferred from knowledge of gel patterns expected for enzymes of a given subunit structure and from agreement of the population genotype frequencies with Hardy-Weinberg expectations (in random mating populations). Where controlled crosses are feasible or pedigree information is known, the allelic basis of banding patterns can be further confirmed, though this is seldom deemed necessary. Electrophoretic variants attributable to simple Mendelian polymorphisms are termed allozymes, to distinguish them from the broader category of isozymes, which includes protein variants whose particular genetic bases may remain unspecified. At a polymorphic locus, a population may exhibit multiple alleles (though a diploid individual is either homozygous or heterozygous for two copies). However, evolutionary relationships among various allozymes of a locus cannot be safely inferred from the observable property, gel mobility. Analyses of allozyme data can be carried out using BIOSYS, PAUP, or PHYLIP software (Swofford and Selander 1989; Swofford 1990; Felsenstein 1993).

Apart from their many uses as single-locus Mendelian markers in such areas as forensic science, parentage assessment, and gene flow estimation among populations, allozyme frequencies observed at multiple loci can also be employed to compute quantitative measures of the genetic distance (D) between populations or other taxa under comparison. Such genetic distances represent composite information (at the protein level) from all loci included in the survey.

Key references. Laboratory techniques: Shaw and Prasad 1970; Selander et al. 1971. *Overview:* Powell 1975; Nevo 1978; Ferguson 1980; Avise and Aquadro 1982.

Protein Immunology (complement fixation). Genetic differences between species can be examined through the use of protein immunology. When a protein, such as serum albumin or transferrin, is purified from a reference species and injected into a rabbit or goat, production of an antiserum is elicited. In a technique called microcomplement fixation, this antiserum is assayed for crossreactivity with serum from another species whose genetic relationship to the reference species is of interest. The greater the degree of crossreactivity, the greater is the inferred structural similarity of the reference and test species (and the lower is their immunological distance, or *I.D.*). Much evidence suggests that for at least some monomeric proteins, such as albumin, I.D. is approximately linearly related to the amount of time elapsed since the common ancestry of the species compared.

Nature of the data. The raw data in microcomplement assays are numerical values of genetic distance between the protein of the reference and test species. Qualitative character states are lacking, and the genetic distance refers to the single gene under observation.

Key references. Laboratory techniques: Champion et al. 1974; Maxson and Wilson 1975; Gahne et al. 1977. *Overview:* Wilson et al. 1977.

Nuclear DNA Analysis

DNA hybridization. This technique is generally used to construct species phylogenies and could be used to determine the relationship between an endangered or extinct species and a congener. Double-stranded (duplex) DNA is isolated from two or more species of interest, sheared into fragments averaging 0.5 kilobases (kb) in length, and boiled to dissociate the strands. When single-stranded DNA from one species is incubated with that from the same or a different species, the homologous regions reassociate to form homo- or hetero-duplexes, respectively. The thermal stability of each duplex is then monitored by gradually increasing the temperature of the mixture, which results in duplex dissociation as hydrogen bonds between the two strands are broken. The closer the base-pair complementarity in the single-stranded DNAs forming a duplex, the higher the temperature at which the duplex remains intact. The difference in thermal stability between homo- and heteroduplexes (ΔTm) is a measure of how far the nucleotide sequences of the two species' DNA have diverged. Reference studies suggest that each increase of 1°C in ΔTm represents approximately one additional percent of mismatch in the DNA sequence.

To avoid the overriding influence that large families of repetitive DNA might have on thermal stability comparisons, DNA/DNA hybridization is normally carried out on the single-copy fraction of the genome. Single-copy DNA refers to gene sequences represented only once (or perhaps a few times) in the genome, in contrast to repeated DNA sequences, which may be present in large numbers of replicates.

Nature of the data. Like the I.D.'s provided by microcomplement fixation, the raw data derived from DNA/DNA hybridization consist of a numerical value of genetic distance (ΔTm) between any pair of species. Thus, qualitative character states are lacking. Unlike I.D.'s, ΔTm's provide a composite view of genetic divergence at a large number of loci.

Key references. Laboratory techniques: Kohne and Britten 1971; Sibley and Ahlquist 1981; Sibley et al. 1988; Kirsch et al. 1990; Werman et al. 1990. *Overview:* Sibley and Ahlquist 1983, 1986; Sibley et al. 1988.

Single-copy RFLP's (restriction fragment-length polymorphisms). Single-copy RFLP's may be useful in examining differences among small populations when allozyme techniques did not reveal sufficient variability for robust comparisons. In this technique, nuclear DNA is isolated and digested with one or more of the many commercially available restriction endonucleases, each of which cleaves duplex DNA at a specific oligonucleotide sequence. For example, *Eco*RI cuts DNA wherever the nucleotide sequence GAATTC occurs. DNA fragments produced by endonuclease digestion are then separated according to molecular size by electrophoresis through an agarose gel. In a total nuclear DNA digest, thousands of fragments are present in the gel (appearing as a continuous smear when stained with ethidium bromide), and the trick is to reveal the simpler digestion profiles of particular loci or stretches of DNA. This is accomplished through "Southern blotting" procedures using labeled DNA as probes to identify DNA sequences complementary to the probe.

Typically, a gene "library" is prepared using recombinant DNA techniques that involve cloning random, single-copy sequences (usually 1–5 kb in length) in a bacterial plasmid vector. In Southern blotting, DNA probes taken from the library are radioactively labeled and then utilized as probes in hybridizations with DNA fragments separated in agarose gels as described above, under conditions where pairing takes place only between the probe and restriction fragments homologous to it. Development of an autoradiograph reveals a gel-banding pattern representing DNA fragments that have hybridized to the probe. Variation in the fragment digestion profiles among individuals reflects polymorphisms in the positions of restriction sites in the DNA region recognized by the probe. Polymorphisms can often be interpreted as simple Mendelian variants, and such information can be accumulated from many enzyme/probe combinations.

Nature of the data. The raw data are, in many respects, analogous to those provided by protein electrophoresis: for each gene region assayed, individuals can be described as homozygous or heterozygous (for various restriction sites of each endonuclease); genotypic descriptions can be accumulated across many enzyme/probe combinations; a population may exhibit multiple alleles at a "locus," and alleles thus identified normally remain unordered with respect to evolutionary relationships. The major advantage over protein electrophoresis is that, in principle, a nearly unlimited pool of genetic variants may be tapped. There are several thousand single- or low-copy regions in most genomes. A vast number of enzyme/probe combinations can be employed, and the polymorphisms reflect variation at both silent and replacement nucleotide positions (as well as variation due to other causes such as insertions of transposable elements). The major disadvantage in comparison to protein electrophoresis is that these methods (particularly the library construction) are extremely tedious and time-consuming. Perhaps for this reason, there have been few applications of nuclear RFLP approaches in population biology (but see Henke et al. 1990, 1991; Karl and Avise 1992; Karl et al. 1992). The method is becoming widespread in the fields of human medicine and quantitative genetics, where the polymorphisms are employed as genetic markers useful in establishing linkage relationships with disease genes and quantitative trait loci, respectively.

Key references. Laboratory techniques: Maniatis et al. 1982; Kochert 1989; Hanotte et al. 1991a. *Overview:* Quinn and White 1987; Burke et al. 1991; Jeffreys et al. 1991.

DNA fingerprinting (profiles). The same basic methods of Southern blotting described above for single-copy RFLP's can also be employed with repeated DNA elements as probes. In DNA fingerprinting (or DNA profiles), detailed questions regarding population structure, mating systems, pedigree definition, and parentage can be addressed. Hence, genetic variation is revealed simultaneously in an entire family of repetitive elements that hybridize to the probe, and the fragment digestion profiles on a gel may be correspondingly more complex. The term DNA fingerprinting has come to be associated specifically with a molecular approach introduced by Jeffreys et al. (1985a, b), in which the probes are conserved core sequences within tandem-repetitive regions of DNA (minisatellites) dispersed in the nuclear genome. The "hypervariability" reflected in Southern blot digestions is thought to result from unequal crossing over during meiosis that alters numbers of tandem repeats at numerous "minisatellite" or "VNTR" (variable number of tandem repeat) loci and from combination among unlinked arrays. Human probes isolated by Jeffreys et al. have hybridized to hypervariable regions in many other animal and plant species. In addition to the sequences described by Jeffreys et al., several additional families of minisatellites have also been discovered and results are generally referred to as DNA profiles, rather than DNA fingerprints (Jarman and Wells 1989; Vassart et al. 1987; Nakamura et al. 1987).

Nature of the data. The raw data in DNA fingerprints consist of complex digestion profiles on gels, often involving twenty or more bands of varying intensity per individual. Individuals are differentiated either by presence or absence of specific bands on an autoradiograph or by comparison of the percent of similar bands shared between individuals (Lynch 1990). In several surveyed species, including humans, variation in band patterns is so great that virtually all individuals are unique, and therein lies the major strength and appeal of the method. On the other hand, in the methods as originally described it is generally unknown which bands belong to which locus, whether bands are linked, and whether alternative "alleles" at a locus can be identified. Consequently, simple Mendelian interpretations of gel patterns are precluded (unlike with allozymes or single-copy RFLP's). This problem and related scoring limitations have serious implications for some projected uses of the original DNA fingerprinting methods to establish genetic relatedness in extended pedigrees (Lynch 1988). Nonetheless, considerable useful information relevant to parentage qualification and kinship in populations for which some pedigree information exists can be established with this technique, when properly applied and interpreted (e.g., Geyer and Thompson, essay 10 in this volume; Gilbert et al. 1991; Jones et al. 1991; Lynch 1991; Packer et al. 1991; Haig et al. 1993b, 1994a, b).

Key references. Laboratory techniques: Burke 1989; Jeffreys et al. 1985a. *Overview:* Hill 1987; White and Lalouel 1988; Lynch 1988; Burke 1989; Lander 1989; Burke et al. 1991; Jeffreys et al. 1991; Geyer et al. 1993.

Individual hypervariable loci. A variant of the two prior procedures is to use particular defined genes as probes in Southern blots. If probes are chosen that reveal highly variable regions at a single locus, such as genes within the MHC complex or particular microsatellite or minisatellite tandem arrays, highly variable banding patterns may be revealed that nonetheless permit simple allelic interpretation. Quite often the polymorphism is due to a variation in the number of small tandem repeats at the short DNA sequence under study. The large number of identifiable alleles at such loci has greatly facilitated studies in human genome mapping, and in principle it could provide a wealth of genetic markers for studies in population biology as well. Relatively little work in this latter area has been carried out thus far. The management of populations explicitly for enhanced MHC polymorphism has been proposed (Hughes 1991), but this suggestion remains controversial (Vrijenhoek and Leberg 1991; Gilpin and Wills 1991; Miller and Hedrick 1991).

Nature of the data. The raw data consist of highly variable gel patterns that can be interpreted as allelic variants at the locus under consideration. Thus, this approach combines certain advantages of DNA fingerprinting (high variability and resolution) with those of single-copy RFLP approaches (simple Mendelian variation). However, unless many such loci are included in a study, the assayed sample of the genome is very small.

Key references. Laboratory techniques: Chakraborty et al. 1991. *Overview:* Nakamura et al. 1987; Jeffreys et al. 1991; Chakraborty et al. 1991, Schreiber and Tichy 1992.

DNA sequencing and the polymerase chain reaction (PCR). All methods discussed thus far provide indirect assessments of nucleotide sequence variation and divergence. Although techniques of nucleotide sequencing have been available for many years (Sanger and Coulson 1975; Maxam and Gilbert 1977), the major limitation in applying these methods to problems in population biology has been the difficulty of isolating homologous pieces of DNA for comparison among many specimens. The recent development of the polymerase chain reaction (PCR) has changed this situation dramatically (Hedrick 1992).

The PCR technique involves three steps: (1) denaturation of double-stranded DNA by heating; (2) annealing of extension primers to sites flanking the region to be amplified; and (3) primer extension, in which strands complementary to the region between the flanking primers are synthesized by a thermostable DNA polymerase (Taq, from *Thermobacillus aquaticus*). The double-stranded products are repeatedly subjected to steps (1)–(3). In each round of denaturation-annealing-extension, the target sequence is roughly doubled in the reaction mixture, so that after twenty or more rounds the product assumes overwhelming preponderance and can be sequenced directly. The PCR procedure can be performed manually, but is laborious. Automated thermal cycler devices are commercially available and are being refined to run faster and with the capability of simultaneously running numerous samples.

DNA primers required to initiate the PCR process are short (twenty to thirty bases) sequences that exhibit homology only to regions surrounding the area to be amplified. Several such evolutionarily conserved sequences useful as PCR primers have been identified in mitochondrial (mt) DNA (see below), which has been the molecule most commonly used in PCR efforts for population biology. There are two primary reasons for this. First, complete nucleotide sequences of mtDNA have been published for several species, so conserved flanking primers could readily be identified. Second, mtDNA is effectively haploid in most organisms, so that a single sequence normally becomes amplified during PCR. In contrast, nuclear genes are diploid, so that PCR of a region heterozygous at multiple nucleotide positions could produce two amplified products. Not only would two alleles need to be distinguished, but the extent of "PCR recombinants" produced by template shifts of the Taq polymerase during a round of synthesis would require assessment. Whether such theoretical concerns will entail significant complications for population applications involving PCR and the sequencing of nuclear genes remains to be seen.

The benefits of PCR over other molecular techniques include: (1) no need to use radioactive probes; (2) a small amount of DNA suffices for analyses; (3) degraded or ancient samples sometimes can be used as templates, allowing for analysis of forensic or museum materials; (4) numerous samples (≥ 40) can be amplified simultaneously; and (5) the purity of the resulting PCR product makes direct sequencing possible without additional steps (Arnheim et al. 1990; Hedrick 1992). The drawbacks of this technique are that samples can easily be contaminated and that prior effort is required to identify suitable primers (Arnheim et al. 1990; Hadrys et al. 1992; Hedrick 1992). PCR-based approaches are evolving rapidly and soon may be widely used by conservation biologists to address such topics as gender determination, phylogeny, parentage and other kin associations, and population differentiation.

Random Amplified Polymorphic DNA (RAPD's) involve a modification of typical PCR in which a single nucleotide primer, approximately ten bases long, is used in the amplification reaction (Williams et al. 1990). The choice of primer sequence is arbitrary in that it does not require prior knowledge of the template DNA sequences. When template sequences homologous to a primer have appropriate spacing and orientation, the PCR amplifies the intervening sequence. A series of products of various sizes is thereby derived from a genomic DNA template. When DNAs from different individuals in a population are used as templates, different products may be generated. The major benefit of this technique is that it is fast and efficient; however, assay repeatability can be a problem, and heterozygosity cannot be established because bands are either present or absent (e.g., dominance is exhibited).

Nature of the data. Data provided by PCR-based sequencing are direct nucleotide sequences of specified regions of DNA, usually several hundred base pairs in length. An obvious advantage is that precise information about the genetic basis of any polymorphisms is obtained. In addition, PCR opens the possibility of genetic studies of individuals in single-celled or simple organisms. Rapidly or slowly evolving regions of DNA can be examined, so the window of resolution required in a given project can be shifted by choice of the DNA to be sequenced. The technique's limitations make it unsuitable for studies attempting to infer genomewide patterns of variation or divergence from data of one or a few genes.

Key references. *Laboratory techniques:* Williams et al. 1990; Casanova et al. 1990; Green et al. 1990. *Overview:* Kocher et al. 1989; Arnheim et al. 1990; Chakraborty et al. 1991; Hadrys et al. 1992; Garner and Ryder 1992; Hoelzel and Green 1992; Bowditch et al. 1993; Quinn and Wilson 1993.

Mitochondrial DNA (mtDNA) Analysis. MtDNA is a small (usually about 16 kb) extranuclear piece of DNA housed within mitochondria in the cell cytoplasm that exhibits strict maternal transmission in most higher animals (Avise and Vrijenhoek 1987). Portions of the molecule evolve very rapidly, so mtDNA methods commonly are applied to phylogenetic issues at the intraspecific level. Because of its uniparental, nonrecombining mode of inheritance (and the usual absence of significant mtDNA sequence heterogeneity among the germ or somatic cells of an individual), mtDNA markers offer some unusual opportunities for phylogenetic analysis.

Assays of mtDNA involve either: (a) nucleotide sequencing of particular gene regions, as described above; or, more commonly, (b) restriction site analyses. Restriction assays sometimes involve Southern blotting procedures as described in the section on single-copy RFLP, using the entire mtDNA molecule or particular mtDNA genes as probes. Alternatively, closed-circular mtDNA can be isolated from each specimen (using dye-buoyant density centrifugation), and the purified mtDNA can be used directly in the generation of restriction digestion profiles that are revealed by staining or radioactive methods.

Nature of the data. Raw data in the restriction approaches consist of mtDNA fragment digestion profiles for particular endonucleases, of which 10–20 may be employed in a given study. A typical survey reveals perhaps 50–100 or more fragments per individual, representing 300–600 base-pairs in a recognition sequence, or roughly 2–4% of the mtDNA genome. Considered in composite, these data provide a description of a mtDNA haplotype for each individual. Differences among digestion profiles can often be attributed to gains or losses of particular restriction sites, and genetic and phylogenetic relationships among haplotypes can be readily inferred (for example, by parsimony methods). From a functional perspective, mtDNA consists of about thirty-seven genes, but from a phylogenetic perspective the entire molecule represents one genealogical unit since mtDNA is nonrecombining. Because mtDNA is maternally inherited, the evolutionary relationships among haplotypes are interpreted as estimates of matriarchal phylogeny. Data derived from direct nucleotide sequencing of mtDNA are interpreted similarly and in addition can often be applied to estimates of phylogenetic relationships at intermediate taxonomic levels.

Key references. Laboratory techniques: Brown 1980; Lansman et al. 1981. *Overview:* Brown 1985; Wilson et al. 1985a; Avise 1986; Avise et al. 1987; Moritz et al. 1987.

APPLICATION OF GENETIC TECHNIQUES TO POPULATION MANAGEMENT

In describing the variety of molecular genetic techniques in the first part of this essay, we do not mean to imply that all have been of comparable utility in addressing issues in population biology and evolution. Some methods (e.g., assays of allozymes and mtDNA restriction sites) have a significant track record of providing informative genetic markers, while some of the more promising new approaches (e.g., assays of nuclear RFLP's and sequencing via PCR) have not yet been employed quite so widely in the field. In the following sections, we use selected examples to highlight some potential conservation applications (and limitations) of molecular genetic data. Recent studies illustrating the use of these techniques at various population levels are listed in table 9.1.

Genetic Identity Versus Nonidentity

One straightforward application of genetic markers is in assessing whether tissue samples derive from a particular individual. For example, such issues arise in human forensics when establishing the source of sperm in rape cases or of blood at crime scenes (Dodd 1985; Gill et al.

1985). The lack of a genetic match between tissue and suspect positively excludes identity, while the presence of a genetic match suggests, but does not prove, the null hypothesis of no genetic differences. In general, genetic inclusions are more difficult to establish than genetic exclusions because they depend on elimination of all suspects except one. Probabilities of exclusion (and hence inclusion) are a function of the numbers and frequencies of allelic markers at independent genetic polymorphisms; inclusions depend additionally on the size (and genetic relationships) of the suspect pool.

Several molecular genetic methods reveal sufficient polymorphism to permit genetic distinctions among conspecific individuals with high probability. DNA fingerprints (from minisatellite probes) are appropriately named because the complex banding patterns on gels are specific to individual humans in much the same way as are conventional fingerprints. For the British population, Jeffreys et al. (1985b) estimate that the probability of unrelated individuals sharing all fragments in the gel patterns for one VNTR probe is less than 3×10^{-11}, and comparable variability in DNA fingerprints has been found in several other species (Burke and Bruford 1987; Jeffreys and Morton 1987; Jeffreys et al. 1987; Wetton et al. 1987). More traditional molecular genetic methods also permit rather fine genetic distinctions. For example, a typical allozyme survey of a vertebrate population conservatively might reveal polymorphisms at six unlinked loci. Suppose that each such locus has two alleles, at frequencies 0.7 and 0.3, such that genotype frequencies (f_i) expected under Hardy-Weinberg equilibrium are 0.49, 0.42, and 0.09. The probability that two individuals share a single-locus genotype is $\Sigma f_i^2 = 0.425$, and the corresponding probability of identity at all assayed loci is $(0.425)^6 = 5.8 \times 10^{-3}$. Variation observed in conventional mtDNA restriction site surveys has also been sufficiently great in some species to yield probabilities of genetic identity of less than 0.05 among unrelated individuals (reviewed in Avise et al. 1989).

Examples. DNA fingerprinting has been used to identify specific individuals in three species of Old World monkeys (Washio et al. 1989) and in the spotted sandpiper (*Actitis macularia;* Oring et al. 1992). In the case of the polyandrous spotted sandpiper, examination of fingerprints from parents and offspring indicated that second and third mates were not fathering all their putative offspring. Further identification of specific individuals from the population using fingerprinting indicated that females' first mates of the year were fathering chicks in subsequent broods. Thus, females were storing sperm and subsequent mates were being cuckolded.

DNA fingerprinting has also been used to identify sex-specific restriction fragments in the brown skua (*Catharacta lonnbergi;* Millar et al. 1992) and a series of other avian species (Longmire et al. 1993).

Several possible applications can be imagined for individual genetic diagnoses in zoos or in other population management contexts. In some cases it might be desirable to establish whether members of a litter are products of mono- or multizygotic development (i.e., whether they are identical or fraternal twins), or to employ genetic markers in various forensic contexts such as establishing the source of sperm in an unobserved insemination. One possible class of applications for wild populations might involve the use of genetically "tagged" individuals in studies of behavior, social structure, or migration patterns. In species not readily observed directly, such as many cetaceans, monitoring individual movements might be facilitated through the use of genetic "fingerprints" obtained from repeated biopsies (Hoelzel and Amos 1988). This approach would also be of use in considering clonal species.

Parentage

Molecular approaches associated with parentage assessment are similar to those described above, with the added complication that processes of genetic assortment and recombination (for autosomal nuclear genes) have intervened between offspring and their putative parents. The most common situation is when the genotypes of a mother and her progeny are known, and paternity is uncertain. Paternity exclusion is established by showing the absence of the offspring's paternal alleles in prospective fathers. Whether paternity can be established positively depends on the pool of prospective fathers and the level of polymorphism in the genetic markers utilized. Traditionally, allozyme markers have been employed successfully for paternity exclusions (Hanken and Sherman 1981; Foltz and Hoogland 1981; Foltz 1981; Schwartz and Armitage 1980). Chromosomal variation, for example in heterochromatin, has also proved useful in humans and related species (Benirschke et al. 1984).

Methods of DNA analysis (RFLP's and fingerprinting) have increased resolution so that paternity inclusions are more closely approached (Birkhead and Moller 1992). In principle, markers on the Y chromosome could provide a more direct assessment of paternity in mammals, but the sex-specific nuclear markers identified thus far do not appear to be highly polymorphic (Bishop et al. 1985).

In oviparous species where embryonic development takes place outside the female's body, maternity may also be in question. Furthermore, the tendency for some female mammals to adopt or steal offspring from other females also raises questions about biological maternity. If the father is known, exclusion of maternity is established by showing the absence of a prospective mother's alleles in the offspring. When neither parent is known, the assessment of parentage by nuclear genes is somewhat more difficult.

Many questions can be addressed through genetic analyses of parentage (Sherman 1981): Which mate(s) are responsible for a litter when females copulate with multiple males? How often do successful extra-pair copulations occur in "monogamous" species? How frequently are litter mates full siblings? What is the variance in reproductive success among males in polygynous species, or among females in polyandrous species? How often do males and females invest resources in rearing progeny other than their own? Since the genetic relationships between adults and the young they attend cannot be determined from behavioral observations alone, genetic analyses of parentage can help describe such single-generation links in a suspected pedigree. The following are among many published examples that illustrate the kinds of applications thus far attempted in parentage analysis.

Examples. *Paternity analysis:* Westneat (1987) used allozymes encoded by nine polymorphic loci to show that 37 of 257 assayed indigo bunting (*Passerina cyanea*) offspring had genotypes incompatible with the putative male parent. Based on Mendelian considerations, the observed frequency of exclusions with these particular genetic markers should have underestimated the actual rate by about 60% (Chakraborty et al. 1974). Results were further substantiated, however, by DNA fingerprinting where 35/63 offspring had one novel fragment not present in the parents and 22/63 offspring had more novel fragments that could be explained by mutation (Westneat 1990). Thus, the high frequency of extra-pair fertilizations demonstrated for this species indicates that "social consortships between males and females do not reflect exclusive mating relationships" (Westneat 1987, 1990).

Burke et al. (1989) used a combination of behavioral observations and DNA fingerprinting methods to study parentage in a banded population of dunnocks (*Prunella modularis*). Their results indicated that virtually all broods were fathered by the resident male or males (some female territories are occupied by multiple resident males) and that maternity was also attributed in all cases to the resident female (that is, there were no cases of intraspecific brood parasitism). Thus, unlike the indigo bunting, in this species' social consortships appear to be an excellent predictor of parentage.

In blue tits (*Parus caeruleus*), data from twelve years of observations from marked birds and single-locus DNA fingerprints of the entire population, showed an asymmetrical assignment of young to breeding males in the population (Kempenaers et al. 1992). Females frequently engaged in successful extra-pair copulations with males of higher quality than their mates. Males that lost paternity were often left by their fertile mates, were smaller, and had lower survival rates than males with higher paternity. Males with high paternity were larger, had more ornaments, and had higher survival rates.

Maternity analysis: McCracken (1984) used two allozyme polymorphisms from blood samples to assess whether female free-tailed bats (*Tadarida brasiliensis*) returning from foraging rounds normally find and nurse their own progeny in the dense creches of pups covering the roosting surfaces of caves. In 167 female-pup pairs sampled during nursing, 7 genotypic combinations incompatible with mother-offspring relationships were observed, whereas about 43 such combinations were expected if nursing had been random with respect to the genetic markers employed. The conclusion was that although mothers occasionally nurse pups that are not their own, nursing is highly nonrandom and presumably selective along kinship lines.

Jeffreys et al. (1985c) used DNA fingerprinting to establish that the putative mother of an immigrant boy to the United Kingdom was indeed his biological parent. Conventional genetic markers (from allozymes and other blood group loci) had shown that the woman and boy were almost certainly related but could not establish whether the woman was the boy's mother or aunt. The paternally and maternally derived DNA bands were inferred by a process of elimination involving comparisons among DNA fingerprints of the boy, his putative mother, and three undisputed sibs. All maternally inherited DNA fragments in the boy were also present in the woman, leading to the conclusion by immigration authorities that "beyond reasonable doubt" she was indeed the mother.

Joint maternity and paternity analysis: Quinn et al. (1987) used Mendelian nuclear RFLP's to examine parentage in four "families" of lesser snow geese (*Anser caerulescens*), each consisting of goslings attended by adults at the nest. Six of 17 goslings exhibited genotypes inconsistent with parentage of one or both nest attendants. Some inconsistencies excluded the male as parent and hence could have arisen from intraspecific brood parasitism (IBP) or extra-pair fertilizations (EPF). Other genetic markers excluded both attendants as parents and presumably resulted from IBP.

In principle, highly polymorphic mtDNA markers can be employed to provide a direct assay of maternity, provided that sufficient mtDNA variation among matrilineal clones is detectable. Use of mitochondrial DNA variation to assist in identification of maternity in combination with the use of multilocus (or a combination of single-locus) probes for producing DNA fingerprints may allow for partial reconstruction of pedigrees in closed breeding groups, as has been discussed for the lion-tailed macaque (*Macaca silenus;* Morin and Ryder 1991).

Genetic Relationships Within a Population's Pedigree

Whereas genetic relatedness among individuals can be estimated if a population pedigree is known, in wild populations more often the pedigree is unknown, and the hope is to employ genetic markers to infer kinship. If reliable estimates of individual relationships could be obtained, they would likely find wide application in such endeavors as filling gaps in knowledge of pedigrees for zoo or other populations, screening for relationships among potential founders in a reintroduction program designed to minimize inbreeding, and assessing the role of kin selection in the evolution of social behavior. Although it is possible to estimate the average relatedness within social or other groups from molecular genetic data (e.g., using the approach of genotypic correlation;

Pamilo 1984; Wilkinson and McCracken 1985), estimating relatedness values for specific individuals is much more problematic.

Lynch (1988) and Pamilo (1989) discuss the considerable theoretical difficulties of attempting individual estimates of genetic relatedness from Mendelian genotypes at small or moderate numbers of loci and from DNA fingerprint data, respectively (but see Geyer and Thompson, essay 10 of this volume). Before various genetic surrogates of kinship (such as proportions of bands shared in DNA fingerprints) are adopted as reliable estimators of individual relationship, additional theoretical and empirical study of such estimation procedures will be necessary. Nonetheless, correlations have been reported between band similarity in DNA fingerprints and relatedness calculated from a pedigree (Packer et al. 1991; Reeve et al. 1992; Piper and Parker Rabenold 1992; Geyer et al. 1993; Haig et al. 1993b; Haig et al. 1994a, b).

Examples. To test the hypothesis that genetically related larvae of the coral reef fish, *Anthias squamipinnis,* might remain together and settle as sibling cohorts, Avise and Shapiro (1986) employed allozyme markers at three polymorphic loci to assess kinship within social groups. The mean genetic relatedness within groups, measured by genotypic correlation, was indistinguishable from zero. This and other analyses of the molecular genetic data demonstrated that juvenile cohorts do not consist exclusively or predominantly of siblings but rather represent a nearly random draw from zygotes of the local gene pool.

McCracken and Bradbury (1977) used allozyme variation at three polymorphic loci to assess kinship within harems of a neotropical bat, *Phyllostomus hastatus.* The distributions of genotypes within and among harems indicated that although individuals form annually stable and cohesive groups, they are not more closely related to one another than to other individuals in the population at large. Apparently, movements of juveniles from parental units to new harems provides an avenue of gene flow sufficient to prevent genetic differentiation among social units.

Haig et al. (1994a) used DNA profiles to test five hypotheses proposed to explain the relatedness among founders of the captive population of Guam rails (*Rallus owstoni*). Band-sharing among founders and their subsequent offspring was correlated with relatedness values calculated from hypothesized pedigrees to determine the accuracy of founder hypotheses and select a founder-relatedness scenario upon which to base future genetic management of the captive population. A similar approach was taken by Ashworth and Parkin (1992) in examining relationships among founders of the British population of Bali mynahs (*Leucopsar rothschildi*). Relatedness was estimated for California Condors (*Gymnogyps californianus*) using DNA fingerprints and a statistical model developed by Geyer and Thompson (1992) that estimates relatedness among unknown individuals (Geyer et al. 1993).

Genetic Variation and Population Viability

Apart from their use in kinship or phylogeny estimation, molecular methods can also be used to assess the levels of genetic variation in a population. In fact, most discussions of genetics in conservation biology have focused on how best to monitor and preserve variability within species, the assumption being that higher variation may enhance a population's viability over ecological or evolutionary timescales. Molecular genetic variation does appear to be significantly reduced in some threatened species (Bonnell and Selander 1974; Lesica et al. 1988; Vrijenhoek et al. 1985), and such reductions are sometimes correlated with lower components of fitness (O'Brien and Evermann 1988; Quattro and Vrijenhoek 1989; Wildt et al. 1987). However, from allozyme methods it is evident that natural populations of various species apparently exhibit a broad range of heterozygosities (Nevo 1978; Powell 1975), and some species reported to lack appreciable variability (e.g. elephant seals, *Mirounga angustirostris*; Bonnell and Selander 1974) are expanding rapidly and appear to be demographically "healthy" at the present time. Thus, in assessing the role of molecular genetic variation in population management, two general questions arise: (1) how reliably do the techniques employed (such as allozymes) monitor genomewide levels of variability; and (2) is there a relationship between genome variation and population viability?

The former question can best be addressed by including a variety of molecular or other assay methods in estimating genetic variation, and the latter question can be approached by comparing various components of fitness in the target population with those of other closely related populations or species with differing heterozygosities. The following examples are among those that have attempted such a thorough characterization.

Example. O'Brien et al. (1985) summarize evidence that the cheetah (*Acinonyx jubatus*) may have undergone a recent population bottleneck followed by inbreeding that severely reduced genetic variation in the species and may have resulted in an increased susceptibility to extinction through disease or other agents. Evidence for low variation comes from a near absence of heterozygosity at a large number of allozyme and other protein loci (other large cats showed "normal" levels of variation) and from reduced genetic variability at the major histocompatibility complex (MHC) as evidenced by the acceptance of skin grafts among individuals not thought to be related. Evidence for diminished reproductive performance in comparison to other cats comes from a high incidence of morphological abnormalities in sperm, lower spermatozoal concentrations, and high juvenile mortality in noninbred matings. In addition, cheetahs exposed to a coronavirus causing feline infectious peritonitis (FIP) showed an extreme sensitivity to infection, possibly due to a lack of variation in products of disease-resistance genes including the MHC.

The red-cockaded woodpecker (RCW) (*Picoides borealis*) is a cooperatively breeding, endangered species in the southeastern U.S. whose populations have declined as a result of the loss of old growth forest habitat. One population at the Savannah River Forest in South Carolina underwent a significant bottleneck so that by 1985 only one breeding pair and two solitary males remained. An electrophoretic survey of twenty-six RCW populations indicated that F_{ST} for RCW's was high (0.14); yet the Savannah River population had levels of heterozygosity equal to other RCW populations (Stangel et al. 1992). Birds were translocated to the Savannah River population from adjacent populations so that by 1990 twenty-five birds were resident. Comparison of DNA profiles from all individuals present since 1985 with relatedness calculated from the pedigree allowed for a delineation of the population structure (Haig et al. 1993b). Additional pedigree and population viability analyses were carried out to determine what management activities could be carried out within ten years to insure a genetically viable population (i.e., 90% heterozygosity for 200 years). Haig et al. (1993a) determined that successful annual translocation of three females and two males for a ten-year period will achieve a 96% probability of survival of that population for 200 years. RAPD analyses of fourteen additional populations indicated that future translocations into this population would best be achieved by using birds from nearby populations, because genetic distance increased significantly with geographic distance (Haig et al. in press). Finally, the recovery objective of attaining effective population sizes of two hundred or more individuals per population was assessed using DNA fingerprinting in the Savannah River and the more northerly Sandhills (North Carolina) populations. Parentage analyses indicated that helpers did not contribute genes to the offspring in either population. Therefore calculations of effective population size must consider that there are many nonbreeding adults in these populations, thus lowering previous estimates (Haig et al. 1994b).

Geographic Population Structure and Intraspecific Phylogeny

For the management of species in nature, it is often desirable to know the extent of gene flow among populations. For example, a biologist charged with protecting a marine fishery could profit from knowing the numbers and geographic distributions of genetic and demographic stocks under exploitation. In addition, since geographic populations that currently exchange few or no genes must have been in contact at various times in the past, their historical relationships are of interest in terms of the conservation biology of distinct gene pools. Molecular genetic data on population structure can add a historical dimension to studies of gene flow and other elements of demography, and hence it can complement the kinds of mark-recapture or direct observational data obtainable from contemporary ecological analyses of natural populations (Slatkin 1985a).

Any molecular method capable of revealing qualitative variation among alleles (such as assays of karyotypes, allozymes, RFLP's, or mtDNA) can provide frequency data for estimating the magnitude of the gene flow between populations. Slatkin (1987) reviews two major statistical approaches employed to estimate gene flow, both of which involve the calculation of Nm, where N is the size of local populations and m is the migration rate in an island model of population structure. In the F_{ST} approach, the standardized variance in allele frequencies among local populations is calculated from the data and used to estimate Nm by the formula $F_{ST} \approx 1/(1 + 4Nm)$ (Wright 1931). In the rare allele method (Slatkin 1985b) the calculation of Nm is based on its expected relationship to the average frequency of "private" alleles (those confined to a single population). These methods are expected to yield comparable estimates on Nm under a wide variety of population structures (Slatkin and Barton 1989). In general, under an island model the reciprocal exchange between populations of more than a single migrant per generation ($Nm > 1$) is theoretically sufficient to prevent substantial allele frequency differentiation by genetic drift alone. In a given survey, estimates of Nm are typically made from a number of independent allozymes or other loci and are often quite consistent (e.g., Slatkin 1987). Loci that significantly vary with the consensus pattern may have been affected by additional factors, such as balancing or diversifying selection resulting in lower or higher than average allele frequency differences, respectively, among populations.

Assays of mtDNA typically provide an additional dimension of information, e.g., evolutionary relationships among the alleles themselves. Slatkin and Maddison (1989) developed a cladistic measure of gene flow inferred from the phylogenies of any such alleles. The approach involves estimating the minimum number of migration events between localities necessary to account for an observed geographic distribution of alleles whose phylogeny is known or hypothesized. Such attempts are valuable because they capitalize on the added knowledge of allelic ancestry. On the other hand, one must exercise caution in inferring the evolutionary histories of populations from the phylogenies of particular genes, since there are many genealogical tracings within any organismal pedigree. Avise (1989a) reviews concepts concerning the relationships between gene trees and organismal histories.

Examples. Meylan et al. (1990) used variation in mtDNA to assess female-mediated gene flow between green turtle (*Chelonia mydas*) rookeries in the Caribbean Sea and Atlantic Ocean. Most rookeries exhibited fixed or nearly fixed mtDNA genotype frequency differences, leading to point estimates of Nm (from the Slatkin/Maddison approach) ranging from 0.0–0.5 between various pairs of colonies. However, all mtDNA genotypes exhibited very low sequence divergence, suggesting that green turtle populations are isolated from one another over ecological, rather than long evolutionary, timescales. The green turtle is an endangered species, and population biologists had long sought evidence of genetic differences among populations that might support the desirability of rookery-specific conservation programs (Carr 1975).

Avise and Nelson (1989) surveyed mtDNA variation among geographic populations of the seaside sparrow (*Ammodramus maritimus*), including the now extinct dusky seaside sparrow (*A.m. nigrescens*), which had been the object of intensive conservation efforts. Two fundamental phylogenetic subdivisions were apparent in the genetic data, and these characterized populations on the Atlantic versus the Gulf Coasts. The phylogenetic split is concordant with genetic patterns also observed in a number of other coastal restricted species in the southeastern U.S. (Avise and Ball 1990); it most likely reflects a vicariant biogeographic subdivision dating to the Pleistocene. Since the phylogenetic split in the seaside sparrow went unrecognized in prior subspecies descriptions, conservation programs had not focused on managing the major population sources of evolutionary genetic diversity in the complex.

Laerm et al. (1982) provide a similar case history in which molecular genetic data call into question the basis for taxonomic recognition of an "endangered species." The colonial pocket gopher (*Geomys colonus*) had been described in the late 1800s as specifically distinct from a widespread and common congener, *G. pinetis*. The range of *G. colonus* was confined to one county in southeast Georgia. The genetic analyses by Laerm et al. included standard karyotypes, allozymes, and mtDNA and showed that *G. colonus* was indistinguishable from surrounding populations of *G. pinetis,* whereas in these same assays, populations of *G. pinetis* in the eastern versus western portions of the range were dramatically divergent.

Taxonomic descriptions inevitably shape perceptions of how biotic diversity is partitioned. We suspect that a widened application of molecular methods will reveal many instances in which current lower-level taxonomies (often derived from small numbers of morphological traits with uncertain genetic basis) have provided inadequate or even misleading guides for management programs (Avise 1989b).

Speciation

Morphologically cryptic species have been identified through studies of zoogeography and behavioral ecology. Perhaps less well recognized have been the identification of speciation events in mammals that are detected by chromosomal and molecular genetic methods.

African dik-diks are dwarf antelopes that are unusual because of their monogamous social structure. In zoological parks, F_1 male sterility with accompanying breakdown of spermatogenesis has been identified in Kirk's dik-dik (*Madoqua kirkii*) individuals that are cytotype hybrids. Several parental cytotypes have been identified, suggesting population subdivision and reproductive isolation as indicated by the chromosomal variance (Ryder et al. 1989b). Although six subspecies of Kirk's dik-dik occur in Kenya, it had not been previously recognized that reproductively isolated subpopulations exist within this single species.

Soemmerring's gazelle (*Gazella soemmerringi*) is rarely represented in captivity, and in North America recent efforts to establish a breeding population of this species have failed due to the chromosomal incompatibility of individuals. In a recent cytogenetics survey of animals in North American zoos, no male possessed the same karyotype as any female in the captive population. Chromosome numbers of 34–39 were observed, and chromosomal incompatibility was clearly implicated as the cause of reproductive failure (Benirschke et al. 1984).

Orangutans (*Pongo pygmaeus*) are known now to occur only on the islands of Borneo and Sumatra. Morphological differences between Bornean and Sumatran orangutans have led to the designation of two separate subspecies, *P. pygmaeus pygmaeus*, and *P. p. abelii*. Individuals in the two populations are distinguishable on the basis of a pericentric inversion in the second chromosome (PPY2). In a study of wild-caught orangutans, no inversion heterozygotes were found in PPY2. A study of mitochondrial DNA restriction maps of individuals whose chromosomal status was known revealed the presence of two distinct mitochondrial DNA lineages corresponding to the two karyotypically distinct populations. The extent of nucleotide sequence divergence based on mitochondrial DNA restriction analysis between Bornean and Sumatran orangutans was similar to that noted for the two species of chimpanzee: *Pan paniscus* and *Pan troglodytes* (Ryder and Chemnick 1993). In a study of isozyme and two-dimensional gel electrophoresis, Janczewski et al. (1990) also observed levels of genetic differentiation between the two recognized subspecies of orangutans, the extent of which was more consistent with differences on the species level rather than that of subspecies.

A highly practical use of molecular markers in deciphering differences between species occurs in cases where conservation officers attempt to identify taxa that have been poached or brought to customs officers for import or export (Thommasen et al. 1989; Cronin et al. 1991). Protein analyses as well as mitochondrial and nuclear DNA techniques have been useful in identifying species from tissue such as hair, skin, organs, or muscle. Some of these techniques can also be used for more detailed appraisals of the geographic or subspecific sources of individuals.

Higher-level Phylogenies

Because some molecular genetic assays, such as DNA/DNA hybridization and protein complement fixation, typically reveal little or no intraspecific divergence, they can be applied only to systematic and evolutionary questions at higher taxonomic levels. Although it is difficult to envision a wide range of applications for such data in the field of conservation biology, some possibilities exist. We will illustrate them by providing an example of how molecular genetic data have reshaped thinking about avian phylogeny and biogeography on a global scale.

Example. From extensive studies of over fifteen hundred avian species using techniques of DNA/DNA hybridization, Sibley and Ahlquist (1986; see also Sibley et al. 1988) reached the startling conclusion that the world's great diversity of oscine songbirds may be traced to two distinct phylogenetic lines, one of which originated in Australia and the other in Africa or Asia. Previous systematic treatments based primarily

Table 9.1 Recent studies using molecular genetic techniques

COMPARISON LEVEL	TECHNIQUE	COMMON NAME	SCIENTIFIC NAME	SOURCE
Among Species	Electrophoresis	Gulls	*Larus*, spp.	Snell 1991
		Owls	*Strigiformes* (7 spp.)	Randi et al. 1991a
		New World Woodpeckers	*Piciformes* (26 spp.)	Lanyon and Zink 1987
		Hawaiian Honeycreeper	*Depranidinae*	Johnson et al. 1988
		Pied Flycatcher	*Ficedula hypoleuca*	Gelter et al. 1989
		Collared Flycatcher	*Ficedula albicollis*	"
		New World Monkeys	*Saguinus midas*	Melo et al. 1992
		"	*S. fuscicollus weddelli*	"
		Marmosets	*Callitrix* (5 spp.)	Meireles et al. 1992
		Chamois	*Rupicapra rupicapra rupicapra*	Randi et al. 1991b
		Caprini	*Capra aegagrus hircus*	"
		"	*C. ibex ibex*	"
		"	*Ovis ammon musimon*	"
		Northern White Rhino	*Ceratotherium simum simum*	Merenlender et al. 1989
		Southern White Rhino	*C. s. cottoni*	"
		Black Rhino	*Diceros bicornis*	"
		Indian Rhino	*Rhinoceros unicornis*	"
		African Elephant	*Loxodonta africana*	Drysdale and Florkiewicz 1989
		Asian Elephant	*Elephus maximus*	"
	DNA Hybridization	Cranes	*Gruidae*	Krajewski 1990; Love and Deininger 1992
		Chickadees, Titmice	*Parus*	Sheldon et al. 1992

mtDNA		
Waterfowl	*Anatidae* (13 spp.)	Madsen et al. 1988
Birds	*Aves*	Sibley and Ahlquist 1986
Red Phalarope	*Phalaropus fulicaria*	Dittman and Zink 1991
Wilson's Phalarope	*P. tricolor*	" "
Red-necked Phalarope	*P. lobatus*	" "
Hawaiian Goose	*Nesochen sandvicensis*	Quinn et al. 1991
Canada Goose	*Branta canadensis*	" "
Pacific Black Brant	*B. bernicula nigricans*	" "
Emperor Goose	*Chen canagica*	" "
Mallard	*Anas platyrhynchos*	Avise et al. 1990, Rhymer et al. 1994
Black Duck	*A. rubripes*	" "
Grey Duck	*A. superciliosis*	Rhymer et al. 1994
Old World Monkeys	Primates	Easteal 1991
" "	Tribe: *Papionini*	Disotell et al. 1992
Primates	Primates (14 spp.)	Wayne et al. 1991d
Carnivores	Carnivora (72 spp.)	Wayne et al. 1991d
Polar Bear	*Ursus maritimus*	Shields and Kocher 1991
Brown Bear	*U. arctos*	" "
Black Bear	*U. americanus*	" "
Gray Wolf	*Canis lupus*	Lehman et al. 1991
Coyote	*C. latrans*	" ", Wayne and Jenks 1991
Red Wolf	*C. rufus*	Wayne and Jenks 1991
African Jackals	*Canis* (3 spp.)	Wayne et al. 1989
South American Foxes	*Dusicyon* (2 spp.)	Wayne et al. 1989
Wood Mouse	*Apodemus sylvaticus*	Tegelstrom and Jaarola 1989
Yellow-necked Mouse	*A. flavicollis*	" "

(continued)

211

Table 9.1 (*Continued*)

COMPARISON LEVEL	TECHNIQUE	COMMON NAME	SCIENTIFIC NAME	SOURCE
		Grasshopper Mice	*Onychomys*	Riddle and Honeycutt 1990
		Blue Whale	*Balaenoptera musculus*	Arnason et al. 1991
		Fin Whale	*B. physalus*	" "
		Menhaden fish	*Brevoortia tyrannus/patronus*	Avise et al. 1989
		Pacific Salmon	*Oncorhynchus* spp.	Thomas et al. 1986
		Death Valley Pupfish	*Cyprinodon* (4 spp.)	Echelle and Dowling 1992
		Sea Urchins	*Strongylocentrotus purpuratus*	Palumbi and Wilson 1990
		Kemp's Ridley Sea Turtle	*Lepidochelys kempi*	Bowen et al. 1991
		Olive Ridley Sea Turtle	*L. olivacea*	
		Desert Tortoise	*Xerobates agassizi*	Lamb et al. 1989
		Firebellied Toad	*Bombina bombina*	Szymura and Barton 1986
		Chuckwalla Lizard	*Sauromalus obesus*	Avise et al. 1989
		Salamanders	*Ambystoma* (4 spp.)	Hedges et al. 1992
DNA Fingerprinting		Mute Swan	*Cygnus olor*	Meng et al. 1990
		Bewick Swan	*C. cygnus*	" "
		Black Swan	*C. columbianus*	" "
Microcomplement Fixation		Carnivores	Carnivora	Wayne et al. 1989, 1991c
		Primates	Primates	Wayne et al. 1991c
		Cats	Felidae	Collier and O'Brien 1985
PCR		Primates	Primates	Rogers et al. 1992
		Whales	Odonotoceti/Mysticeti	Schlötterer et al. 1991
		Whalebone Whale	Mysticeti (10 spp.)	Arnason and Best 1991
		Blue Whale	*Balaenoptera musculus*	Arnason and Gullberg 1993

212

mtDNA	Fin Whale	*B. physalus*	" "
Karyotyping	Chickadees	*Parus* spp.	Gill et al. 1993
	Parrots	*Psittacidae*	Christidis et al. 1991
	Lorikeets	*Loridae*	" "
	Cockatoo	*Cacatridae*	" "
	New World Monkeys	*Aotus vociferans*	Pieczarka et al. 1992
		A. nancymai	" "
	Chimpanzee	*Pan paniscus*	Ryder and Chemnick 1993
	"	*Pan troglodytes*	" "
	Grevy Zebra	*Equus grevyi*	Breen and Gill 1991
	Domestic Horse	*E. caballus*	" "
	African Plains Zebra	*E. burchelli*	" "
	Horses/Zebra/Ass	*Equus* (6 sp.)	Wichman et al. 1991
	Asiatic Wild Asses	*E. przewalskii*	Ryder and Chemnick 1990
	Soemmerring's Gazelle	*Gazelle soemmerringi*	Benirschke et al. 1984
	Lechwe	*Kobus leche*	Benirschke and Kumamoto 1991
	Nile Lechwe	*K. megaceros*	" "
	Octodontid Rodents	*Octodontidae*	Gallardo 1992
	Blue Wildebeest	*Connochaetes taurinus*	Corbet and Robinson 1991
	Black Wildebeest	*C. gnou*	" "
Among Populations	Electrophoresis	African Bats	*Vestertilionid*	Ruedas et al. 1990
		Kirk's Dik-dik	*Madoqua kirkii*	Ryder et al. 1989b
		Wood Stork	*Mycteria americana*	Stangel et al. 1990
		Brant	*Branta bernicla brota*	Novak et al. 1989
		Lesser Snow Goose	*Chen caerulescens c.*	Cooke et al. 1988
		Piping Plover	*Charadrius melodus*	Haig and Oring 1988
		Common Tern	*Sterna hirundo*	Burson 1990

(continued)

Table 9.1 (*Continued*)

COMPARISON LEVEL	TECHNIQUE	COMMON NAME	SCIENTIFIC NAME	SOURCE
		Willow Ptarmigan	*Lagopus lagopus*	Rorvik and Steen 1989
		Red-cockaded Woodpecker	*Picoides borealis*	Stangel et al. 1992
		Spotted Owl	*Strix occidentalis*	Barrowclough and Gutierrez 1990
		Common Myna	*Acridotheres tristis*	Fleischer et al. 1991c
		Common Chaffinch	*Fringella coelebs*	Baker et al. 1990a, 1992
		Blue Chaffinch	*F. teydea*	" "
		Laysan Finch	*Telespiza cantans*	Fleischer et al. 1991a
		Fox Sparrow	*Passerella iliaca*	Burns and Zink 1990
		Kakapo	*Strigops habroptilus*	Triggs et al. 1989
		Japanese Macaque	*Macaca fuscata*	Nozawa et al. 1991
		Rhesus Macaque	*M. mulatta*	Gill et al. 1992
		Cebus Monkey	*Cebus appella paraguayanus*	Sampaio et al. 1991
		Orangutan	*Pongo pygmaeus*	Janczewski et al. 1990
		Black Lemur	*Eulemur macaco macaco*	Arnaud et al. 1992
		Bandicoot	*Perimeles gunii*	Sherwin et al. 1991
		Florida Manatee	*Trichechus manatus*	McClenaghan and O'Shea 1988
		Dall's Porpoise	*Phocoenoides dalli*	Winans and Jones 1988
		Coyote	*Canis latrans*	Hamilton and Kennedy 1986
		Gray Wolf	*C. lupus*	Wayne et al. 1991b
		Eastern Cottontail	*Sylvilagus floridanus*	Scribner et al. 1983
		North Am. Pronghorn	*Antilocapra americana*	Lee et al. 1989
		Red Deer	*Cervus elaphus*	Hartl et al. 1991, Herzog et al. 1991

	Common name	Scientific name	Reference
	Chinook Salmon	*Oncorhynchus tshawytscha*	Beacham et al. 1989, Waples and Teel 1990
	Pecos Gambusia	*Gambusia nobilis*	Echelle et al. 1989
	Greek Brown Trout	*Salmo trutta*	Karakousis and Triantaphyllidis 1990
	Cutthroat Trout	*S. clarki*	Allendorf and Leary 1988
	Paddlefish	*Polyodon spathula*	Carlson et al. 1982
	Colorado Squawfish	*Ptychocheilus lucius*	Ammerman and Morizot 1989
	Land Snail	*Chondrina clienta*	Baur and Klemm 1989
	Littorine Snail	*Bembicium vittatum*	Johnson and Black 1991
	Crustaceans	*Hyale plumulosa*	McDonald 1991
	Noble Crayfish	*Astacus astacus*	Fevolden and Hessen 1989
	Water Strider	*Aquarius remigis*	Preziosi and Fairbairn 1992
	Alpine Grasshopper	*Aeropedellus clavatus*	Hamrick and Hamrick 1989
	Desert Tortoise	*Gopherus agassizi*	Rainboth et al. 1989
	Common Frog	*Rana temporaria*	Reh and Seitz 1990
	Watersnake	*Nerodia barteri*	Rose and Selcer 1989
	Zebratail lizard	*Callisaurus draconoides*	Adest 1987
mtDNA	Pacific Black Brant	*Branta bernicla nigricans*	Shields 1990
	Canada Goose	*B. canadensis*	Shields and Wilson 1987
	Snow Goose	*Chen caerulescens*	Avise et al. 1992
	Northern Flicker	*Colaptes auratus*	Moore et al. 1991
	Blue Tit	*Parus caeruleus*	Taberlet et al. 1992
	Streaked Saltator	*Saltator albicollis*	Seutin et al. 1993
	Common Grackle	*Quiscalus quiscula*	Zink et al. 1991
	Brown-headed Cowbird	*Molothrus ater*	Fleischer et al. 1991b
	Song Sparrow	*Melospiza melodia*	Zink and Dittmann 1993
	Dusky Seaside Sparrow	*Ammodramus maritimus nigrescens*	Avise and Nelson 1989

(continued)

215

Table 9.1 (*Continued*)

COMPARISON LEVEL	TECHNIQUE	COMMON NAME	SCIENTIFIC NAME	SOURCE
		Japanese Macaque	*Macaca fuscata*	Hayasaka et al. 1991
		Killer Whale	*Orcinus orca*	Hoelzel and Dover 1991
		Humpback Whale	*Megaptera novaeangliae*	Baker et al. 1990b
		Black Rhinoceros	*Diceros bicornis*	Ashley et al. 1990
		Mule Deer	*Odocoileus hemionus*	Cronin 1992
		White-tailed Deer	*O. virginianus*	" "
		Moose	*Alces alces*	" "
		Elk	*Cervus elaphus*	" "
		Caribou	*Rangifer tarandus*	" "
		Gray Wolf	*Canis lupus*	Wayne et al. 1991b, 1992
		Channel Island Deer Mouse	*Peromyscus maniculatus*	Ashley and Wills 1989
		Columbian Ground Squirrel	*Spermophilus columbianus*	MacNeil and Strobeck 1987
		Trinidad Guppy	*Poecilia reticulata*	Fajen and Breden 1992
		Walleye	*Stizostedion vetreum*	Billington and Hebert 1988
		Rainbow Trout	*Salmo gairdneri*	Wilson et al. 1985a
		Steelhead Trout	*S. gairdneri*	" "
		Cutthroat Trout	*S. clarki*	" "
		Striped Bass	*Morone saxatilis*	Chapman 1990
		White Perch	*M. americana*	Mulligan and Chapman 1989
		Killifish	*Fundulus heteroclitus*	Brown and Chapman 1991
		Lake Whitefish	*Coregonus clupeaformis*	Bernatchez and Dodson 1990
		American Eel	*Anguilla rostrata*	Avise et al. 1986
		Sea Urchin	*Strongylocentrotus pallidus*	Palumbi and Kessing 1991
		Monarch Butterfly	*Danaus plexippus*	Brower and Boyce 1991

	Green Turtle	*Chelonia mydas*	Meylan et al. 1990; Bowen et al. 1992
DNA Fingerprinting	Mole Salamander	*Ambystoma* spp.	Splosky et al. 1992
	Blue Duck	*Hymenolaimus malacorhynchos*	Triggs et al. 1992
	Guam Rail	*Rallus owstoni*	Haig et al. 1994a
	Peregrine Falcon	*Falco peregrinus*	Longmire et al. 1991
	California Condor	*Gymnogyps californa*	Geyer et al. 1993, Geyer and Thompson, essay 10, this vol.
	Red-cockaded Woodpecker	*Picoides borealis*	Haig et al. 1993a, 1994b
	Rothschild's Mynah	*Leucopsar rothschildi*	Ashworth and Parkin 1992
	Striped-backed Wren	*Campylorhynchus nuchalis*	Rabenold et al. 1991
	Red-winged Blackbird	*Agelaius phoeniceus*	Reeve et al. 1992
	Killer Whale	*Orcinus orca*	Hoelzel and Dover 1991
	Humpback Whales	*Megaptera novaeangliae*	Baker et al. 1993
	Channel Island Fox	*Urocyon littoralis*	Gilbert et al. 1990, Wayne et al. 1991a
PCR	Gray Wolf	*Canis lupus*	Wayne et al. 1991b
	Thick-billed Murre	*Uria lomvia*	Birt-Friesen et al. 1992
	Snow Goose	*Chen caerulescens*	Quinn 1992
	Dunlin	*Calidris alpina*	Wenick et al. 1993
	Japanese Macaque	*Mucaca fuscata*	Hayasaka et al. 1991
	Killer Whale	*Orcinus orca*	Hoelzel and Dover 1991
	Pilot Whale	*Globicephala melas*	Amos et al. 1993
	African Elephant	*Loxodonta africana*	Bischof 1992
	Gorilla	*Gorilla gorilla*	Garner and Ryder 1992
	Green Turtle	*Chelonia mydas*	Karl et al. 1992
	New Zealand Frog	*Leiopelma hochstetteri*	Zeyl and Green 1992

(continued)

Table 9.1 (*Continued*)

COMPARISON LEVEL	TECHNIQUE	COMMON NAME	SCIENTIFIC NAME	SOURCE
	Karyotyping	Northern Flicker	*Colaptes auratus*	Grudzien et al. 1987
		Pocket Gopher	*Geomys bursarius*	Dowler 1989
		Common Shrew	*Sorex araneus*	Hatfield et al. 1992
		Salt-marsh Harvest Mouse	*Reithrodontomys raviventris*	Hood et al. 1984
		Orangutan	*Pongo pygmaeus*	Ryder and Chemnick 1993
		New England Cottontail	*Sylvilagus transitionalis*	Ruedas et al. 1989
		Lake Trout	*Salvelinus namaycush*	Phillips et al. 1989
		Rainbow Trout	*Salmo gairdneri*	Thorgaard 1983
		Liolaimus Lizard	*Liolaimus monticola*	Lamborot 1991
	Single-locus DNA	Indian Peafowl	*Pavo cristatus*	Hanotte et al. 1991a,b
Within populations	Electrophoresis	Hawaiian Duck	*Anas wyvilliana*	Browne et al. 1993
		Laysan Duck	*A. laysanensis*	" "
		Mallard	*A. platyrhynchos*	" "
		Willow Ptarmigan	*Lagopus lagopus*	Rorvik et al. 1990
		Acorn Woodpecker	*Melanerpes formicivorus*	Joste et al. 1985, Mumme et al. 1985
		Common Myna	*Acridotheres tristis*	Fleischer et al. 1991c
		Marten	*Martes americana*	Mitton and Raphael 1990
		Toque Macaque	*Macaca sinica*	Shotake et al. 1991
		Red Howler Monkey	*Alouatta seniculus*	Pope 1992
		One-horned Rhinoceros	*Rhinoceros unicornis*	Dinerstein and McCracken 1990
		Pronghorn	*Antilocapra americana*	Lee et al. 1989
		Plains Bison	*Bison bison*	McClenaghan et al. 1990, Braend and Stormont 1963

Method	Common Name	Scientific Name	Reference
	Black-tailed Prairie Dog	*Cynomys ludovicianus*	Daley 1992
	Atlantic Walrus	*Odobenus rosmarus rosmarus*	Simonsen et al. 1982
	Polar Bear	*Thalarctos maritimus*	Allendorf et al. 1979
	Elephant Seal	*Mirounga angustirostris*	Bonnell and Selander 1974
	Virginia River Chub	*Gila seminuda*	Demarais et al. 1993
	Colorado Squawfish	*Ptychocheilus lucius*	Ammerman and Morizot 1989
	Coho Salmon	*Oncorhynchus kisutch*	Wehrhahn and Powell 1987
	Sonoran Topminnow	*Poeciliopsis occidentalis*	Vrijenhoek et al. 1985
	Sea Lamprey	*Petromyzon marinus*	Krueger 1980
	Marine Bivalve	*Ruditapes decussatus*	Borsa et al. 1991
	Alpine Grasshopper	*Aeropedellus clavatus*	Hamrick and Hamrick 1989
mtDNA	Lion-tailed Macaque	*Macaca silenus*	Morin and Ryder 1991
	Black-backed Jackal	*Canis mesomelas*	Wayne et al. 1991c
	Meadow Vole	*Microtus pennsylvanicus*	Plante et al. 1989
	Dwarf Cisco	*Coregonus artedii*	Shields et al. 1990
	White Perch	*Morone americana*	Mulligan and Chapman 1989
	Atlantic Salmon	*Salmo salar*	Birt et al. 1986
	Chuckwalla Lizard	*Sauromalus obesus*	Avise et al. 1989
	Salamander	*Desmognathus quadramaculatus*	Stiven and Bruce 1988
PCR	Marine Mussels	*Mytilus edulis*	Zouros et al. 1992
	"	*M. trossulus*	"
DNA Fingerprinting	Pilot Whales	*Globicephala melas*	Amos et al. 1993
	Guam Rail	*Rallus owstoni*	Haig et al. 1994a
	Hispaniolan Parrot	*Amazona ventralis*	Brock and White 1991
	Red-cockaded Woodpecker	*Picoides borealis*	Haig et al. 1993a, 1994b
	House Sparrow	*Passer domesticus*	Wetton et al. 1987
	Lion-tailed Macaque	*Macaca silenus*	Morin and Ryder 1991
	Prairie Vole	*Microtus ochrogaster*	Hoagland et al. 1991

(continued)

Table 9.1 (*Continued*)

COMPARISON LEVEL	TECHNIQUE	COMMON NAME	SCIENTIFIC NAME	SOURCE
		Naked Mole Rat	*Heterocephalus glaber*	Faulkes et al. 1990; Reeve et al. 1990
		Banner-tailed Kangaroo Rat	*Dipodomys spectabilis*	Keane et al. 1991
		House Mouse	*Mus domesticus*	Everitt et al. 1991
		Asian Elephant	*Elaphus maximus*	Bischof 1992
		Lion	*Panthera leo*	Gilbert et al. 1991; Packer et al. 1991;
	Karyotyping	Poeciliid fish	*Limia perugiae*	Schartl et al. 1993
		Schistome-vector snail	*Bulinus globosus*	Jarne et al. 1992
		Honeybee	*Apis mellitera*	Blanchetot 1991
		Galapagos Tortoise	*Testudo elaphantopus*	Ryder et al. 1989a
		Lesser Snow Geese	*Chen caerulescens c.*	Quinn et al. 1990
		White-throated Sparrow	*Zonotrichia albicollis*	Thorneycroft 1975
		Dwarf Cisco	*Coregonus artedii*	Shields et al. 1990
		Coho Salmon	*Oncorhynchus kisoteh*	Lozano et al. 1991
		Dwarf Cisco	*Coregonus artedii*	Shields et al. 1990
		Lake Trout	*Salvelinus namaycush*	Phillips et al. 1989
Parentage	Electrophoresis	Mallard	*Anas platyrhynchos*	Evarts and Williams 1987
		European Starling	*Sturnus vulgaris*	Romagnano et al. 1989
		Eastern Bluebird	*Sialis sialis*	Gowaty and Karlin 1984, Karlin et al. 1990
		Field Sparrow	*Spizella pusilla*	Petter et al. 1990
		White-crowned Sparrow	*Zonotrichia leucophrys oriantha*	Sherman and Morton 1988

220

	Common Name	Species	Reference
	Eastern Kingbird	*Tyrannus tyrannus*	McKitrick 1990
	House Wren	*Troglodytes aedon*	Price et al. 1989
	Feral Horse	*Equus caballus*	Bowling and Touchberry 1990
mtDNA	White-footed Mouse	*Peromyscus leucopus*	Xia and Millar 1991
DNA Fingerprinting	Poeciliid Fish	*Poecilia latipinna*	Travis et al. 1990
	Garter Snake	*Thamnophis sirtalis*	Schwartz et al. 1989
	Speke's Gazelle	*Gazella spekei*	Templeton et al. 1987
	Northern Fulmar	*Fulmaris gracialis*	Hunter et al. 1992
	Lesser Snow Goose	*Chen caerulescens c.*	Quinn et al. 1989
	Spotted Sandpiper	*Actitis macularia*	Oring et al. 1992
	Black Vulture	*Coragyps atratus*	Decker et al. 1993
	Red-cockaded Woodpecker	*Picoides borealis*	Haig et al. 1993a, in press.
	Barn Swallow	*Hirundo rustica*	Smith et al. 1991
	Tree Swallow	*Tachycineta bicolor*	Lifjeld et al. 1993
	Pied and Collared Flycatcher	*Ficedula hypoleuca and F. albicollis*	Gelter et al. 1992; Gelter and Tegelstrom 1992
			" "
	Purple Martin	*Progne subis*	Morton et al. 1990
	House Sparrow	*Passer domesticus*	Burke and Bruford 1987
	Indigo Bunting	*Passerina cyanea*	Westneat 1987, 1990
	Willow Warbler	*Phylloscopus trochilus*	Gyllensten et al. 1990
	Wood Warbler	*P. sibilatrix*	" "
	Hooded Warbler	*Wilsonia citrina*	Stutchbury et al. 1994
	Striped-backed Wren	*Campylorhynchus nuchalis*	Rabenold et al. 1990
	Dunnocks	*Prunella modularis*	Burke et al. 1989
	White-fronted Bee-Eater	*Merops bullockoides*	Emlen and Wrege 1992
	European Bee-Eater	*M. apiaster*	Jones et al. 1991
	Zebra Finch	*Taeniopygia guttata*	Birkhead et al. 1990

(*continued*)

221

Table 9.1 (*Continued*)

COMPARISON LEVEL	TECHNIQUE	COMMON NAME	SCIENTIFIC NAME	SOURCE
		Red-winged Blackbird	*Agelaius phoeniceus*	Gibbs, et al. 1990; Westneat 1993
		Bull-headed Shrike	*Lanius bucephalus*	Yamagishi et al. 1992
		Muskrat	*Ondatra zibethicus*	Marinelli et al. 1992
		Old World Monkeys	*Macaca silenus*	Weiss et al. 1988
		"	*M. fuscata*	"
		"	*Erythrocebus patas*	"
		"	*Colobus guereza*	"
		Japanese Macaque	*Macaca fuscata*	Inoue et al. 1991
		Chimpanzee	*Pan troglodytes*	Ely and Ferrell 1990
		Long-finned Pilot Whale	*Globicephala melaena*	Amos and Dover 1990
		"	*G. melas*	Amos et al. 1991
		Lion	*Panthera leo*	Gilbert et al. 1991
		Common Shrew	*Sorex araneus*	Tegelstrom et al. 1991
		Bush Cricket	*Poecilimon veluchianus*	Achmann et al. 1992
	Single-locus DNA	Blue Tit	*Parus caeruleus*	Kempenaers et al. 1992
	PCR/RAPD	Chacma Babboon	*Papio cynocephalus*	Riedy et al. 1992
		Aeshnid Dragonfly	*Anax parthenope*	Hadrys et al. 1993
		Libellulid Dragonfly	*Orthethrum coerulescens*	"

on morphology had allied many of the Australian songbirds with their supposed nearest relatives elsewhere, but the DNA data suggest that such morphological similarities may sometimes have been due to convergent evolution. If Sibley et al. are correct, the radiation in Australian songbirds may have paralleled the better-known radiation there of marsupial mammals. To the extent that phylogenetic methods can contribute to our knowledge of the origins and patterns of biotic diversity, such data are relevant to the broader concerns of conservation biology.

CONCLUSIONS

A variety of descriptive molecular techniques are now available for estimating genetic variation and divergence among biological units ranging from individuals to higher taxa. Thus these descriptive molecular studies can, in combination with more traditional studies in natural history, ecology, morphometrics, and zoogeography, provide additional information of relevance to the management of compromised species and populations (Ryder 1986; Haig and Nordstrom 1991; Amos and Hoelzel 1992).

Acknowledgments
We thank Judy Rhymer for providing useful comments.

References

Achmann, R., K. G. Heller, and J. T. Epplen. 1992. Last-male sperm precedence in the bushcricket *Poecilimon veluchianus* (Orthoptera, Tettigonioidea) demonstrated by DNA fingerprinting. *Molecular Ecology* 1:47–54.

Adest, G. A. 1987. Genetic differentiation among populations of the zebratail lizard, *Callisaurus draconoides* (Sauria: Iguanidae). *Copeia* 1987:854–59.

Allendorf, F. W. and R. F. Leary. 1988. Conservation and distribution of genetic variation in a polytypic species, the cutthroat trout. *Conservation Biology* 2:170–84.

Allendorf, F. W., F. B. Christiansen, T. Dobson, W. F. Eanes, and O. Frydenberg. 1979. Electrophoretic variation in large mammals, I: The polar bear, *Thalarctos maritimus*. *Hereditas* 91:19–22.

Ammerman, L. K. and D. C. Morizot. 1989. Biochemical genetics of endangered Colorado squawfish populations. *Transactions of the American Fisheries Society* 118:435–40.

Amos, B. and G. A. Dover. 1990. DNA fingerprinting and the uniqueness of whales. *Mammal Review* 20:23–30.

Amos, B. and A. R. Hoelzel. 1992. Applications of molecular genetic techniques to the conservation of small populations. *Biological Conservation* 61:133–44.

Amos, B., J. Barrett, and G. A. Dover. 1991. Breeding behaviour of pilot whales revealed by DNA fingerprinting. *Heredity* 67:49–55.

Amos, B., C. Schlotter, and D. Tautz. 1993. Social structure of pilot whales revealed by analytical DNA profiling. *Science* 260:670–72.

Arnason, U. and P. B. Best. 1991. Phylogenetic relationships within the Mysticeti (whalebone whales) based upon studies of highly repetitive DNA in all extant species. *Hereditas* 114:263–69.

Arnason, U. and R. Gullberg. 1993. Comparison between the complete mtDNA sequences of blue and fin whales: Two species that hybridize in nature. *Molecular Evolution* 37:312–22.

Arnason, U., R. Spilliaert, A. Palsdottir, and A. Arnason. 1991. Molecular identification of hybrids between the two largest whale species, the blue whale (*Balaenoptera musculus*) and the fin whale (*B. physalus*). *Hereditas* 115:183–89.

Arnaud, J., B. Meier, J. M. Dugoujon, and Y. Rumpler. 1992. Study of the variability of erythrocyte enzymes in captive and wild populations of the black lemur (*Eulemur macaco macaco*): An indispensable preliminary in captive breeding programmes. *Primates* 33:139–46.

Arnheim, N., T. White, and W. E. Rainey. 1990. Application of PCR: Organismal and population biology. *BioScience* 40:174–82.

Ashley, M. V. and C. Wills. 1989. Mitochondrial-DNA and allozyme divergence patterns are correlated among island deer mice. *Evolution* 43:646–50.

Ashley, M. V., D. J. Melnick, and D. Western. 1990. Conservation genetics of the black rhinoceros (*Diceros bicornis*), I: Evidence from the mitochondrial DNA of three populations. *Conservation Biology* 4:71–77.

Ashworth, D. and D. T. Parkin. 1992. Captive breeding: Can genetic fingerprinting help? In H. D. M. Moore, W. V. Holt, and G. M. Mace, eds., *Biotechnology and the Conservation of Genetic Diversity. Zoological Society of London Symposium 64*, pp. 135–50. London, England: Oxford Scientific.

Avise, J. C. 1986. Mitochondrial DNA and the evolutionary genetics of higher animals. *Proceedings Royal Society London* B312:325–42.

Avise, J. C. 1989a. Gene trees and organismal histories: A phylogenetic approach to population biology. *Evolution* 43:1192–1208.

Avise, J. C. 1989b. A role for molecular genetics in the recognition and conservation of endangered species. *Trends in Ecology and Evolution* 4:279–81.

Avise, J. C. 1994. *Molecular Markers, Natural History, and Evolution.* New York: Chapman and Hall.

Avise, J. C. and C. F. Aquadro. 1982. A comparative summary of genetic distances in the vertebrates. *Evolutionary Biology* 15:151–85.

Avise, J. C. and R. M. Ball, Jr. 1990. Principles of genealogical concordance in species' concepts and taxonomy. *Oxford Surveys in Evolutionary Biology* 7:45–67.

Avise, J. C. and W. S. Nelson. 1989. Molecular genetic relationships of the extinct Dusky seaside sparrow. *Science* 243:646–48.

Avise, J. C. and D. Y. Shapiro. 1986. Evaluating kinship of newly settled juveniles within social groups of the coral reef fish, *Anthias squamipinnis. Evolution* 40:1051–59.

Avise, J. C. and R. C. Vrijenhoek. 1987. Mode of inheritance and variation of mitochondrial DNA in hybridogenetic fishes of the genus *Poeciliopsis*. *Molecular Biology and Evolution* 4:514–25.

Avise, J. C., R. T. Alisauskas, W. S. Nelson, and C. D. Ankney. 1992. Matriarchical population genetic structure in an avian species with female natal philopatry. *Evolution* 46:1084–96.

Avise, J. C., C. D. Ankney, and W. S. Nelson. 1990. Mitochondrial gene trees and the evolutionary relationship of mallard and black ducks. *Evolution* 44:1109–19.

Avise, J. C., J. Arnold, R. M. Ball, Jr., E. Bermingham, T. Lamb, J. E. Neigel, C. A. Reeb, and N. C. Saunders. 1987. Intraspecific phylogeography: The mitochondrial DNA bridge between population genetics and systematics. *Annual Review of Ecology and Systematics* 18:489–522.

Avise, J. C., B. W. Bowen, and T. Lamb. 1989. DNA fingerprints from hypervariable mitochondrial genotypes. *Molecular Biology and Evolution* 6:258–69.

Avise, J. C., G. S. Helfman, N. C. Saunders, and L. S. Hales. 1986. Mitochondrial DNA differentiation in north Atlantic eels: Population genetic consequences of an unusual life history pattern. *Proceeding of the National Academy of Sciences* 83:4350–54.

Baker, A. J. 1992. Genetic and morphometric divergence in ancestral European and descendent New Zealand populations of chaffinches (*Fringella coelebs*). *Evolution* 46:1784–1800.

Baker, A. J., M. D. Dennison, A. Lynch, and G. Le Grand. 1990a. Genetic divergence in peripherally isolated populations of chaffinches in the Atlantic islands. *Evolution* 44:981–99.

Baker, C. S., D. A. Gilbert, M. T. Weinrich, R. Lambertsen, J. Calambokidis, B. McArdle, G. K. Chambers, and S. K. O'Brien. 1993. Population characteristics of DNA fingerprints in humback whales (*Megaptera novaeangliae*). *Journal of Heredity* 84:281–90.

Baker, C. S., S. R. Palumbi, R. H. Lambertsen, M. T. Weinrich, J. Calambokidis, and S. J. O'Brien. 1990b. Influence of seasonal migration on geographic distribution of mitochondrial DNA haplotypes in humpback whales. *Nature* 344:238–40.

Barrowclough, G. F. and R. J. Gutierrez. 1990. Genetic variation and differentiation in the spotted owl (*Strix occidentalis*). *Auk* 107:737–44.

Baur, B. and M. Klemm. 1989. Absence of isozyme variation in geographically isolated populations of the land snail *Chondrina clienta*. *Heredity* 63:239–44.

Beacham, T. D., C. B. Murray, and R. E. Withler. 1989. Age, morphology, and biochemical genetic variation of Yukon River chinook salmon. *Transactions of the American Fisheries Society* 118:46–63.

Benirschke, K. and A. T. Kumamoto. 1991. Mammalian cytogenetics and conservation of species. *Journal of Heredity* 82:187–91.

Benirschke, K., A. T. Kumamoto, J. H. Olsen, M. M. Williams, and J. E. Oosterhuis. 1984. On the chromosomes of *Gazella sommerringi Cretschmar*, 1826. *Z. Säugetierk.* 49:368–73.

Bernatchez, L. and J. J. Dodson. 1990. Allopatric origin of sympatric populations of lake whitefish (*Coregonus clupeaformis*) as revealed by mitochondrial DNA restriction analysis. *Evolution* 44:1263–71.

Billington, N. and P. D. Hebert. 1988. Mitochondrial DNA variation in Great Lakes walleye (*Stizostedion vitreum*) populations. *Canadian Journal of Fisheries and Aquatic Sciences* 45:643–54.

Birkhead, T. R. and A. P. Moller. 1992. *Sperm Competition in Birds: Causes and Consequences.* London: Academic Press.

Birkhead, T. R., T. Burke, R. Zann, F. M. Hunter, and A. P. Krupa. 1990. Extra-pair paternity and intraspecific brood parasitism in wild zebra finches (*Taeniopygia guttata*) revealed by DNA fingerprinting. *Behavioral Ecology and Sociobiology* 27:315–24.

Birt, T. P., J. M. Green, and W. S. Davidson. 1986. Analysis of mitochondrial DNA in allopatric anadromous and nonanadromous Atlantic salmon, *Salmo salar. Canadian Journal of Zoology* 64:118–19.

Birt-Friesen, V. L., W. A. Montevecchi, A. J. Gaston, and W. S. Davidson. 1992. Genetic structure of thick-billed murre (*Uria Lomvia*) populations examined using direct sequence analysis of amplified DNA. *Evolution* 46:267–72.

Bischof, L. L. 1992. Genetics and elephant conservation. *Endangered Species Update* 9 (7 & 8): 1–4.

Bishop, C. E., P. Boursot, B. Baron, F. Bonhomme, and D. Hatat. 1985. Most classical *Mus musculus domesticus* laboratory mouse strains carry a *Mus musculus musculus* Y chromosome. *Nature* 315:70–72.

Blanchetot, A. 1991. Genetic relatedness in honeybees as established by DNA fingerprinting. *Journal of Heredity* 82:391–96.

Bonnell, M. L. and R. K. Selander. 1974. Elephant seals: Genetic variation and near extinction. *Science* 184:908–9.

Borsa, P., M. Zainuri, and B. Delay. 1991. Heterozygote deficiency and population structure in the bivalve *Ruditapes decussatus. Heredity* 66:1–8.

Bowditch, B. M., D. G. Albright, J. G. K. Williams, and M. J. Braun. 1993. Use of randomly amplified polymorphic DNA markers in comparative genome studies. *Methods in Enzymology* 224:294–309.

Bowen, B. W., A. B. Meylan, and J. C. Avise. 1991. Evolutionary distinctiveness of the endangered Kemp's Ridley sea turtle. *Nature* 352:709–11.

Bowen, B. W., A. B. Meylan, J. P. Ross, C. J. Limpus, G. H. Balasz, and J. C. Avise. 1992. Global population structure and natural history of the green turtle (*Chelonia mydas*) in terms of matriarchal phylogeny. *Evolution* 46:865–81.

Bowling, A. T. and R. W. Touchberry. 1990. Parentage of Great Basin feral horses. *Journal of Wildlife Management* 54:424–29.

Braend, M. and C. Stormont. 1963. Haemoglobin and transferrin types in the American buffalo. *Nature* 197:910–11.

Breen, M. and J. J. B. Gill. 1991. The chromosomes of two horse x zebra hybrids: *E. caballus* x *E. grevyi* and *E. burchelli. Hereditas* 115:169–75.

Brock, M. K. and B. N. White. 1991. Multifragment alleles in DNA fingerprints of the parrot, *Amazona ventralis. Journal of Heredity* 82:209–12.

Brower, A. V. Z. and T. M. Boyce. 1991. Mitochondrial DNA variation in monarch butterflies. *Evolution* 45:1281–86.

Brown, W. M. 1980. Polymorphism in mitochondrial DNA of humans as revealed by restriction endonuclease analysis. *Proceedings of the National Academy of Sciences USA* 77:3605–9.

Brown, W. M. 1985. The mitochondrial genome of animals. In R. J. MacIntyre, ed., *Molecular Evolutionary Genetics,* pp. 95–130. New York: Plenum Press.

Brown, B. L. and R. W. Chapman. 1991. Gene flow and mitochondrial DNA variation in the killifish, *Fundulus heteroclitus. Evolution* 45:1147–61.

Burke, T. 1989. DNA fingerprinting and other methods for the study of mating success. *Trends in Ecology and Evolution* 4:139–44.

Burke, T. and M. W. Bruford. 1987. DNA fingerprinting in birds. *Nature* 327:149–52.

Burke, T., N. B. Davies, M. W. Bruford, and B. J. Hatchwell. 1989. Parental care and mating behaviour of polyandrous dunnocks *Prunella modularis* related to paternity by DNA fingerprinting. *Nature* 338:249–51.

Burke, T., O. Hanotte, M. W. Bruford, and E. Cairns. 1991. Multilocus and single locus minisatellite analysis in population biological studies. In T. Burke, G. Dolf, A. J. Jeffreys, and R. Wolff, eds., *DNA Fingerprinting: Approaches and Applications,* pp. 154–68. Basel: Birkhauser Verlag.

Burns, K. J. and R. M. Zink. 1990. Temporal and geographic homogeneity of gene frequencies in the fox sparrow (*Passerella iliaca*). *Auk* 107:421–25.

Burson, S. L., III. 1990. Population genetics and gene flow of the common tern. *Condor* 92:182–92.

Carlson, D. M., M. K. Kettler, S. E. Fisher, and G. S. Whitt. 1982. Low genetic variability in paddlefish populations. *Copeia* 1982:721–25.

Carr, A. F. 1975. The Ascension Island green turtle colony. *Copeia* 1975:547–55.

Casanova, J. L., L. Pannetier, C. Javlin, and P. Kourilsky. 1990. Optimal conditions for directly sequencing double-stranded PCR products with sequenase. *Nucleic Acids Research* 18:4028.

Chakraborty, R., M. Fornage, R. Gueguen, and E. Boerwinkle. 1991. Population genetics of hypervariable loci analysis of PCR based VNTR polymorphism within a population. In T. Burke, G. Dolf, A. J. Jeffreys, and R. Wolff, eds., *DNA Fingerprinting: Approaches and Applications,* pp. 127–43. Basel: Birkhauser Verlag.

Chakraborty, R., M. Shaw, and W. J. Schull. 1974. Exclusion of paternity: The current state of the art. *American Journal of Human Genetics* 26:477–88.

Champion, A. B., E. M. Prager, D. Wachter, and A. C. Wilson. 1974. Microcomplement fixation. In C. A. Wright, ed., *Biochemical and Immunological Taxonomy of Animals,* pp. 397–416. London: Academic Press.

Chapman, R. W. 1990. Mitochondrial DNA analysis of striped bass populations in Chesapeake Bay. *Copeia* 2:355–66.

Christidis, L., D. D. Shaw, and R. Schodde. 1991. Chromosomal evolution in parrots, lorikeets, and cockatoos (Aves:Psittaciformes). *Hereditas* 114:47–56.

Collier, G. J. and S. J. O'Brien. 1985. A molecular phylogeny of the Felidae: Immunologic distance. *Evolution* 39:473–87.

Cooke, F., D. T. Parkin, and R. F. Rockwell. 1988. Evidence of former allopatry of the two color phases of lesser snow geese (*Chen caerulescens caerulescens*). *Auk* 105:467–79.

Corbet, S. W. and T. J. Robinson. 1991. Genetic divergence in South African wildebeest: Comparative cytogenetics and analysis of mitochondrial DNA. *Journal of Heredity* 82:447–52.

Cram, L. S., M. F. Bartholdi, F. A. Ray, G. L. Travis, and P. M. Kraemer. 1983. Spontaneous neoplastic evolution of Chinese hamster cells in culture: Multistep progression of karyotype. *Cancer Research* 43:4828–37.

Cronin, M. A. 1992. Intraspecific variation in mitochondrial DNA of North American cervids. *Journal of Mammalogy* 73:70–82.

Cronin, M. A., D. A. Palmisciano, E. R. Vyse, and D. G. Cameron. 1991. Mitochondrial DNA in wildlife forensic science: Species identification of tissues. *Wildlife Society Bulletin* 19:94–105.

Daley, J. G. 1992. Population reductions and genetic variability in black-tailed prairie dogs. *Journal of Wildlife Management* 56:212–20.

Decker, M. D., P. G. Parker, D. J. Minchella, and K. N. Rabenold. 1993. Monogamy in black vultures: Genetic evidence from DNA fingerprinting. *Behavioral Ecology* 4:29–35.

Demarais, B. D., T. E. Dowling, and W. L. Minckley. 1993. Post-perturbation genetic changes in a population of endangered Virginia chubs. *Conservation Biology* 7:334–41.

Dinerstein, E. and G. F. McCracken. 1990. Endangered greater one-horned rhinoceros carry high levels of genetic variation. *Conservation Biology* 4:417–22.

Disotell, T. R., R. L. Honeycutt, and M. Ruvolo. 1992. Mitochondrial DNA phylogeny of the Old-World monkey tribe Papionini. *Molecular Biology and Evolution* 9:1–13.

Dittmann, D. L. and R. M. Zink. 1991. Mitochondrial DNA variation among Phalaropes and allies. *Auk* 108:771–79.

Dodd, B. E. 1985. DNA fingerprinting in matters of family and crime. *Nature* 318:506–7.

Dowler, R. C. 1989. Cytogenetic studies of three chromosomal races of pocket gophers (*Geomys bursarius complex*) at hybrid zones. *Journal of Mammalogy* 70:253–66.

Drysdale, T. A. and R. F. Florkiewicz. 1989. Electrophoretic variation within and between the two extant elephant species (Mammalia:Proboscidea). *Journal of Mammalogy* 70:381–83.

Easteal, S. 1991. The relative rate of DNA evolution in primates. *Molecular Biology and Evolution* 8:115–27.

Echelle, A. A. and T. E. Dowling. 1992. Mitochondrial DNA variation and evolution of the Death Valley pupfishes (*Cyprinodon,* Cyprinodontidae). *Evolution* 46:193–206.

Echelle, A. F., A. A. Echelle, and D. R. Edds. 1989. Conservation genetics of a spring-dwelling desert fish, the Pecos gambusia (*Gambusia nobilis,* Poeciliidae). *Conservation Biology* 3:159–69.

Ely, J. and R. E. Ferrell. 1990. DNA "Fingerprints" and paternity ascertainment in chimpanzees (*Pan troglodytes*). *Zoo Biology* 9:91–98.

Emlen, S. T. and P. H. Wrege. 1992. Parent-offspring conflict and the recruitment of helpers among bee-eaters. *Nature* 356:331–33.

Evarts, S. and C. J. Williams. 1987. Multiple paternity in a wild population of mallards. *Auk* 104:597–602.

Everitt, J., J. L. Hurst, D. Ashworth, and C. J. Barnard. 1991. Aggressive behavior among wild-caught house mice, *Mus domesticus Rutty,* correlates with a measure of genetic similarity using DNA fingerprinting. *Animal Behaviour* 42:313–16.

Fajen, A. and F. Breden. 1992. Mitochondrial DNA sequence variation among natural populations of the Trinidad Guppy. *Evolution* 46:1457–65.

Faulkes, C. G., D. H. Abbott, and A. L. Mellor. 1990. Investigation of genetic diversity in wild colonies of naked mole-rats (*Heterocephalus glaber*) by DNA fingerprinting. *Journal of Zoology, London* 221:87–97.

Felsenstein, J. 1993. *PHYLIP:* Phylogeny Inference Package. Seattle, Wa.: University of Washington.

Ferguson, A. 1980. *Biochemical Systematics and Evolution.* New York: Wiley.

Fevolden, S. E. and D. O. Hessen. 1989. Morphological and genetic differences among recently founded populations of noble crayfish (*Astacus astacus*). *Hereditas* 110:149–58.

Fleischer, R. C., S. Conant, and M. P. Morin. 1991a. Genetic variation in native and translocated populations of the Laysan finch (*Telespiza cantans*). *Heredity* 66:125–30.

Fleischer, R. C., S. I. Rothstein, and L. S. Miller. 1991b. Mitochondrial DNA variation indicates gene flow across a zone of known secondary contact between two subspecies of the brown-headed cowbird. *Condor* 93:185–89.

Fleischer, R. C., R. N. Williams, and A. J. Baker. 1991c. Genetic variation within and among populations of the common myna (*Acridotheres tristis*) in Hawaii. *Journal of Heredity* 82:205–8.

Foltz, D. W. 1981. Genetic evidence for long-term monogamy in a small rodent, *Peromyscus polionotus. American Naturalist* 117:665–75.

Foltz, D. W. and J. L. Hoogland. 1981. Analysis of the mating system in the black-tailed prairie dog (*Cynomys ludovicianus*) by the likelihood of paternity. *Journal of Mammalogy* 62:706–12.

Gahne, G., R. K. Juneja, and J. Grolmus. 1977. Horizontal polyacrylamide gel electrophoresis for the simultaneous phenotyping of transferrin, post transferrin, albumin, and post albumin in the blood plasma of cattle. *Animal Blood Groups, Biochemistry, and Genetics* 8:127–37.

Gallardo, M. H. 1992. Karyotypic evolution in octodontid rodents based on C-Band analysis. *Journal of Mammalogy* 73:89–98.

Garner, K. J. and O. A. Ryder. 1992. Some applications of PCR to studies in wildlife genetics. *Symposium of the Zoological Society of London* 64:167–81.

Gelter, H. P. and H. Tegelstrom. 1992. High frequency of extra-pair paternity in Swedish pied flycatchers revealed by allozyme electrophoresis and DNA fingerprinting. *Behavioral Ecology and Sociobiology* 30:1–7.

Gelter, H. P., H. Tegelstrom, and L. Gustafsson. 1992. Evidence from hatching success and DNA fingerprinting for the fertility of hybrid pied x collared flycatchers *Ficedula hypoleuca x albicollis. Ibis* 134:62–68.

Gelter, H. P., H. Tegelstrom, and G. Stahl. 1989. Allozyme similarity between the pied and collared flycatchers (Aves:*Ficedula hypoleuca* and *F. albicollis*). *Hereditas* 111:65–72.

Geyer, C. J. and E. A. Thompson. 1992. Constrained Monte Carlo maximum likelihood for dependent data. *Journal of the Royal Statistical Society* B54:657–99.

Geyer, C. J., O. A. Ryder, L. G. Chemnick, and E. A. Thompson. 1993. Analysis of relatedness in the California condors from DNA fingerprints. *Molecular Biology and Evolution* 10:571–89.

Gibbs, H. L., P. J. Weatherhead, P. T. Boag, B. N. White, L. M. Tabak, and D. J. Hoysak. 1990. Realized reproductive success of polygynous red-winged blackbirds revealed by DNA markers. *Science* 250:1394–97.

Gilbert, D. A., N. Lehman, S. J. O'Brien, and R. K. Wayne. 1990. Genetic fingerprinting reflects population differentiation in the California Channel Island fox. *Nature* 344:764–66.

Gilbert, D. A., C. Packer, A. E. Pusey, J. C. Stephens, and S. J. O'Brien. 1991. Analytical DNA fingerprinting in lions: Parentage, genetic diversity, and kinship. *Journal of Heredity* 82:378–86.

Gill, F. B., A. M. Mostrom, and A. L. Mack. 1993. Speciation in North American Chickadees, I: Patterns of mtDNA genetic divergence. *Evolution* 47:195–212.

Gill, P. S., J. Blangero, G. S. Manis, J. Scheffler, M. E. Keeling, and W. H. Stone. 1992. Genetic structure of three populations of rhesus macaques (*Macaca mulatta*): Implications for genetic management. *American Journal of Primatology* 27:85–92.

Gill, P., A. J. Jeffreys, and D. J. Werrett. 1985. Forensic application of DNA "fingerprints." *Nature* 318:577–79.

Gilpin, M. and C. Wills. 1991. MHC and captive breeding: A rebuttal. *Conservation Biology* 5:554–55.

Gowaty, P. A. and A. A. Karlin. 1984. Multiple maternity and paternity in single broods of apparently monogamous Eastern bluebirds (*Sialia sialis*). *Behavioral Ecology and Sociobiology* 15:91–95.

Green, A., A. Roopra, and M. Vaudin. 1990. Direct single-stranded sequencing from agarose of PCR products. *Nucleic Acids Research* 18:61–63.

Grudzien, T. A., W. S. Moore, J. R. Cook, and D. Tagle. 1987. Genic population structure and gene flow in the Northern flicker (*Colaptes auratus*) hybrid zone. *Auk* 104:654–64.

Gyllensten, U. B., S. Jakobsson, and H. Temrin. 1990. No evidence for illegitimate young in monogamous and polygynous warblers. *Nature* 343:168–70.

Hadrys, H., M. Balick, and B. Schierwater. 1992. Applications of random amplified polymorphic DNA (RAPD) in molecular ecology. *Molecular Ecology* 1:55–63.

Hadrys, H., B. Schierwater, S. L. Dellaporta, R. DeSalle, and L. W. Buss. 1993. Determination of paternity in dragonflies by random amplified polymorphic DNA fingerprinting. *Molecular Ecology* 2:79–87.

Haig, S. M. and L. H. Nordstrom. 1991. Genetic management of small populations. In D. J. Decker, M. E. Krasny, G. R. Goff, C. R. Smith, and D. W. Gross, eds., *Challenges in the Conservation of Biological Resources*, pp. 119–38. Boulder: Westview Press.

Haig, S. M. and L. W. Oring. 1988. Genetic differentiation of piping plovers across North America. *Auk* 105:260–67.

Haig, S. M., J. D. Ballou, and N. J. Casna. 1994a. Identification of kin structure among Guam rail founders using DNA profiles. *Molecular Ecology* 3:109–19.

Haig, S. M., J. D. Ballou, and S. R. Derrickson. 1990. Management options for preserving genetic diversity: Reintroduction of Guam rails to the wild. *Conservation Biology* 4:290–300, 464.

Haig, S. M., J. R. Belthoff, and D. H. Allen. 1993a. Examination of population structure in red-cockaded woodpeckers using DNA profiles. *Evolution* 47:185–94.

Haig, S. M., J. R. Belthoff, and D. H. Allen. 1993b. Population viability analysis for a small population of red-cockaded woodpeckers and an evaluation of population enhancement strategies. *Conservation Biology* 7:289–301.

Haig, S. M., J. M. Rhymer, and D. G. Heckel. In press. Population differentiation in red-cockaded woodpeckers using random amplified polymorphic DNA. *Molecular Ecology.*

Haig, S. M., J. R. Walters, and J. H. Plissner. 1994b. Genetic evidence for monogamy in the cooperatively breeding red-cockaded woodpecker. *Behavioral Ecology and Sociobiology* 34:295–303.

Hamilton, M. J. and M. L. Kennedy. 1986. Genic variation in the coyote, *Canis latrans* in Tennessee, U.S.A. *Genetica* 71:167–73.

Hamrick, K. J. and J. L. Hamrick. 1989. Genetic variation within and among populations of an alpine grasshopper, *Aeropedellus clavatus. Journal of Heredity* 80:186–92.

Hanken, J. and P. Sherman. 1981. Multiple paternity in Belding's ground squirrel litters. *Science* 212:351–53.

Hanotte, O., T. Burke, J. A. L. Armour, and A. J. Jeffreys. 1991a. Cloning, characterization, and evolution of Indian Peafowl *Pavo cristatus* minisatellite loci. In T. Burke, G. Dolf, A. J. Jeffreys, and R. Wolff, eds., *DNA Fingerprinting: Approaches and Applications,* pp. 193–216. Basel: Birkhauser Verlag.

Hanotte, O., T. Burke, J. A. L. Armour, and A. J. Jeffreys. 1991b. Hypervariable minisatellite DNA sequences in Indian peafowl *Pavo cristatus. Genomics* 9:587–97.

Hartl, G. B., G. Lang, F. Klein, and R. Willing. 1991. Relationships between allozymes, heterozygosity, and morphological characters in red deer (*Cervus elaphus*), and the influence of selective hunting on allele frequency distributions. *Heredity* 66:343–50.

Hatfield, T., N. Barton, and J. B. Searle. 1992. A model of a hybrid zone between two chromosomal races of the common shrew (*Sorex araneus*). *Evolution* 46:1129–45.

Hayasaka, K., T. Ishida, and S. Horai. 1991. Heteroplasmy and polymorphism in the major noncoding region of mitochondrial DNA in Japanese monkeys: Association with tandemly repeated sequences. *Molecular Biology and Evolution* 8:399–415.

Hedges, S. B., J. P. Bogart, and L. R. Maxson. 1992. Ancestry of unisexual salamanders. *Nature* 356:708–10.

Hedrick, P. 1992. Shooting the RAPDs. *Nature* 355:679–80.

Henke, J., L. Henke, and S. Cleef. 1990. Segregation of single-locus DNA fragments in a large family. In H. F. Polesky and W. R. Mayr, eds., *Advances in Forensic Haemogenetics,* pp. 75–76. Berlin: Springer.

Henke, L., S. Clef, M. Zakrzewska, and J. Henke. 1991. Population genetic data determined for five different single locus minisatellite probes. In T. Burke, G. Dolf, A. J. Jeffreys, and R. Wolff, eds., *DNA Fingerprinting: Approaches and Applications,* pp. 144–53. Basel: Birkhauser Verlag.

Herzog, S., C. Mushovel, H. H. Hattemer, and A. Herzog. 1991. Transferrin polymorphism and genetic differentiation in *Cervus elaphus* L. (European red deer) populations. *Heredity* 67:231–39.

Hill, W. G. 1987. DNA fingerprints applied to animal and bird populations. *Nature* 327:98–99.

Hoagland, D. B., N. Tilakaratne, R. F. Weaver, and M. S. Gaines. 1991. "DNA fingerprinting" of prairie voles (*Microtus ochrogaster*). *Journal of Mammalogy* 72:422–26.

Hoelzel, A. R. and W. Amos. 1988. DNA fingerprinting and "scientific" whaling. *Nature* 333:305.

Hoelzel, A. R. and G. A. Dover. 1991. Genetic differentiation between sympatric killer whale populations. *Heredity* 66:191–95.

Hoelzel, A. R. and A. Green. 1992. Analysis of population level variation by sequencing PCR-amplified DNA. In A. R. Hoelzel, ed., *Molecular Genetic Analysis of Populations: A Practical Approach,* pp. 159–87. Oxford: Oxford University Press.

Hood, C. S., L. W. Robbins, R. J. Baker, and H. S. Shellhammer. 1984. Chromosomal studies and evolutionary relationships of an endangered species, *Reithrodontomys raviventris*. *Journal of Mammalogy* 65:655–67.

Hsu, T. C. and K. Benirschke. 1967–1977. *Mammalian Chromosomal Atlas.* Volumes 1–10. New York: Springer-Verlag.

Hubby, J. L. and R. C. Lewontin. 1966. A molecular approach to the study of genic heterozygosity in natural populations, I: The number of alleles at different loci in *Drosophila pseudoobscura*. *Genetics* 54:577–94.

Hughes, A. L. 1991. MHC polymorphism and the design of captive breeding programs. *Conservation Biology* 5:249–51.

Hunter, F. M., T. Burke, and S. E. Watts. 1992. Frequent copulation as a method of paternity assurance in the northern fulmar. *Animal Behavior* 44:149–56.

Hutchins, M. and R. J. Wiese. 1991. Beyond genetic and demographic management: The future of the species survival Plan and related AAZPA conservation efforts. *Zoo Biology* 10:285–92.

Inoue, M., F. Mitsunaga, H. Ohsawa, A. Takenaka, Y. Sugiyama, S. Gaspard, and O. Takenaka. 1991. Male mating behaviour and paternity discrimination by DNA fingerprinting in a Japanese macaque group. *Folia Primatologia* 56:202–10.

Janczewski, D. N., D. Goldman, and S. J. O'Brien. 1990. Molecular genetic divergence of orangutan (*Pongo pygmaeus*) subspecies based on isozyme and two-dimensional gel electrophoresis. *Journal of Heredity* 81:375–87.

Jarman, A. P. and R. A. Wells. 1989. Hypervariable minisatellites: Recombinators or innocent bystanders. *Trends in Genetics* 5:367–71.

Jarne, P., B. Delay, C. Bellec, G. Roizes, and G. Cuny. 1992. Analysis of mating systems in the schistosome-vector hermaphrodite snail *Bulinus globosus* by DNA fingerprinting. *Heredity* 68:141–46.

Jeffreys, A. J. and D. B. Morton. 1987. DNA fingerprints of dogs and cats. *Animal Genetics* 18:1–15.

Jeffreys, A. J., J. F. Y. Brookfield, and R. Semeonoff. 1985c. Positive identification of an immigration test-case using human DNA fingerprints. *Nature* 317:818–19.

Jeffreys, A. J., N. J. Royle, I. Patel, J. A. L. Armour, A. MacLeod, A. Collick, I. C. Gray, R. Neumann, M. Gibbs, M. Crosier, M. Hill, E. Signer, and D. Moncton. 1991. Principles and recent advances in human DNA fingerprinting. In T. Burke, G. Dolf, A. J.

Jeffreys, and R. Wolff, eds., *DNA Fingerprinting: Approaches and Applications*, pp. 1–20. Basel: Birkhauser Verlag.

Jeffreys, A. J., V. Wilson, R. Kelly, B. A Taylor, and G. Bulfield. 1987. Mouse DNA "fingerprints": Analysis of chromosome localization and germ-line stability of hypervariable loci in recombinant inbred strains. *Nucleic Acids Research* 15:2823–36.

Jeffreys, A. J., V. Wilson, and S. L. Thein. 1985a. Hypervariable "minisatellite" regions in human DNA. *Nature* 314:67–73.

Jeffreys, A. J., V. Wilson, and S. L. Thein. 1985b. Individual-specific "fingerprints" of human DNA. *Nature* 316:76–79.

Johnson, M. S. and R. Black. 1991. Genetic subdivision of the intertidal snail *Bembicium vittatum* (Gastropoda:Littorinidae) varies with habitat in the Houtman Abrolhos Islands, Western Australia. *Heredity* 67:205–13.

Johnson, N. K., J. A. Marten, and C. J. Ralph. 1988. Genetic evidence for the origin and relationships of Hawaiian honeycreepers (Aves:Fringillidae). *Condor* 91:379–96.

Jones, C. S., C. M. Lessells, and J. R. Krebs. 1991. Helpers-at-the-nest in European bee-eaters (*Meriops apiaster*): A genetic analysis. In T. Burke, G. Dolf, A. J. Jeffreys, and R. Wolff, eds., *DNA fingerprinting: Approaches and Applications*, pp. 169–92. Basel: Birkhauser Verlag.

Joste, N., J. D. Ligon, and P. B. Stacey. 1985. Shared paternity in the acorn woodpecker (*Melanerpes formicivorus*). *Behavioral Ecology and Sociobiology* 17:39–41.

Karakousis, Y. and C. Triantaphyllidis. 1990. Genetic structure and differentiation among Greek brown trout (*Salmo trutta L.*) populations. *Heredity* 64:297–304.

Karl, S. A. and J. C. Avise. 1992. Balancing selection at allozyme loci in oysters: Implications from nuclear RFLPs. *Science* 256:100–2.

Karl, S. A., B. W. Bowen, and J. C. Avise. 1992. Global population structure and male-mediated gene flow in the green turtle (*Chelonia mydas*): RFLP analyses of anonymous nuclear loci. *Genetics* 131:163–73.

Karlin, A. A., K. G. Smith, M. C. Stephens, and R. A. Barnhill. 1990. Additional evidence of multiple parentage in Eastern bluebirds. *Condor* 92:520–21.

Keane, B., P. M. Waser, L. Danzl-Tauer, and D. J. Minchella. 1991. DNA fingerprinting: Estimating background band-sharing in banner-tailed kangaroo rats. *Animal Behavior* 42:141–43.

Kempenaers, B., G. R. Verheyen, M. Van den Broeck, T. Burke, C. Van Broeckhoven, and A. A. Dhondt. 1992. Extra-pair paternity results from female preference for high quality males in the blue tit. *Nature* 357:494–96.

Kirsch, J. A. W., R. J. Ganje, K. G. Olesen, D. W. Hoffman, and A. H. Bledsoe. 1990. TED: An improved thermal elution device for the simultaneous hydroxyapatite chromatography of solution DNA/DNA hybrids. *BioTechniques* 8:505–6.

Kocher, T. D., W. K. Thomas, A. Meyer, S. V. Edwards, S. Paabo, F. X. Villablanca, and A. C. Wilson. 1989. Dynamics of mitochondrial DNA evolution in animals: Amplification and sequencing with conserved primers. *Proceedings of the National Academy of Sciences USA* 86:6196–6200.

Kochert, G. 1989. *Introduction to RFLP Mapping and Plant Breeding Applications*. Special publication. New York: Rockefeller Foundation.

Kohne, D. E. and R. J. Britten. 1971. Hydroxyapatite techniques for nucleic acid reassociation. In G. L. Cantoni and D. R. Davies, eds., *Procedures in Nucleic Acid Research,* vol. 2, pp. 500–12. New York: Harper and Row.

Krajewski, C. 1990. Relative rates of single-copy DNA evolution in cranes. *Molecular Biology and Evolution* 7:65–73.

Krueger, C. C. 1980. Detection of variability at isozyme loci in sea lamprey *Petromyzon marinus. Canadian Journal of Fisheries and Aquatic Sciences* 37:1630–34.

Laerm, J., J. C. Avise, J. C. Patton, and R. A. Lansman. 1982. Genetic determination of the status of an endangered species of pocket gopher in Georgia. *Journal of Wildlife Management* 46:513–18.

Lamb, T., J. C. Avise, and J. W. Gibbons. 1989. Phylogeographic patterns in mitochondrial DNA of the Desert Tortoise (*Xerobates agassizi*) and evolutionary relationships among the North American gopher tortoises. *Evolution* 43:76–87.

Lamborot, M. 1991. Karyotypic variation among populations of *Liolaemus monticola* (Tropiduridae) separated by riverine barriers in the Andean range. *Copeia* 4:1044–59.

Lander, E. S. 1989. DNA fingerprinting on trial. *Nature* 339:501–5.

Lansman, R. A., R. O. Shade, J. F. Shapira, and J. C. Avise. 1981. The use of restriction endonucleases to measure mitochondrial DNA sequence relatedness in natural populations, III: Techniques and potential applications. *Journal of Molecular Evolution* 17:214–26.

Lanyon, S. M. and R. M. Zink. 1987. Genetic variation in piciform birds: Monophyly and generic and familial relationships. *Auk* 104:724–32.

Leberg, P. L. 1992. Effects of population bottlenecks on genetic diversity as measured by allozyme electrophoresis. *Evolution* 46:477–95.

Lee, T. E., Jr., J. N. Derr, J. W. Bickham, and T. L. Clark. 1989. Genetic variation in pronghorn from west Texas. *Journal of Wildlife Management* 53:890–96.

Lehman, N., A. Eisenhawer, K. Hansen, L. D. Mech, R. O. Peterson, P. J. P. Gogan, and R. K. Wayne. 1991. Introgression of coyote mitochondrial DNA into sympatric North American gray wolf populations. *Evolution* 45:104–19.

Lesica, P., R. F. Leary, F. W. Allendorf, and D. E. Bilderback. 1988. Lack of genic diversity within and among populations of an endangered plant, *Howellia aquatilis. Conservation Biology* 2:275–82.

Lifjeld, J. T., P. O. Dunn, R. J. Robertson, and P. T. Boag. 1993. Extra-pair paternity in monogamous tree swallows. *Animal Behavior* 45:213–29.

Longmire, J. L., R. E. Ambrose, N. C. Brown, T. J. Cade, T. L. Maechtle, S. W. Seegar, F. P. Ward, and C. M. White. 1991. Use of sex-linked minisatellite fragments to investigate genetic differentiation and migration of North American populations of the peregrine falcon (*Falco peregrinus*). In T. Burke, G. Dolf, A. J. Jeffreys, and R. Wolff, eds., *DNA Fingerprinting: Approaches and Applications,* pp. 217–29. Basel: Birkhauser Verlag.

Longmire, J. L., M. Maltbie, R. W. Pavelka, L. M. Smith, S. M. Witte, O. A. Ryder, D. L. Ellsworth, and R. J. Baker. 1993. Gender identification in birds using microsatellite DNA fingerprint analysis. *Auk* 110:378–81.

Love, J. and P. Deininger. 1992. Characterization and phylogenetic significance of a repetitive DNA sequence from whooping cranes (*Grus americana*). *Auk* 109:73–79.

Lozano, R., C. R. Rejon, and M. R. Rejon. 1991. An analysis of Coho salmon chromatin by means of C-banding, AG and fluorochrome staining, and *in situ* digestion with restriction endonucleases. *Heredity* 66:403–9.

Lynch, M. 1988. Estimation of relatedness by DNA fingerprinting. *Molecular Biology and Evolution* 5:584–99.

Lynch, M. 1990. The similarity index and DNA fingerprinting. *Molecular Biology and Evolution* 7:478–84.

Lynch, M. 1991. Analysis of population structure by DNA fingerprinting. In T. Burke, G. Dolf, A. J. Jeffreys, and R. Wolff, eds., *DNA Fingerprinting: Approaches and Applications*, pp. 113–26. Basel: Birkhauser Verlag.

MacNeil, D. and C. Strobeck. 1987. Evolutionary relationships among colonies of Columbian ground squirrels as shown by mitochondrial DNA. *Evolution* 41:873–81.

Madsen, C. S., K. P. McHugh, and S. R. De Kloet. 1988. A partial classification of waterfowl (Anatidae) based on single-copy DNA. *Auk* 105:542–49.

Maniatis, T., E. F. Fritsch, and J. Sambrook. 1982. *Molecular Cloning: A Laboratory Manual*. Cold Spring Harbor: Cold Spring Harbor Laboratory.

Marinelli, L., F. Messier, and Y. Plante. 1992. Use of DNA fingerprinting to determine parentage in muskrats (*Ondatra zibethicus*). *Journal of Heredity* 83:356–60.

Maxam, A. M. and W. Gilbert. 1977. A new method for sequencing DNA. *Proceedings of the Natural Academy of Sciences USA* 74:560–64.

Maxson, L. R. and A. C. Wilson. 1975. Albumin evolution and organismal evolution in tree frogs (Hylidae). *Systematic Zoology* 24:1–15.

McClenaghan, L. R., Jr. and T. J. O'Shea. 1988. Genetic variability in the Florida manatee (*Trichechus manatus*). *Journal of Mammalogy* 69:481–88.

McClenaghan, L. R., Jr., J. Berger, and H. D. Truesdale. 1990. Founding lineages and genic variability in plains bison (*Bison bison*) from Badlands National Park, South Dakota. *Conservation Biology* 4:285–89.

McCracken, G. F. 1984. Communal nursing in Mexican free-tailed bat maternal colonies. *Science* 223:1090–91.

McCracken, G. F. and J. W. Bradbury. 1977. Paternity and genetic heterogeneity in the polygynous bat *Phyllostomus hastatus*. *Science* 198:303–29.

McDonald, J. H. 1991. Contrasting amounts of geographical variation as evidence for direct selection: The Mpi and Pgm loci in eight crustacean species. *Heredity* 67:215–19.

McKitrick, M. C. 1990. Genetic evidence for multiple parentage in Eastern kingbirds (*Tyrannus tyrannus*). *Behavioral Ecology and Sociobiology* 26:149–55.

Meireles, C. M. M., M. I. C. Sampaio, H. Schneider, and M. P. C. Schneider. 1992. Protein variation, taxonomy, and differentiation in five species of marmosets. *Primates* 33:227–38.

Melo, A. C. A., M. I. C. Sampaio, M. P. C. Schneider, and H. Schneider. 1992. Biochemical diversity and genetic distance in two species of the genus *Saguinus*. *Primates* 33:217–25.

Meng, A., R. E. Carter, and D. T. Parkin. 1990. The variability of DNA fingerprints in three species of swan. *Heredity* 64:73–80.

Merenlender, A. M., D. S. Woodruff, O. A. Ryder, R. Kock, and J. Vahala. 1989. Allozyme variation and differentiation in African and Indian rhinoceroses. *Journal of Heredity* 30:377–82.

Meylan, A. B., B. W. Bowen, and J. C. Avise. 1990. A genetic test of "natal homing" versus "social facilitation" in green sea turtle migration. *Science* 248:724–27.

Millar, C. D., D. M. Lambert, A. R. Bellamy, P. M. Stapleton, and E. C. Young. 1992. Sex-specific restriction fragments and sex ratios revealed by DNA fingerprinting in the brown skua. *Journal of Heredity.* 83:350–55.

Miller, P. S. and P. W. Hedrick. 1991. MHC polymorphisms and the design of captive breeding programs: Simple solutions are not the answer. *Conservation Biology* 5:556–58.

Mitton, J. B. and M. C. Raphael. 1990. Genetic variation in the marten, *Martes americana. Journal of Mammalogy* 71:195–97.

Moore, W. S., J. H. Graham, and J. T. Price. 1991. Mitochondrial DNA variation in the northern flicker (*Colaptes auratus,* Aves). *Molecular Biology and Evolution* 8:327–44.

Morin P. A. and O. A. Ryder. 1991. Founder contribution and pedigree inference in a captive breeding colony of lion-tailed macaques, using mitochondrial DNA and DNA fingerprint analysis. *Zoo Biology* 10:341–52.

Moritz, C., T. E. Dowling, and W. M. Brown. 1987. Evolution of animal mitochondrial DNA: Relevance for population biology and systematics. *Annual Review of Ecology and Systematics* 18:269–92.

Morton, E. S., L. Forman, and M. Braun. 1990. Extra-pair fertilizations and the evolution of colonial breeding in purple martins. *Auk* 107:275–83.

Mulligan, T. J. and R. W. Chapman. 1989. Mitochondrial DNA analysis of Chesapeake Bay white perch, *Morone americana. Copeia* 3:679–88.

Mumme, R. L., W. D. Koenig, R. M. Zink, and J. A. Marten. 1985. Genetic variation and parentage in a California population of acorn woodpeckers. *Auk* 102:305–12.

Nakamura, Y., M. Leppert, P. O'Connell, R. Wolff, T. Holm, M. Culver, C. Martin, E. Fujimoto, M. Hoff, E. Kumlin, and R. White. 1987. Variable number of tandem repeat (VNTR) markers for human genome mapping. *Science* 235:1616–22.

Nevo, E. 1978. Genetic variation in natural populations: Patterns and theory. *Theoretical Population Biology* 13:121–77.

Novak, J. M., L. M. Smith, and L. D. Vangilder. 1989. Genetic variability within and among wintering populations of Brant. *Journal of Heredity* 80:160–63.

Nozawa, K., T. Shotake, M. Minezawa, Y. Kawamoto, K. Hayasaka, S. Kawamoto. 1991. Population genetics of Japanese monkeys, III: Ancestry and differentiation of local populations. *Primates* 32:411–35.

O'Brien, S. J. and J. F. Evermann. 1988. Interactive influence of infectious disease and genetic diversity in natural populations. *Trends in Ecology and Evolution* 3:254–59.

O'Brien, S. J., M. E. Roelke, L. Marker, A. Newman, C. A. Winkler, D. Meltzer,

L. Colly, J. F. Evermann, M. Bush, and D. E. Wildt. 1985. Genetic basis for species vulnerability in the cheetah. *Science* 227:1428–34.

Oring, L. W., R. C. Fleischer, J. M. Reed, and K. E. Marsden. 1992. Cuckoldry via stored sperm in the sequentially polyandrous spotted sandpiper. *Nature* 359:631–33.

Packer, C., D. A. Gilbert, A. E. Pusey, and S. J. O'Brien. 1991. A molecular genetic analysis of kinship and cooperation in African lions. *Nature* 351:562–65.

Palumbi, S. R. and B. D. Kessing. 1991. Population biology of the trans-arctic exchange: MtDNA sequence similarity between Pacific and Atlantic sea urchins. *Evolution* 45:1790–1805.

Palumbi, S. R. and A. C. Wilson. 1990. Mitochondrial DNA diversity in the sea urchins *Strongylocentrotus purpuratus* and *S. droebachiensis. Evolution* 44:403–15.

Pamilo, P. 1984. Genotypic correlation and regression in social groups: Multiple alleles, multiple loci, and subdivided populations. *Genetics* 107:307–20.

Pamilo, P. 1989. Estimating relatedness in social groups. *Trends in Ecology and Evolution* 4:353–55.

Petter, S. C., D. B. Miles, and M. M. White. 1990. Genetic evidence of mixed reproductive strategy in a monogamous bird. *Condor* 92:702–8.

Phillips, R. B., K. D. Zajicek, and P. E. Ihssen. 1989. Population differences in chromosome-banding polymorphisms in lake trout. *Transactions of the American Fisheries Society* 118:64–73.

Pieczarka, J. C., R. M. D. Barros, C. Y. Nagamachi, R. Rodrigues, and A. Espinel. 1992. *Aotus vociferans x Aotus nancymai:* Sympatry without chromosomal hybridation. *Primates* 33:239–45.

Piper, W. H. and P. Parker Rabenold. 1992. Use of fragment-sharing estimates from DNA fingerprinting to determine relatedness in a tropical wren. *Molecular Ecology* 1:69–78.

Plante, Y., P. T. Boag, and B. N. White. 1989. Microgeographic variation in mitochondrial DNA of meadow voles (*Microtus pennsylvanicus*) in relation to population density. *Evolution* 43:1522–37.

Pope, T. R. 1992. Influence of dispersal patterns and mating system on genetic differentiation within and between populations of the red howler monkey (*Alouatta seniculus*). *Evolution* 46:1112–28.

Powell, J. R. 1975. Protein variation in natural populations of animals. *Evolutionary Biology* 8:79–119.

Preziosi, R. F. and D. J. Fairbairn. 1992. Genetic population structure and levels of gene flow in the stream dwelling waterstrider, *Aquarius remigis* (Hemiptera:Geridae). *Evolution* 46:430–44.

Price, D. K., G. E. Collier, and C. F. Thompson. 1989. Multiple parentage in broods of house wrens: Genetic evidence. *Journal of Heredity* 80:1–5.

Quattro, J. M. and R. C. Vrijenhoek. 1989. Fitness differences among remnant populations of the endangered Sonoran topminnow. *Science* 245:976–78.

Quinn, T. W. 1992. The genetic legacy of Mother Goose: Phylogenetic patterns of the lesser snow goose *Chen c. caerulescens* maternal lineage. *Molecular Ecology* 1:105–17.

Quinn, T. W. and B. N. White. 1987. Analysis of DNA sequence variation. In F. Cooke and P. A. Buckley, eds., *Avian Genetics: A Population and Ecological Approach,* pp. 163–98. New York: Academic Press.

Quinn, T. W. and A. C. Wilson. 1993. Sequence evolution in the mitochondrial genome of birds. *Journal of Molecular Evolution* 37:417–25.

Quinn, T. W., F. Cooke, and B. N. White. 1990. Molecular sexing of geese using a cloned Z chromosome sequence with homology to the W chromosome. *Auk* 107:199–200.

Quinn, T. W., J. C. Davies, F. Cooke, and B. N. White. 1989. Genetic analysis of offspring of a female-female pair in the lesser snow goose (*Chen c. caerulescens*). *Auk* 106:177–84.

Quinn, T. W., J. S. Quinn, F. Cooke, and B. N. White. 1987. DNA marker analysis detects multiple maternity and paternity in single broods of the lesser snow goose. *Nature* 326:392–94.

Quinn, T. W., G. F. Shields, and A. C. Wilson. 1991. Affinities of the Hawaiian goose based on two types of mitochondrial DNA data. *Auk* 108:585–93.

Rabenold, P. P., K. N. Rabenold, W. H. Piper, J. Haydock, and S. W. Zack. 1990. Shared paternity revealed by genetic analysis in cooperatively breeding tropical wrens. *Nature* 348:538–40.

Rabenold, P. P., K. N. Rabenold, W. H. Piper, and D. J. Minchella. 1991. Density-dependent dispersal in social wrens: Genetic analysis using novel matriline markers. *Animal Behavior* 42:144–46.

Rainboth, W. J., D. G. Buth, and F. B. Turner. 1989. Allozyme variation in Mojave populations of the desert tortoise, *Gopherus agassizi. Copeia* 1:115–23.

Randi, E., G. Fusco, R. Lorenzini, and F. Spina. 1991a. Allozyme divergence and phylogenetic relationships within the Strigiformes. *Condor* 93:295–301.

Randi, E., G. Fusco, R. Lorenzini, S. Toso, and G. Tosi. 1991b. Allozyme divergence and phylogenetic relationships among *Capra, Ovis,* and *Rupicapra* (Artyodactyla, Bovidae). *Heredity* 67:281–86.

Reeve, H. K., D. F. Westneat, W. A. Noon, P. W. Sherman, and C. F. Aquadro. 1990. DNA "fingerprinting" reveals high levels of inbreeding in colonies of the eusocial naked mole-rat. *Proceedings of the National Academy of Sciences USA* 87:2496–2500.

Reeve, H. K., D. F. Westneat, and D. C. Queller. 1992. Estimating within-group relatedness from DNA fingerprinting. *Molecular Ecology* 1:223–32.

Reh, W. and A. Seitz. 1990. The influence of land use on the genetic structure of populations of the common frog *Rana temporaria. Biological Conservation* 54:239–49.

Rhymer, J. M., M. J. Williams, and M. J. Braun. 1994. Mitochondrial analysis of gene flow between New Zealand mallards (*Anas platyrhynchos*) and grey ducks (*A. superciliosa*). *Auk* (in press).

Riddle, B. R. and R. L. Honeycutt. 1990. Historical biogeography in North American arid regions: An approach using mitochondrial-DNA phylogeny in grasshopper mice (Genus *Onychomys*). *Evolution* 44:1–15.

Roed, K. H., I. M. H. Eikelmann, M. Jacobsen, and O. Pedersen. 1991. Chromosome aberrations in Norwegian reindeer calves exposed to fallout from the Chernobyl accident. *Hereditas* 115:201–6.

Rogers, J., G. Ruano, and K. K. Kidd. 1992. Variability in nuclear DNA among non-human primates: Application of molecular genetic techniques to intra- and interspecies genetic analyses. *American Journal of Primatology* 27:93–105.

Romagnano, L., T. R. McGuire, and H. W. Power. 1989. Pitfalls and improved techniques in avian parentage studies. *Auk* 106:129–36.

Rorvik, K. and J. B. Steen. 1989. The genetic structure of Scandinavian willow ptarmigan (*Lagopus l. lagopus*) populations. *Hereditas* 110:139–44.

Rorvik, K., H. C. Pedersen, and J. B. Steen. 1990. Genetic variation and territoriality in willow ptarmigan (*Lagopus l. lagopus*). *Evolution* 44:1490–97.

Rose, F. L. and K. W. Selcer. 1989. Genetic divergences of the allopatric populations of *Nerodia harteri*. *Journal of Herpetology* 23:261–67.

Ruedas, L. A., R. C. Dowler, and E. Aita. 1989. Chromosomal variation in the New England cottontail, *Sylvilagus transitionalis*. *Journal of Mammalogy* 70:860–64.

Ruedas, L. A., T. E. Lee, Jr., J. W. Bickham, and D. A. Schlitter. 1990. Chromosomes of five species of Vespertilionid bats from Africa. *Journal of Mammalogy* 71:94–100.

Ryder, O. A. 1986. Species conservation and systematics: The dilemma of subspecies. *Trends in Ecology and Evolution* 1:9–10.

Ryder, O. A. and L. G. Chemnick. 1990. Chromosomal and molecular evolution in Asiatic wild asses. *Genetica* 83:67–72.

Ryder, O. A. and L. G. Chemnick. 1993. Chromosomal and mitochondrial DNA variation in orangutans. *Journal of Heredity* 84:405–9.

Ryder, O. A. and L. G. Chemnick, S. F. Schafer, and A. L. Shima. 1989a. Individual DNA fingerprints from Galapagos tortoises. *International Zoo Yearbook* 28:84–87.

Ryder, O. A., A. T. Kumamoto, B. S. Durrant, and K. Benirschke. 1989b. Chromosomal divergence and reproductive isolation in dik-diks (genus *Madoqua*, Mammalia, Bovidae). In D. Otte and J. A. Endler, eds., *Speciation and its Consequences*, pp. 208–225. Sunderland, Mass.: Sinauer.

Sampaio, M. I. C., C. M. L. Barroso, B. T. F. Da Silva, H. Seuanez, T. Matayoshi, E. Howllin, N. Nassazi, C. Nagle, H. Schneider. 1991. Genetic variability in *Cebus appella paraguayanus*: Biochemical analysis of seven loci and variation in Glyoxalase I (E.C.4.4.1.5.). *Primates* 32:105–9.

Sanger, F. and A. R. Coulson. 1975. A rapid method for determining sequences in DNA by primed synthesis with DNA polymerase. *Journal of Molecular Biology* 94:441–48.

Schartl, M., C. Erbelding, S. Denk, S. Holter, I. Nanda, M. Schmid, J. H. Schroder, J. T. Emlen. 1993. Reproductive failure of dominant males in the poeciliad fish *Limia perugiae* determined by DNA fingerprinting. *Proceedings of the National Academy of Sciences, USA* 90:7064–68.

Schlötterer, C., B. Amos, and D. Tautz. 1991. Conservation of polymorphic simple sequence loci in cetacean species. *Nature* 354:63–65.

Schreiber, A. and H. Tichy. 1992. MHC polymorphisms and the conservation of endangered species. In H. D. M. Moore, W. V. Holt, and G. M. Mace, eds., *Biotechnology and the Conservation of Genetic Diversity*. Zoological Society of London Symposium 64, pp. 103–21. London: Oxford Scientific Publications.

Schwartz, J. M., G. F. McCracken, and G. M. Burghardt. 1989. Multiple paternity in wild populations of the garter snake, *Thamnophis sirtalis*. *Behavioral Ecology and Sociobiology* 25:269–73.

Schwartz, O. A. and K. B. Armitage. 1980. Genetic variation in social mammals: The marmot model. *Science* 207:666–67.

Schwartz, O. A. and K. B. Armitage. 1983. Problems in the use of genetic similarity to show relatedness. *Evolution* 37:417–20.

Scribner, K. T., R. K. Chesser, and R. J. Warren. 1983. Spatial and temporal genetic variability of the Eastern cottontail on west Texas playa basins. *Journal of Mammalogy* 64:287–94.

Selander, R. K., M. H. Smith, S. Y. Yang, W. E. Johnson, and J. B. Gentry. 1971. Biochemical polymorphism and systematics in the genus *Peromyscus*, II: Genic heterozygosity and genetic similarity among populations of the old-field mouse (*Peromyscus polionotus*). *Studies in Genetics* 7103:49–90.

Seutin, G., J. Brawn, R. E. Ricklefs, E. Bermingham. 1993. Genetic divergence among populations of a tropical passerine, the streaked saltator (*Saltator albicollis*). *Auk* 110:117–26.

Shaw, C. R. and R. Prasad. 1970. Starch gel electrophoresis of enzymes: A compilation of recipes. *Biochemical Genetics* 4:297–320.

Sheldon, F. H., B. Slikas, M. Kinnarney, F. B. Gill, E. Zhao, and B. Silverin. 1992. DNA-DNA hybridization evidence of phylogenetic relationships among major lineages of *Parus*. *Auk* 109:173–85.

Sherman, P. W. 1981. Electrophoresis and avian genealogical analyses. *Auk* 98:419–22.

Sherman, P. W. and M. L. Morton. 1988. Extra-pair fertilizations in mountain white-crowned sparrows. *Behavioral Ecology and Sociobiology* 22:413–20.

Sherwin, W. B., N. D. Murray, J. A. M. Graves, and P. R. Brown. 1991. Measurement of genetic variation in endangered populations: Bandicoots (Marsupialia: Peramelidae) as an example. *Conservation Biology* 5:103–8.

Shields, B. A., K. S. Guise, and J. C. Underhill. 1990. Chromosomal and mitochondrial DNA characterization of a population of dwarf cisco (*Coregonus artedii*) in Minnesota. *Canadian Journal of Fisheries and Aquatic Sciences* 47:1562–69.

Shields, G. F. 1982. Comparative avian cytogenetics: A review. *Condor* 84:45–48.

Shields, G. F. 1987. Chromosomal variation. In F. Cooke and P. A. Buckley, eds., *Avian Genetics*, pp. 79–104. London: Academic Press.

Shields, G. F. 1990. Analysis of mitochondrial DNA of Pacific black brant (*Branta bernicla nigricans*). *Auk* 107:620–23.

Shields, G. F. and T. D. Kocher. 1991. Phylogenetic relationships of North American ursids based on analysis of mitochondrial DNA. *Evolution* 45:218–21.

Shields, G. F. and A. C. Wilson. 1987. Subspecies of the Canada goose (*Branta canadensis*) have distinct mitochodrial DNA's. *Evolution* 41:662–66.

Shotake, T., K. Nozawa, and C. Santiapilai. 1991. Genetic variability within and between the troops of toque macaque, *Macaca sinica*, in Sri Lanka. *Primates* 32:283–99.

Sibley, C. G. and J. E. Ahlquist. 1981. The phylogeny and relationships of the ratite birds as indicated by DNA-DNA hybridization. In G. G. E. Scudder and J. R. Reveal, eds., *Evolution Today: Proceedings of the Second International Congress on Systematics and Evolutionary Biology,* pp. 301–35. Pittsburgh: Hunt Institute for Botanical Documentation.

Sibley, C. G. and J. E. Ahlquist. 1983. Phylogeny and classification of birds based on the data of DNA-DNA hybridization. In R. F. Johnston, ed., *Current Ornithology,* vol. 1, pp. 245–92. New York: Plenum Press.

Sibley, C. G. and J. E. Ahlquist. 1986. Reconstructing bird phylogeny by comparing DNA's. *Scientific American* 254:82–93.

Sibley, C. G., J. E. Ahlquist, and B. L. Monroe, Jr. 1988. A classification of the living birds of the world based on DNA-DNA hybridization studies. *Auk* 105:409–23.

Simonsen, V., E. W. Born, and T. Kristensen. 1982. Electrophoretic variation in large mammals: The Atlantic walrus, *Odobenus r. rosmarus. Hereditas* 97:91–94.

Slatkin, M. 1985a. Gene flow in natural populations. *Annual Review of Ecology and Systematics* 16:393–430.

Slatkin, M. 1985b. Rare alleles as indicators of gene flow. *Evolution* 39:53–65.

Slatkin, M. 1987. Gene flow and the geographic structure of natural populations. *Science* 236:787–92.

Slatkin, M. and N. H. Barton. 1989. A comparison of three indirect methods for estimating average levels of gene flow. *Evolution* 43:1349–68.

Slatkin, M. and W. P. Maddison. 1989. A cladistic measure of gene flow inferred from the phylogenies of alleles. *Genetics* 123:603–13.

Snell, R. R. 1991. Interspecific allozyme differentiation among North Atlantic white-headed Larid gulls. *Auk* 108:319–28.

Stangel, P. W., M. R. Lennartz, and M. H. Smith. 1992. Genetic variation and population structure of red-cockaded woodpeckers. *Conservation Biology* 6:283–92.

Stangel, P. W., J. A. Rodgers, Jr., and A. L. Bryan. 1990. Genetic variation and population structure of the Florida wood stork. *Auk* 107:614–19.

Stiven, A. E. and R. C. Bruce. 1988. Ecological genetics of the salamander (*Desmognathus quadramaculatus*) from disturbed watersheds in the Southern Appalachian biosphere reserve cluster. *Conservation Biology* 2:195–205.

Stutchbury, B. J., J. M. Rhymer, and E. S. Morton. 1994. Extra-pair paternity in hooded warblers. *Behavioral Ecology* 5:384–392.

Swofford, D. L. 1990. *PAUP: Phylogenetic analysis using parsimony.* Champaign, Ill.: Illinois Natural History Survey.

Swofford, D. L. and R. B. Selander. 1989. *BIOSYS-1: A computer program for the analysis of allelic variation in population genetics and biochemical systematics.* Champaign, Ill.: Illinois Natural History Survey.

Szymura, J. M. and N. H. Barton. 1986. Genetic analysis of a hybrid zone between the fire-bellied toads, *Bombina bombina* and *B. variegata,* near Cracow in southern Poland. *Evolution* 40:1141–59.

Taberlet, P., A. Meyer, and J. Bouvet. 1992. Unusual mitochondrial DNA polymorphism in two local populations of blue tit, *Parus caerulescens. Molecular Ecology* 1:27–36.

Tegelstrom, H. and M. Jaarola. 1989. Genetic divergence in mitochondrial DNA between the wood mouse (*Apodemus sylvaticus*) and the yellow necked mouse (*A. flavicollis*). *Hereditas* 111:49–60.

Tegelstrom, H., J. Searle, J. Brookfield, and S. Mercer. 1991. Multiple paternity in wild common shrews (*Sorex araneus*) is confirmed by DNA fingerprinting. *Heredity* 66:373–79.

Templeton, A. R., S. K. Davis, and B. Read. 1987. Genetic variability in a captive herd of Speke's gazelle (*Gazella spekei*). *Zoo Biology* 6:305–13.

Thomas, W. K., R. E. Withler, and A. T. Beckenbach. 1986. Mitochondrial DNA analysis of Pacific salmonid evolution. *Canadian Journal of Zoology* 64:1058–64.

Thommasen, H. V., M. J. Thomson, G. G. Shutler, and L. T. Kirby. 1989. Development of DNA fingerprints for use in wildlife forensic science. *Wildlife Society Bulletin* 17:321–26.

Thorgaard, G. H. 1983. Chromosomal differences among rainbow trout populations. *Copeia* 1983:659–52.

Thorneycroft, H. B. 1975. A cytogenetic study of the white-throated sparrow, *Zonotricha albicollis* (Gmelin). *Evolution* 29:611–21.

Travis, J., J. C. Trexler, and M. Mulvey. 1990. Multiple paternity and its correlates in female *Poecilia latipinna* (Poeciliidae). *Copeia* 3:722–29.

Triggs, S. J., R. G. Powlesland, C. H. Daugherty. 1989. Genetic variation and conservation of kakapo (*Strigops habroptilus*: Psittaciformes). *Conservation Biology* 3:92–96.

Triggs, S. J., M. J. Williams, S. J. Marshall, and G. K. Chambers. 1992. Genetic structure of blue duck (*Hymenolaimus malacorhynchos*) populations revealed by DNA fingerprinting. *Auk* 109:80–89.

Vassart, G., M. Georges, R. Monsieur. H. Brocas, A. S. Lequarre, and D. Christophe. 1987. A sequence in M13 phage detects hypervariable minisatellites in human and animal DNA. *Science* 235:683–84.

Vrijenhoek, R. C. and P. L. Leberg. 1991. Lets not throw the baby out with the bathwater: A comment on management for MHC diversity in captive populations. *Conservation Biology* 5:252–54.

Vrijenhoek, R. C., M. E. Douglas, and G. K. Meffe. 1985. Conservation genetics of endangered fish populations in Arizona. *Science* 229:400–2.

Waples, R. S. and D. J. Teel. 1990. Conservation genetics of Pacific salmon, I: Temporal changes in allele frequency. *Conservation Biology* 4:144–56.

Washio, K., S. Misawa, and S. Ueda. 1989. Individual identification of non-human primates using DNA fingerprinting. *Primates* 30:217–21.

Wayne, R. K. and S. M. Jenks. 1991. Mitochondrial DNA analysis implying extensive hybridization of the endangered red wolf *Canis rufus*. *Nature* 351:565–68.

Wayne, R. K., S. B. George, D. Gilbert, P. W. Collins, S. D. Kovach, D. Girman, and N. Lehman. 1991a. A morphologic and genetic study of the Island fox, *Urocyon littoralis*. *Evolution* 45:1849–68.

Wayne, R. K., D. A. Gilbert, N. Lehman, K. Hansen, A. Eisenhawer, D. Girman, R. O. Peterson, L. D. Mech, P. J. P. Gogan, U. S. Seal, and R. J. Krumenaker. 1991b. Conservation genetics of the endangered Isle Royale gray wolf. *Conservation Biology* 5:41–51.

Wayne, R. K., N. Lehman, M. W. Allard, and R. L. Honeycutt. 1992. Mitochondrial variability of the gray wolf: Genetic consequences of population decline and fragmentation. *Conservation Biology* 6:559–69.

Wayne, R. K., A. Meyer, N. Lehman, B. Van Valkenburgh, P. W. Kat, T. K. Fuller, D.

Girman, and S. J. O'Brien. 1991c. Large sequence divergence among mitochondrial DNA genotypes within populations of East African black-backed jackals. *Proceedings of the National Academy of Sciences USA* 87:1772–76.

Wayne, R. K., B. Van Valkenburgh, P. W. Kat, T. K. Fuller, W. E. Johnson, and S. J. O'Brien. 1989. Genetic and morphological divergence among sympatric canids. *Journal of Heredity* 80:447–54.

Wayne, R. K., B. Van Valkenburgh, and S. J. O'Brien. 1991d. Molecular distance and divergence time in carnivores and primates. *Molecular Biology and Evolution* 8:297–319.

Wehrhahn, C. F. and R. Powell. 1987. Electrophoretic variation, regional differences, and gene flow in the Coho salmon (*Oncorhynchus kisutch*) of southern British Columbia. *Canadian Journal of Fisheries and Aquatic Sciences* 44:822–30.

Weiss, M. L., V. Wilson, C. Chan, T. Turner, and A. J. Jeffreys. 1988. Application of DNA fingerprinting probes to Old World monkeys. *American Journal of Primatology* 16:73–79.

Wenick, P. W., A. J. Baker, and M. G. J. Tilanus. 1993. Hypervariable control-region sequences reveal global population structure in a long distant migrant shorebird, the dunlin (*Calidris alpina*). *Proceedings of the National Academy of Science of the USA* 90:94–98.

Werman, S. D., M. S. Springer, and R. J. Britten. 1990. Nucleic acids, I: DNA-DNA hybridization. In D. M. Hillis and C. Moritz, eds., *Molecular Systematics,* pp. 204–49. Sunderland, Mass.: Sinauer.

Westneat, D. F. 1987. Extra-pair fertilizations in a predominantly monogamous bird: Genetic evidence. *Animal Behavior* 35:877–86.

Westneat, D. F. 1990. Genetic parentage in the indigo bunting: A study using DNA fingerprinting. *Behavioral Ecology and Sociobiology* 27:67–76.

Westneat, D. F. 1993. Polygyny and extra-pair fertilizations in eastern red-winged blackbirds (*Agelaius phoeniceus*). *Behavioral Ecology* 4:49–60.

Wetton, J. H., R. E. Carter, D. T. Parkin, and D. Walters. 1987. Demographic study of a wild house sparrow population by DNA fingerprinting. *Nature* 327:147–49.

White, R. and J. M. Lalouel. 1988. Chromosome mapping with DNA markers. *Scientific American* 258:40–48.

Wichman, H. A., C. T. Payne, O. A. Ryder, M. J. Hamilton, M. Maltbie, and R. J. Baker. 1991. Genomic distribution of heterochromatic sequences in equids: Implications to rapid chromosomal evolution. *Journal of Heredity* 82:369–77.

Wildt, D. E., M. Bush, K. L. Goodrowe, C. Packer, A. E. Pusey, J. L. Brown, P. Joslin, and S. J. O'Brien. 1987. Reproductive and genetic consequences of founding isolated lion populations. *Nature* 329:328–30.

Williams, J. G. K., A. R. Kubelik, K. L. Livak, J. A. Rafalski, and S. R. Tingey. 1990. DNA polymorphisms amplified by arbitrary primers are useful as genetic markers. *Nucleic Acids Research* 18:6531–35.

Wilkinson, G. S. and G. F. McCracken. 1985. On estimating relatedness using genetic markers. *Evolution* 39:1169–74.

Wilson, A. C., R. L. Cann, S. M. Carr, M. George, Jr., U. B. Gyllensten, K. M. Helm-Bychowski, R. G. Higuchi, S. R. Palumbi, E. M. Prager, R. D. Sage, and M. Stoneking.

1985a. Mitochondrial DNA and two perspectives on evolutionary genetics. *Biological Journal of the Linnaean Society* 26:375–400.

Wilson, A. C., S. S. Carlson, and T. J. White. 1977. Biochemical evolution. *Annual Review of Biochemistry.* 46:573–639.

Wilson, G. M., W. K. Thomas, and A. T. Beckenbach. 1985b. Intra- and interspecific mitochondrial DNA sequence divergence in salmon: Rainbow, steelhead, and cutthroat trouts. *Canadian Journal of Zoology* 63:2088–94.

Winans, G. A. and L. L. Jones. 1988. Electrophoretic variability in Dall's porpoise (*Phocoenoides dalli*) in the North Pacific Ocean and Bering Sea. *Journal of Mammalogy* 69:14–21.

Wright, S. 1931. Evolution in Mendelian populations. *Genetics* 16:97–159.

Xia, X. and J. S. Millar. 1991. Genetic evidence of promiscuity in *Peromyscus leucopus*. *Behavioral Ecology and Sociobiology* 28:171–78.

Yamagishi, S., I. Nishiumi, and C. Shimoda. 1992. Extra-pair fertilizations in monogamous bull-headed shrikes revealed by DNA fingerprinting. *Auk* 109:711–21.

Zeyl, C. W. and D. M. Green. 1992. Heteromorphism for a highly repeated sequence in the New Zealand frog *Leiopelma hochstetteri*. *Evolution* 46:1891–99.

Zink, R. M. and D. L. Dittmann. 1993. Gene flow, refugia, and evolution of geographic variation in the song sparrow (*Melospiza melodia*). *Evolution* 47:717–29.

Zink, R. M., W. L. Rootes, and D. L. Dittmann. 1991. Mitochondrial DNA variation, population structure, and evolution of the common grackle (*Quiscalus quiscula*). *Condor* 93:318–29.

Zouros, E., K. R. Freeman, A. Oberhauser Ball, G. H. Pogson. 1992. Direct evidence for extensive paternal mitochondrial DNA inheritance in the marine mussel *Mytilus*. *Nature* 359:412–14.

10

A New Approach to the Joint Estimation of Relationship from DNA Fingerprint Data

■■

Charles J. Geyer and Elizabeth A. Thompson

In the management and reestablishment of populations of endangered species, it may be important to estimate the patterns of relationship among surviving individuals; the California condor, *Gymnogyps californianus*, provides a case in point. Knowledge of the relationships among individuals has implications for breeding strategies that conserve maximal genetic variation. If the relationship structure is known, matings between closely related individuals can be avoided, and underrepresented components of the founder gene pool can be protected. In the selection of individuals for release, a propagule more genetically representative of that founder pool can be constructed, while at the same time avoiding risk to founder genes that may be replicated in only a few current individuals.

On the one hand, multilocus DNA fingerprint data are increasingly available and are becoming the data of choice for many analyses (Avise et al., essay 9 of this volume). On the other hand, questions have been raised as to the usefulness of these data for genealogical inference (Lynch 1988); it is clear that they have much less power to resolve genealogical relationships than single-locus polymorphic Mendelian markers. It is important to understand the limitations of inferences from such data and to develop models and methods of analysis that use the available information to maximum effect. Modeling the multi-locus genotypes underlying a band-sharing pattern is not a feasible approach (Lynch 1988); there are too many unknowns. Moreover, if the group of individuals in question constitutes the entire species, even familiar population genetic concepts, such as allele frequencies, have little relevance. A band will have some frequency within the group of related individuals, but there is no large population of "unrelated" individuals from which a "population frequency" can be estimated.

Additionally, it is not a matter of determining the simple maternity and paternity of specified offspring. In the case of the California condor, these latter relationships are well known and can be readily validated from the genetic data. Rather, the questions concern the patterns of relationships among the adult birds brought into captivity. These individuals may not be closely related but might be as closely related as cousins or even siblings. The number of alternative genealogical hypotheses is huge, and subsetting the data to facilitate analysis results in loss of information. There is information on relatedness not just in the pairwise similarity of individuals but also in their joint pattern of similarity to others.

Instead of modeling the genetic processes that give rise to the band patterns under alternative genealogical scenarios, we adopt a phenomenological approach. The statistical model developed here describes the observed patterns of relative similarities between individuals. The model permits analyses of the similarity of band patterns, while adjusting for the differing frequencies of bands and the different numbers of bands expected in differentially inbred individuals. The theory underlying the methods of estimation is described in detail elsewhere (Geyer and Thompson 1992), as is the analysis of the California condor data, which motivated the work (Geyer et al. 1993). Here the objective is to motivate the model and to demonstrate that, if analyzed appropriately, multilocus DNA fingerprint data can provide information on the detailed population structure of a small group of individuals. For this purpose, we use simulated data that mimic some of the features of the California condor population, pedigree, and genetic data. The results are discussed.

METHODS

The Simulated Data

A complex pedigree of 40 interrelated individuals over 5 generations, with some inbreeding, was constructed. Genes at 25 pairs of loosely linked Mendelian loci (recombination = 0.25) were simulated throughout the pedigree. Founder genes were assigned allelic types in accordance with varying frequencies, some loci being assumed highly polymorphic (e.g., alleles at frequencies 0.3, 0.2, 0.2, 0.1, 0.1, 0.05, 0.05) and others having one predominant allele (e.g., a frequency of 0.9). A set of 13 individuals was chosen from the final 2 generations of the pedigree. A total of 93 alleles were present among these 13 individuals. Each allele was then assumed to give rise to a uniquely identifiable band with a probability of 0.5; the other alleles were discarded. This resulted in a list of 45 bands, each present in some, but not all, of the 13 individuals. To remove any obvious patterns between adjacently labeled bands or individuals, the set of 45 bands was randomly relabeled, as were the 13 individuals.

The objective was to provide data that might mimic the recent demographic and genetic history of the California condor up to 1980. From 1980 on, the condor population was closely monitored, eggs were taken, and chicks hatched and reared in captivity. In 1986–87 the surviving wild population was brought into captivity, following the death of some 50% of the individuals in the winter of 1984–85. This study is concerned with the relationships among these adult birds and also those among the birds identified as parents of chicks hatched since 1982. Data are available for most of these individuals even if they did not survive to be brought into captivity. There are a total of 13 such birds (Geyer et al. 1993). For the condors, there are additional data on the offspring generations, but here the objective was to mimic the data among the adults whose interrelationships are almost completely unknown.

The Model and its Statistics

The underlying genetic model for a multilocus DNA fingerprint is complex and contains many unknown parameters. Rather than adopting the direct approach, we take the reverse philosophy of identifying the important statistics and using the canonical model for which these functions of the data are the minimal sufficient statistics (Lauritzen 1988).

If we assume the DNA band pattern is clear, then we have binary data; $X_{ij} = 1$ if individual i ($i = 1, . . ., m$) has observable band j ($j = 1, . . ., n$) and $X_{ij} = 0$ otherwise. More recent analyses (Geyer et al. 1993) have extended the model to accommodate uncertainty in the scoring of bands; if presence/absence is unclear, or if some individuals are missing from some gels, the relevant X_{ij} can be treated as missing data. For the present study, however, we assume there are no missing data.

The number of observable bands shared by a pair of individuals i and k, $S_{ik} = \sum_j X_{ij} X_{kj}$, is clearly a relevant statistic. The number of shared bands, however, accounts neither for inbreeding (which affects the number of distinct observable bands in an individual), nor for differential population frequencies of bands. We therefore use, in addition to the S_{ik}, the number of observable bands in each individual $\left(U_i = \sum_j X_{ij}, i = 1, \ldots, m \right)$ and the number of individuals who exhibit each band $\left(V_j = \sum_i X_{ij}, j = 1, \ldots, n \right)$. These statistics have no terms linking different bands, so the model they generate has no dependence among bands; genetic factors, such as possible allelism and linkage, are not considered. Although modeling band dependence would be possible in theory, the number of statistics, and hence parameters, already introduced precludes this as a practical proposition.

The model generated by the statistics

$$U_i, i = 1, . . . , m; V_j, j = 1, . . . , n; \text{ and}$$
$$S_{ik}, i = 1, . . . , m - 1, k = i + 1, . . . , m \qquad (10.1)$$

is an autologistic model (Besag 1974). It has a large number of parameters, one corresponding to each statistic. For our small simulated data set, $m = 13$ and $n = 45$, and there are thus 136 parameters. The probability model is most easily understood through the conditional probability of the presence of a given band j in a given individual i, given the pattern of presence of band j in other individuals $k \neq i$:

$$P(X_{ij} = 1 \mid X_{kj}, k \neq i) = \frac{\exp\left(\alpha_i + \beta_j + \sum_{k \neq i} \gamma_{ik} X_{kj}\right)}{1 + \exp\left(\alpha_i + \beta_j + \sum_{k \neq i} \gamma_{ik} X_{kj}\right)} \quad (10.2)$$

where, for convenience, we define γ_{ik} for $i > k$ to be identical to γ_{ki}. This logistic regression form for each variable conditional upon all the others is the origin of the name "autologistic." Other things being equal, the higher the value of α_i, the more likely individual i is to have any given band; the parameter α_i, $i = 1, \ldots, m$, corresponds to a measure of outbreeding for individual i. Likewise, the higher the value of β_j, the more likely an individual is to have the band j; β_j, $j = 1, \ldots, n$ corresponds to a measure of population frequency for band j. The parameters principally of interest are the relationship parameters γ_{ik}. If individual k has band j ($X_{kj} = 1$), then the higher the value of γ_{ik}, the more likely individual i is to have the band also. Genealogical relatedness introduces positive dependence between individuals, whereas unrelated individuals are independent. On average, relatives cannot be "less alike" than unrelated individuals. We impose, therefore, the constraint $\gamma_{ik} \geq 0$; the sign of γ_{ik} is that of the conditional covariance between X_{ij} and X_{kj}. In fact, the constraint does not correspond exactly to non-negativity of unconditional covariances. For example, an unrelated pair may have negative covariance, conditional on the bands in a common offspring (see the discussion in Geyer and Thompson 1992). It does, however, provide a close approximation, and the level of approximation involved will not impact inferences of the relationship structure of the group. Some bounds on the parameter space are necessary so that there will be sufficient information (statistically) for inferences to be made.

Methods of Estimation

Likelihood analysis in autologistic models of this size has previously been considered infeasible, but, in fact, a new approach using Markov chain Monte Carlo (Hastings 1970) makes it possible to find maximum likelihood estimates of the parameters and to evaluate likelihood ratios of alternative hypotheses. The methods will not be described in detail here, although three questions that shaped their development will be described briefly in this section. A more complete discussion can be found in Geyer and Thompson (1992), and details of the theoretical development are given by Geyer (1990).

Maximum likelihood estimates (MLEs) of the parameters α_i, β_j, and γ_{ik} were the first objective. One difficulty that arises with maximum likelihood estimates in this and in many other problems is that, although the limiting likelihood is well defined, some parameter estimates may be infinite. One time-honored way (dating back to Laplace) to prevent this is to add minimal "data" to ensure finiteness of MLEs. For the current model, this can be achieved by assigning each individual a band not shared by any other individual (a "name-tag" band). It can be proved that on the basis of these augmented data the MLEs are necessarily finite. The additional bands serve to identify the individuals; in fact, individuals are uniquely identifiable, and with sufficient genetic data are presumably genetically uniquely identifiable.

A second difficulty concerns the reduction of the parameter space. We have already described the big reduction accomplished by requiring $\gamma_{ik} \geq 0$, but these inequality parameters do not reduce the dimension of the parameter space. Since it is relationships (measured by parameters γ_{ik}) and inbreeding (measured via parameters α_i) that are primarily of interest, perhaps one should make inferences based on the likelihood conditional on the values of V_j, the numbers of copies of each band. The "nuisance parameters" β_j then disappear from the likelihood function. Unfortunately, this conditioning results in the parameters γ_{ik} being identifiable only up to an additive constant, thus preventing the imposition of the constraints $\gamma_{ik} \geq 0$ (Geyer and Thompson 1992). Without this constraint, the precision of the estimation is lost and the results are not interpretable. It seems there is no choice other than joint analysis of all the parameters.

Although it is possible to evaluate likelihoods and find MLEs, intensive computation is required. One may ask whether another method of parameter estimation might serve as well. One way previously suggested (Besag 1975) is that of maximum pseudolikelihood estimation (MPLE), in which the product of conditional distributions (equation 10.2) is maximized. For comparison, maximum pseudolikelihood estimates were also made, and the results were compared with the MLEs. As will emerge below, the MPLEs are unsatisfactory. Despite the computational difficulties, the likelihood analysis of the full joint model seems to be the only route to useful inferences of the relationship structure.

RESULTS

The data on the presence of the "visible bands" in each of the 13 individuals resulting from the simulation described above are shown in figure 10.1. The MLEs of the parameters α_i and γ_{ik} are given in table 10.1. There was virtually no difference between the MLEs (allowing infinite parameter values) and the "name-tag MLEs" (figure 10.2). The "name-tag" procedure reduced the infinite estimates to large, but finite, values, but probability distributions under the two parameter sets were almost identical. Thus, this procedure, which facilitates analysis (Geyer 1990), seems to be statistically justified.

Figure 10.1 Simulated DNA fingerprint data for 13 individuals. *From Geyer and Thompson 1992.*

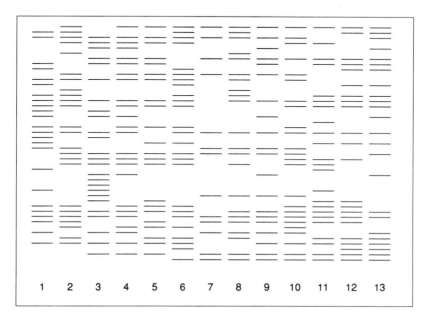

Table 10.1 Maximum likelihood estimates of α's and γ's

INDIVIDUAL	1	2	3	4	5	6	7	8	9	10	11	12	13
α_i	0.0	−2.1	−0.5	−2.1	−2.2	−1.4	*	−1.2	−2.3	−2.2	−1.4	−2.8	−1.3
$\gamma_{1\cdot}$		−	−	−	−	−	−	0.9	−	1.1	−	0.2	0.2
$\gamma_{2\cdot}$			−	1.1	0.4	2.0	−	−	0.5	−	−	−	−
$\gamma_{3\cdot}$					1.3	−	−	−	0.5	1.8	−	−	−
$\gamma_{4\cdot}$						0.5	−	−	−	0.9	0.9	−	−
$\gamma_{5\cdot}$							−	*	*	*	−	0.9	−
$\gamma_{6\cdot}$							−		−	−	−	−	−
$\gamma_{7\cdot}$										−	−	−	−
$\gamma_{8\cdot}$											−	−	−
$\gamma_{9\cdot}$												−	1.3
$\gamma_{10\cdot}$												−	−
$\gamma_{11\cdot}$												2.2	−
$\gamma_{12\cdot}$													1.8

Note: The dashes (−) show zero estimates; the * denotes a ±∞ estimate.
From Geyer and Thompson 1992.

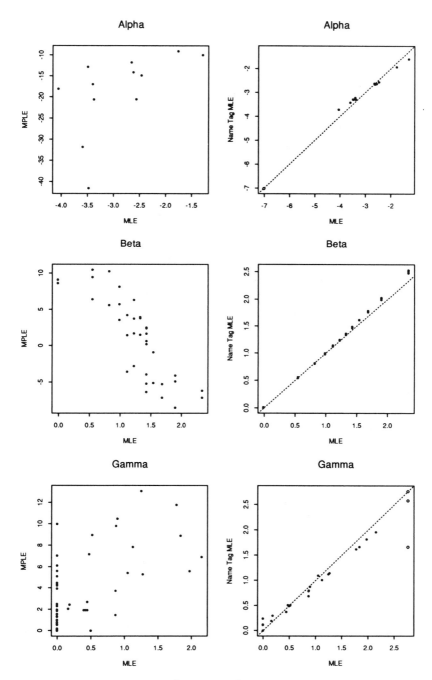

Figure 10.2 Comparison of MLEs with "name-tag" MLE estimates, and with MPLEs. *From Geyer and Thompson 1992.*

This is in contrast to a comparison of the MLEs (or of the name-tag MLEs) with the estimates obtained by the method of maximum pseudolikelihood (MPLE) (figure 10.2). For this problem, the MPLE method performs very poorly, overestimating correlations and providing predictions that bear little relation to the observed data. MPLE reverses the estimates of the β frequency parameters, giving high values for low-frequency estimates, and vice versa. For this type of data there is no satisfactory way to avoid the computation required by a full likelihood analysis.

Although the parameters α_i, β_j, and γ_{ik} specify the probabilities of the presence of bands jointly in all members of the population, these parameters do not have any direct genealogical interpretation. In order to interpret the maximum likelihood model, therefore, other functions of the model are required. Here we focus on two sets of functions. One is the set of covariances, under the estimated model, between pairs of individuals. These are surrogates for the genetic covariances of classical quantitative genetics. The second set of functions presents probabilities of the presence of a band in each individual separately as a function of the β-parameter, which measures the band frequency in the group.

Due to the constraint $\gamma_{ik} \geq 0$, many of the MLEs of these relationship parameters are 0 (table 10.1); conditionally on other individuals the pair i,k is independent. This does not, however, imply overall independence or absence of relationship. (This situation may be compared to the usual Mendelian situation, where grandparent and grandchild are independent, conditional upon the genotype of the intervening parent. Unconditionally, however, a grandparent and grandchild are positively correlated.) The degree of pairwise relationship is more readily assessed from unconditional covariances than directly from the parameter values. Table 10.2 shows the covariance in the presence of a band of typical intermediate frequency ($\beta = 1.25$). All covariances are strictly positive in this small group of highly interrelated individuals. Individual 1 has low covariance with all others; by contrast, individuals 2 and 5 are highly correlated, and individual 10 seems closely related to several other population members.

Another way of viewing the different individuals is to consider the probability of band presence in an individual as a function of the band frequency (i.e., of β_j). Figure 10.3 shows these probabilities. Individual 7 is highly inbred and has few bands; this is reflected in the low proba-

Table 10.2 Unconditional covariances of band sharing between individuals i AND k ($\times$ 1000)

k =	2	3	4	5	6	7	8	9	10	11	12	13	i
	3	1	2	3	4	3	2	5	3	8	15	16	1
		20	57	70	120	49	72	43	94	29	3	25	2
			70	31	13	27	20	44	41	10	11	15	3
				103	39	55	45	66	27	29	26	27	4
					60	41	38	43	98	61	42	27	5
						28	38	29	54	38	60	31	6
							102	113	89	18	24	37	7
								78	73	16	21	28	8
									79	25	39	74	9
										31	30	30	10
											125	56	11
												10	12

Modified from Geyer and Thompson 1992.
Note: Computed for a maximally informative band ($\beta = 1.25$).

bility of the presence of a band in individual 7. Individual 1 is not closely related to other members of the population. Relative to other individuals, individual 1 has a high probability of having the low frequency bands and a low probability of having the bands that are present in the majority of individuals. To a lesser extent, the same is true of individual 3. By contrast, individual 10 is highly related to several other individuals. This is reflected in the steep curve for individual 10, or in the high probability of high frequency bands and the low probability of low frequency bands. Individuals 8 and 9 are highly related to individual 7 who has few bands; their curves are also distinctive and are labeled in figure 10.3.

Once one has an estimate of the relationship of the set of individuals, it is useful to represent it graphically. Given a measure of pairwise distance, any of the standard methods can then be used. One suitable measure of distance is $-\log_2 C_{ik}$, where C_{ik} is the unconditional covariance between individuals i and k, and under the model it is evaluated at maximum likelihood values of α and γ and for some maximally informative value of β. From figure 10.3, we see that $\beta = 1.25$ provides maximal differentiation between individuals in probabilities of possession of the

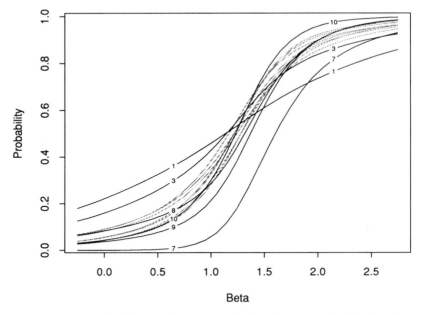

Figure 10.3 Probabilities of presence of a band in an individual and the function of the population frequency parameter (β) of that band. *From Geyer and Thompson 1992.*

band. Each step in a pedigree represents a factor of one half in genetic covariance, so the proposed measure is a surrogate for the degree of relationship. For this small group of individuals, there is little substructure to the population. We have therefore chosen to use a traditional cluster analysis method to represent the structure rather than a more complex procedure such as multidimensional scaling. Figure 10.4 shows the result of applying an average-link hierarchical clustering algorithm (Sokal and Sneath 1963) to the distance matrix. The figure confirms the lack of relationship of individuals 1 and 3 to other members of the population and to the closely related group of which individual 10 is a key member.

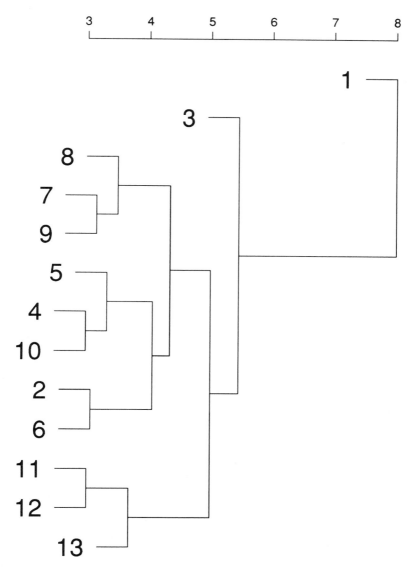

Figure 10.4 An average-link hierarchical clustering representation of the relationships among individuals, using a pairwise distance measure based on the covariances between individuals under the estimated model.

DISCUSSION

The objective of this study has been to motivate a phenomenological probability model for multilocus DNA fingerprint data and to demonstrate its application. The autologistic model provides a basis for estimation of relationships in a way that analyzes all the data jointly and adjusts for the differing frequencies of bands and for the differing numbers of bands in individuals. Although the data used to illustrate the approach are simulated, the simulation was constructed to mimic the genealogical and genetic processes giving rise to actual data on the remnant groups of an endangered species. This is not a "simulation study" of the power of the method; there is no measure of the end result's accuracy. Such a study would require an analysis of multiple simulated data sets and also a measure of similarity between estimates under the model and the simulation genealogy. (It may be noted, however, that individual 1 was indeed unrelated to all other sampled members of the pedigree.) The result of our analysis is not an estimated genealogy but an inference of the population structure that can identify individuals whose genes are important to the conservation of genetic variation.

Even in optimal circumstances, the power available to assess relationships from this type of data is slight. The smaller nonzero γ estimates are not significantly different from 0. Unless there is sufficient information on individuals of known relationship to detect allelism and linkage of bands and on that basis to build a precise genetic model for the data, precise estimation of relationship will remain impractical. The most closely related groups of individuals, however, are well distinguished, and some individuals are identified as less related to the group. In the context of the California condor data, for example, this is the type of assessment required. In that case, relationships among birds reared in captivity are known and can be used as a base point for comparison, providing an absolute scale to our distance measure, which is unavailable in our present example. The unknown patterns of relationship among the adult birds are of interest, but it is necessary to identify members as "less related" or "more related" to each other and to the group as a whole. The analysis approach taken here serves that purpose.

It is important that figure 10.4 not be interpreted as a direct representation of a pedigree. Inference of detailed pedigree structure is not practicable. Nonetheless, the representation does provide useful information for a breeding strategy aiming at conservation of genetic variation, such as could be obtained were a true pedigree available. For example, it shows that individuals 1 and 3 are key individuals in any breeding program—they are likely to have genes not represented in others. Conversely, overrepresentation of the group 2, 6, 10, 4, and 5 should be avoided; they likely duplicate many genes.

Recently there has been active discussion in the literature of breeding strategies for maintenance of genetic variation in small populations. Hughes (1991) has advocated the use of observable variation at the major histocompatibility locus. Vrijenhoek and Leberg (1991) and Miller and Hedrick (1991) have warned against this overly simplistic strategy. However representative (or otherwise) any specific chosen locus may be, it provides information only at a single point in the genome. Breeding strategies based on computations of gene survival in a given pedigree structure reflect expected genetic variation over the whole genome. Despite the imperfections of inferred relationships and reconstructed pedigrees, the use of the inferred structure provides a broader base for developing a breeding strategy than the direct use of observable molecular variation.

Computational complexity limits the application of our approach. While the analysis of the 13 individuals in the example of this study is not too computationally intensive and the methods have now been applied to the data on 32 California condors (Geyer et al. 1993), each new data set presents additional challenges. While the approach is useful where only multilocus DNA fingerprint data are available, these data are not the data of choice for genealogical analysis. Although having the advantage of representing genetic differences and similarities from a spectrum of gene loci, the absence of a genetic model results in a substantial loss of information. Single-locus DNA fingerprints provide much more information on patterns of gene identity by descent at those loci, but a large number of loci are required to obtain precise estimates of relationship (Thompson 1991). Genealogical relationships are characterized by the probabilities of gene identity they exhibit. At each locus there either is or is not gene identity by descent. With the exception of a parent-offspring relationship, where the probability of sharing a gene identical by descent is 1, a single locus cannot provide information on the relevant probabilities. It is of interest, therefore, to speculate on the potential for use of other novel molecular data such as RAPDs (Avise et al., essay 9 of this volume). A large number of markers will be available; however (particularly with dominance), each will provide little information. However, relatively uninformative markers may be combined to give much more informative haplotypes when they form closely linked sets. The molecular data of the future provide many interesting challenges for genealogical analysis.

Acknowledgment

This research was supported in part by NSF grants DMS–9007833 (CJG) and BSR–8921839 (EAT).

REFERENCES

Besag, J. E. 1974. Spatial interaction and the statistical analysis of lattice systems (with discussion). *Journal of the Royal Statistical Society* B36:192–236.

Besag, J. E. 1975. Statistical analysis of non-lattice data. *Statistician* 24:179–95.

Geyer, C. J. 1990. Maximum likelihood in exponential families. Ph.D. diss., University of Washington, Seattle.

Geyer, C. J. and E. A. Thompson. 1992. Constrained Monte Carlo maximum likelihood for dependent data (with discussion). *Journal of the Royal Statistical Society* B54:657–99.

Geyer, C. J., O. A. Ryder, L. Chemnick, and E. A. Thompson. 1993. Analysis of relatedness of the California condors from DNA fingerprints. *Molecular Biology and Evolution* 10:571–89

Hastings, W. K. 1970. Monte Carlo sampling methods using Markov chains and their applications. *Biometrika* 57:97–109.

Hughes, A. I. 1991. MHC polymorphism and the design of captive breeding programs. *Conservation Biology* 5:249–51.

Lauritzen, S. L. 1988. *Extremal Families and Systems of Sufficient Statistics.* New York: Springer-Verlag.

Lynch, M. 1988. Estimation of relatedness by DNA fingerprinting. *Molecular Biology and Evolution* 5:584–99.

Miller, P. S. and P. W. Hedrick. 1991. MHC polymorphism and the design of captive breeding programs: Simple solutions are not the answer. *Conservation Biology* 5:556–58.

Sokal, R. R. and P. H. A. Sneath. 1963. *Principles of Numerical Taxonomy.* San Francisco: Freeman.

Thompson, E. A. 1991. Estimation of relationships from genetic data. In C. R. Rao and R. Chakraborty, eds., *Handbook of Statistics, Volume 8: Statistical Methods in Biological and Medical Sciences,* pp. 255–70. New York: North Holland.

Vrijenhoek, R. C. and P. I. Leberg. 1991. Let's not throw out the baby with the bathwater: A comment on management for MHC diversity in captive populations. *Conservation Biology* 5:252–54.

11

Genotypic Inference with the Gibbs Sampler

■■

Alun Thomas

The pedigree of the Przewalski's horse, *Equus przewalskii* (Volf 1959 et seq.), is much used for illustrating methods for pedigree analysis. This highly structured pedigree, descended from 13 founders, has several inbred lines in its early history that have been interbred more recently. These features are shown in figure 11.1. This is a marriage node graph—the terminology comes from human pedigree analysis (Cannings and Thompson 1981)—of that part of the Przewalski's horse pedigree ancestral to tested horses. Two particularly interesting founders are DOM, a domestic mare, and 231, the most recent animal captured from the wild.

Over the past twelve years, 147 of the horses have been typed for at least one of 16 allozyme polymorphisms (Mace and Whitehouse, personal communication). These animals are colored gray in figure 11.1. Of the sixteen polymorphisms, nine had two alleles, four had three alleles, one had four, one had five, and one had six alleles. For reasons

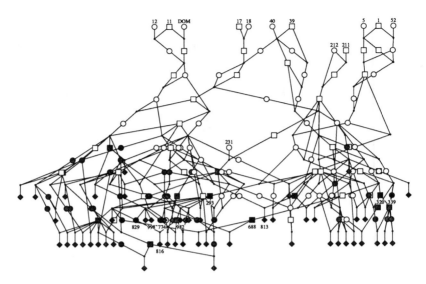

Figure 11.1 A marriage node pedigree of the captive Przewalski's horse population. Squares represent males, circles females, and diamonds individuals who have not yet reproduced. Diamonds may represent several sibs. Matings are represented by black dots; these are connected upward to parents and downward to offspring. The ten horses with the highest estimated heterozygosity are labeled and colored black. The thirteen founders (individuals without connections to ancestors) have been labeled. Individuals typed for allozyme polymorphisms are colored gray.

explained below, only the nine diallelic polymorphisms were considered in this work. These data make it possible to compare the observed heterozygosity of the tested individuals for these polymorphisms with their inbreeding coefficients calculated relative to the founders of the pedigree. However, not all animals were tested for all markers. The problem that arises, then, is to estimate the missing genotypes, in particular, to estimate the probability that each animal is heterozygous for each marker.

METHOD

Sheehan (1989) outlines the way in which several techniques from the field of image reconstruction can be used in pedigree analysis. This is possible because of a conditional independence property that is common to both areas, which is demonstrated in figure 11.2, the close-up of part of a pedigree. Suppose that we are interested in the individual colored black but don't have data on his genotype. If we are given the genotypes of his neighbors, that is, parents, mates, and offspring (shaded gray), inferences about his genotype are independent of any information about the rest of the pedigree (colored white) and of its structure. In image processing, pixels correspond to individuals, and the neighbors of a pixel are usually those adjacent on a square lattice. This conditional independence defines a Markov random field. It is a somewhat more natural concept in pedigree analysis than in image processing, as it is a consequence of Mendelian segregation rather than a convenient assumption. This property is widely exploited when calculating proba-

Figure 11.2 Neighbors of an individual in a pedigree.

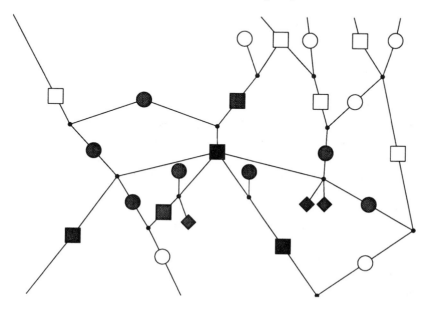

bilities on pedigrees using the general peeling method of Cannings et al. (1978).

The peeling process is a recursive procedure that allows us to make probability calculations on arbitrary complex pedigrees. Individuals in the pedigree are successively peeled off and their genotype information is converted into a function on other individuals remaining in the pedigree (Cannings et al. 1978). The problem of genotype inference could be addressed by peeling to groups of individuals and summing over the joint genotype probability distribution obtained to get marginal posterior probability distributions for the genotypes of the individuals for whom we wish to estimate data. The Przewalski's horse pedigree is just about at the limit of complex pedigrees for which this would be computationally feasible. This would, however, require several applications of the program for each polymorphism, and each application would take a considerable amount of computer time. The method we will employ, called the Gibbs Sampler (Geman and Geman 1984), will allow us to simultaneously estimate, by simulation, the marginal probability distributions for the genotypes that we require for each individual in the pedigree. The method, as described by Sheehan (1989), proceeds as follows.

To begin with, each individual whose genotype is unknown is given an initial genotype such that the starting configuration of genotypes in the pedigree is consistent with Mendelian segregation and with the data that have been observed. In the case of a diallelic trait, this can be done by assigning the heterozygous genotype to all ancestors of observed individuals. This ensures that the parental genotypes can give rise to any observed offspring genotypes with positive probability. Descendants of observed individuals can also be given the heterozygous genotype unless the genotypes of their parents make them homozygous. This method does not extend to traits with more than two alleles, which is why only the nine diallelic traits are considered in this study.

The pedigree is then scanned and the genotypes of all individuals are updated in succession as follows. The conditional probability distribution of the genotype of the individual is calculated given the currently assigned genotypes of its neighbors, as defined above, and any observed data for that individual. This calculation can be considered as a local peeling calculation. For each genotype we simply multiply together any probability functions involving the individual being updated, using the currently assigned genotype values for any other individuals involved in these functions.

The required functions are: the penetrance if the individual's phenotype has been observed; the probability of transmission from its parents if it is not a founder; a prior genotype frequency if it is a founder; and the transmission function to each offspring. The result of this is for each genotype a number proportional to the required conditional probability. Then, using a pseudorandom number generator, a genotype is simulated from this distribution and assigned to the individual. The order in which individuals are scanned is not important.

Straightforward theorems for Markov chains (Sheehan and Thomas 1993) show that if the updating described above is done repeatedly, then the configuration of the pedigree's genotype will converge to a realization from the posterior distribution of all configurations given the pedigree structure and observed data. In particular, an individual genotype in the configuration is a realization from the marginal distribution we wish to estimate. We can, therefore, estimate the probabilities in the marginal distributions by making several simulations, observing the outcomes, and simply dividing the number of occurrences of each genotype by the number of simulations. The irreducibility of the underlying Markov process, necessary to make this method work, was proved for this special case by Sheehan (1989).

In practice, we make a large number of updating passes through the pedigree and observe the genotypes at each pass. This gives a large number of highly dependent observations from the posterior distribution of genotype configurations from which we can readily get estimates but not estimated standard errors.

RESULTS

The Przewalski's horse pedigree was analyzed using the above method to estimate each individual's probability of being heterozygous for each of the nine diallelic markers. A Sun 4–260 computer was used to run 10,000 scans for each marker. The programs used were extensions to the PEDPACK pedigree analysis package. Each application used about twenty-one to twenty-two minutes of processing time. Table 11.1 gives the estimated probability of being heterozygous for each marker for

Table 11.1 Probability of heterozygosity at each diallelic locus for the 10 most heterozygous horses

						HORSE				
MARKER	320	339	688	813	982	816	829	998	293	774
Alb	.6994	.7773	1.0000	.0000	.9999	.9999	.0000	.9999	1.0000	.9999
CAI	.0405	.0631	.0219	.9999	.0000	.0000	.0000	.0000	.0000	.0000
GBG	.0000	.0000	.0000	.0000	.0000	.0000	1.0000	1.0000	.0000	1.0000
GPI	.2982	.3753	.3794	.9999	.0000	.0000	.0000	.0000	.0000	.0000
Hb	.4348	.3808	.3190	.0000	.9999	.9999	.0000	.0000	.0000	.0000
MPI	.4576	.4425	.4326	.0000	.9999	.9999	.9999	.9999	1.0000	.9999
PEPB	.6111	.4915	.4704	.9999	.0000	.0000	.0000	.0000	.0000	.0000
PEPD	.2216	.2302	.3208	.9999	.0000	.0000	.9999	.9999	1.0000	.9999
PGMI	.4126	.4173	.4038	.0000	.9999	.9999	.9999	.0000	1.0000	.9999
Mean	.3529	.3531	.3720	.4444	.4444	.4444	.4444	.4444	.4444	.5555

each of the ten horses with the highest estimated heterozygosity averaged over all markers. These horses are colored black in figure 11.1.

Those entries in table 11.1 that are either 0 or 1 (or .9999) correspond to observed data, while those in between correspond to estimates of the probability of being heterozygous. The results range from clear cut (e.g., 320, 339, and 688 are very likely to be homozygous for CAI) to vague (e.g., the results for PGM1 and MPl on these same horses). Such results can indicate which horses, if available, it would be most informative to test for which markers. For instance, little extra information would be gained by testing 688 for CAI; it would be better to test it for PEPB.

Figure 11.3 gives a scatterplot of the average estimated heterozygosity against inbreeding coefficient for each horse in the pedigree. The expected reduction in heterozygosity with increased inbreeding is, however, less striking than might be expected and the variation in heterozygosity for any particular level of inbreeding is large.

Figure 11.3 Mean estimated heterozygosity as calculated by the Gibbs Sampler (averaged over nine diallelic loci) by inbreeding coefficient for each individual in the Przewalski's horse pedigree.

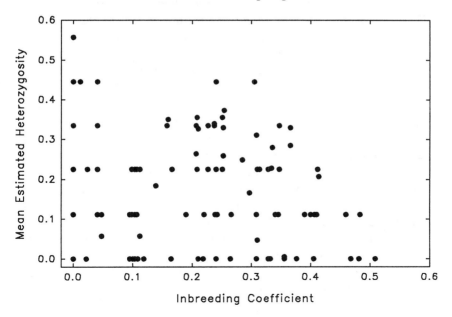

DISCUSSION

The application of the Gibbs Sampler in pedigree analysis is still experimental. These early results, and those of Sheehan (1989), however, indicate that this is a method of great potential, with possibilities for generalizations in many directions. For instance, in the process of producing the marginal distributions for the genotypes of tested individuals, similar distributions for all the other individuals in the pedigree, including the founders, were also calculated. This opens up the possibility for ancestral inference. Equally, genetic counseling can be addressed, as can assessment of breeding programs. Furthermore, joint distributions on genotypes of sets of individuals could have been estimated, allowing, for example, the examination of interactions of descent from the founders. It might also be possible to detect founders coming from different subpopulations in the wild, however, with six to ten generations between data and founders, there is not likely to be enough power to make confident inferences.

The potential of the Gibbs Sampler can perhaps be best appreciated when compared with the standard methods of gene-dropping and peeling. Gene-drop simulation, which uses Monte Carlo methods to simulate genotypes based on the rules of Mendelian segregation (MacCluer et al. 1986), is essentially useless when simulating pedigree genotype configurations consistent with any significant amount of observed data. This would involve generating random genotypes and rejecting those inconsistent with the data. With up to 147 observed genotypes to match, as in this study, the rejection rate would be impracticably high. Peeling, however, is equally limited in the Przewalski's horse pedigree for any genetic trait with more than three genotypes, as the necessary calculations would become computationally infeasible. On the other hand, it is conceivable that the Gibbs Sampler could be used for linkage analysis, possibly even multipoint linkage analysis (with the highly complex genetic models that this would involve) on this complex pedigree.

Several problems need to be addressed before the full potential of this method can be achieved. Most urgently, the question of the number of iterations required to attain a certain accuracy, or equivalently, of getting estimated standard errors of estimates, needs to be considered. Perhaps this can be answered by a rule of thumb such as "each one-hundredth observation is approximately independent," but the autocorrelations within sequences of simulations need further investigation.

Second, just as the underlying Markov chain must be irreducible—that is, it must be possible to go to any genotype configuration that is consistent with the observed data to any other—so it is vital that the process starts in a state consistent with the observations. For diallelic traits this is straightforward, but for more general traits a method for finding an initial consistent state is needed.

Third, there are theoretical considerations. Although the underlying Markov chain induced by this method is known to be irreducible for any realistic diallelic traits, the irreducibility of the chain for multi-allelic traits needs further investigation. Even when it is irreducible, does the Markov chain allow sufficient ease of transition between states to make use of convergence theorems in finite computing time?

The intention of this study has been to illustrate the potential benefits of applying methods from image analysis to pedigree analysis. This is worth much further consideration. Other related methods from image analysis, such as simulated annealing, iterated conditional modes, pseudolikelihoods, and pixel aggregation, may also prove of value either in the maximization of likelihoods or in resampling schemes.

POSTSCRIPTUM

Since this largely experimental work was done, the methodology of Gibbs sampling for pedigrees has progressed significantly. Sheehan and Thomas (1992) have extended the method to traits with any number of alleles and an arbitrary penetrance structure by incorporating a rejection sampling step. This paper also gives a fuller description of the method. With this extension, the problem of finding an initial consistent configuration is also solved. However, despite its theoretical validity and successful use for traits with small numbers of alleles (see Sheehan 1992), the method is still computationally intensive for complex traits with large numbers of alleles, and current research aims at speeding up convergence by updating groups of individuals simultaneously.

Acknowledgments

I am grateful to Georgina Mace, of the London Zoological Society, and David Whitehouse, of University College London, for allowing me access to their data.

REFERENCES

Cannings, C. and E. A. Thompson. 1981. *Genealogical and Genetic Structure.* Cambridge: Cambridge University Press.

Cannings, C., E. A. Thompson, and M. H. Skolnick. 1978. Probability functions on complex pedigrees. *Advances in Applied Probability* 10:26–61.

Geman, S. and D. Geman. 1984. Stochastic relaxation, Gibbs distributions, and the Bayesian restoration of images. *IEEE Transactions on Pattern Analysis and Machine Intelligence* 6:721–41.

MacCluer, J. W., J. L. VandeBerg, B. Read, and O. A. Ryder. 1986. Pedigree analysis by computer simulation. *Zoo Biology* 5:147–60.

Sheehan, N. A. 1989. Image processing procedures applied to the estimation of genotypes on pedigrees. *Technical Report 176,* Department of Statistics, University of Washington, Seattle.

Sheehan, N. A. 1992. Sampling genotypes on complex pedigrees with phenotypic constraints: The origin of the B allele among Polar Eskimos. *IMA Journal of Mathematics Applied in Medicine and Biology* 9:1–18.

Sheehan, N. A. and A. Thomas. 1993. On the irreducibility of a Markov chain defined on a space of genotype configurations by a sampling scheme. *Biometrics* 49:163–75.

Volf, J. 1959 et seq. *Pedigree Book of the Przewalski's Horse (Equus przewalskii).* Prague Zoo, Czechoslovakia.

PART FOUR

Conservation Strategies

12

Conservation Management Strategies Based on Viable Populations

■■

Thomas J. Foose, Leobert de Boer,
Ulysses S. Seal, and Russell Lande

Conservation has traditionally concentrated on ecosystems and on protection. This volume is predicated on the premise that conservation
must be increasingly based on management and on populations. It is
also the case that the most frequent and formidable conservation problems are political not biological. This volume is about biology.

The paramount concern of conservation is the survival or recovery of
ecosystems. However, ecosystems are often exasperatingly complex.
Therefore, they do not often provide a practicable framework for defining conservation action with enough explicitness and simplicity to be

feasible. Conservation of carefully selected populations can provide the best method to insure the survival and recovery of not only individual taxa but also their ecosystems. The linkage is provided by the use of umbrella and keystone taxa. An umbrella taxon is one for which the habitat required to sustain viable populations is sufficiently large to encompass appreciable parts of natural ecosystems. A keystone species is one whose ecology is crucial to the operation of the entire ecosystem. Umbrella species are also frequently keystone species, although the converse is not normally the case. The most common umbrella taxa are the so-called charismatic megavertebrates (Janzen 1988; Terborgh 1988; Redford 1992). Their function as umbrella species can in part ameliorate the concern that investing so much money for the preservation of a few megavertebrates is unjustified as long as the greater number of perhaps more important but less charismatic species may be neglected.

Protection, while necessary, is often insufficient to ensure the survival and recovery of ecosystems and their component populations. Management is necessary because the populations that can be maintained under the pressures of unsustainable exploitation and habitat degradation are small, i.e., a few tens to a few hundreds, or at best a few thousands, depending on the species. Small populations are vulnerable to stochastic, or random, problems that can imperil their survival just as much as the more deterministic threats of habitat degradation and unsustainable exploitation. Protection can mitigate the deterministic problems. Management is required to mitigate the stochastic problems.

In this essay we discuss methods for developing management-orientated conservation strategies based on the concept of viable populations. This concept emphasizes the benefits of formulating explicit quantitative goals as conservation objectives for both wild and captive populations. The process of developing these conservation strategies is greatly facilitated through the use of population and habitat viability analyses (PHVAs) computer models (Boyce 1992; Lacy 1993). Often, these analyses emphasize the need for managing multiple populations (i.e., metapopulations) to enhance population viability. Frequently, an important component of the management strategy for a metapopulation is captive propagation. Thus, management objectives and strategies for captive propagation programs are briefly discussed. Finally, based on the experiences of the Captive Breeding Specialist Group

(CBSG), we present an outline of how conservation strategies for endangered taxa can be prioritized and formulated in a comprehensive and integrated action plan.

PROBLEMS OF SMALL POPULATIONS

Stochastic problems affecting the long-term persistence of small populations can be environmental, demographic, and/or genetic in nature. Environmentally, small populations can be devastated by catastrophes or decimated by less drastic fluctuations in environmental conditions that can impair the survival and fertility of individuals. Catastrophes (e.g., droughts, floods, epidemics) are increasingly recognized as severe threats to small populations (Thorne and Oakleaf 1991). Demographically, even in the absence of deleterious fluctuations in the environment, small populations may develop intrinsic demographic problems (e.g., biased sex ratios, unstable age distributions, or random failures in survival and fertility) that can fatally disrupt propagation and persis-

Figure 12.1 Extinction vortex: interaction between demographic (reduced reproduction, survival) and genetic (inbreeding depression, increased susceptibility to disease) factors reduces population size, causing further genetic and demographic problems. *From Seal et al. 1990*

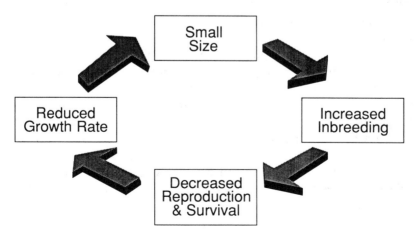

tence (Goodman 1987). Genetically, small populations also can rapidly lose the heritable diversity necessary for fitness under existing environmental conditions and for their adaptation to changed environments in the future (Lacy et al., essay 4 of this volume; Hedrick et al. 1986). The smaller the population and the more limited its distribution, the greater these stochastic risks will be. Further, the genetic and demographic problems can interact (figure 12.1) to create what is known as an extinction vortex (Gilpin and Soulé 1986). These problems apply to small populations whether they still occur in the natural habitat of the species or are maintained in more artificial environments (i.e., captivity).

Given their stochastic nature, the occurrence and effect of these problems in small populations is difficult to predict with accuracy. However, management actions must be developed to address these concerns. Furthermore, conservation strategies should be formulated on the basis of worst-case scenarios to maximize options and minimize regrets (Starfield et al., essay 8 of this volume). Such strategies can be developed by basing them on the concept of viable populations.

VIABLE POPULATION CONSERVATION STRATEGIES

It has been proposed that the ultimate goal of conservation strategies should be the survival or recovery of populations large enough to permit evolution through natural selection to occur (Soulé 1987b). There have been a number of attempts to provide general guidelines on the population sizes this will require (Franklin 1980; Lande 1988, essay 14 of this volume).

More intermediate or pragmatic goals, however, may be necessary for species that are currently threatened with extinction, are reduced in number, and most probably will remain that way for a long time. Conservation strategies for these species must be based on maintaining viable populations, i.e., populations sufficiently large and well distributed to ensure a high probability (e.g., 99%) of survival for a long period of time (e.g., 100 years; Shaffer 1987) and/or to retain as much of the genetic variation of a defined set of organisms (geographic population, subspecies, species) to maximize options for the future (Foose 1991; Soulé et al. 1986; Lande, essay 14 of this volume). These options will include eventual recovery of the larger population sizes that will permit evolution by natural selection to occur. Hence, conservation strategies need to be based on population viability theory and goals (Soulé 1987a).

A critical characteristic of a viable population strategy is that it provides explicit and quantitative objectives, for example:

- 99% probability of survival over, and recovery of evolutionary potential by the end of, the next 100 years; or
- 99% probability of survival and 95% preservation of diversity for the next 100 years; and,
- Consequently, populations of a quantitatively specified size and distribution to achieve these objectives.

There are at least two major reasons to be as numerate or as quantitative as possible. Action plans (for captive and wild populations) ultimately must establish numerical objectives for population sizes and distribution as countermeasures to the stochastic problems if populations are to be viable. Numbers also provide for more objectivity, less ambiguity, more comparability, better communication and, hence, cooperation.

There is no single magic number that represents a viable population size for all taxa (Soulé 1987a). Indeed, there is no single number that represents a minimum viable population for any one taxon all the time. Rather, viable population size depends on several sets of factors:

1. Genetic and demographic objectives of the conservation program
   (A) The probability of demographic survival of the population
   (B) Genetic goals of evolution by natural selection or preservation of a defined high level of genetic variation (for the latter goal, there is then the issue of the kinds and amounts of genetic diversity to be preserved; Lande and Barrowclough 1987; Lande, essay 14 of this volume);
   (C) The period of time over which this genetic diversity and survival probability are to be maintained
2. The kinds and levels of stochasticity operating
3. Biological characteristics of the population, which include:
   (A) Size and geographic distribution
   (B) Life-history characteristics
   (C) Intrinsic growth rate and its variation over time

(D) Number of founders

(E) Ratio of genetically effective size (N_e) to the total size (N)

(F) The degree of subdivision or fragmentation

While the exact sizes for population viability will vary depending on these factors, it may be possible to provide some useful generalizations and guidelines (Franklin 1980; Soulé et al. 1986; Mace and Lande 1991; Lande, essay 14 of this volume). These criteria are formulated in terms of both effective and total population sizes. Effective size is critical with respect to the stochastic problems, in particular the loss of genetic diversity. N_e may be as low as 10 to 25% of the total population number. Mace and Lande (1991) use a general N_e/N ratio of .2, which may be low for some taxa. But conservatism is prudent. Thus, using the Mace-Lande guidelines, a recommended N_e of 500 may require that a population of at least 2500, or better more, actually be maintained. It is important to realize that the minimum scientifically recommended as necessary for long-term survival under the best information available is just that, a minimum. More is always better and safer.

Population viability theory can contribute to the development of conservation strategies at the level of both the single taxon and the multiple taxa. When applied to keystone or umbrella species, population viability theory can also be the foundation for conservation strategies for ecosystems and reserve design (Armbruster and Lande 1993).

POPULATION AND HABITAT VIABILITY ANALYSIS

At the population, taxon, or ecosystem level, the population viability approach to formulating conservation strategies is made possible by population and habitat viability analyses (PHVAs; Boyce 1992; Clark et al. 1990; Lindenmayer et al. 1991; Lacy 1993). PHVA is the process of systematically and quantitatively evaluating: (1) the extinction processes that operate on small and often fragmented populations of threatened taxa, and (2) the probable consequences for the viability of the population of various management actions or inactions (Soulé 1987c, Gilpin and Soulé 1986, Boyce 1992).

Computer modeling is an important part of this process (Lacy 1993). The models incorporate information on the geographic distribution, demographic, and genetic characteristics of the population, and conditions in the environment to simulate probable fates (especially probability of extinction and loss of genetic variation) under these circumstances. However, no computer model can be expected to provide exact quantitative predictions of extinction because of the complexity of the extinction process, our lack of understanding of the specific processes involved, and, often, lack of data. Nevertheless, computer models have proven extremely useful in the PHVA process because they can be used to:

1. Focus attention and discussion on the biological and ecological problems affecting the population, which is facilitated by the quantitative approach

2. Quantitatively describe and evaluate a range of scenarios for the populations under a variety of management (or nonmanagement) regimes

3. Identify gaps in our knowledge in areas that may be important for the survival of the populations

4. Help formulate specific management actions that maximize the probability of the population's survival or recovery

The management actions deriving from the PHVA process may include: establishment, enlargement, or more management of protected areas; poaching control; reintroduction or translocation; sustainable use programs; education efforts; and initiation or maintenance of captive breeding programs. The PHVA process can also be used to recommend quantitative objectives for population and metapopulation conservation strategies that provide acceptable levels of probability of the taxon's survival and preservation of its genetic diversity. These management actions and conservation objectives can assist in formulating action plans at the level of both the individual taxon and multiple taxa (Seal and Foose 1989; Seal et al. 1990).

METAPOPULATION STRATEGIES

It will be difficult or impossible to maintain single, contiguous populations in the hundreds or thousands required for viability. However, it is possible for smaller populations and sanctuaries to be viable if they are managed interactively as a so-called metapopulation. Hence, viable

population strategies will often require the development of metapopulations (figure 12.2) to achieve populations that are sufficiently large
and widely distributed to have an acceptable probability of surviving
stochastic risks (Gilpin 1987; Gilpin and Soulé 1986; Hanski 1991).

Metapopulation strategies will entail interactively managing the
subpopulations to maximize the probability of the species' survival.
Any small, isolated population is at high risk of extinction. In a system
of such small populations, the same factors of extinction still operate
but not all at the same time or in the same way. Hence, the overall system, the metapopulation, has a higher probability of survival (Hanski
1991). Moreover, subdivided populations can potentially preserve
much higher levels of genetic variation than can single panmictic populations (Lande, essay 14 of this volume).

A metapopulation strategy (or survival plan) must recommend the
number, sizes, and distribution of the subpopulations and the level of
interchange among them to achieve the goals of the conservation pro-

Figure 12.2 Metapopulation management strategies can include captive and wild population components.

METAPOPULATION

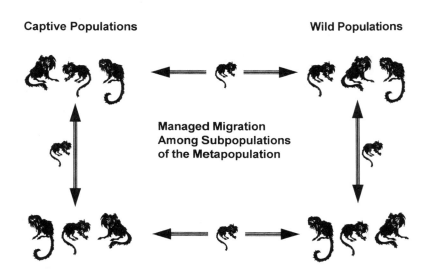

Captive Populations

Wild Populations

**Managed Migration
Among Subpopulations
of the Metapopulation**

gram. PHVAs can provide recommendations on the number, size, and interaction of the separate subpopulations that are being managed collectively and interactively to constitute the metapopulation.

As an example of applying this kind of strategy, the International Union for the Conservation of Nature's (IUCN) Species Survival Commission (SSC) in its Asian Rhino Action Plan for each of the three species of Asian rhinos recommends (Khan 1989):

Total Effective Population Size $(N_e) \geq 500$
Total Population Size ≥ 2500
Number of Subpopulations ≥ 10
Size of Each Subpopulation ≥ 100.

Similar recommendations have been provided for species ranging in size and situation from the black-footed ferret (*Mustela nigripes;* Brussard and Gilpin 1989) to the African elephant (*Loxodonta africana;* Armbruster and Lande 1993)

Reproductive technology, i.e., artificial insemination and embryo transfer techniques could greatly facilitate the management of populations in the wild as well as in captivity, especially in interactions between the two (Moore et al. 1992). Reproductive technology may also greatly facilitate the "readaptation" process from captivity to the wild. There may be significant difficulties for captive-bred animals to readapt to wild conditions (Arnold, essay 13 of this volume). However, where remnant natural populations survive, it may be possible to infuse "new blood," in the form of semen or embryos, from the genetic reservoirs in captivity into individuals in the wild that still retain survival skills acquired by experience rather than inheritance. Thus, reproductive technology may permit conservation management to achieve the best of both worlds.

ZOOS AND MEGAZOOS

Conservation strategies to achieve viable populations often entail metapopulation management strategies in which there is: (1) protection of larger populations in the "wild"; (2) intensive *in situ* management of smaller populations in the "wild"; and (3) *ex situ* programs to reinforce wild populations (de Boer 1992). In actuality, captive (*ex situ*) and wild (*in situ*) are really poles of a spectrum. To a great extent, there is no longer any wild, at least for the larger species (Conway, preface to this volume). For them and for many other species, what survives on the planet is a spectrum of situations and scenarios that vary only in the level of human exploitation and management applied to them. It will still be convenient to refer to populations more or less free-ranging in natural habitats as being in the wild but only while realizing that these species are not in unexploited or unmanaged situations. Mark Stanley-Price (1993) has recently suggested a visualization of this spectrum as depicted in figure 12.3.

Managed migration is one example of the kinds of intensive management and protection of viable populations in the wild. More intensive management may also be possible and needed for small wild populations so that corrective measures can be applied if and when stochastic problems are detected (Foose 1989). Some examples might be to accelerate the turnover of dominant males that might be monopolizing the breeding of multiple females and thereby causing distortion of sex ratios and depression of N_e, to translocate otherwise doomed dispersing young animals to available habitat to which they could not migrate naturally, and to relocate animals to prevent reproduction by close relatives and to improve survival of the young.

As traditional zoos become larger and more naturalistic, sanctuaries

Figure 12.3 The spectrum of focus of conservation strategies, ranging from *ex situ* genome banking to *in situ* conservation of wild populations. *Modified from Stanley-Price 1993*

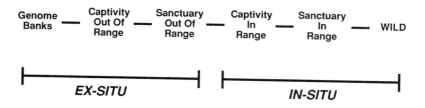

OPTIONS FOR WILDLIFE CONSERVATION

in the wild are becoming smaller and more artificial. In essence they are becoming megazoos. The same kinds of intensive management in genetic and demographic terms will need to be applied to both zoo and wild populations. For example, in Kenya, the five hundred or so surviving rhino are mostly in sanctuaries that are now completely enclosed with fences and are further protected by frequent guard patrols (Conway, preface to this volume). Intensive management will require much sophisticated genetic and demographic analysis of populations and will demand the compilation of more detailed data on wild populations including the possible compilation of studbooks (Lacy et al., essay 4 of this volume). Studbooks are already being compiled and applied to these megazoo situations (e.g., golden lion tamarins *Leontopithecus rosalia*, J. Ballou, personal communication).

Managed metapopulations will also frequently incorporate captive populations. There are a number of advantages to captivity: animals can be protected from poachers; environmental variance can be moderated; there can be more intensive genetic management, specifically the effective population size can be increased; and numbers can be securely expanded, ultimately to provide stock for return to natural habitats.

The paramount goal of captive propagation programs is to contribute to the survival and recovery of populations in the wild, i.e., less intensively managed habitats within the natural or historic range of the taxon (Foose et al. 1986). Captive populations are support, not a substitute, for wild populations. This support can be the restoration of populations that have been extinguished or the revitalization of populations that are debilitated genetically or demographically. Indeed, what appears optimal and inevitable are conservation strategies incorporating both captive and wild populations that are interactively managed for mutual support and survival.

IUCN, the World Conservation Union, has recognized the importance of captive programs with a policy statement that recommends initiation of a captive propagation program for any taxon whose wild population declines below one thousand, an admittedly simplistic and arbitrary number but one that at least provides a point of departure (IUCN 1987). The new Mace-Lande categories suggest that this threshold should in general perhaps be twenty-five hundred (Mace and Lande 1991).

In general, captive populations and captive propagation programs can serve three roles in holistic conservation strategies (IUDZG 1993):

1. Living ambassadors that can educate the public at all levels and can generate funds for *in situ* conservation

2. Scientific resources and opportunities for research that can provide information and technologies beneficial to protection and management of populations in the wild

3. Genetic and demographic reservoirs that can be used to reinforce the survival of taxa in the wild either by revitalizing populations that are languishing in natural habitats or by reestablishing populations that have become extinct

The third of these roles may often be a benefit only for the longer term as return to the wild may not be a prospect for the immediate future. However, it is proposed that captive and wild populations should and can be intensively and interactively managed with interchanges of animals occurring as needed and as feasible to genetically and demographically enhance the survival of wild populations. The PHVA process can be used to define specific objectives and management actions (e.g., frequency of interchanges) for such interactive management of wild and captive populations. It is important to note that there may be many problems with such interchanges including epidemiologic risks, logistic difficulties, financial limitations, etc. But with effort, based on limited but growing experience, these problems can be resolved (Gipps 1991). The bottom line is that strategies and priorities should try to maximize options and minimize regrets.

Formally coordinated and scientifically managed captive propagation programs have been developed at both regional and global levels to breed and manage over 160 designated, usually threatened, taxa (see, e.g. Wiese et al. 1993). Regional programs now exist in North America (the American Association of Zoological Parks and Aquariums' Species Survival Plan; Hutchins and Wiese 1991), continental Europe (Europäisches Erhaltungszucht Programm; de Boer 1992) the United Kingdom (the British Federation of Zoos' Joint Management of Species Group), Australasia (the Australasian Regional Association of Zoological Parks and Aquaria's Australasian Species Management Program), Japan, India, and Sub-Saharan Africa (de Boer and Foose 1992).

Each region is also actively involved in coordinating its breeding programs at the international level with the facilitation of the Captive Breeding Specialist Group (CBSG) of the IUCN (Foose et al. 1992; Seal et al. 1994). Such coordination will assist regional programs in:

1. Adopting global conservation goals for the species involved in regional programs

2. Dividing responsibility, e.g., especially target population sizes, for achieving global goals

3. Arranging interactions, especially animal or germplasm exchanges, among the regional programs

However, even maximal participation and coordination of the world's zoos may not provide enough captive habitat and resources to assist all the taxa in need (e.g., Maguire and Lacy 1990). The problem is formidable: Soulé et al. (1986) estimate that two thousand species of large vertebrates will need captive propagation assistance to avoid extinction. Captive propagation programs must be not merely internationalized but also recognized as an important conservation tool and applied by governmental wildlife departments and other nonzoo organizations: captive propagation need not occur only in traditional zoos. There is great merit in wildlife departments developing captive propagation programs, often in collaboration with traditional zoos, especially within or near the natural habitat of a taxon. A major problem is that such endeavors will divert resources that might otherwise be applied to free-ranging populations. Quantitative cost benefit analyses must be conducted to resolve the conflicts.

The basic population management objectives of these regional and global propagation programs are to propagate and manage *ex situ* populations of highly threatened taxa with prescribed levels of demographic stability and genetic diversity for defined periods of time to prevent the taxa's extinction and to fulfill the goal of establishing or restoring viable populations in the wild. The formal programs operate through masterplans that perform sophisticated genetic and demographic analyses to formulate animal-by-animal recommendations for the entire managed captive population (Foose and Ballou 1988; Ballou and Foose in press).

All conservation-orientated captive propagation programs attempt to minimize the amount of genetic change that may occur in a taxon during its time in captivity (Arnold, essay 13 of this volume; Lacy et al., essay 4 of this volume). The challenge is to insure that the animals emerge from the ark in some semblance of how they entered (Lacy et al., essay 4 of this volume). Because the loss of genetic diversity and vulnerability to stochasticity is a function of population size, an important part of every program is establishing a target population size (also known as the captive carrying capacity) large enough to achieve acceptable genetic and demographic objectives. In terms of the genetic and demographic problems, more is always better. However, captive habitat is limited, so target populations must be compromises between maxima large enough for viability and minima that do not exclude other taxa from programs.

The role of captive propagation in the conservation strategy for a taxon and its genetic and demographic objectives will, therefore, depend to a large part on the status and prospects of the taxon in the wild. Some taxa need large captive populations for a long time; others need small incipient nuclei or reduced gene pools that can be expanded later if needed. To reflect the varying role that captive propagation may play in conservation strategies, the CBSG has defined five categories, or levels, of captive propagation programs (table 12.1). These range from the immediate establishment of captive populations in the case of severely endangered species (90%/100 YEARS I in figure 12.1) to captive populations that can be disbanded to make room for other, more needy, species (category ELIMINATE in figure 12.1).

The program goals for taxa categorized as either 90%/100 YEARS I and II are different from the general guideline recommended for captive programs in the past, i.e., 90% of genetic diversity for 200 years (Soulé et al. 1986). A shorter time period is proposed for two reasons. First, it buys time for more taxa that might be excluded from captive programs if a longer time period (e.g., 200 years) is adopted. Second, it maintains more incentive to secure or restore viable populations *in situ*.

It is often a useful fiction to visualize the history and development of captive populations as expanding from a base of founders to a target size (Ralls and Ballou 1992). Ideally, this expansion should be as rapid as possible for both demographic security and genetic diversity although some details of genetic management may require less than maximal growth in some instances. For example, in the black-footed ferret program, genetic management was considered a priority only after the captive population attained sufficient size for modest security (Ballou and Oakleaf 1989). In general, once the population has attained its target size, there is an attempt to stabilize it at approximately this number by regulating the reproduction and survival of individuals.

As new populations (captive or wild) are established or reestablished, a very important consideration is the number of founders. A founder is an animal from a source population (e.g., an existing wild population) that establishes a derived population (e.g., a captive or translocated wild population). There must be care to insure that the founders represent a viable genetic sample from the source population. In the case of captive populations, the founders from the wild represent the sample of the wild gene pool that the captive program can then try to preserve. The number of founders can affect the target size required (Soulé et al. 1986). To a point, the more founders the better, although there may be a point of diminishing returns at about twenty to thirty effective founders (Lacy 1987, 1989). However, the number of founders does depend in part on the kind of diversity from the wild gene pool that is of concern. Founder numbers in the range between twenty and thirty are adequate to contain 95% or more of the source gene pool's average heterozygosity, which in a sense represents the more common alleles (Denniston 1978). If rare alleles (which may be important for future adaptation) are of concern, the number of founders required will be much larger (Gregorius 1980).

Whatever the number of founders, it is useful to visualize the attempt to preserve genetic variation in captive or other intensively managed small populations in terms of the relative representation of founder lineages over time. Ideally, this representation should be equal. However, uneven production of offspring and hence transmission of genes through lineages causes disparity in the representation of lineages and loss of the genomes of the various founders (Lacy 1989). Hence, instead of equality, the goal of genetic management becomes proportionate parity. In other words, a target distribution of desired founder representations is established to reflect the relative proportion of each founder's genome that still survives in the population. Conceptually, reproduction is managed to move the founder representations in the population toward this target distribution (Ballou and Lacy, essay 5 of this volume).

Actual management to achieve the genetic and demographic goals translates into establishing offspring objectives for both individuals and the population. Animals that will actually be bred in any year are selected based on their genetic and demographic importance. Mean kinship has emerged along with measures of genome uniqueness as the primary criteria of genetic importance (Ballou and Lacy, essay 5 of this volume; Thompson, essay 6 of this volume). The bottom line is that formal captive propagation programs try to provide institution-by-institution and animal-by-animal recommendations for propagation and management to achieve specific genetic and demographic objectives.

This simplistic overview has emphasized methods that require good data on pedigrees and vital statistics. Often in captive and usually in wild populations, such data are deficient. Hence, alternative models less sensitive to such incomplete data need to be developed (Lacy et al., essay 4 of this volume; Princée, essay 7 of this volume). Many of the papers in this volume are devoted to this problem.

IDENTIFYING PRIORITIES: CONSERVATION ACTION PLANS

Population viability theory can also be used systematically and comprehensively to develop priorities for action and hence the allocation of resources. Terms such as triage have been used in the past to describe such processes. An important part of this process is assessing the degree of threat. Mace and Lande (1991) propose the use of population viability concepts as a basis for categorizing taxa according to the degree of threat facing a taxon. They suggest that the IUCN Red Data Categories (threatened, vulnerable, and endangered) be reformulated in a more quantitative way to reflect the problems of small populations. The Mace-Lande scheme provides quantitative criteria for assessing the degree of threat in terms of population sizes, distribution, trends, and deterministic and stochastic threats confronting the populations.

The CBSG, in collaboration with other IUCN Specialist Groups and conservation organizations, has developed and applied a Conservation Assessment and Management Plan (CAMP) process to formulate a strategic guide for intensive conservation action for a particular taxon or taxa (Foose et al. 1992; Seal et al. 1994). This process:

1. Reviews the wild and captive status of each taxon in a defined broad group of taxa (e.g., an order, family, subfamily, community)

2. Assesses the degree of threat for each taxon according to the Mace-Lande categories

3. Recommends intensive management and information collection action to mitigate the threat. This may include conducting

PHVA workshops, *in situ* management, conservation oriented research (surveys, taxonomy, etc.), captive breeding, and/or genome banking

If captive propagation is appropriate, an important outcome of the CAMP process is a global captive breeding action plan. This plan:

1. Recommends:
    (A) which taxa in captivity should remain there
    (B) which taxa in captivity need not be maintained there for conservation reasons
    (C) which taxa not yet in captivity should be there to assist conservation efforts

2. Proposes levels for captive breeding programs in terms of genetic and demographic objectives that translate into recommendations about global captive target populations (see table 12.1)

3. Suggests how responsibilities for captive programs might be

Table 12.1 Five levels of captive propagation programs used by the Captive Breeding Specialist Group (CBSG) to assign conservation status to captive populations

LEVEL	CAPTIVE POPULATION OBJECTIVES
90% / 100 Years I	Immediately establish (within 1–5 years) and maintain a captive population of sufficient size to preserve 90% of the average heterozygosity of the wild gene pool for 100 years.
90% / 100 Years II	Establish a captive population of sufficient size to preserve 90% of the average heterozygosity of the wild gene pool for 100 years within the next 5–10 years.
Nucleus I	Establish a captive nucleus (50–100 individuals) to continuously represent 98% of the wild gene pool's heterozygosity. This type of program will require periodic, but in most cases modest, immigration/importation of individuals from the wild to maintain this high level of genetic diversity in such a limited captive population (Willis and Wiese 1993). Reproductive technology will facilitate this strategy.
Nucleus II	Maintain a well-managed captive nucleus (25–100) for taxa not of conservation concern but otherwise of interest (e.g., maintained for educational or research purposes).
Elimination	Taxa are not of conservation concern and are not otherwise of interest. The captive population should be managed to extinction to make room for other, more needy taxa.

distributed among the regional programs (i.e., this function translates into recommendations for regional captive target population sizes)

4. Identifies priorities for technology transfer and for financial and other support for *in situ* conservation

A similar process should occur at a regional level (e.g., North America) to reflect regional goals and priorities (e.g., Baker in press; Koontz in press; Hutchins and Wiese 1991).

CONCLUSIONS

The CBSG, in collaboration with governmental and nongovernmental conservation agencies has applied the PHVA process in workshop settings to develop comprehensive and integrated conservation strategies for over thirty taxa. These include the Florida panther (*Felis concolor coryi;* Seal and Lacy 1989), lion tamarins (*Leontopithecus* spp.; Seal et al. 1990), Javan rhinoceros (*Rhinoceros sondaicus,* Seal and Foose 1989), and numerous others. Our experience, and the experiences of others involved in similar challenges, demonstrates that the PHVA process has proven most successful when conducted *in situ* in a workshop format, bringing together all relevant experts knowledgeable in the biology, ecology, conservation, and administration of the taxon (taxa) of concern (Lacy 1993; Lindenmayer et al. 1991; Clark et al. 1990).

In summary, concepts from population viability theory can be used to help formulate conservation strategies for populations and their ecosystems in both captivity and the wild at both the level of a single taxon and that of multiple taxa. As wild populations continue to be limited in size and distribution, they will increasingly require the intensive levels of management now commonly applied only to captive populations. Thus, conservation strategies for small populations in nature will become increasingly similar to those in captivity. This reality must be recognized by all those concerned with the continuing survival of the species now facing extinction.

References

Armbruster, P. and R. Lande. 1993. A population viability analysis for the African elephant (*Loxodonta africana*): How big should reserves be? *Conservation Biology* 7:602–10.

Baker, A., ed. In press. *AZA New World Primate Regional Collection Plan.* Syracuse, New York: Burnet Park Zoo.

Ballou, J. D. and T. J. Foose. In press. Demographic and genetic management of captive populations. In D. G. Kleiman, S. Lumpkin, M. Allen, H. Harris, and K. Thompson, eds., *Wild Mammals in Captivity.* Chicago: University of Chicago Press.

Ballou, J. D. and R. Oakleaf. 1989. Demographic and genetic captive-breeding recommendations for black-footed ferrets. In U. S. Seal, E. T. Thorne, M. A. Bogan, and S. H. Anderson, eds., *Conservation Biology and the Black-footed Ferret,* pp. 247–67. New Haven: Yale University Press.

Boyce, M. S. 1992. Population viability analysis. *Annual Review of Ecology and Systematics* 23:481–506.

Brussard, P. F. and M. E. Gilpin. 1989. Demographic and genetic problems of small populations. In U. S. Seal, E. T. Thorne, M. A. Bogan, and S. H. Anderson, eds., *Conservation Biology and the Black-footed Ferret,* pp. 37–48. New Haven: Yale University Press.

Clark, T. W., G. N. Backhouse, and R. C. Lacy. 1990. The population viability assessment workshop: A tool for threatened species management. *Endangered Species Update* 8 (2): 1–5.

de Boer, L. E. M. 1992. *Ex situ* propagation programmes as a contribution to the conservation of biodiversity. In O. T. Sandlund, K. Hindar, and A. H. D. Brown, eds., *Conservation of Biodiversity for Sustainable Development,* pp. 214–29. Oslo: Scandinavian University Press.

de Boer, L. E. M. and T. J. Foose. 1992. Analysis of breeding programmes in other regions. In K. Brouwer, S. Smits, and L. E. M. de Boer, eds., *EEP Yearbook 1991/92,* pp. 215–16. Amsterdam: EAZA/EEP Executive Office.

Denniston, C. 1978. Small population size and genetic diversity. Implications for endangered species. In S. A. Temple, ed., *Endangered Birds: Management Techniques for Preserving Threatened Species,* pp. 281–89. Madison, Wisconsin: University of Wisconsin Press.

Foose, T. J. 1989. Globalization of species survival programs: The world as a megazoo. In B. L. Dresser, R. W. Reece, and E. J. Maruska, eds., *Proceedings: 5th World Conference on Breeding Endangered Species in Captivity,* pp. 383–92. Cincinnati, Ohio: Cincinnati Zoo & Botanical Garden, Center for Reproduction of Endangered Wildlife.

Foose, T. J. 1991. Viable population strategies for reintroduction programmes. *Symposium of the Zoological Society of London* 62:165–72.

Foose, T. J. and J. D. Ballou. 1988. Management of small populations. *International Zoo Yearbook* 27:26–41.

Foose, T. J., R. Lande, N. R. Flesness, G. Rabb, and B. Read. 1986. Propagation plans. *Zoo Biology* 5:139–46.

Foose, T. J., S. Ellis-Joseph, and U. S. Seal. 1992. Conservation assessment and management plans (CAMPs) progress report. *SPECIES* 18:73–75.

Franklin, I. R. 1980. Evolutionary changes in small populations. In M. E. Soulé and B. A. Wilcox, eds., *Conservation Biology: An Evolutionary-Ecological Perspective,* pp. 135–49. Sunderland, Mass.: Sinauer.

Gilpin, M. E. 1987. Spatial structure and population vulnerability. In M. E. Soulé, ed., *Viable Populations for Conservation,* pp. 125–39. Cambridge: Cambridge University Press.

Gilpin, M. E. and M. E. Soulé. 1986. Minimum viable populations: Processes of species extinction. In M. E. Soulé, ed., *Conservation Biology: The Science of Scarcity and Diversity,* pp. 19–34. Sunderland, Mass.: Sinauer.

Gipps, J. H. W. 1991. *Beyond Captive Breeding.* New York: Oxford University Press.

Goodman, D. 1987. The demography of chance extinction. In M. E. Soulé, ed., *Viable Populations for Conservation,* pp. 11–34. Cambridge: Cambridge University Press.

Gregorius, H. 1980. The probability of losing an allele when diploid genotypes are sampled. *Biometrics* 36:643–52.

Hanski, I. 1991. Single-species metapopulation dynamics: Concepts, models, and observations. *Biological Journal of the Linnean Society* 42:17–38.

Hedrick, P. W., P. F. Brussard, F. W. Allendorf, J. A. Beardmore, and S. Orzack. 1986. Protein variation, fitness, and captive propagation. *Zoo Biology* 5:91–99.

Hutchins, M. and R. J. Wiese. 1991. Beyond genetic and demographic management: The future of the Species Survival Plan and related AAZPA Conservation Efforts. *Zoo Biology* 10:285–92.

IUCN. 1987. *IUCN Policy Statement on Captive Breeding.* Gland, Switzerland: International Union for the Conservation of Nature (IUCN).

IUDZG/CBSG (IUCN/SSC). 1993. *The World Zoo Conservation Strategy: The Role of the Zoos and Aquaria of the World in Global Conservation.* Brookfield, Ill.: Chicago Zoological Society.

Janzen, D. H. 1988. Management of habitat fragments in a tropical dry forest: Growth. *Annals of the Missouri Botanical Garden* 75:105–16.

Khan, M. 1989. *Asian Rhinos: An Action Plan for Their Conservation.* Gland, Switzerland: IUCN.

Koontz, F., ed. In press. *AZA Old World Monkey Regional Collection Plan.* Bronx, New York: New York Zoological Society.

Lacy, R. C. 1987. Loss of genetic diversity from managed populations: Interacting effects of drift, mutation, immigration, selection, and population subdivision. *Conservation Biology* 1:143–58.

Lacy, R. C. 1989. Analysis of founder representation in pedigrees: Founder equivalents and founder genome equivalents. *Zoo Biology* 8:111–24.

Lacy, R. C. 1993. Vortex: A computer simulation model for population viability analysis. *Wildlife Research* 20:45–65.

Lande, R. 1988. Genetics and demography in biological conservation. *Science* 241:1455–60.

Lande, R. and G. F. Barrowclough. 1987. Effective population size, genetic variation, and their use in population management. In M. E. Soulé, ed., *Viable Populations for Conservation,* pp. 87–124. Cambridge: Cambridge University Press.

Lindenmayer, D. B., V. C. Thomas, R. C. Lacy, and T. W. Clark. 1991. *Population Viability Analysis (PVA): The Concept and its Applications, with a Case Study of Lead-*

beater's Possum, Gymnobelideus leadbeateri. Report to the Resource Assessment Commission. Melbourne: Department of Conservation and Environment.

Mace, G. M. and R. Lande 1991. Assessing extinction threats: Towards a reevaluation of IUCN Threatened Species Categories. *Conservation Biology* 5:148–57.

Maguire, L. A. and R. C. Lacy. 1990. Allocating scarce resources for conservation of endangered subspecies: Partitioning zoo space for tigers. *Conservation Biology* 4:157–66.

Moore, H. D. M., W. V. Holt, and G. M. Mace. 1992. *Biotechnology and the Conservation of Genetic Diversity.* Oxford: Clarendon Press.

Ralls, K. and J. D. Ballou. 1992. Managing genetic diversity in captive breeding and reintroduction programs. *Transactions of the 57th North American Wildlife and Natural Resources Conference:* 263–82.

Redford, K. H. 1992. The empty forest. *Bioscience* 42:412–22.

Seal, U. S. and T. J. Foose. 1989. *Javan Rhinoceros: Population Viability Analysis.* Apple Valley, Minn.: IUCN Captive Breeding Specialist Group (CBSG).

Seal, U. S. and R. C. Lacy. 1989. *Florida panther population viability analysis.* Report to the U.S. Fish and Wildlife Service. Apple Valley, Minn.: IUCN Captive Breeding Specialist Group (CBSG).

Seal, U. S., J. D. Ballou, and C. V. Padua. 1990. *Leontopithecus: Population Viability Analysis Workshop Report.* Apple Valley, Minn.: IUCN Captive Breeding Specialist Group (CBSG).

Seal, U. S., T. J. Foose, and S. Ellis. 1994. Conservation assessment and management plans (CAMPs) and Global Captive Action Plans (GCAPs). In P. J. S. Olney, G. M. Mace, and A. T. C. Feistner, eds., *Creative Conservation,* pp. 312–23. London: Chapman and Hall.

Shaffer, M. 1987. Minimum viable populations: Coping with uncertainty. In M. E. Soulé, ed., *Viable Populations for Conservation,* pp. 69–86. Cambridge: Cambridge University Press.

Soulé, M. E. 1987a. Introduction. In M. E. Soulé, ed., *Viable Populations for Conservation,* pp. 1–10. Cambridge: Cambridge University Press.

Soulé, M. E. 1987b. Where do we go from here? In M. E. Soulé, ed., *Viable Populations for Conservation,* pp. 175–84. Cambridge: Cambridge University Press.

Soulé, M. E., ed. 1987c. *Viable Populations for Conservation.* Cambridge: Cambridge University Press.

Soulé, M. E., M. Gilpin, W. Conway, and T. Foose. 1986. The millennium ark: How long a voyage, how many staterooms, how many passengers? *Zoo Biology* 5:101–13.

Stanley-Price, M. R. 1993. What will it take to save the rhino? In O. A. Ryder, ed., *Rhinoceros Biology and Conservation,* pp. 48–67. San Diego: Zoological Society of San Diego.

Terborgh, J. 1988. The big things that run the world: A sequel to E. O. Wilson. *Conservation Biology* 2:402–3.

Thorne, E. T. and B. Oakleaf. 1991. Species rescue for captive breeding: Black-footed ferret as an example. In J. Gipps, ed., *Beyond Captive Breeding,* pp. 241–62. Oxford: Oxford University Press.

Willis, K. and R. Wiese. 1993. Effect of new founders on retention of gene diversity in captive populations. *Zoo Biology* 12:535–48.

Wiese, R. J., K. Willis, J. Bowdoin, and M. Hutchins. 1993. *AAZPA Annual Report on Conservation and Science, 1992–1993*. Bethesda, Maryland: American Association of Zoological Parks and Aquariums.

13

Monitoring Quantitative Genetic Variation and Evolution in Captive Populations

■■

Stevan J. Arnold

This essay focuses on the genetic aspects of captive management that might ultimately affect the success of reintroduction. Many other aspects influencing the success of reintroduction have recently been discussed by Griffith et al. (1989) and Kleiman (1989). The first consideration is whether the reintroduced population will be able to respond to selection pressures in the wild. Response to selection depends on both the selection that is imposed and the nature and amount of genetic variation in the population (Fisher 1958; Lewontin 1974; Falconer 1981). What types of genetic variation are likely to be important to the population's fate and how can these be monitored and enhanced? Second, the fate of the population may depend on how different the average captive animal has become relative to the average wild progenitor. Adaptation to the captive regime may mean maladaptation in the wild. What kinds of genetic and environmental modifications can be anticipated under captive propagation and how can they be minimized?

MONITORING GENETIC VARIATION IN CAPTIVE POPULATIONS

What Kinds of Genetic Variation Should Be Monitored?

Not all genetic variation will be equally important in determining whether the reintroduced population can respond to selection in the wild. Genetic variation for selectively neutral traits, for example, will have no bearing on the population's fate. For this reason, most allozyme variation, monitored by protein electrophoresis, has no direct bearing on possible responses to selection, although it may have an indirect bearing. If the population lacks electrophoretic variation, it may have recently gone through a bottleneck and therefore, may also lack genetic variation for adaptively important traits. Abundant electrophoretic variation, however, does not mean abundant genetic variation for the size of the camel's hump, the cheetah's fleetness, or the panda's dentition.

Once the decision is made to monitor genetic variation in traits likely to be important to the population in nature, the problem of choosing them remains. One approach would be to focus on traits likely to be important to any population. The HLA loci are a case in point. The liability here is the potential to miss traits that make tigers different from lions, or dogs different from wolves. Another approach would be to monitor a large number of traits, chosen on largely arbitrary grounds, in the hope that they might be indicators of variation in important traits or that there might be some important traits in the sample. This approach seems only slightly better than focusing on an arbitrary set of allozymes. A third approach, the one that is discussed in this essay, is to tailor the choice of traits to the systematics and ecology of the taxon in question. Even this approach is likely to entail a large amount of guesswork.

Ecological and systematic studies can be used to suggest the choice of traits for genetic monitoring. Consider three examples. Golden cats (*Felis aurata*) show much geographic variation in their coloration pattern (Kingdon 1977), suggesting that matching the local background plays an important role in prey capture and predator evasion. Lions (*Panthera leo*) displayed pronounced geographic variation in size when they had a nearly world-wide distribution at the end of the Pleistocene (Kurtén and Anderson 1980). Thus, the ability to adapt in body size has apparently been important in the history of lions, and so it is likely to be important in their future. Garter snakes (*Thamnophis elegans*) show polymorphisms and geographic variation in feeding reactions to prey (Arnold 1981). Consequently, genetic variation in feeding reactions is likely to be crucial for adaptation to local ecological circumstances. Pelage and size of felids, or feeding reactions in snakes, are easily scored and could be routinely monitored in captive populations.

Environmental differences between long-term propagation sites and reintroduction sites may suggest traits for monitoring. For example, at the reintroduction site, the population will commonly face a greater variety of predators and greater predation intensity than it did at the propagation site. Does the population show genetic variation for antipredator tactics (Arnold and Bennett 1984; Brodie 1989, 1993)?

The feasibility of monitoring quantitative genetic variation in captive colonies has already been established in the case of primates and rodents. Skeletal remains from rhesus macaques (*Macaca mulatta*) in the Cayo Santiago colony have been systematically preserved over a twenty-five-year period (Buettner-Janusch et al. 1974; Sade et al. 1977). This material was used by Cheverud (1982a, b) to assess the genetic variation in a large number of cranial and postcranial traits. In a similar program, the carcasses of animals dying natural deaths were regularly frozen in a colony of two species of tamarins (*Saguinus fuscicollis* and *S. oedipus*). The skeletal remains of a few hundred animals were later prepared and used in studies of quantitative inheritance (Cheverud 1994; Cheverud et al. 1994). As a third example, skulls and museum skins were routinely prepared from animals in Lee R. Dice's White-footed Mouse (*Peromyscus*) colony at the University of Michigan. Lofsvold (1986, 1988) used that material in comparative studies of morphological inheritance.

Monitoring Genetic Variation in Polygenic Traits

The individual traits that make or break the population in its struggle for reestablishment are likely to be affected by many genes (Wright 1968). In such polygenic or multifactorial traits, most genes have such small phenotypic effects that detection is difficult. Despite the difficulty of assaying individual genes (as in protein electrophoresis), the ensemble properties of the many genes that affect a particular trait can be detected (Fisher 1918) by quantifying the phenotypic resemblance between parents and offspring. The essential points are perhaps easiest to see with hypothetical data.

The resemblance between parents and their offspring reflects genetic variance and covariance if there are no confounding environmental sources of resemblance. With hypothetical data, such confounding is removed by assertion, but in the real world it can be controlled by experimental design (e.g., randomization of rearing environments, cross-fostering). Suppose a particular phenotypic attribute—say, skull width—is scored in a set of parents and their offspring. The trait must be scored at the same age in all individuals or at any age after the skull has stopped growing. If the average skull width of each set of siblings is plotted against the average skull width of their parents, any of the relationships shown in figure 13.1 might be obtained. No resemblance is an indication of no genetic variance in skull width; a strong resemblance is a sign of abundant genetic variance. The significance of genetic variance in skull width is that it enables one to predict the genetic consequences of selection on skull width (figure 13.2).

The resemblance between different attributes can also be examined. To do this, one attribute in offspring (e.g., skull depth) is plotted against a different attribute in parents (e.g., skull width). The cross-resemblance in such a plot is an indication of genetic covariance (figure 13.3) and reflects the influence of particular genes on both traits as well as nonrandom association between genes (i.e., between genes that affect skull width and those that affect skull depth). The genetic covariance between two traits may be negative (e.g., fig. 13.3, graph A), positive, or zero. The significance of genetic covariance is that it enables one to predict whether selection on one trait will have ramifications on other traits (figure 13.3, graph B).

The Mendelian basis of the concepts of genetic variance and covari-

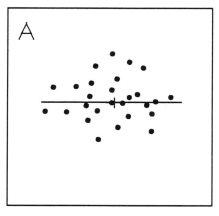

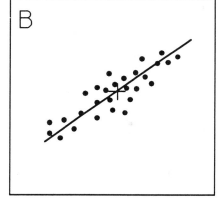

OFFSPRING SKULL WIDTH

Figure 13.1 Resemblance between parents and their offspring is a reflection of additive genetic variance. Hypothetical data are shown in which the average skull width of offspring is plotted against the average skull width of their parents. The least squares regression of offspring values on parental values estimates the standardized genetic variance (heritability) of the trait. The three plots represent different populations with (A) no, (B) abundant, and (C) modest additive genetic variance for skull width.

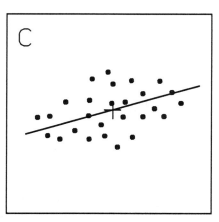

PARENT SKULL WIDTH

Figure 13.2 Response to selection is proportional to additive genetic variance. The three panels correspond to the panels in figure 13.1. The horizontal arrows represent the difference between the mean skull width of all potential parents and the mean skull width of parents selected for breeding (open symbols), a measure of the intensity of selection on skull width. (A) With no additive genetic variance, selection produces no shift in the mean of the offspring generation. (B) With abundant additive genetic variance, selection produces a large response in the offspring generation (vertical arrow). (C) With modest additive genetic variance, selection produces a small response (vertical arrow).

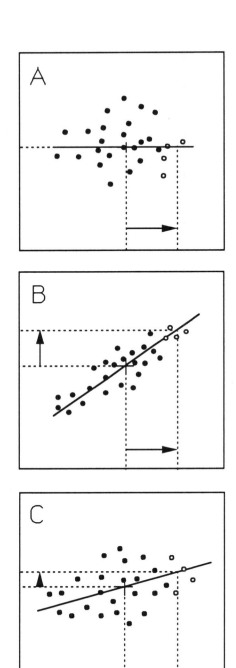

OFFSPRING SKULL WIDTH

PARENT SKULL WIDTH

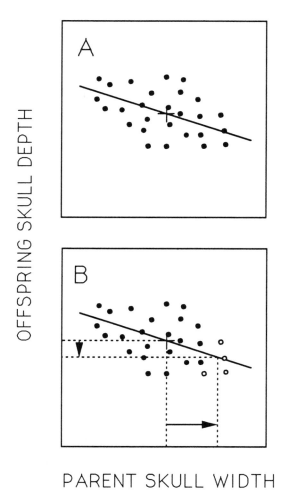

Figure 13.3 One trait can respond to selection on another trait if the two traits are genetically coupled. (A) Association between the average skull depth of offspring and the average skull width of their parents is a sign of genetic coupling (genetic covariance). In the case shown the association is negative. (B) Because skull depth and width are genetically coupled, selection on skull width in the parental generation (horizontal arrow) will shift the mean skull length in the offspring generation (vertical arrow). Because the genetic coupling is negative, selection for increased skull width in the parental generation results in reduced skull depth in the offspring generation.

ance are lucidly discussed by Falconer (1981). Using these two concepts and the concept of selective force shown in figures 13.2 and 13.3, the simultaneous evolution of multiple traits can be modeled (Lande 1979, 1988). Moving from two to three to dozens of traits requires no new concepts. Furthermore, a large body of techniques developed for genetic analysis of economically important traits in commercial animal breeding (Turner and Young 1969) could be applied to captive propagation programs.

The concepts of genetic variance and covariance, and their consequences, are easiest to understand from plots comparing offspring with their parents, but these genetic parameters can be estimated from other combinations of relatives (e.g., sets of full sibs, sets of half sibs, etc.). Some kinds of relationships give much better estimates of genetic variance and covariance than others (e.g., parent-offspring data are usually better than just full-sib data). The estimation theory was developed by Kempthorne (1954) and Cockerham (1954, 1963), building on Fisher's seminal 1918 paper, and it is reviewed by Falconer (1981). Complications arising from maternal effects have been recently discussed by Lande and Price (1989) and Kirkpatrick and Lande (1989, 1992). Genetic variances and covariances can also be estimated from pedigrees if the scores of polygenic traits are known for all or most individuals. For overviews of theory and methodology see Barton and Turelli (1989) and Arnold (1992, 1994).

It is difficult to say how many sets of relatives will be required to estimate genetic variances and covariances because standard errors of these parameters depend on the magnitude of the parameters themselves. Small genetic variances have large standard errors; large genetic variances have small standard errors. The usual approach in planning a quantitative genetic analysis is to work on a worst-case basis. Suppose that genetic variance is only 10% of the phenotypic variance (10% heritability). How many families would be needed to show that genetic variance is nonzero at the 0.05 level? Robertson (1959a, b) and Falconer (1981) give formulas for solving this and similar problems. Generally speaking, one can expect to need dozens or scores of families to detect heritabilities as low as 10 or 20%. If heritability is as high as 70% (as is often the case for linear dimensions in large mammals), only a couple of dozen families would be needed. On the dark side, if only one or a few offspring are available in each family, hundreds of families may be needed to detect low heritabilities (Klein et al. 1973; Arnold 1994).

How Often Should Genetic Variation Be Monitored and When?

Because of the sample sizes needed, it may be possible to estimate genetic variation only periodically, pooling data over several or many generations. In the case of intensively managed, small populations of large vertebrates, traits might be scored from photographs or from records taken at autopsy. Many generations might elapse before records are compiled on, say, a set of fifty parents and their offspring. In animals maintained in larger populations, it may be possible, with appropriate planning, to estimate quantitative genetic variation in any particular generation. In this case, it would be possible to track genetic variation. In either case, however, the crucial juncture for estimation may be the generations that precede reintroduction. If genetic variation should turn out to be discouragingly low, the manager would have the option of supplementing variation by infusion from other captive or wild populations (Lande, essay 14 of this volume).

EVOLUTION IN CAPTIVE POPULATIONS

Will the Population Evolve in Response to the Captive Situation?

In experimental studies, it is not uncommon to detect responses to selection after only three or four generations. Furthermore, the response may be sustained over many generations (Robertson 1980). Selection on body size in flour beetles (*Tribolium*) increased the mean by over 17 phenotypic standard deviations over a period of 108 generations (Enfield 1980). In a worst-case scenario, therefore, a population might evolve appreciably in just a few generations of captive propagation. Consistent selection, even if not deliberate, could produce sustained change for a hundred generations or more.

Even more troubling is the possibility that substantial genetic change might occur during the first generation or two of captive management (Briscoe et al. 1992). To the extent that traits (e.g., athletic ability, shyness, and nervousness) are heritable, the population may experience considerable response to the unconscious selection imposed during capture and transport, because these procedures usually involve escapes and mortality at nearly every stage. It is, therefore, easy to imagine that founders of the captive stock are a biased sample of the native population. In addition, the means of other traits may be shifted by the small sample of founders (Wright 1931, 1948; Lynch and Lande 1993). By chance sampling, the mean of the captive population may drift away from the mean of the wild population. Such changes are usually greatest during the first few generations, when the population is small.

Once the captive population builds in numbers, the propagation regime may impose selective pressures different from those in nature and so induce a steady, but artificial, evolution. Effects of the latter kind are the easiest to anticipate and counteract.

How to Determine Whether the Captive Population Has Evolved

By monitoring the means of quantitative traits each generation, changes in the captive population can be detected. The evolutionary change might be erratic or progressive. In intensively managed small populations, the best strategy might be to score several traits on every animal. Autopsy is one conspicuous occasion for trait scoring. If the veterinarian or pathologist is unable to do more than routine photography (for coloration traits) and measurement, the skull and other body parts might be frozen for later preparation and scoring. If the population is so large that it is not feasible to score every animal, a sample of even ten to twenty animals per generation would provide considerable statistical power to detect trends.

In light of the possibility that substantial change may occur in the first few generations, it is especially critical to score the traits of founders and their immediate descendants. Since the numbers are likely to be small, perhaps the best policy is to preserve as much of each specimen as is feasible (photographs, skins, skulls, postcranial skeletons, and frozen tissue samples). This could be accomplished at autopsy after natural death without jeopardizing the propagation program. Should genetic change be suspected after several or many generations of propagation, the traits in question could be examined in founders and their immediate descendants.

The wild population of origin is also an important reference in testing for progressive change, so traits might be scored in animals not brought into captivity (e.g., by photography of free-ranging animals or by measurement in the course of field work involving capture). Such nondestructive scoring in the wild population is especially important if the taxon is not well represented in museums. Most large research museums maintain a computer inventory of vertebrate holdings and can quickly respond to inquiries.

A shift in the phenotypic mean of the captive population from generation to generation or in relation to the wild progenitor may have environmental as well as genetic causes. Rearing temperature, for example, can have dramatic effects on body proportions in domestic swine (Weaver and Ingram 1969). The usual tests for environmental effects on the mean are either to rear populations in the same environment and then compare means (common garden experiment) or to cross the populations and see if the first and second generations of hybrids meet Mendelian expectations (East 1916; Turesson 1922). Generally, only tests of the first kind will be a feasible supplement to a captive propagation program. A variety of the common garden experiment is to contrast the mean of wild stock during the first few generations in captivity with the mean of long-propagated stock kept under the same environmental conditions during the same time period. Under the environmental effect hypothesis, the phenotypic mean of the wild stock should immediately converge on the mean of the captive stock. Another form of data analysis is to test for shifts in the mean of the captive stock while holding the environment constant or to restrict tests to time blocks within which conditions are constant, or virtually so.

What Sorts of Phenotypic Change Might Occur Under Captive Propagation?

Trends Under Domestication. The study of domestication provides some expectations about the kinds of change that might accompany captive propagation. Captive propagation with the intent of eventual release should produce less extreme effects than domestication. Nevertheless, a consideration of trends under domestication is illuminating (Darwin 1882). Zeuner (1963), for example, lists the following common trends in domesticated species: (a) smaller size; (b) greater variation in size; (c) coloration altered and more variable; (d) facial part of skull shortened relative to cranial part; (e) limb bones usually shorter but sometimes longer; f) length of hair changed (shorter or longer); (g) skin more flabby (skin folds characteristic of juveniles retained in adults); (h) smaller relative brain size; (i) reduced musculature (but sometimes hypertrophied); (j) increased docility. This list suggests three generalizations: (1) characters are often favored that would be pathological in nature; (2) growth rates are often affected with resultant change in body proportions; (3) juvenile characters persist in adults. The last two kinds of trends have been studied for many years by researchers at the Russian Academy of Science's Institute of Animal Morphology in Moscow. Scott (1954) stresses the point that an increase in variability among breeds has accompanied the domestication of dogs from wolf ancestors. Some dog breeds are less vocal than wolves, but some are more vocal. The same observation applies to among-breed variation in size, aggressiveness, and many other attributes (Darwin 1882). Domestication seems to have quantitative rather than qualitative effects on behavior, e.g., by changing response thresholds (Ratner and Boice 1975; Price 1984).

In an experimental study of the domestication process in rats (*Rattus norvegicus*), King (1939) and King and Donaldson (1929) founded a laboratory colony from 20 female and 16 male wild-caught rats and then tracked changes in behavior and morphology for 40 generations. After this long period of captive propagation, the colony showed an earlier age of first reproduction in females, longer duration of reproductive life, an increase in adult mass, and an increase in docility. But, even after 40 generations, the colony rats were not as docile as typical laboratory stock. Behavioral change (e.g., increased docility) is a major concern in captive propagation.

Environmental and Hereditary Wildness. Wildlife managers often anticipate a loss of wildness during captive propagation. Leopold (1944) defined the general meaning of wildness as "the sum of the various behavior patterns and other inherent adaptations which permit the successful existence of a free population." Wildness is an ensemble of attributes, not a single, unitary characteristic. Rearing conditions can affect some aspects of wildness without affecting others (Galef 1970); an animal or population can be tame in some aspects and still wild in others. The tragedy of tameness (the loss of wildness) is that the population, as well as the individual, may be ill-suited to sustain itself in nature. A few studies of rearing effects on wildness and of hereditary transmission have been conducted, but we know almost nothing about how wildness promotes fitness in nature or, conversely, how tameness results in maladaptation.

An exception is Leopold's (1944) study of why the release of 14,000 hybrid turkeys in Missouri failed to produce sustaining populations. Leopold compared the behavior of wild and hybrid turkeys (*Meleagris gallopavo*) in the field. He concluded that the failure of hybrid birds could be attributed to their tranquility, early breeding, and the scattering, rather than hiding, response of chicks to the warning note of the hen.

> Wild turkeys are wary and shy, which are advantageous characteristics in eluding natural and human enemies. They breed at a favorable season of the year. The hens and young automatically react to danger in ways that are self-protective. Reproductive success is high. Collectively these and associated actions and reactions literally adapt the native wild birds to existence in their ancestral environment. . . . Birds of the domestic strain, on the other hand, are differently adapted. Many of their physiological reactions and psychological characteristics are favorable to existence in the barnyard but many preclude success in the wild. (Leopold 1944)

In studies lacking a field component (such as the ones discussed below), we can only guess about the adaptive significance of wildness.

Studies with rodents indicate that some aspects of wildness can be quickly restored simply by changing rearing conditions. Clark and Galef (1977, 1980, 1981) found that shelter can be important for morphological and behavioral development in rodents. Gerbils (*Meriones unguiculatus*) reared without shelters showed accelerated development, lacked a fear response to novel stimuli, and were easier to handle than gerbils that had access to shelters during rearing. Galef (1970) found that handling during rearing affects some aspects of wildness in wild rats but not others. Rearing wild rats with domesticated mothers had no effect on any aspect of wildness.

Although rearing conditions can have immediate effects on wildness, heredity can have effects as well. Environmental and genetic effects are not mutually exclusive. Most genetic studies of wildness have been conducted with rodents, including the earliest studies in the discipline of behavioral genetics. Yerkes (1913) compared the behavior of domestic and wild-caught rats (*Rattus norvegicus*) as well as the behavior of their first and second generation hybrids by scoring a variety of responses to handling by a human investigator (e.g., biting, teeth gnashing, defecation, etc.). F_1 hybrids were intermediate in behavior but also more variable than either parental population. F_2 hybrids were more docile than F_1s, but very few F_2s were as wild as rats in the wild-caught parental population.

Coburn (1922) patterned a study of behavior in mice after Yerkes' study. Here, F_1 hybrids showed intermediate behavior with a mean shifted toward the wild parental population and hardly any mice showing scores typical of domestic parents. Both grandparental types were recovered in the F_2 generation, which showed more variance than the F_1. Dawson (1932) compared the running speed in wild and domestic mice as well as in first and second generation hybrids. F_1 hybrids resembled wild mice. The expansion of variance in the F_2 generation indicated that at least three segregating factors (genes or blocks of genes) were responsible for the differences between the wild and domestic strains. Selection for slower speed over four generations produced a response, but selection for faster speed did not. The results of these studies suggest polygenic inheritance, sometimes with directional dominance for wildness.

Change in Fitness Components and Other Traits Due to Inbreeding Depression. Some degree of inbreeding is inevitable in captive populations because of their small size. Inbreeding has a systematic effect on the means of traits affected by dominant genes; the mean shifts progressively downward (Crow and Kimura 1970; Falconer 1981). This downward shift is known as inbreeding depression. Polygenic traits in which a preponderance of loci show dominance (directional dominance) as well as single-locus traits are susceptible to inbreeding depression. Fitness components (juvenile mortality, longevity, fertility, fecundity) are notoriously prone to inbreeding depression (Darwin 1882; Slatis 1960; Ralls et al. 1979; Falconer 1981; Charlesworth and Charlesworth 1987). Traits that are the immediate determinants of survival and reproductive success are thus prime candidates for monitoring in captive populations, as is any trait showing dominance or directional dominance. For example, in a survey of genetic literature on activity in mice, Henderson (1986) found that many behaviors (nipple attachment in pups; jumping, running, and pole climbing in older mice) show directional dominance in crosses between strains. Usually F_1 hybrids resemble the more active parental strain. Consequently, on inbreeding a mouse population, we might expect nipple attachment in pups and activity at various ages to decline in succeeding generations.

At present, there is no reliable way to predict which traits (aside from fitness components) are likely to show directional dominance and hence inbreeding depression. One school of thought argues that traits long exposed to directional selection will show directional dominance, whereas traits long under stabilizing selection will not (Mather 1949, 1955). The prediction is based on Fisher's theory of the evolution of dominance, which is still fraught with controversy (Fisher 1928, 1929, 1934; Wright 1929 a–c; Charlesworth 1979). Empirical tests of the directional selection/directional dominance prediction are plagued with failure to actually measure the selection that is being predicted a posteriori from the genetic architecture. The best guide to traits showing directional dominance is the genetic literature in which dominance is directly accessed.

How Can Methodical, Unconscious, and Incidental Selection in the Captive Situation Be Minimized?

Selection in Captivity. Darwin (1882) distinguished two kinds of artificial selection: methodical and unconscious. Methodical selection prevails when the breeder directs the stock toward some conscious goal. Unconscious selection prevails when the breeder selects the best stock and prevents the worst from breeding, not with the aim of improving the stock, but of simply maintaining it. To these categories we might add a third, namely, incidental selection, to refer to the artificial selection resulting from the captive environment rather than from the direct actions of the propagator. These modes of selection overlap, but the distinctions are useful if they alert the manager to deleterious ongoing selection. Finally, as Darwin (1882) points out, natural selection is not suspended in captivity; it continues to act, either in line with or against the direction of artificial selection.

Minimizing artificial selection is an important goal during captive propagation (Lacy et al., essay 4 of this volume), but one that requires constant vigilance. Methodical selection is worrisome because it holds the threat of gradually shaping the animal into an unnatural form. Even without a stated phenotypic goal for the stock, the threat of methodical selection remains. The stock managers may have their own ideas, for example, of what a Przewalski's horse (*Equus przewalskii*) should look like or how it should behave. A standard strategy in captive breeding programs is to minimize both selection and drift by equalizing family sizes (Lande and Barrowclough 1987; Allendorf 1993; Borlase et al. 1993; Lande, essay 14 of this volume).

Unconscious selection is almost inevitable, since, for example, malformities are bound to arise. Perhaps the safest guideline is to curtail the breeding of only those individuals that would certainly die or fail to breed in nature. The middle ground is the most treacherous. In a large sample of newborn snakes, for example, a few percent will inevitably have slightly kinked vertebral columns. Should these individuals be excluded from the breeding stock? Probably they should since only a small percentage of the newborns are involved, even though it is by no means clear that the trait is heritable. What about variants that are less obviously deleterious, e.g., melanism and other pigment variations, pattern variants, etc.? A good guide here is the natural population. If the variants exist in nature, there may be no reason to weed them out of the captive population. In general, the best practice may be to ask whether a particular form of methodical or unconscious selection, if practiced over a long time period, is likely to transform the population away from the natural phenotype. That natural phenotype, of course, may be variable and polymorphic.

Unconscious selection can arise from the most pragmatic aspects of propagation. Spurway (1955) notes that the practice of breeding just those pairs judged to be in the best sexual condition, with swapping of partners if pairs do not breed, will impose selection for phenotypes that are: (a) the least disturbed by transplantation and human proximity; (b) the least exacting about environmental requirements; (c) the least disturbed by separation from previous partners; (d) the least dependent on social facilitation; (e) the least discriminating in mate choice; and (f) the most stimulating to sexual partners. Many of these differences distinguish domestic strains from their wild ancestors (Lorenz 1940). On the morphological side, many of the changes in body proportions associated with domestication (see Zeuner's list, above) may be a consequence of selection for early sexual maturity (Berry 1969). Alteration of developmental timing can have far-reaching consequences on adult form (Alberch et al. 1979), with the captive animal gradually becoming a paedomorph.

The artificiality of caging, food, and social contacts could exert incidental selection. In simple cages, some behaviors are never expressed. Gerbils do not show foot-thumping, a form of social communication, unless provided with tunnels (Clark and Galef 1977). Behaviors that are not expressed may eventually deteriorate because natural selection does not maintain them. Other aspects of captivity may evoke evolutionary change in the direction of adaptation to captivity and maladaptation to the wild. Domestic turkey hens vocalize in response to approaching danger and their chicks disperse. Perhaps this signal-response system has benefits in the barnyard, but in the field it alerts and attracts predators. Wild turkey hens and their chicks crouch and hide in response to danger at a distance (Leopold 1944).

Countering or Minimizing Artificial Selection. Could we impose methodical selection to reverse deleterious trends observed in captive stock? In theory yes, but in practice probably not. Genetic coupling between traits presents a serious obstacle in methodical selection. With accurate estimates of the genetic covariances among traits (and their genetic variances), we could, in theory, design a selection protocol to accomplish almost any desired objective; however, the requisite genetic information is unlikely to be available. The more practical and safer alternatives are to reverse the trends by infusion of new stock or by letting natural selection do its work.

Artificial selection can be minimized by implementing a captive breeding program that focuses on maintaining genetic diversity by maximizing effective population size (Lacy et al., essay 4 of this volume). Careful control of which animals breed, with an emphasis on equalizing reproduction among all breeders, will mitigate the effects of methodical and unconscious selection.

Propagation in large natural or seminatural enclosures has the advantage of eliminating some forms of artificial selection while maintaining many forms of natural selection. The most pernicious aspects of methodical, unconscious, and incidental selection arise because breeding is in the hands of the manager and because of the artificiality of the environment. In a population of reasonable size, housed in a sufficiently large enclosure, success in life and in reproduction could be more directly determined by the form and behavior of the animals themselves without the selective hand of the manager. Furthermore, if selection is eliminated, a smaller effective population size is required to maintain genetic variation (Lande, essay 14 of this volume).

SUMMARY

Genetic variation for phenotypic traits, such as body size, skull shape, or coloration pattern, could be monitored in captive populations in order to determine whether the population could respond to selection in nature and whether genetic variation should be supplemented (e.g., by bringing in additional stock from nature). An arbitrary set of phenotypic traits could be monitored in the hope that representative genetic variation will be assessed. Alternatively, the choice of traits for monitoring could be tailored to the population in question. Traits that are liable to evolution in nature or are ecologically important could be monitored so that the loss of critical kinds of genetic variation can be minimized. Genetic variation can be estimated by assessing the phenotypic resemblance between offspring and parents or between other sets of relatives. A large body of techniques developed for genetic analysis of economically important traits in commercial animal breeding could be applied in captive propagation programs.

In addition to monitoring genetic variation, the phenotypic means of important traits could be scored in each generation to determine whether the captive population is evolving. The results of long-term selection experiments provide some basis for predicting how much evolution might occur per generation. In general, we can expect a captive population to change by only a fraction of a phenotypic standard deviation in each generation. More pronounced evolutionary change, however, might occur during the first few generations in captivity due to the inevitable bottleneck attending establishment of the captive population and to unconscious selection under the new regime in captivity. The literature on common evolutionary trends in domesticated species provides some clues about the kinds of traits that are likely to evolve in captivity (e.g., tameness, fatness, etc.). These traits might be included in the monitoring program as well as traits liable to inbreeding depression (e.g., fitness components and behaviors that tend to show directional dominance).

Artificial selection could have the twofold disadvantage of depleting genetic variation and causing unfortunate evolutionary responses. Usually there is not enough genetic information to design a selection program to counteract these evolutionary trends. Furthermore, the captive population is usually so small that measurement of artificial selection becomes imprecise or impossible. Under these circumstances, the best remedy may be to minimize selection as much as possible or, at least, to avoid manifestly artificial selection. This can best be achieved through a captive breeding program that emphasizes the maintenance of genetic variability and equal reproduction. In addition, large natural or seminatural enclosures have many advantages over small, unnatural enclosures or cages.

Acknowledgments

The preparation of this paper was supported by N.S.F. grants BSR 89–06703, BSR 89–18581 and BSR 91–19588. I am grateful to Sharon Emerson and the Department of Biology at the University of Utah, to Victor Orlov at the Institute of Animal Morphology in Moscow, and to Brad Shaffer and the Section of Ecology and Evolutionary Biology at the University of California, Davis, for hospitality at their respective institutions. James Cheverud and Bennett Galef provided advice and counsel.

REFERENCES

Alberch, P., S. J. Gould, G. F. Oster, and D. B. Wake. 1979. Size and shape in ontogeny and phylogeny. *Paleobiology* 5:296–317.

Allendorf, F. W. 1993. Delay of adaptation to captive breeding by equalizing family size. *Conservation Biology* 7:416–25.

Arnold, S. J. 1981. The microevolution of feeding behavior. In A. Kamil and T. Sargent, eds., *Foraging Behavior: Ecological, Ethological, and Psychological Approaches*, pp. 409–53. New York: Garland Press.

Arnold, S. J. 1992. Constraints on phenotypic evolution. *American Naturalist* 140:S85–S107.

Arnold, S. J. 1994. Multivariate inheritance and evolution: A review of concepts. In C. R. P. Boake, ed., *Quantitative Genetic Studies of the Evolution of Behavior*, pp. 18-48. Chicago: University of Chicago Press.

Arnold, S. J. and A. F. Bennett. 1984. Behavioural variation in natural populations,

III: Antipredator displays in the garter snake *Thamnophis radix*. *Animal Behaviour* 32:1108–18.

Barton, N. H. and M. Turelli. 1989. Evolutionary quantitative genetics: How little do we know? *Annual Review of Genetics* 23:337–70.

Berry, R. J. 1969. The genetical implications of domestication in animals. In P. J. Ucko and G. W. Dimbleby, eds., *The Domestication and Exploitation of Plants and Animals*, pp. 207–17. Chicago: Aldine.

Borlase, S. C., D. A. Loebel, R. Frankham, R. K. Nurthen, D. A. Briscoe, and G. E. Daggard. 1993. Modeling problems in conservation genetics using captive *Drosophila* populations: Consequences of equalization of family sizes. *Conservation Biology* 7:122–31.

Briscoe, D. A., J. M. Malpica, A. Robertson, G. J. Smith, R. Frankham, R. G. Banks, and J. S. F. Barker. 1992. Rapid loss of genetic variation in large capture populations of *Drosophila* flies: Implications for the genetic management of captive populations. *Conservation Biology* 6:416–25.

Brodie, E. D., III. 1989. Genetic correlations between morphology and antipredator behaviour in natural populations of the garter snake *Thamnophis ordinoides*. *Nature* 342:542–43.

Brodie, E. D., III. 1993. Homogeneity of the genetic variance-covariance matrix for antipredator traits in two natural populations of the garter snake *Thamnophis ordinoides*. *Evolution* 47:844–54.

Buettner-Janusch, J., G. Mason, L. Dame, V. Buettner-Janusch, and D. Sade. 1974. Genetic studies of serum transferrin of free-ranging rhesus macaques of Cayo Santiago. *American Journal of Physical Anthropology* 41:217–32.

Charlesworth, B. 1979. Evidence against Fisher's theory of dominance. *Nature* 278:878–79.

Charlesworth, D. and B. Charlesworth. 1987. Inbreeding depression and its evolutionary consequences. *Annual Review of Ecology and Systematics* 18:237–68.

Cheverud, J. M. 1982a. Phenotypic, genetic, and environmental morphological integration in the cranium. *Evolution* 36:499–516.

Cheverud, J. M. 1982b. Relationships among ontogenetic, static, and evolutionary allometry. *American Journal of Physical Anthropology* 59:139–49.

Cheverud, J. M. 1994. Morphological integration in the saddle-back tamarin (*Saguinus fuscicollis*) cranium. *American Naturalist* (in press).

Cheverud, J. M., E. Routman, C. Jaquish, S. Tardif, G. Petersen, N. Belfiore, and L. Forman. 1994. Quantitative and molecular genetic variation in captive cotton-top tamarins (*Saguinus oedipus*). *Conservation Biology* 8:95–105.

Clark, M. M. and B. G. Galef, Jr. 1977. The role of physical rearing environment in the domestication of the Mongolian gerbil (*Meriones unguiculatus*). *Animal Behavior* 25:298–316.

Clark, M. M. and B. G. Galef, Jr. 1980. Effects of rearing environment on adrenal weights, sexual development, and behavior in gerbils: An examination of Richter's domestication hypothesis. *Journal of Comparative and Physiological Psychology* 94:857–63.

Clark, M. M. and B. G. Galef, Jr. 1981. Environmental influence on development, behavior, and endocrine morphology of gerbils. *Physiology & Behavior* 27:761–65.

Coburn, C. A. 1922. Heredity and wildness and savageness in mice. *Behavioral Monographs* 4:1–71.

Cockerham, C. C. 1954. An extension of the concept of partitioning hereditary variance for analysis of covariances among relatives when epistasis is present. *Genetics* 39:859–82.

Cockerham, C. C. 1963. Estimation of genetic variances. *Statistical Genetics and Plant Breeding: National Academy of Sciences - National Research Council Publ.* 982:53–93.

Crow, J. F. and M. Kimura. 1970. *An Introduction to Population Genetics Theory.* Minneapolis: Burgess.

Darwin, C. 1882. *The Variation of Animals and Plants under Domestication.* London: Murray.

Dawson, W. M. 1932. Inheritance of wildness and tameness in mice. *Genetics* 17:296–326.

East E. M. 1916. Studies on size inheritance in Nicotiana. *Genetics* 1:164–76.

Enfield, F. D. 1980. Long-term effects of selection to response. In A. Robertson, ed. *Selection Experiments in Laboratory and Domestic Animals,* pp. 69–86. Slough, U.K.: Commonwealth Agricultural Bureau.

Falconer, D. S. 1981. *Introduction to Quantitative Genetics.* 2d ed. London: Longman.

Fisher, R. A. 1918. The correlation between relatives on the supposition of Mendelian inheritance. *Transactions of the Royal Society of Edinburgh* 52:399–433.

Fisher, R. A. 1928. The possible modification of the wild type to recurrent mutations. *American Naturalist* 62:115–26.

Fisher, R. A. 1929. The evolution of dominance; Reply to Professor Sewall Wright. *American Naturalist* 63:553–56.

Fisher, R. A. 1934. Professor Wright on the theory of dominance. *American Naturalist* 68:370–74.

Fisher, R. A. 1958. *The Genetical Theory of Natural Selection.* 2d ed. New York: Dover.

Galef, B. G., Jr. 1970. Aggression and timidity: Responses to novelty in feral Norway rats. *Journal of Comparative and Physiological Psychology* 70:370–81.

Griffith, B., J. M. Scott, J. W. Carpenter, and C. Reed. 1989. Translocation as a species conservation tool: Status and strategy. *Science* 245:477–80.

Henderson, N. D. 1986. Predicting relationships between psychological constructs and genetic characters: An analysis of changing genetic influences on activity in mice. *Behavior Genetics* 16:201–20.

Kempthorne, O. 1954. The correlation between relatives in a random mating population. *Proceedings of the Royal Society of London* B143:103–13.

King, H. D. 1939. Life processes in gray Norway rats during fourteen years in captivity. *American Anatomical Memoirs* 17:1–77.

King, H. D. and H. H. Donaldson. 1929. Life processes and size of body and organs of the gray Norway rat during ten generations in captivity. *American Anatomical Memoirs* 14:1–106.

Kingdon, J. 1977. *East African Mammals: An Atlas of Evolution in Africa. Vol. III: Part A (Carnivores).* London: Academic Press.

Kirkpatrick, M. and R. Lande. 1989. The evolution of maternal characters. *Evolution* 43:485–503.

Kirkpatrick, M. and R. Lande. 1992. The evolution of maternal characters: Errata. *Evolution* 46:284.

Kleiman, D. G. 1989. Reintroduction of captive mammals for conservation. *Bioscience* 39:152–61.

Klein, T. W., J. C. DeFries, and C. T. Finkbeiner. 1973. Heritability and genetic correlation: Statistical power, population parameters, and sample size. *Behavior Genetics* 3:355–64.

Kurtén, B. and E. Anderson. 1980. *Pleistocene Mammals of North America.* New York: Columbia University Press.

Lande, R. 1979. Quantitative genetic analysis of multivariate evolution, applied to brain: Body size allometry. *Evolution* 33:402–16.

Lande, R. 1988. Quantitative genetics and evolutionary theory. In B. Weir, E. Eisen, M. Goodman, and G. Namkoong, eds., *Proceedings of the Second International Conference on Quantitative Genetics,* pp. 71–84. Sunderland, Mass.: Sinauer.

Lande, R. and G. F. Barrowclough. 1987. Effective population size, genetic variation, and their use in population management. In M. Soulé, ed., *Viable Populations for Conservation,* pp. 87–123. New York: Cambridge University Press.

Lande, R. and T. Price. 1989. Genetic correlations and maternal effect coefficients obtained from offspring-parent regression. *Genetics* 122:915–22.

Leopold, A. S. 1944. The nature of heritable wildness in turkeys. *Condor* 46:133–97.

Lewontin, R. C. 1974. *The Genetic Basis of Evolutionary Change.* New York: Columbia University Press.

Lofsvold, D. 1986. Quantitative genetics of morphological differentiation in *Peromyscus,* I: Tests of homogeneity of genetic covariance structure among species and subspecies. *Evolution* 40:559–73

Lofsvold, D. 1988. Quantitative genetics of morphological differentiation in *Peromyscus,* II: Analysis of selection and drift. *Evolution* 42:54–67.

Lorenz, K. Z. 1940. Durch Domestikation verursachte Störungen arteigenen Verhaltens. *Zeitschrift für angewandte Psychologie und Charakterkunde* 59:2–82.

Lynch, M. and R. Lande. 1993. Evolution and extinction in response to environmental change. In P. M. Kareiva, J. G. Kingsolver, and R. B. Huey, eds., *Biotic Interactions and Global Change,* pp. 234–50. Sunderland, Mass.: Sinauer.

Mather, K. 1949. *Biometrical Genetics.* London: Methuen.

Mather, K. 1955. The genetical basis of heterosis. *Proceedings of the Royal Society of London* B144:143–50.

Price, E. O. 1984. Behavioral aspects of animal domestication. *Quarterly Review of Biology* 59:1–32.

Ralls, K., K. Brugger, and J. Ballou. 1979. Inbreeding and juvenile mortality in small populations of ungulates. *Science* 206:1101–3.

Ratner, S. C. and R. Boice. 1975. Effects of domestication on behaviour. In E. S. E. Hafez, ed., *The Behaviour of Domestic Animals,* 3d ed., pp. 3–19. Baltimore: Williams and Williams.

Robertson, A. 1959a. Experimental design in the evaluation of genetic parameters. *Biometrics* 15:219–26.

Robertson, A. 1959b. The sampling variance of the genetic correlation coefficient. *Biometrics* 15:469–85.

Robertson, A., ed. 1980. *Selection Experiments in Laboratory and Domestic Animals.* Slough, U.K.: Commonwealth Agricultural Bureau.

Sade, D., K. Cushing, P. Cushing, J. Dunaif, A. Figuero, J. Kaplan, C. Lauer, D. Rhodes, and J. Schneider. 1977. Population dynamics in relation to social structure on Cayo Santiago. *Yearbook of Physical Anthropology* 20:252–62.

Scott, J. P. 1954. The effects of selection and domestication upon the behavior of the dog. *Journal of the National Cancer Institute* 15:739–58.

Slatis, H. M. 1960. An analysis of inbreeding in the European bison. *Genetics* 45:273–85.

Spurway, H. 1955. The causes of domestication: An attempt to integrate some ideas of Konrad Lorenz with evolution theory. *Journal of Genetics* 53:325–62.

Turesson, G. 1922. The species and the variety as ecological units. *Hereditas* 3:100–13.

Turner, H. N. and S. S. Y. Young. 1969. *Quantitative Genetics in Sheep Breeding.* South Melbourne: MacMillan.

Weaver, M. E. and D. L. Ingram. 1969. Morphological changes in swine associated with environmental temperature. *Ecology* 50:710–13.

Wright, S. 1929a. The evolution of dominance: Comment on Dr. Fisher's reply. *American Naturalist* 63:1–5.

Wright, S. 1929b. Fisher's theory of dominance. *American Naturalist* 63:274–79.

Wright, S. 1929c. The evolution of dominance. *American Naturalist* 63:556–61.

Wright, S. 1931. Evolution in Mendelian populations. *Genetics* 16:97–159.

Wright, S. 1948. On the roles of directed and random changes in gene frequency in the genetics of populations. *Evolution* 2:279–94.

Wright, S. 1968. *Evolution and the Genetics of Populations, vol. 1: Genetic and Biometric Foundations.* Chicago: University of Chicago Press.

Yerkes, R. M. 1913. The heredity of savageness and wildness in rats. *Journal of Animal Behavior* 3:286–96.

Zeuner, F. E. 1963. *A History of Domesticated Animals.* London: Hutchinson.

14

Breeding Plans for Small Populations Based on the Dynamics of Quantitative Genetic Variance

■■

Russell Lande

Habitat destruction and fragmentation often make it necessary to protect small populations in nature preserves or to establish captive breeding programs to prevent their extinction. In most wild populations, ecological factors are likely to be more important than genetic factors in determining the probability of persistence into the foreseeable future. This is because a wild population that can avoid extinction from Allee effects, edge effects, demographic and environmental stochasticity, and local extinction and colonization is also likely to be large enough to prevent appreciable inbreeding depression or loss of genetic variability from random genetic drift (Lande 1988). In wild populations, however, that are artificially reduced to a small size, genetic factors and their interactions with ecological factors become increasingly important.

In the captive environment, demographic fluctuations caused by predation, diseases, weather, and food supply can be at least partially controlled. If the goal of the captive breeding program is release into the wild at a later date, the breeding structure and size of the population can be managed to maintain a high proportion of the original genetic variability of the wild population. This is likely to increase the population's chance of survival upon reintroduction into the wild, since additive genetic variance is necessary for adaptation to a changing environment. Genetic considerations, therefore, should play a dominant role in breeding plans for captive populations with this goal. Even in a carefully controlled environment, however, demographic factors, such as population growth rate, age distribution, and sex ratio should not be ignored (Foose 1980).

Soulé et al. (1986) proposed maintaining 90% of the genetic variability present in the original (base) population for a period of 200 years as the management goal for captive populations. Using a model of an ideal population with discrete, nonoverlapping generations, and a Poisson distribution of progeny numbers, they computed by numerical methods the final, or equilibrium, population size that would be necessary to achieve the goal with a certain initial number of founders for a species with a given population growth rate and generation time, assuming geometric growth of the population up to the final size. Their model accounted for the loss of genetic variability (i.e., heterozygosity or purely additive genetic variance in quantitative traits) caused by random genetic drift in a finite population. This or similar goals and the breeding plans recommended by Soulé et al. (1986) to meet them have already been adopted in management plans for captive populations of several endangered species (e.g., for the gorilla, *Gorilla gorilla gorilla;* cheetah, *Acinonyx jubatus;* addax, *Addax nasomaculatus;* Przewalski's horse, *Equus przewalskii;* scimitar-horned oryx, *Oryx dammah;* greater one-horned Asian rhinoceros, *Rhinoceros unicornis;* and Florida panther, *Felis concolor coryi* (Foose et al., essay 12 of this volume; Wiese et al. 1993).

Most morphological, behavioral, and physiological measurements are genetically complex (polygenic) quantitative traits, which are generally thought to be of critical importance in adaptation to natural environments (Franklin 1980; Lande and Barrowclough 1987). Here we investigate the influence of additional factors affecting the maintenance of additive genetic variance in quantitative characters, i.e., mutation, immigration from the wild, selection in the captive environment, and population subdivision. It is shown that due to these factors smaller final population sizes and founder numbers are needed to achieve the goal of preserving a certain fraction of the original genetic variability for a particular period of time. By using a continuous time model, which is probably more accurate than the discrete generation model for most real populations with overlapping generations, it is possible to derive general analytical solutions that allow breeding plans to be specified for management goals involving the maintenance of any fraction of the original genetic variability for any time period. The text develops the general models and provides explicit evaluations in graphical form for the particular management goal suggested by Soulé et al. (1986). Analytical formulas are presented in the appendix.

DYNAMICS OF ADDITIVE GENETIC VARIANCE IN QUANTITATIVE TRAITS

In the captive environment, natural selection on most traits is likely to be greatly reduced or absent, so that random genetic drift and mutation are the most important factors affecting genetic variation in a population closed to immigration. Nevertheless, there may be substantial selection on some characters for adaptation to captivity, and evolutionary changes resembling domestication are likely to occur in captive populations, for example, selection for docility and high reproduction (Arnold, essay 13 of this volume). We first analyze random genetic drift and mutation in a population founded from a given initial number of individuals that grows to a constant final number. Immigration, selection, and subdivision in a population of constant size are then analyzed.

Random Genetic Drift and Mutation

Let V_g be the (purely) additive genetic variance in a quantitative character. The input of additive genetic variance from mutation in each generation, V_m, is assumed to be a constant independent of the amount of genetic variance already in the population. This can be justified by a detailed model of mutation in which there is a wide range of possible allelic effects at each locus, with each allele mutating at the same rate with the same distribution of mutational changes in effect, although these parameters may differ between loci (Kimura 1965; Lande 1975). In a diploid, randomly mating population, the expected rate of loss of heterozygosity, or additive genetic variance in a quantitative trait, due to random genetic drift in the absence of selection is $1/(2N_e)$ per generation, where N_e is the effective population size (Wright 1931, 1951; Latter and Novitski 1969). Measuring time, t, in generations, the dynamics of the expected value of the additive genetic variance, $\bar{V}_g$, under random genetic drift and mutation obey:

$$\frac{d\bar{V}_g}{dt} = -\frac{\bar{V}_g}{2N_e} + V_m \qquad (14.1)$$

(Clayton and Robertson 1955; Lande 1979).

The effective population size may change with time. Here we assume that it is always a constant multiple of the actual population size (N_e/N = constant), and starting from an effective number of founders, $N_e(0)$ the population grows exponentially at the rate r per generation until it reaches the final effective size, K_e. Thus the time in generations to reach the final size is $\tau = r^{-1}ln[K_e/N_e(0)]$ and the effective population size follows

$$N_e(t) = \begin{cases} N_e(0)e^{rt} & \text{for } t < \tau \\ K_e & \text{for } t \geq \tau \end{cases} \qquad (14.2)$$

To account for the age distribution of the founders, $N_e(0)$ can be approximated using standard (discrete generation) formulas involving sex ratio and distributions of progeny numbers (Crow and Kimura 1970; Lande and Barrowclough 1987), starting with the initial total reproductive values of males and females (Fisher 1958; Pollard 1973) instead of the actual numbers of each sex.

For a population with overlapping generations, the generation time, T, is defined as the average age of mothers and fathers of newborn individuals in a population with a stable age distribution (assuming that the sex ratio of offspring is independent of parental age) (Leslie 1966; Hill

1979). With a constant life history (age-specific mortality and fecundity rates independent of time), T depends on the growth rate of the population, being smaller for populations that are more rapidly increasing (Leslie 1966). Because the change in generation time within species is likely to be small in comparison to the range in generation times among species managed by a single breeding program and to simplify the analysis and facilitate comparison of the general results with those obtained by Soulé et al. (1986), we assume that T is approximately constant and ignore other complications caused by changes in age structure.

Figure 14.1 displays results accounting for random genetic drift, but ignoring mutation (assuming $V_m = 0$). The upper right panel with $r = 0.5$ is nearly identical to figure 1 of Soulé et al. (1986) except that the axes have been reversed to emphasize that we wish to determine the final effective population size, K_e, necessary to preserve 90% of the original additive genetic variance in the base population after 200 years, given T, $N_e(0)$ and r. An important feature of figure 14.1 is that when mutation is neglected, the final effective population sizes needed to achieve this goal are extremely large for species with generation times of a few years or less. Note that when $r = 0.2$ and $N_e(0) = 20$, the management goal cannot be attained for species with generation times less than 21.6 years.

Figure 14.2 shows analogous results incorporating a typical level of mutation that has been observed in quantitative characters in a variety of organisms, $V_m = 10^{-3} V_e$ where V_e is the environmental variance in the character that would be expressed in a genetically uniform population (Lande 1975; Hill 1982; Lynch 1988a). We assume that the typical quantitative character in the base population has a heritability $h^2 = V_g(0)/[V_g(0) + V_e] = 0.5$ so that $V_g(0) = V_e$. Franklin (1980) apparently chose these same values for mutability and heritability when he suggested that in the absence of selection a population with $N_e = 500$ would maintain typical levels of additive genetic variance (Lande and Barrowclough 1987). It should therefore come as no surprise that even for species with very short generation times the value of K_e needed to achieve the management goal never exceeds 450 (or 90% of Franklin's number).

A comparison of figures 14.1 and 14.2 reveals that accounting for mutation allows the management goal to be met with a smaller number of founders. In the discrete generation model, Soulé et al. (1986) point

Random genetic drift: $V_m = 0$

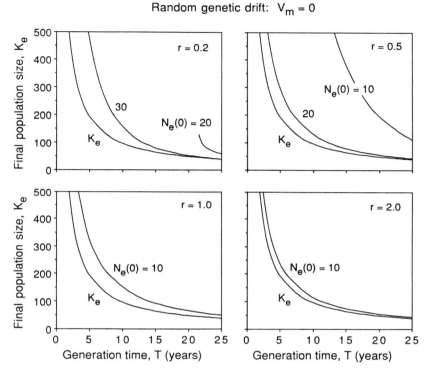

Figure 14.1 Final effective size of a captive population, K_e, necessary to expect 90% of the original heterozygosity, or additive genetic variance in quantitative characters, in the base (wild) population after 200 years, as a function of the generation time, for various values of the effective number of founders, $N_e(0)$, and population growth rate per generation, r. From equations (14.1) and (14.2), assuming no mutation.

out that $N_e(0)$ must be greater than five to preserve 90% of the genetic variability in the base population since if $N_e(0) = 5$, then $1/(2N_e(0)) = 0.1$ of the genetic variability will be lost in the first generation. The accumulation of genetic variance by mutation over several generations can compensate for a loss of this magnitude; thus, founder numbers smaller than previously proposed may be acceptable.

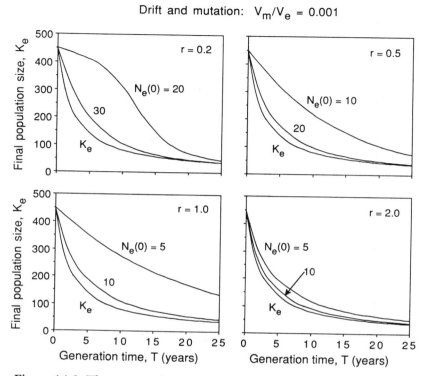

Figure 14.2 The same as figure 14.1 but for a typical quantitative character with additive genetic variance created by mutation at the rate $V_m/V_e = 0.001$ per generation, and a heritability in the base (wild) population of $h^2 = 0.5$.

Immigration from the Wild

Loss of genetic variance in a small captive population can be offset by immigration from the wild, assuming that the wild population remains large enough to maintain its original genetic variability. For a given effective population size, immigration from the wild also has the effect of retarding random genetic drift in the mean phenotype of the captive population away from that in the wild population. In an equilibrium analysis of the "island model," Wright (1931, 1951, 1969) showed that immigration of a few individuals per generation will prevent substantial loss of genetic variability or differentiation by random genetic drift. Here we analyze a relatively simple model of the dynamics of additive genetic variance and random genetic drift in the mean phenotype of a small captive population subject to immigration from a large wild population.

The immigration rate from the wild to the captive population is defined as m, such that a proportion m of the captive population is replaced by wild individuals matched for sex and age. Let the wild population have additive genetic variance $V_g(0)$ in a quantitative character with mean phenotype $\bar{z}(0)$, which are assumed to remain constant. The variance in the probability distribution of the mean phenotype in the captive population caused by random genetic drift is denoted as $V_{\bar{z}} = E[(\bar{z}(t) - \bar{z}(0))^2]$. In this definition, it is assumed that the mean phenotype is measured on a hypothetical large number of progeny; measurement of the actual population with effective size N_e would increase the expected variance in $\bar{z}(t)$ by an amount $(\bar{V}_g + V_e)/N_e$. The dynamics of the expected additive genetic variance within the captive population and the expected random genetic drift in its mean phenotype follow the coupled pair of equations

$$\frac{d\bar{V}_g}{dt} = -\frac{\bar{V}_g}{2N_e} + V_m + m[V_g(0) - \bar{V}_g] + \frac{m(1 - m)}{2} V_{\bar{z}} \quad (14.3)$$

$$\frac{dV_{\bar{z}}}{dt} = -2mV_{\bar{z}} + \frac{\bar{V}_g}{N_e} \qquad \text{assuming } m \ll 1.0 \quad (14.4)$$

(Lande 1979; Lynch 1988b). The last two terms in equation (14.3) correspond respectively to the genetic variance carried by the immigrants and the genetic variance that is produced by hybridization between populations. For simplicity, we assume that N_e is constant and equal to the size of the founder population. We also assume that immigration occurs at a small constant rate, $m \ll 1.0$.

The left side of figure 14.3 shows that with typical levels of mutation even one effective migrant every few generations ($N_e m = 1/4, 1/2,$ or 1) substantially reduces the effective population size necessary to achieve the management goal. The actual number of immigrants, Nm, differs from the effective number of immigrants. $N_e m$ can be estimated from the expected reproductive value of the immigrants times N_e/N for the captive population.

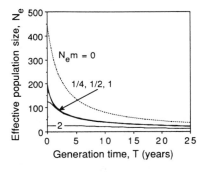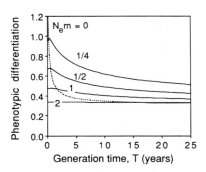

Figure 14.3 *Left*: Effective population size, N_e, needed to expect 90% of the original additive genetic variance after 200 years, as a function of the generation time, for various values of the effective number of immigrants per generation from the wild, $N_e m$, assuming $V_m / V_e = 0.001$ and $h^2 = 0.5$. *Right*: Expected amount of random genetic drift in the mean phenotype, in units of phenotypic standard deviations in the wild population, as a function of the generation time, when N_e is kept for 200 years at the size given in the left graph. From equations (14.3) and (14.4).

The right side of figure 14.3 depicts the amount of random genetic drift in the mean phenotype for populations managed to maintain 90% of the original genetic variance after 200 years (as shown in the left side of figure 14.3). The mean phenotype in the population is expected to drift less than one phenotypic standard deviation in 200 years, except for populations with generation times less than half a year in the absence of immigration. When $N_e m$ is in the range of 1/4 to 1, more phenotypic differentiation is expected to occur than in the absence of immigration, unless the generation time is less than one or two years. This result, which at first seems counterintuitive, occurs because these immigration rates allow the management goal to be met with smaller effective population sizes, which increases the rate of random genetic drift in the mean phenotype. With $N_e m > 2$, there is expected to be less phenotypic differentiation than in the absence of immigration because the stabilizing influence of immigration on the mean phenotype is stronger than the random genetic drift caused by reduced N_e.

Selection in the captive environment

Newly established captive populations often experience substantial selection to adapt to the captive environment. This includes novel physical conditions, such as confinement, and new social and biotic factors, such as isolation or crowding, and exposure to an altered set of pathogens. There may be additional artificial selection by the managers (consciously or unconsciously) for docility and high reproductive rate, especially during the early history of the population. In addition, the relaxation of natural selection may result in the gradual deterioration of some characters subject to directional mutation and maintained by a mutation-selection balance in wild populations, especially traits most closely related to fitness in the wild, e.g., sensory acuity, agility, and cognitive function. Higher animal species may also experience a loss of culturally transmitted information during a period of a generation or more in captivity (Arnold, essay 13 of this volume).

The effect of selection in the captive environment on the additive genetic variance of a particular trait can be modeled crudely by the loss of a constant proportion s per generation, so that equation (14.1) is modified to

$$\frac{\mathrm{d}\overline{V}_g}{\mathrm{d}t} = -\left(\frac{1}{2N_e} + s\right)\overline{V}_g + V_m. \qquad (14.5)$$

The left side of figure 14.4 reveals that with typical rates of mutation, if s is as small as 1%, even an infinitely large population will not maintain 90% of the original genetic variance for 200 years unless the generation time of the species is rather long. It may therefore be impossible to meet the management goal for characters under appreciable selection in captivity. Instead of causing despair, this conclusion can be turned around, in the manner of the right side of figure 14.4. For species with short generation times, populations with a moderate effective size will maintain nearly as much genetic variance in selected characters as an infinitely large population.

Deleterious or undesirable evolution in captive populations, caused by adaptation to captivity or by mutation and random genetic drift, can be counteracted by immigration from the wild or by artificial selection

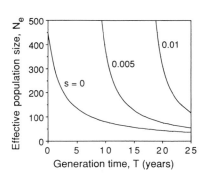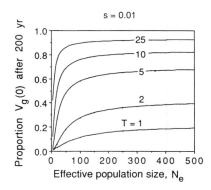

Figure 14.4 *Left*: Effective size of a captive population, N_e, necessary to expect 90% of the initial additive genetic variance after 200 years, as a function of the generation time, for various values of the rate of selective loss of genetic variance, s. *Right*: Expected proportion of additive genetic variance maintained after 200 years as a function of N_e, for various values of the generation time, assuming $s = 0.01$. From equation (14.5).

imposed by managers. To have much effect in this context, the rate of immigration would have to be comparable to the strength of selection ($m \geq s$). The imposition of artificial selection to counteract natural selection in captivity would help to prevent changes in the mean phenotype, but it may also increase the rate of loss of additive genetic variance. Another way of reducing evolutionary changes in a captive population is by increasing generation time and equalizing progeny numbers. Any required artificial selection should be exerted within progeny groups, with readjustment to equal size after selection (Lande and Barrowclough 1987).

Population Subdivision

Subdivision of a population and random genetic drift within the subpopulations converts the original genetic variation within the base population into genetic variation between subpopulations. Population subdivision also allows genetic variation between populations to accumulate by random genetic drift and fixation of new mutations. Once alternative alleles at a locus are fixed in different subpopulations, this component of genetic variability is permanently maintained and cannot be lost as long as the subpopulations persist. Splitting a population into separate subpopulations with no gene flow or migration among them is therefore a powerful way of maintaining genetic variability, even though the total population size may be small.

Consider a panmictic population with an effective population size N_e that is divided at time 0 into n separate subpopulations, each with constant effective size N_e/n. The additive genetic variance maintained by this population structure after t generations can be measured by the amount that would exist if all subpopulations were randomly mated and allowed to attain linkage equilibrium (e.g., after several generations at a large population size). Since purely additive genetic variance within populations is expected to double when converted by random genetic drift to variation among populations (Wright 1951), the total additive genetic variance in the population after panmixia, V_{gP}, is expected to be

$$\overline{V}_{gP}(t) = \overline{V}_g(t) + \frac{1}{2}\left(1 - \frac{1}{n}\right)V_{\bar{z}}(t) \qquad (14.6)$$

where $\overline{V}_g(t)$ and $V_{\bar{z}}(t)$ are respectively the expected genetic variance within subpopulations and the expected differentiation among subpopulations, as defined above in equations (14.3) and (14.4).

The preservation of heterozygosity, or additive genetic variance, in a subdivided population is most easily illustrated when there is no mutation, migration, or selection. Although smaller subpopulations lose genetic variance faster, figure 14.5 shows that splitting a population of a given total size into more subpopulations is expected to result in the preservation of more genetic variance. After a few times N_e/n generations, the amount of additive genetic variance preserved among n subpopulations approaches $(1 - 1/n)V_g(0)$.

With mutation, but no migration or selection, the subpopulations will continue to differentiate, and, after many generations have elapsed, the total genetic variance as measured by equation (14.6) will actually exceed that originally contained in the base population. The left side of figure 14.6 gives the total population size, N_e, needed to maintain 90% of the initial genetic variance in a typical quantitative character after

200 years, with various numbers of subpopulations. The curves for $n >$ 2 are truncated because species with generation times less than a few years are always expected to maintain *more* than 90% of the original genetic variance, regardless of the total population size, because of the accumulation of new mutations among populations.

Subdivision can also help to counteract the erosion of genetic variability by selection in the captive environment if subpopulations are small enough so that random genetic drift and fixation of alternate alleles in different subpopulations occurs faster than selection. For example, the right side of figure 14.6 depicts the simple case where direction-

Figure 14.5 Expected proportion of original heterozygosity or additive genetic variance maintained as a function of time, for various numbers of subpopulations, n. Time is scaled in units of $2N_e$ where N_e is the total effective size if the population were panmictic. There is no mutation or selection, and no gene flow or migration among subpopulations. From equation (14.6).

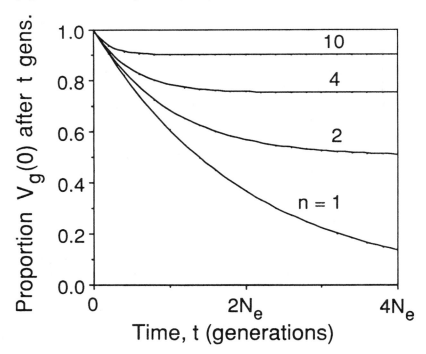

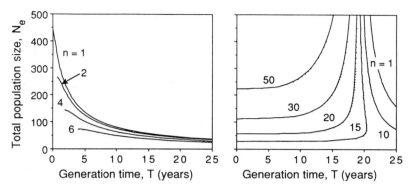

Figure 14.6 *Left*: Total population size, N_e, needed to maintain 90% of the initial additive genetic variance after 200 years, as a function of the generation time, for various numbers of subpopulations, n. Evaluated for a character with $V_m/V_e = 0.001$ and $h^2 = 0.5$, but with no selection and no migration among subpopulations. *Right*: Same as the left side, but there is selection, $s = 0.01$ and no mutation, $V_m = 0$. From equations (14.5) and (14.6).

al selection operates with the same intensity on all subpopulations, regardless of their mean phenotype (e.g., due to unconscious artificial selection for tameness). It can be seen that for species with intermediate generation times, splitting the population into many very small subpopulations makes the management goal attainable with feasible total population sizes. Stabilizing selection toward the same phenotype in all subpopulations would retard their differentiation and reduce the impact of subdivision, whereas diversifying selection toward different phenotypes in different subpopulations would accelerate their differentiation and enhance the influence of subdivision in comparison to that shown in the right side of figure 14.6.

SUMMARY AND DISCUSSION

Breeding plans for captive populations should be designed to meet a specific goal. Possible goals range from the establishment of a permanent captive population for public display in zoos or arboreta to captive breeding for later release into the wild (Frankham et al. 1986; Foose et al. 1986). The present study concerns captive breeding for later release into the wild. For many species, especially large mammals and birds, or species with specialized habitat requirements, continued habitat alteration (directly or indirectly by human exploitation) will cause extinction or near extinction in the wild, necessitating a period of captive propagation to produce stock for later release into natural or restored areas. Soulé et al. (1986) suggested the management goal of maintaining 90% of the initial heterozygosity for 200 years. We derived an analytical framework for the development of breeding plans designed to meet this goal for additive genetic variance in typical quantitative characters. Results are presented in the figures. General analytical formulas in the appendix allow the construction of breeding plans to meet other goals, such as the maintenance of 75% of the original genetic variability for 100 years (Foose et al., essay 12 of this volume).

Building on the model of Soulé et al. (1986), which includes the number of founders, exponential growth of the population to its final size, and random genetic drift, the present results demonstrate that the management goal can be achieved with smaller population sizes if account is taken of mutation in typical quantitative traits. This is especially important for species with short generation times, as can be seen from comparison of figures 14.1 and 14.2. Immigration from the wild of one effective individual every few generations would also permit substantial reduction in the size of the managed population necessary to meet the goal (figure 14.3), but this option is not possible if the wild population is extinct, and it may not be desirable if the wild population has been severely reduced in size for several generations so that it is highly inbred and depauperate of genetic variability.

These models analyze the dynamics of genetic variability, assuming that in the captive environment there is no selection on most characters. For some traits, however, such as tameness or fecundity, natural or artificial selection for adaptation to captivity may occur. With appreciable selection in the captive environment, the management goal cannot be met using a single panmictic population, except for species with rather long generation times. In this situation, a population with an effective size of a few hundred individuals can maintain nearly as much genetic variability as an indefinitely large population, as is shown in figure 14.4.

Breeding plans for closely managed populations often have a single (nearly) panmictic population with an effective size large enough to avoid severe inbreeding depression and to maintain substantial amounts of selectively neutral heterozygosity or additive genetic variance in quantitative traits for long periods of time (Franklin 1980; Foose et al. 1986; Soulé et al. 1986; Lacy et al., essay 4 of this volume). Random exchange of one effective immigrant every few generations between subdivisions of a population renders it nearly panmictic with respect to selectively neutral variation (Wright 1951; Foose et al. 1986). Most of the deleterious effects of inbreeding depression can be avoided if each subpopulation has an effective size of more than a few dozen individuals (Lande and Barrowclough 1987). This degree of subdivision also has the advantage of reducing the chance of catastrophic extinction (e.g., by epidemics) and regionalizing logistical problems including transportation costs (Foose et al. 1986).

Complete subdivision of a population acts to permanently maintain genetic variability between subpopulations rather than within them. Subdivision of a population into noninterbreeding units may be appropriate if the management goal cannot be met with a single randomly mating population because of space limitations (figures 14.5 and 14.6, left side). Extreme subdivision into numerous very small subpopulations may be the only method of maintaining a high proportion of the original genetic variation for characters that are under appreciable selection for adaptation to captivity. The subpopulations, however, should not be so small that they experience severe inbreeding depression. The choice of the degree of subdivision (e.g., figure 14.6, right side) should be based on a consideration of the intensity of selection and the magnitude of inbreeding depression. Stronger selection requires more subdivision, but a larger subpopulation size allows selection to counteract inbreeding depression more efficiently by eliminating deleterious recessive mutations when they become homozygous.

In addition to the goal of maintaining genetic variability, breeding plans should also limit evolution of the mean phenotype in the captive population by random genetic drift or selection in the captive environment. The appendix and figure 14.3 show that for the breeding plans described above, random genetic drift in the mean phenotype is not expected to be substantial, unless the generation time of the species is much less than one year (e.g., on the order of one month). Aside from reducing the intensity of selection (by equalizing family sizes, maximizing generation time, and eliminating conscious selection) or continually introducing immigrants from the wild, extreme population subdivision may be the most powerful method of reducing the influence of selection in the captive environment. To counteract deleterious mutations or undesirable evolutionary changes in quantitative traits, Lande and Barrowclough (1987) recommend artificial selection within families by maintaining equal family sizes after selection.

When a captive population is released into a natural or restored area, the initial founders must reproduce sufficiently fast for the population to grow and become established at a size large enough to avoid extinction due to ecological and genetic factors. The number of individuals released should be sufficiently large to prevent substantial inbreeding and loss of genetic variability and to overcome Allee effects such as the difficulty of finding a mate in a sparse population. The period of captive propagation should encompass as few generations as possible to minimize loss of genetic variation, loss of cultural information, and domestication effects. The environment of the release site should be similar to that of the original natural habitat to reduce the difficulty of adaptation. In many cases, multiple releases at various localities will be necessary for successful reestablishment in the wild (Griffith et al. 1989).

Acknowledgments
I thank S. J. Arnold, J. D. Ballou, and M. Lynch for stimulating discussions. This work was supported by U.S. Public Health Service Grant GM27120.

REFERENCES
Abramowitz, M. and I. A. Stegun. 1972. *Handbook of Mathematical Functions.* New York: Dover.
Clayton, G. and A. Robertson. 1955. Mutation and quantitative genetic variation. *American Naturalist* 89:151–58.
Crow, J. F. and M. Kimura. 1970. *An Introduction to Population Genetics Theory.* New York: Harper and Row.
Fisher, R. A. 1958. *The Genetical Theory of Natural Selection,* 2d ed. New York: Dover.
Foose, T. 1980. Demographic management of endangered species in captivity. *International Zoo Yearbook* 20:154–66.
Foose, T. J., R. Lande, N. R. Flesness, G. Rabb, and B. Read. 1986. Propagation plans. *Zoo Biology* 5:139–46.

Frankham, R., H. Hemmer, O. A. Ryder, E. G. Cothran, M. E. Soulé, N. D. Murray, and M. Snyder. 1986. Selection in captive populations. *Zoo Biology* 5:127–38.

Franklin, I. R. 1980. Evolutionary changes in small populations. In M. E. Soulé and B. A. Wilcox, eds., *Conservation Biology: An Evolutionary-Ecological Approach,* pp. 135–49. Sunderland, Mass.: Sinauer.

Griffith, B., J. M. Scott, J. W. Carpenter, and C. Reed. 1989. Translocation as a species conservation tool: Status and strategy. *Science* 245:477–80.

Hill, W. G. 1979. A note of effective population size with overlapping generations. *Genetics* 92:317–22.

Hill, W. G. 1982. Predictions of response to artificial selection from new mutations. *Genetical Research* 40:255–78.

Kimura, M. 1965. A stochastic model concerning the maintenance of genetic variability in quantitative characters. *Proceedings of the National Academy of Sciences of the U.S.A.* 54:731–36.

Lande, R. 1975. The maintenance of genetic variation by mutation in a quantitative character with linked loci. *Genetical Research* 26:221–35.

Lande, R. 1979. Quantitative genetic analysis of multivariate evolution, applied to brain: Body size allometry. *Evolution* 33:402–16.

Lande, R. 1980. Genetic variation and phenotypic evolution during allopatric speciation. *American Naturalist* 116:463–79.

Lande, R. 1988. Genetics and demography in biological conservation. *Science* 241:1455–60.

Lande, R. and G. F. Barrowclough. 1987. Effective population size, genetic variation, and their use in population management. In M. Soulé, ed., *Viable Populations for Conservation,* pp. 87–123. New York: Cambridge University Press.

Latter, B. D. H. and C. E. Novitski. 1969. Selection in finite populations with multiple alleles, I: Limits to directional selection. *Genetics* 62:859–76.

Leslie, P. H. 1966. The intrinsic rate of increase and the overlap of successive generations in a population of guillemots (*Uria aalge* Pont.). *Journal of Animal Ecology* 25:291–301.

Lynch, M. 1988a. The rate of polygenic mutation. *Genetical Research* 51:137–48.

Lynch, M. 1988b. The divergence of neutral quantitative characters among partially isolated populations. *Evolution* 42:455–66.

Pollard, J. H. 1973. *Mathematical Models for the Growth of Human Populations.* New York: Cambridge University Press.

Soulé, M., M. Gilpin, W. Conway, and T. Foose. 1986. The millennium ark: How long a voyage, how many staterooms, how many passengers? *Zoo Biology* 5:101–14.

Wiese, R. J., K. Willis, J. Bowdoin, and M. Hutchins, eds. 1993. *AAZPA Annual Report on Conservation and Science, 1992–93.* Bethesda, Maryland: American Association of Zoological Parks and Aquariums.

Wright, S. 1931. Evolution in Mendelian populations. *Genetics* 16:97–159.

Wright, S. 1951. The genetical structure of populations. *Annals of Eugenics* 15:323–54.

Wright, S. 1969. *Evolution and the Genetics of Populations, Vol. 2: The Theory of Gene Frequencies.* Chicago: University of Chicago Press.

APPENDIX

Random Genetic Drift and Mutation

Equation (14.1) is first order and linear, with nonconstant coefficient $1/(2N_e(t))$ given by equation (14.2). It can be solved using an integrating factor. From the solution, given $V_g(0)$, $N_e(0)$, r and T, we wish to derive the value of K_e that will satisfy the management goal. Thus we require that the final effective population size has been reached, $t \geq \tau$, and that after $t = 200/T$ generations an expected proportion p (here $p = 0.9$) of the initial additive genetic variance is maintained, $\bar{V}_g(200/T) = pV_g(0)$. The solution of equation (14.1) at $t = \tau$ is

$$\bar{V}_g(\tau) = I(\tau) \left[V_g(0) + V_m \int_0^\tau [I(u)]^{-1} du \right] \qquad (14.A1)$$

where the integrating factor is

$$I(\tau) = \exp \left\{ - \frac{1 - e^{-r\tau}}{2N_e(0) \, r} \right\} \qquad (14.A2)$$

and $\tau = r^{-1} \ln[K_e/N_e(0)]$. For $t \geq \tau$, the solution is

$$\bar{V}_g(t) = 2K_e V_m + [\bar{V}_g(\tau) - 2K_e V_m] \exp \left\{ - \frac{t - \tau}{2K_e} \right\}. \qquad (14.A3)$$

Although it is not possible to obtain an explicit expression for K_e from these formulas, t can be expressed in terms of K_e as

$$t = \tau + 2K_e \ln \left\{ \frac{\bar{V}_g(\tau) - 2K_e V_m}{pV_g(0) - 2K_e V_m} \right\} \qquad (14.A4)$$

in which $\bar{V}_g(\tau)$ is given by equation (14.A1). Generation times are then obtained from $T = 200/t$.

In the absence of mutation ($V_m = 0$) the term in brackets in equation (14.A4) becomes simply $I(\tau)/p$ as was used to construct figure 14.1. With mutation, it is convenient to divide numerator and denominator in the bracketed term by $V_g(0)$, setting $V_m/V_g(0) = (V_m/V_e)(1 - h^2)/h^2$ in which h^2 is the heritability of the character in the base population (see text). To construct figure 14.2 the integral in equation (14.A1) was evaluated by substituting $y = \alpha e^{-ru}$ with $\alpha = [2N_e(0)r]^{-1}$,

$$\int_0^T [I(u)]^{-1}du = r^{-1}e^\alpha[E_1(\alpha e^{-r\tau}) - E_1(\alpha)] \qquad (14.A5)$$

where $E_1(x) = \int_x^\infty y^{-1}e^{-y}dy$ is the exponential integral. In the range $0 \le x \le 1$ (if $r > 0$ this requires that $2N_e(0)r \ge 1$), the exponential integral can be approximated with an error less than 2×10^{-7} by the function (Abramowits and Stegun 1972)

$$E_1(x) = \ln x + a_0 + a_1x + a_2x^2 + a_3x^3 + a_4x^4 + a_5x^5 \qquad (14.A6)$$

with

$$
\begin{aligned}
a_0 &= -0.57721566 & a_3 &= 0.05519968 \\
a_1 &= 0.99999193 & a_4 &= -0.00976004 \\
a_2 &= -0.24994055 & a_5 &= 0.00107857.
\end{aligned}
$$

Immigration from the Wild

Equations (14.3) and (14.4) constitute a coupled pair with constant coefficients, which can be solved by finding the eigenvalues and eigenvectors of the system. Since we have assumed that $m \ll 1$, the last coefficient in equation (14.3) can be approximated as $m(1 - m)/2 \cong m/2$. We must analyze separately the cases of positive migration rate and no migration since the solution changes discontinuously as m approaches 0.

For $m > 0$, the equilibrium values of the variables are

$$\overline{V}_g(\infty) = \frac{4N_e[V_m + mV_g(0)]}{4N_em + 1} \qquad (14.A7)$$

$$V_{\bar z}(\infty) = \frac{\overline{V}_g(\infty)}{2N_em}. \qquad (14.A8)$$

Defining $\delta(t) = \overline{V}_g(t) - \overline{V}_g(\infty)$ and $\epsilon(t) = V_{\bar z}(t) - V_{\bar z}(\infty)$ equations 14.3 and 14.4 become

$$\frac{d}{dt}\begin{pmatrix} \delta \\ \epsilon \end{pmatrix} = \begin{pmatrix} -m - 1/(2N_e) & m/2 \\ 1/N_e & -2m \end{pmatrix}\begin{pmatrix} \delta \\ \epsilon \end{pmatrix} \qquad (14.A9)$$

The eigenvalues of the matrix in (14.A9) are $-m$ and $\lambda = -1/(2N_e) - 2m$, with corresponding eigenvectors in transposed form $(N_em, 1)$ and $(-1/2, 1)$. Then

$$\overline{V}_g(t) = \overline{V}_g(\infty) + c_1 N_e m e^{-mt} - (c_2/2)e^{\lambda t} \tag{14.A10}$$

$$V_{\tilde{z}}(t) = V_{\tilde{z}}(\infty) + c_1 e^{-mt} + c_2 e^{\lambda t} \tag{14.A11}$$

where, using $V_{\tilde{z}}(0) = 0$ and (14.A8),

$$c_1 = \frac{\overline{V}_g(\infty) - 2\overline{V}_g(0)}{2N_e m + 1}$$

$$c_2 = \frac{2\left[\overline{V}_g(0) - \overline{V}_g(\infty) \left(1 + \dfrac{1}{4N_e m} \right) \right]}{2N_e m + 1}.$$

Setting $\overline{V}_g(t) = p V_g(0)$ in equation (14.A10), and dividing all genetic variances by $V_g(0)$ as after (14.A4), Newton's method of iteration was used to find numerical values of t for given values of N_e, $N_e m$, V_m/V_e and the initial heritability h^2. Numerical values of t were converted to generation times using $T = 200/t$ to plot the solid curves in figure 14.3a, and they were also substituted into equation (14.A11) to construct the solid curves in figure 14.3b.

For $m = 0$, the solutions of equations (14.3) and (14.4) are

$$\overline{V}_g(t) = 2N_e V_m + [V_g(0) - 2N_e V_m]e^{-t/(2N_e)} \tag{14.A12}$$

$$V_{\tilde{z}}(t) = 2[V_g(0) - 2N_e V_m][1 - e^{-t/(2N_e)}] + 2tV_m \tag{14.A13}$$

(Lande 1980). These formulas were used to plot the dashed curves in figures 14.3a and 14.3b, proceeding as with equations (14.A10) and (14.A11), except that an analytical expression for t can be easily obtained from equation (14.A12).

Selection in captivity

Equation (14.5) is linear with constant coefficients. Setting $\lambda = 1/(2N_e) + s$ the solution is

$$\overline{V}_g(t) = \lambda^{-1} V_m + [V_g(0) - \lambda^{-1} V_m]e^{-\lambda t}. \tag{14.A14}$$

Setting $\overline{V}_g(t) = p V_g(0)$ and solving for t yields

$$t = \lambda^{-1}\ln\left\{ \frac{V_g(0) - V_m/\lambda}{p V_g(0) - V_m/\lambda} \right\}. \tag{14.A15}$$

Again $T = 200/t$ and the variances in the bracketed term can be expressed in units of $V_g(0)$ as after equation (14.A4). Equations (14.A15) and (14.A14) were used respectively to produce the left and right sides of figure 14.4.

Population Subdivision

From equation (14.6) using equations (14.A12) and (14.A13) with N_e divided by n, we find that with no mutation, and no selection or migration

$$\overline{V_{gP}}(t) = V_g(0)[1 - (1 - e^{\frac{-nt}{2N_e}})/n] \qquad (14.A16)$$

which was used to construct figure 14.5. With a constant intensity of directional selection on each subpopulation, regardless of its mean phenotype, equation (14.5) with N_e divided by n describes the dynamics of $\bar{V}_g$ and the expected differentiation among subpopulations is given by $dV_{\bar{z}}/dt = n\bar{V}_g/N_e$. The expected total genetic variance after panmixia in generation t, with selection and mutation but no migration, is then

$$\overline{V_{gP}}(t) = [V_g(0) - V_m/\lambda][c/\lambda + (1 - c/\lambda)e^{-\lambda t}] \qquad (14.A17)$$
$$+ (1 + ct)V_m/\lambda$$

where $\lambda = n/(2N_e) + s$ and $c = (n - 1)/(2N_e)$. Setting $\bar{V}_{gP}(t)/V_g(0) = 0.9$, this equation was evaluated as above for typical character with $h^2 = 0.5$ and $V_m/V_e = 0.001$. Newton's method was employed to obtain numerical solutions for t which were converted to generation times using $T = 200/t$ for the construction of figure 14.6.

Random Genetic Drift in the Mean Phenotype

For completely additive genetic variance, Wright (1951) showed that random drift in the mean phenotype of a single population is expected to cause a squared deviation between the initial and final mean phenotypes of $2V_g(0)$ based on fixation of the original genetic variation. Random genetic drift and fixation of new mutations are expected to add a quantity less than $2tV_m$, regardless of $N_e(t)$ (Lande 1980; equation [14.A13]). Defining $V_{\bar{z}}(t) = V_{\bar{z}}(t)/[V_g(0) + V_e]$ then

$$v_{\bar{z}}(t) < 2h^2 + 2t(V_m/V_e)(1 - h^2). \qquad (14.A18)$$

At $t = 200/T$, the mean phenotype of a typical character with heritability $h^2 = 0.5$ and $V_m/V_e = 0.001$ is not expected to drift more than one phenotypic standard deviation because of fixation of genetic variation in the base population and less than an additional $1/(5T)$ phenotypic standard deviations based on new mutations. Thus, unless $T \ll 1$, random genetic drift in the mean phenotype is not likely to be substantial in breeding plans for a single population carried out on a timescale of 200 years.

The same conclusion holds true for population subdivision, regardless of the sizes of the subpopulations or the migration rates between them. Let the ith subpopulation have mean phenotype $\bar{z}_i$ (measured in a large number of offspring), additive genetic variance V_{gi}, and effective size N_{ei}. The ratio of actual to effective size is assumed to be the same in all subpopulations, so that the total effective size in the absence of subdivision would be $N_e = \Sigma N_{ei}$. The grand mean phenotype and the weighted average genetic variance within subpopulations are

$$\bar{z} = \sum N_{ei}\bar{z}_i/N_e \quad \text{and} \quad \overline{V}_g = \sum N_{ei}V_{gi}/N_e \qquad (14.A19)$$

The increased variance in the probability distribution of $\bar{z}$ due to one generation of random genetic drift is

$$\text{Var}_{\text{drift}}[\bar{z}] = \sum (N_{ei}/N_e)^2 V_{gi}/N_{ei} = \overline{V}_g/N_e. \qquad (14.A20)$$

This result is not influenced by migration among subpopulations, provided that individuals do not incur reduced fitness during migration, because with purely additive genetic variance migration does not alter $\bar{z}$. Thus random genetic drift in $\bar{z}$ occurs at the same rate as if the population were panmictic with additive genetic variance $\bar{V}_g$. Because population subdivision is expected to decrease the additive genetic variance within subpopulations (Wright 1951; Lynch 1988b), the rate of genetic drift in the grand mean phenotype of a subdivided population must be less than that for a single panmictic population with the same total effective size, analyzed in equation (14.A18).

15

Introgression, Supportive Breeding, and Genetic Conservation

■■

Nils Ryman, Fred Utter, and Kjetil Hindar

Releasing captive-bred animals and cultivated plants is an increasingly common practice in the management of biological resources (e.g., IUCN 1987a; Conant 1988; Griffith et al. 1989). For example, endangered species are bred in captivity with the ultimate goal of restocking or reintroduction into the wild. Many game species as well as commercially important species are bred for release into and harvest from natural settings. Modern forestry is likewise dependent upon the planting of large numbers of cultivated seedlings derived from an often small number of nonautochthonous parental trees grown in seed orchards. Furthermore, the recent expansion of confined rearing of fish within the field of aquaculture has resulted in unintentional releases through escapes of large numbers of individuals.

There are a number of potential genetic problems associated with such captive breeding and release programs, and the problems may differ for programs with different purposes such as introduction, reintroduction, or enhancement. This study focuses on the potential impact on natural gene pools of releasing captive-bred animals and plants into the wild for the purpose of supporting natural populations, i.e., problems related to the genetic effects of enhancement or stocking (restocking in the nomenclature of IUCN [1987a]).

Problems relating to the genetic effects of enhancement have been largely deferred within the context of classical conservation genetics, most likely because of the urgent need to focus on other matters such as the risk of immediate extinction and the development of genetically sound captive breeding programs. These concerns, however, will become increasingly topical with the growing awareness of the need for biological conservation (IUCN 1987b); they are presently under consideration within the domains of fisheries and forestry, for example, where recent advances in artificial production have made them increasingly more apparent. For instance, it has been noted for Atlantic salmon (*Salmo salar*) that in some rivers in Norway about 80% of the spawning fish are escapes from net-pens, and there is justifiable concern that the consequent reproduction will rapidly destroy valuable and irreplaceable gene pools (Moen and Gausen 1989).

There are two types of potential genetic concerns associated with this kind of release, whether intentional or not. The most obvious one concerns introgression and occurs when the genetic characteristics of the captive populations differ from those of the wild ones. When released individuals breed with wild ones, the genetic characteristics of the natural populations may be compromised. The second problem refers to the effects on the genetically effective population size that arises within a population subjected to supportive breeding. It occurs without introduction of exogenous genes and independently of possible adaptations to the captive environment; it is caused by the manipulation of reproductive rates inherent in any captive breeding program.

Clearly, the first type of concern extends to any program where the released animals are genetically different from those they will interact with in nature. In such cases there are three issues to be considered: (1) Do genetic changes that have occurred in captivity have an appreciable effect on performance under natural conditions? (2) If so, are these undesirable characteristics transferred to the natural population(s)? and

(3) What fraction of the original genes can be replaced by exogenous ones before the genetic characteristics of the natural population must be considered compromised? The second type of concern raises questions relating to potentially negative impacts of manipulating reproductive rates within a population that is supported by captive breeding.

Of course, there is no single answer to these questions. The management goals, and thus the justified concerns about enhancement, are quite different for different situations. At one extreme we may envision an almost extinct species with only a few remnant individuals existing in nature. In this case, the major goal most likely is to increase the size of the population in the wild through, among other things, releasing captive-reared individuals. The survival of the species depends primarily upon raising the numbers by almost any means available. In addition, the gene pool of the natural population may justifiably be considered to be severely depleted through bottlenecking to the point that any influx of new genes should be beneficial.

At the other extreme we may consider salmonid fishes, which are typically not considered threatened at the species level. They are, however, characterized by the existence of a number of local populations that exhibit a large degree of genetic differentiation between them. For these local populations, releases or escapes from aquaculture may constitute a serious threat to local adaptations and to unique alleles or gene combinations of individual populations as well as to the overall genetic structuring of the species itself (e.g., Ryman 1981, 1983; Allendorf and Leary 1988).

Between these extremes are an indefinite number of intermediate cases where the potential problems of releases may require attention in the context of conservation biology. Factors to be considered include: (1) the amount of genetic divergence between the captive and wild populations; (2) the genetic population structure of the species; (3) the number of animals released and the size of the recipient populations; and (4) the probability that introgression will occur.

In this essay we discuss various genetic aspects of enhancement, and we use examples from the growing body of information obtained in the context of the management of captive and wild salmonid fish populations. We have focused on salmonids because to our knowledge the most extensive set of empirical data that is relevant to the present issues has been obtained for this group of organisms. Salmonid fishes have been particularly targeted for genetic investigations, among other things because of their distinct population structure, which makes them excellent models for population genetic studies. Consequently, good genetic descriptions of natural salmonid populations exist, which in some cases permit monitoring of the genetic effects of releases of cultured fishes into those populations.

PREDICTING THE GENETIC EFFECTS OF INTROGRESSION

In the context of introgression we are concerned about genetic changes in wild populations receiving exogenous genes. Intentional or incidental releases of individuals bred in captivity into areas inhabited by naturally reproducing populations constitute a threat (1) by loss of adapted genes or gene complexes through interbreeding, (2) by loss of entire populations as a result of displacement (or eradication through disease introduction), or (3) by homogenization of a previously genetically structured population through swamping a region with a common gene pool. In addition, continual flooding of an area with exogenous genes may prevent readaptation after the first introduction of exogenous genes.

In order to predict the effects and to identify critical levels of introgression from exogenous to wild populations, we need to be able to predict the biological implications of manipulating patterns and rates of gene flow among wild and captive populations (figure 15.1). Such predictions can be made on the basis of population genetics theory provided that all necessary parameters are known (e.g., Crow and Kimura 1970; Nei 1975, 1987; Endler 1977; Hartl 1980; Falconer 1981). Unfortunately, they are never known in real situations. This dilemma is a reality that must be accepted and dealt with. We do not know the current genetic characteristics of either the wild or the captive populations of concern (figure 15.1). Likewise, we do not know the mode and magnitude of present and past selective forces acting upon those populations, their size, migration patterns, or their evolutionary history. For instance, the majority of genes for any species are still to be identified, and we have very little knowledge about the numbers of genes, their functions, and their interactions. Thus, we have almost no idea of the extent to which most genes are subjected to selection and genetic drift.

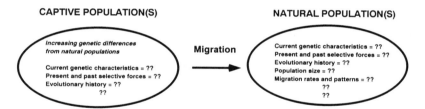

CAPTIVE POPULATION(S)   NATURAL POPULATION(S)

Increasing genetic differences
from natural populations   **Migration**

Current genetic characteristics = ??
Present and past selective forces = ??
Evolutionary history = ??
??

Current genetic characteristics = ??
Present and past selective forces = ??
Evolutionary history = ??
Population size = ??
Migration rates and patterns = ??
??
??

Figure 15.1 Schematic representation of information necessary for a priori predictions of effects on natural gene pools when releasing individuals bred in captivity into the wild.

Furthermore, the genetic basis for the variation of most behavioral and morphological traits remains largely unknown.

The major part of the information that currently does exist concerning the genetic structure of most higher organisms is based on a very limited set of genes that are identified by means of various biochemical and molecular techniques (Utter et al. 1987; Avise et al., essay 9 of this volume). Among others, these techniques include protein electrophoresis, restriction enzyme analysis, and direct sequencing of DNA. Some of these techniques (e.g., protein electrophoresis) permit the identification of both functional genes (loci) as well as variants within loci (alleles). Although a few of these loci have been shown to be directly or indirectly affected by natural selection, it appears from a wealth of empirical observations that much of the variation is selectively neutral or under weak selection (e.g., Kimura 1983; Nei 1987). During the past two decades a great abundance of this type of biochemical genetic information has accumulated for a wide variety of organisms. Most of what is presently known about the genetics of natural animal and plant populations is based on this type of data on allelic variation at biochemically detectable loci (e.g., Nevo 1978; Hamrick 1983; Avise et al. 1987; Nei 1987).

It must be stressed, however, that the kind of genetic information provided by molecular data is very limited with respect to adaptive characteristics of a population. Because molecular data appear largely to reflect the segregation of genes that are not strongly subjected to the forces of natural selection, those loci generally provide little or no information on the amount of genetically determined ecological, ethological, and morphological differentiation among populations. We would expect, therefore, that loci subjected to selection would exhibit a greater degree of genetic differentiation among populations than is observed at, e.g., protein coding loci detected by electrophoresis. For instance, fixation for alternate alleles is rarely observed among conspecific populations for protein coding loci whereas such fixations may be much more frequent for genetically determined morphological traits.

Generally, we know a bit more about a captive population than we do about a natural one. For instance, the actual population size, the number of breeding individuals of each sex, and even the population's pedigree are frequently known. If the captive population has been maintained for more than a few generations, we also suspect that the genetic composition has been altered as a consequence of restricted population size and adaptation to the captive environment (Arnold, essay 13 of this volume). However, in spite of this greater knowledge, we remain very ignorant about its genetic details. We still cannot identify the loci that affect various characters, nor do we know their number or the mode of interaction between them. Regardless of our ignorance about the genetic details of a captive population, it is obvious that over time such a population is becoming increasingly different from its ancestors as well as from any natural population (Lande, essay 14 of this volume).

It is obvious from the above that we do not currently have the pertinent information for anything more than very general a priori predictions concerning the genetic effects of releasing captive-bred individuals into natural environments inhabited by wild populations of the same species. Thus, we are faced with the problem of not being able to predict the genetic consequences of possible introgression when management aims at conserving the genetic characteristics of the wild populations.

Given the difficulty (or even impossibility) of making these a priori predictions, it is necessary to obtain as much empirical information as possible on the actual results of releases under various conditions. The best set of data that we are aware of in the above context has been obtained as a result of large-scale releases of commercially grown salmonid fishes. This information can provide a growing body of knowledge for better understanding of possible interactions in release situations. In the following section we summarize some of these data we consider pertinent to the overall question of inadvertent introgression and genetic conservation.

OBSERVATIONS OF GENETIC EFFECTS
FROM RELEASES OF SALMONID FISHES

It is hard to find parallels among other vertebrates for the massive, continuous, and frequently uncontrolled spread of genetic material over
large areas that became possible through the development of hatchery
procedures in the past century (Allendorf et al. 1987). In particular, the
artificial rearing of salmonid fishes has expanded dramatically during
the twentieth century. The destruction of spawning sites and the loss of
migratory passages caused by pollutants and hydroelectric power sta-
tions has necessitated the development of hatchery programs aimed at
reducing ecological and economical damage caused by the reduction or
complete eradication of salmonid populations. Massive releases of
hatchery fish into natural waters is frequently practiced to compensate
for the loss of natural reproduction and to support commercial and
sport fisheries.

In addition, the development of technologies for large-scale rearing
has made possible the breeding and rearing of large numbers of salmonids in captivity for their high commercial value. As the commercial
rearing industry grows, a simultaneous growth has also been observed
in escapes from open-water rearing facilities. In Norway, for instance,
the production of farmed Atlantic salmon has approximately doubled
every two years since 1970 to 115,000 tons in 1989, while the yield of
wild salmon has remained stable at about 1,500 tons (Anon. 1989).
During the winter of 1988–89, accidents resulted in net-pen escapements of approximately 1,500 tons, i.e., escapements from culture facilities were of the same magnitude as the entire annual harvest of wild
fish!

We focus our attention here on examples reported in the literature
that relate to the behavior under natural conditions of salmonid fish
bred in captivity. The examples are compiled from an extensive review
of the effects of aquaculture on natural fish populations (Hindar et al.
1991). At the time and point of release, the captive-bred populations
represent a broad variety of man-mediated genetic differences from indigenous populations. These differences include loss of genetic variability due to founder effects, inbreeding, preexisting adaptations to
other natural environments, and selection (intentional or unintentional) for adaptation to a captive environment as well as for economically

important morphological traits. In most cases it is impossible to tell the exact kind and magnitude of the genetic differences involved. Thus, these populations exhibit the genetic characteristics that typify many, if not most, captive-bred populations of a wide range of organisms (Arnold, essay 13 of this volume).

Table 15.1 presents examples relating to the fitness of introduced fish in relation to that of the local population. Two important points can be made. First, genetic factors appear to be important determinants in the performance of released individuals. Second, it appears that the genetic differences mediated by human involvement (whatever their kind) result in reduced performance in every case where a comparison has been made. The most frequent observation concerns reduced survival rates, which have been reported for a number of species including chum salmon (Altukhov and Salmenkova 1987), coho salmon (Nickelson et al. 1986), brown trout (Schuck 1948), Atlantic salmon (Ritter 1975), and rainbow trout (Reisenbichler and McIntyre 1977). In addition, modified behavior implying reduced fitness has also been noted for released fish (Norman 1987; Vincent 1960; Bams 1976).

It is noteworthy that we have been unable to find examples of improved performance of released fish. This does not reflect a conscious bias from our selection of references; rather, it appears to point to a lack of observations in the opposite direction (cf. Ricker [1972] for a similar conclusion). Naturally, this is by no means unexpected. Most local populations should be adapted to their particular environmental conditions, and it is very unlikely that any intentional or unintentional genetic manipulation would result in anything but poorer adaptation to those conditions.

Given that the genetic differences discussed above appear to result in reduced performance of a detectable magnitude, it is imperative to find out to what extent the genes involved are transmitted to the natural populations. Table 15.2 summarizes the examples relating to such introgression we have found in the literature. The most striking observation is that it appears to be very difficult to predict whether or not introgression will occur. Examples ranging from no introgression at all (e.g., Wishard et al. 1984) to complete introgression (Campton and Johnston 1985) have been reported within the same species (rainbow trout), and the releases appear to have been made under reasonably similar circumstances. The same variation of results has also been reported for the cut-

Table 15.1 Examples of observations relating to the fitness of introduced fish relative to that of the local population

SPECIES (REGION)	OBSERVATION	REFERENCE
Chum salmon (*Oncorhynchus keta*; Sakhalin, USSR)	Total stock size declines to 5% of original number after mass introduction of eggs from foreign stocks.	Altukhov and Salmenkova 1987
Coho salmon (*O. kisutch*; Oregon, USA)	Decline in juvenile densities in stocked streams despite high densities of wild plus stocked juveniles in the previous generation.	Nickelson et al. 1986
Brown trout (*Salmo trutta*; New York, USA)	Survival of wild fingerlings higher than that of hatchery produced fingerlings.	Schuck 1948
Rainbow trout (*O. mykiss*; Washington, USA)	Fry of wild origin have higher survival than either fry of hatchery origin or hybrid fry.	Reisenbichler and McIntyre 1977
Atlantic salmon (*S. salar*; Sweden)	Weaker territorial behavior in offspring from hatchery stock than from wild stock.	Norman 1987
Brook trout (*Salvelinus fontinalis*; New York, USA)	Offspring of domestic fish do not seek shelter and are less frightened by human presence than offspring of wild fish.	Vincent 1960
Atlantic salmon (Canada)	Hatchery-reared salmon have lowered survival when released in rivers other than their own.	Ritter 1975
Coho salmon (Oregon and Washington, USA)	Negative correlation between recapture rate and distance transferred from natal stream.	Reisenbichler 1988
Pink salmon (*O. gorbuscha*; Canada)	Lower straying rate in offspring from local stock than in either foreign stock or hybrid offspring.	Bams 1976

throat trout (*Oncorhynchus clarki;* Allendorf and Leary 1988), including cases where donor and recipient populations exhibit considerable genetic divergence. This variation in results is not confined to the genus *Oncorhynchus* but is also seen in the *Salmo* species native to the Atlantic Ocean (e.g., Vuorinen and Berg 1989; Ryman 1981; Taggart and

Table 15.2 Examples of observations relating to hybridization between released hatchery fish and local populations

SPECIES (REGION)	OBSERVATION	REFERENCE
Atlantic salmon (Norway)	Landlocked salmon not detectably affected by releases of offspring of anadromous salmon.	Vuorinen and Berg 1989
Brown trout (N. Ireland)	Released hatchery stock reproduces successfully and interbreeds with local stock.	Taggart and Ferguson 1986
Brown trout (Sweden)	Local genetic structure broken down, presumably as a result of releases of hatchery stock.	Ryman 1981
Chinook salmon (*Oncorhynchus tshawytscha*; USA and Canada)	Genetic homogenization in areas of intense culture; heterozygosity and number of alleles the same in comparable wild and hatchery populations.	Utter et al. 1989
Chum salmon (Sakhalin, USSR)	Significant gene frequency changes following mass introduction of eggs from foreign stocks.	Altukhov and Salmenkova 1987
Rainbow trout (Kootenai R., Montana, USA)	Some native populations persist in spite of introduced stocks; admixture also seen.	Allendorf et al. 1980
Rainbow trout (Yakima R., Washington, USA)	Local genetic structure represents an admixture of introduced and native stocks.	Campton and Johnston 1985
Rainbow trout (Washington, USA)	Little genetic differentiation probably a result of releases of hatchery stocks.	Reisenbichler and Phelps 1989
Rainbow trout (Idaho, USA)	Local genetic structure not detectably affected by introduction of hatchery rainbow trout.	Wishard et al. 1984

Ferguson 1986). It is apparent that any prediction of results is very difficult. Of course, this conclusion is not very surprising in view of our lack of knowledge of all of the genetic and environmental variables involved (figure 15.1).

These experiences from salmonid fishes strongly suggest that the genetic aspects of interactions between wild and captive-bred animals cannot be neglected. A very important observation is that the effects are of a magnitude that is actually detectable under field testing conditions. The situation is extreme in salmonid fishes because of the numbers being released, and consequently the statistical power for detection of the effects is greater than for many other organisms. In the absence of further knowledge, however, we must accept that such effects are probably generally prevalent even in species where smaller numbers are involved and where the effects may be more difficult or even impossible to detect at the level of statistical significance. Nevertheless, it is important that monitoring for such effects be a component of any release program.

HOW MUCH GENETIC INPUT CAN BE ALLOWED?

It is evident from the preceding sections that guidelines are needed with respect to the amount of input of genes from individuals bred in captivity into wild populations. Such guidelines are presently being requested by fishery agencies and have led to some legislation. It is imperative that such guidelines and legislation be based on proper scientific knowledge rather than on guesses or potentially misguided intuition in order to prevent actions that may be detrimental to the resources in question.

For example, recently passed legislation in Sweden limits the contribution of hatchery fish to about 10% of the total offspring (smolt) production of Atlantic salmon in a particular river (Anon. 1988). This seemingly restrictive guideline would, nevertheless, severely compromise the genetic integrity of the receiving (stocked) population within a few generations. New genes would be continuously added to the receiving population and thus replace the original ones (cf. Chakraborty and Leimar 1987). After ten generations this stocking rate (10%) would lead to the replacement of most of the genes of the original population by those from the donor population.

Similarly, a recently published Norwegian guideline limits the contribution of hatchery fish to the total population as a function of the effective number of parents producing the hatchery fish to be released (Korsen et al. 1988). This guideline pertains to a typical salmonid stock enhancement situation where the total production of offspring is enhanced by spawning some of the fish artificially and raising their offspring in a protective hatchery environment prior to their release. In this situation, no exogenous genes are introduced into the population; it is only a matter of increasing the survival of some of the parents' offspring.

There is, however, the possibility of reducing the effective size of the overall population and of altering the genetic characteristics of an excessively large fraction of the population through adaptation to the hatchery environment. In order to place a restriction on the total contribution of hatchery-reared progeny, Korsen et al. (1988) recommend that for n effective hatchery parents, a fraction ($0.5n\%$) of the total offspring production of that population is permitted to be of hatchery origin, i.e., thirty effective hatchery parents would result in a recommended maximum of 15% of the total juvenile production to be of hatchery origin. In the extreme case (but still realistic for many salmonid species), two hundred or more effective hatchery parents would allow the entire production to consist of hatchery fish. Among other consequences, long-term use of such a regime could result in the entire population being adapted to the artificial hatchery environment. We will return to the subject of genetic effects of this type of supportive breeding (i.e., without introducing exogenous genes) later in this section.

A clear scientific basis for both of the above guidelines appears to be lacking. Such potentially harmful recommendations are not only dangerous to natural populations of fish, they can easily radiate to other organisms once they become established within the fields of fishery management and fish population conservation.

INTROGRESSION

How much introgression can be accepted before the genetic characteristics of the natural population are compromised? For large and healthy indigenous populations, we see no apparent reason for permitting any artificial introduction of alien genes. Such an attitude, however, might lead to an unrealistically conservative strategy since a certain amount of spontaneous gene flow is occurring, or has recently occurred, among conspecific populations of many species (e.g., Slatkin 1987). From the perspective of genetic conservation, we consider it more realistic and biologically sound to relate acceptable levels of introgression to that occurring naturally.

Such a strategy implies that some means of estimating the degree of recent or ongoing gene flow is available. There are several complications associated with obtaining such estimates (e.g., Slatkin 1987; Waples 1987). Observations of actual migration may produce severely biased estimates in either direction. Gene flow may be underestimated in situations where migration is relatively infrequent and does not occur at the sites or during the period of study; it may be overestimated when actual migrants are less successful in reproduction than nonmigrants. Furthermore, such observations provide no information about past migration events pertinent to the issue of the degree of relatedness between populations.

Alternatively, the genetic effects of past and present migration may be estimated from observations of genetic differentiation patterns. These procedures are to some extent limited by the requirement that estimates must be based on neutral or nearly neutral genes. Further, the sampling properties of the parameters involved imply that multiple loci must be studied for accurate estimates (e.g., Allendorf 1983). Nevertheless, it appears that these kinds of estimates provide more accurate information about actual gene flow than can be obtained through direct observations of migrating individuals (Slatkin 1987). Of course, as much information as possible should be used to assess levels of gene flow, including actual observations of migration. But if different procedures yield widely different results, we recommend that the genetically based ones be considered the more appropriate in the context of genetic conservation.

The most commonly used procedure for estimating gene flow from genetic differentiation patterns is based on the so called fixation index (F_{ST}) of Wright (1943). This quantity is a measure of the variation of gene frequencies at individual loci, such that

$$F_{ST} = \frac{\sigma^2(p)}{\bar{p}(1 - \bar{p})} \qquad (15.1)$$

where $\bar{p}$ and $\sigma^2(p)$ are the mean and variance of gene frequencies among populations, respectively. (More recently, the quantity G_{ST}, that is largely equivalent to F_{ST}, has been introduced and is now more commonly used when combining information from multiple loci and alleles (Nei 1975)). When the homogenizing effect of migration (gene flow) is in balance with the diversifying effect of genetic drift, the amount of genetic differentiation at a selectively neutral locus is approximated by:

$$F_{ST} = \frac{1}{4Nm + 1} \qquad (15.2)$$

where N = the effective population size, m = the migration rate, and Nm is the number of effective migrants per generation (Wright 1969). Strictly speaking, the above relation between F_{ST} and migration refers to an island model of migration and a large number of populations (Wright 1943), but the approximation also appears quite robust under relaxed conditions (e.g., Nei 1987; Chakraborty and Leimar 1987; and references therein). It should be noted that it is the number of migrants (Nm) rather than migration rate (m) that is the critical parameter. This may appear counterintuitive but is the result of the balancing effect of migration and drift. A small number of migrants has little effect on a large population, but in such a population the effects of drift are small and need only a few migrants to be balanced, whereas the opposite is true for a small population.

In most cases the quantity F_{ST} between the donor and the recipient populations can be readily estimated from various biochemical genetic data sets (e.g., Ryman 1983; Waples 1987; Nei 1987). We suggest that the corresponding estimated number of migrants per generation (i.e., Nm) be used as a guideline for acceptable levels of introgression in the context of genetic conservation. It follows that such a strategy would result in a greater amount of acceptable gene flow between populations that are genetically similar than between more divergent ones. For example, an average F_{ST} (or G_{ST}) of 0.10, commonly observed between conspecific populations, would result in an estimated acceptable introgression rate of about 2 individuals per generation. Similarly, an F_{ST} of 0.01, a value less than that observed in most species, would correspond to an acceptable migration rate of about 25 individuals per generation.

It must be emphasized that even a very small amount of differentiation (e.g., F_{ST} = 0.01) permits only a quite limited amount (from a demographic perspective) of genetically effective migration under this guideline. Thus, it is evident that only minor levels of introgression can be accepted in any situation where conservation aims at preserving the characteristics of a genetically distinct recipient population. Moreover, it is obvious that we cannot discuss rates of introgression without relating them to the amount of genetic differentiation between the donor and the recipient populations. Finally, we are concerned with numbers of migrants rather than with rates of migration. Regulations such as the above-mentioned Swedish legislative recommendation of a maximum of 10% migrants should be avoided; limits or recommendations that do not relate to genetically meaningful parameters are dangerous in the context of genetic conservation because they provide a false impression of addressing conservation matters while actually failing to do so.

Our suggestion to relate acceptable levels of introgression to the observed amount of genetic differentiation should be considered a first attempt to establish a baseline recommendation for conservation of particular gene pools. Of course, we do not suggest that this recommendation be followed blindly without consideration of other available information. First, it must be stressed that a low F_{ST} value observed for presumably neutral loci does not necessarily imply an absence of genetic divergence at other loci that are subjected to natural selection (e.g., Chakraborty and Leimar 1987); thus, the estimate obtained via F_{ST} should be considered an upper limit to permissible migration. Second, F_{ST} is a measure of differentiation that relates to migration only under a particular set of assumptions and may not apply to many particular situations. Any additional pertinent information that may be available should, therefore, be used when attempting to assess the pattern of naturally occurring past and present gene flow between populations. Nevertheless, in the absence of such information, we suggest that decisions concerning acceptable levels of introgression be made on the basis of spontaneously occurring gene flow estimated from reliable genetic data using parameters such as F_{ST} or similar ones.

Supportive Breeding

A special case of genetic influence on the wild population occurs when a fraction of the breeders (or their offspring) are brought into captivity for purposes of reproduction or preferential survival. The offspring under these circumstances are released into the wild environment as soon as possible so that adaptation to the captive environment is minimized. In the present context we will refer to this practice as supportive breeding in order to stress that no exotic genes are introduced into the overall population. Supportive breeding is frequently practiced in wildlife management and conservation biology for the management of endangered populations and in fisheries management for the enhancement of particular wild stocks supporting commercial or sport fisheries.

In the context of genetic conservation, previously published recommendations on this kind of supportive breeding have focused on the need to identify the genetic structure within the region in question to assure that the appropriate population is targeted for propagation and release (Brambell 1977; Ryman et al. 1979; Ryman 1981; Ehrlich 1983; Sale 1986; Stromberg and Boyce 1986; Templeton 1986; Templeton et al. 1986; Allendorf et al. 1987; Lyles and May 1987; Allendorf and Leary 1988). There is, however, an additional aspect of supportive breeding that has as yet been largely unrecognized, namely, the impact on the genetically effective size of the entire (wild and captive) population being managed (see Ryman and Laikre [1991] for a more detailed discussion of this concept). Supportive breeding implies manipulating the reproductive rate of a segment of the overall population resulting in a change of the variance of family size, a parameter of critical importance to the genetically effective size of the population.

The relation between effective population size (N_e) and the variance of family size ($\sigma^2(k)$) is approximated by

$$N_e = \frac{4N - 2}{\sigma^2(k) + 2} \tag{15.3}$$

where N is the number of breeders (Wright 1931). Through increasing the survival rates of the artificially bred and reared segment of the population, $\sigma^2(k)$ is increased, which inevitably results in a reduction of the total effective size. The more successful the artificial breeding, the larger the effect on $\sigma^2(k)$ and N_e. Consider, for instance, a situation where an effective number of N_w wild individuals are reproducing naturally, N_c effective ones from the same population and generation are bred in captivity, and the captive-reared offspring are released to mix with the wild ones. In such a case the total effective size (N_e) of the wild and captive parents in combination is given by the relation

$$\frac{1}{N_e} = \frac{x^2}{N_C} + \frac{(1 - x)^2}{N_W} \tag{15.4}$$

where x is the relative contribution of offspring from the captive parents and $(1 - x)$ that of the wild ones (Ryman and Laikre 1991). Note that N_c and N_w refer to the effective numbers of parents, which may be substantially smaller than the actual numbers. For instance, an uneven sex ratio within either group of parents may reduce their effective number (N_p) according to the relation $N_p = (4 \times N_m \times N_f)/(N_m + N_f)$, where N_m and N_f are the actual number of male and female breeders, respectively (Wright 1931). Thus, a captive population of, say, 50 breeders consisting of 5 males and 45 females constitutes less than 20 effective parents.

Figure 15.2 reflects a situation that may exemplify a supportive breeding program in a threatened species. It is assumed that an effective

Figure 15.2 Total effective population size (wild + captive) when a natural population of 200 effective parents is supported by offspring from different effective numbers of captive parents (shown as different curves). The x-axis represents the proportion of offspring contributed by captive breeding.

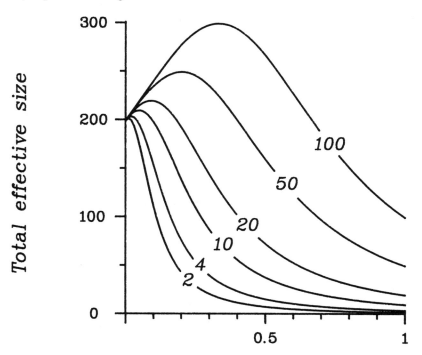

Relative captive contribution

number of 200 wild parents are reproducing naturally. To support this population, an additional number of individuals (N_c effective parents) are bred in captivity and their offspring released to supplement the naturally produced ones. The fraction of captive-reared offspring contributing to the overall number of offspring varies, and the resulting total effective size under this regime is presented as a function of this fraction of artificially produced progeny. The extremes of the curves indicate the respective total production of wild (on the left) and captive parents (on the right).

The total effective size equals the sum of the effective numbers of wild and captive breeders only when the offspring contributions are proportional to the effective sizes. In all other cases, the total effective size is smaller. More striking, and potentially more serious, is that supportive breeding can decrease the total effective number far below what it would have been without any supportive breeding at all. For example, consider a supportive breeding (captive) population of 20 effective parents contributing 40% of the total number of offspring; under these conditions, the total effective size is about 100, i.e., only half of that of the wild population alone.

Supportive breeding, particularly when it is successful, thus results in a trade-off. There is a gain in the total production of offspring, but there is a simultaneous reduction in the effective size of the total population that results in the loss of genetic variability (heterozygosity). In the above-mentioned example the loss of heterozygosity may not be considered very drastic when the effective size drops to 100, and the gain in overall production may be justified. When the absolute size of the wild population is small, however, as it is in cases where supportive breeding may be most warranted, supportive breeding may seriously affect the genetic variability of the overall population.

It is frequently recommended that a minimum of 50 effective parents be maintained in any wild or captive population in order not to result in too rapid a loss of genetic variability. For a population that is not substantially larger than this minimal number of 50, supportive breeding may lead to a serious depletion of genetic variability. We recognize that a one-generation boost of such a population through supportive breeding may be necessary to reduce the probability of extinction. Nevertheless, it must be realized that there is a cost associated even with such a one-generation amplification because the manipulation of reproductive rates may result in a genetic bottleneck, and the trade-off must be carefully evaluated. For instance, in such a situation it may be preferable to attempt to capture all of the wild population for a single generation multiplication, thus avoiding the differential reproductive rates of wild and captive parents.

Considering the above, it is instructive to reexamine previously mentioned published or legislative recommendations relating to supportive breeding. It is clear (figure 15.2) that recommendations such as the Swedish one stating that a maximum of 10% of the offspring may be of hatchery origin can be seriously disadvantageous to the population. Such recommendations fail to consider the effective numbers in both the wild and captive populations and may lead to unwanted genetic effects because they are based on parameters that are independent of, or only weakly related to, those determining the genetic characteristics of the population. The Norwegian recommendation of relating the proportion of offspring released into the wild to the effective number of captive parents represents a step in the right direction. Its failure to consider the effective size of the natural population, however, makes it similarly dubious in many situations. Although the concerns about supportive breeding are currently most evident in the context of fisheries management and fish conservation, they must be considered an important part of any captive breeding and release program.

CONCLUSIONS

We do not intend to advocate an excessively "purist" perspective (Soulé et al. 1986) with regard to gene flow or the release of animals bred in captivity. Clearly, there are situations where introgression might provide input of beneficial genetic material, for example, when a natural population has been genetically depleted over an extended period due to small population size. Similarly, when managing a group of closely related subpopulations, a small amount of migration has been suggested in order to ensure that a suitable level of genetic variation persists in all local demes while also allowing genetic differentiation among subpopulations in response to local selective pressures (Allendorf 1983; Nelson and Soulé 1987). Rather, we want to point out the potential danger that may be associated with thoughtless introgression through human intervention that violates the principal goals of conservation biology.

It has been proposed, for example, that hybrids between specifically adapted cultured fish stocks and wild populations could be used to add new genetic variation to wild populations and thereby increase the potential of the wild populations to adapt to conditions of environmental instability and genetic depletion (Moav et al. 1978; Wohlfarth 1986). Nelson and Soulé (1987) argue against this proposal, citing numerous instances where naturally adapted gene complexes of salmonids have been irreversibly compromised by introgressive hybridization with introduced exogenous stocks. They point out that while a very limited degree of introgression may provide a beneficial stimulus to a wild population through providing new alleles without destroying local adaptation, the loss of genotypic variance resulting from the massive hybridization of two populations is as irreversible as the loss of alleles from a population. Furthermore, it is not likely that cultured stocks possess advantageous alleles unavailable to a local population through immigrants from other wild fish populations (Reisenbichler 1984).

One of the basic purposes of this essay is to emphasize that there are numerous situations where gene flow from captive populations must be completely avoided, exercised with very great care, or at least closely monitored to permit the timely detection of possible negative effects. We consider monitoring to be a minimum requirement for any release program involving stocks that are of exogenous origin or that are otherwise genetically altered.

Monitoring that provides information on the genetic effects from interaction with wild populations can only come from observations of genetic change in those wild populations. Such observations require easily observed genetic differences between the wild and the captive populations so that invading genes are readily detected. Such genetic differences commonly exist (e.g., at protein coding loci), but they must be identified and quantified prior to any release if effective monitoring of the gene flow is to occur. It is therefore very important that adequate amounts of this kind of genetic information be available both for captive populations and for wild populations that may be affected.

Few, if any, populations bred in captivity have been established with the consideration of creating detectable genetic differences from wild populations. Such genetic differences, however, can often be straightforwardly induced without altering the important characteristics of the captive population (e.g., Fournier et al. 1984; Pella and Milner 1987; Parker et al. 1990, for examples relating to fish). Ideally, such "genetic marking" should be a requirement for captive populations that are not otherwise genetically identifiable. We consider this action the most important step to be taken if the genetic effects of the releases are to be understood in a timely manner. Without such a step, these effects will always remain conjectural, and we will never be able to produce anything but more or less meaningless speculations not based on empirical evidence.

A systematic monitoring of wild populations for gene flow can proceed once adequate genetic distinction exists between captive and wild populations. This process permits a posteriori actions following the detection of successful breeding of released animals. Details concerning the appropriate actions to be taken following the detection of gene flow to wild populations lie beyond the scope of this study. The detection of a substantial genetic intrusion into wild populations, however, is a very serious matter that requires immediate attention.

There are situations, of course, where genetic marking is superfluous or even inadvisable as a means of monitoring. One such situation is represented by the most idealized case of supportive breeding when no exogenous genes are introduced into the population and when the possibility of selection within the captive environment can be more or less safely ignored. In such a case, the major genetic concern refers to effective population size rather than to introgression. However, monitoring is nevertheless needed in such situations not only as a means of evaluating the fate of the released individuals but also as a way to obtain estimates of the relative reproductive success of wild and captive parents. Traditional physical marking procedures may be applied in such cases to provide information on parameters necessary for evaluating the genetic and demographic effects of the supportive breeding program.

Acknowledgments
The Swedish Natural Science Research Council and the Norwegian Directorate for Nature Management provided funding for Nils Ryman and Kjetil Hindar, respectively, during the preparation of the manuscript. The U.S. National Marine Fisheries Service provided office space and logistical support for Fred Utter.

REFERENCES

Allendorf, F. W. 1983. Isolation, gene flow, and genetic differentiation among populations. In C. M. Schonewald-Cox, S. M. Chambers, B. MacBryde, and W. L. Thomas, eds., *Genetics and Conservation*, pp. 51–65. Menlo Park: Benjamin-Cummings.

Allendorf, F. W. and R. F. Leary. 1988. Conservation and distribution of genetic variation in a polytypic species: The cutthroat trout. *Conservation Biology* 2:170–84.

Allendorf, F., N. Ryman, and F. Utter. 1987. Genetics and fishery management: Past, present, and future. In N. Ryman and F. Utter, eds., *Population Genetics and Fishery Management*, pp. 1–19. Seattle: University of Washington Press.

Allendorf, F. W., D. M. Espeland, D. T. Snow, and S. Phelps. 1980. Coexistence of native and introduced rainbow trout in the Kootenai River drainage. *Proceedings of the Montana Academy of Science* 39:28–36.

Altukhov, Y. P. and E. A. Salmenkova. 1987. Stock transfer relative to natural organization, management, and conservation of fish populations. In N. Ryman and F. Utter, eds., *Population Genetics and Fishery Management*, pp. 333–43. Seattle: University of Washington Press.

Anon. 1988. Fiskeristyrelsens kungörelse med föreskrifter och allmänna råd om utplantering och flyttning av fisk. *Fiskeristyrelsens författningssamling, FIFS* 1988:10. (Legislative note on release and translocation of fish. The Swedish National Board of Fisheries.).

Anon. 1989. *Fishing and Rearing of Salmon etc.* 1987. Oslo: Central Bureau of Statistics of Norway (In Norwegian, English summary)

Avise, J. C., J. Arnold, R. M. Ball, E. Bermingham, T. Lamb, J. E. Neigel, C. A. Reeb, and N. C. Saunders, 1987. Intraspecific phylogeny: The mitochondrial DNA bridge between population genetics and systematics. *Annual Review of Ecology and Systematics* 18:489–522.

Bams, R. A. 1976. Survival and propensity for homing as affected by presence or absence of locally adapted paternal genes in two transplanted populations of pink salmon (*Oncorhynchus gorbuscha*). *Journal of the Fisheries Research Board of Canada* 33:2716–25.

Brambell, M. R. 1977. Reintroduction. *International Zoo Yearbook* 17:112–16.

Campton, D. E. and J. M. Johnston. 1985. Electrophoretic evidence for a genetic admixture of native and nonnative rainbow trout in the Yakima River, Washington. *Transactions American Fisheries Society* 114:782–93.

Chakraborty, R. and O. Leimar. 1987. Genetic variation within a subdivided population. In N. Ryman and F. Utter, eds., *Population Genetics and Fishery Management*, pp. 89–120. Seattle: University of Washington Press.

Conant, S. 1988. Saving endangered species by translocation. *BioScience* 38:254–57.

Crow, J. F. and M. Kimura. 1970. *An Introduction to Population Genetics Theory*. New York: Harper and Row.

Endler, J. A. 1977. *Geographic Variation, Speciation, and Clines*. Princeton: Princeton University Press.

Ehrlich, P. R. 1983. Genetics and the extinction of butterfly populations. In C. M. Schonewald-Cox, S. M. Chambers, B. MacBryde, and W. L. Thomas, eds., *Genetics and Conservation*, pp. 152–63. Menlo Park: Benjamin-Cummings.

Falconer, D. S. 1981. *Introduction to Quantitative Genetics.* 2d ed. London: Longman.

Fournier, D. A., T. D. Beacham, B. E. Riddell, and C. A. Busack. 1984. Estimating stock composition in mixed stock fisheries using morphometric, meristic, and electrophoretic characteristics. *Canadian Journal of Fisheries and Aquatic Sciences* 41:400–8.

Griffith, B., J. M. Scott, J. W. Carpenter, and C. Reed. 1989. Translocation as a species conservation tool: Status and strategy. *Science* 245:477–80.

Hamrick, J. L. 1983. The distribution of genetic variation within and among natural plant populations. In C. M. Schonewald-Cox, S. M. Chambers, B. MacBryde, and W. L. Thomas, eds., *Genetics and Conservation,* pp. 335–48 and 500–8. Menlo Park: Benjamin-Cummings.

Hartl, D. L. 1980. *Principles of Population Genetics.* Sunderland, Mass.: Sinauer.

Hindar, K., N. Ryman, and F. Utter. 1991. Genetic effects of cultured fish on natural fish populations. *Canadian Journal of Fisheries and Aquatic Sciences* 48:945–57.

IUCN (International Union for Conservation of Nature and Natural Resources). 1987a. *IUCN Position Statement on Translocation of Living Organisms: Introductions, Reintroductions and Restocking.* IUCN Council, Gland, Switzerland, September 4, 1987.

IUCN (International Union for Conservation of Nature and Natural Resources). 1987b. *IUCN Policy Statement on Captive Breeding.* IUCN Council, Gland, Switzerland, September 4, 1987.

Kimura, M. 1983. The neutral theory of molecular evolution. In M. Nei and R. K. Koehn, eds., *Evolution of Genes and Proteins,* pp. 208–33. Sunderland, Mass.: Sinauer.

Korsen, I., J. Mork, O. Johansen, and A. Weiseth, 1988. Vurdering av kultiveringsvirksomheten, og bruk av stedegen fiskestamme till utsettinger: Instilling fra stamfiskutvalget. Report from Direktoratet for naturforvaltning, Trondheim, Norway. (In Norwegian).

Lyles, A. M. and R. M. May, 1987. Problems in leaving the ark. *Nature* 326:245–46.

Moav, R., T. Brody, and G. Hulata. 1978. Genetic improvements of wild fish populations. *Science* 201:1090–94.

Moen, V. and D. Gausen. 1989. Rømt oppdrettsfisk i vassdrag 1988. Direktoratet for naturforvaltning, Trondheim, Rapport 3–1989. (In Norwegian).

Nei, M. 1975. *Molecular Population Genetics and Evolution.* Amsterdam: North-Holland.

Nei, M. 1987. *Molecular Evolutionary Genetics.* New York: Columbia University Press.

Nelson, K. and M. Soulé. 1987. Genetical conservation of exploited fishes. In N. Ryman and F. Utter, eds., *Population Genetics and Fishery Management,* pp. 345–68. Seattle: University of Washington Press.

Nevo, E. 1978. Genetic variation in natural populations: Patterns and theory. *Theoretical Population Biology* 13:121–77.

Nickelson, T. E., M. F. Solazzi, and S. L. Johnson. 1986. Use of hatchery coho salmon (*Oncorhynchus kisutch*) to rebuild wild populations in Oregon coastal streams. *Canadian Journal of Fisheries and Aquatic Sciences* 43:2443–49.

Norman, L. 1987. Stream aquarium observations of territorial behaviour in young salmon (*Salmo salar* L.) of wild and hatchery origin. *Salmon Research Institute, Report.* 1987:2, Älvkarleby. (In Swedish, English summary).

Parker, N. C., A. E. Giorgi, R. C. Heidinger, D. B. Jester, Jr., E. D. Prince, and G. A. Winans, eds. 1990. Fish-marking techniques. *American Fisheries Society Symposium 7.*

Pella, J. J. and G. B. Milner. 1987. Use of genetic marks in stock composition analysis. In N. Ryman and F. Utter, eds., *Population Genetics and Fishery Management,* pp. 247–76. Seattle: University of Washington Press.

Reisenbichler, R. R. 1984. Outplanting: Potential for harmful genetic change in naturally spawning salmonids. In J. M. Walton and D. B. Houston, eds., *Proceedings of the Olympic Wild Fish Conference,* pp. 33–39. Port Angeles, Wash.: Peninsula College, Fisheries Technology Program.

Reisenbichler, R. R. 1988. Relation between distance transferred from natal stream and recovery rate for hatchery coho salmon. *North American Journal of Fisheries Management* 8:172–74.

Reisenbichler, R. R. and J. D. McIntyre. 1977. Genetic differences in growth and survival of juvenile hatchery and wild steelhead trout. *Journal of the Fisheries Research Board of Canada* 34:123–28.

Reisenbichler, R. R. and S. R. Phelps. 1989. Genetic variation in steelhead (*Salmo gairdneri*) from the north coast of Washington. *Canadian Journal of Fisheries and Aquatic Sciences* 46:66–73.

Ricker, W. E. 1972. Hereditary and environmental factors affecting certain salmonid populations. In R. C. Simon and P. R. Larkin, eds., *The Stock Concept in Pacific Salmon,* pp. 19–160. Vancouver, B.C.: H. R. MacMillan Lectures in Fisheries, University of British Columbia.

Ritter, J. A. 1975. Lower ocean survival rates for hatchery-reared Atlantic salmon (*Salmo salar*) stocks released in rivers other than their native streams. *ICES Ana. Cat. Comm. C.M.* 1975/M:26, Copenhagen, Denmark.

Ryman, N. (ed.) 1981. *Fish Gene Pools.* Ecological Bulletins (Stockholm) 34. Stockholm: Editorial Services, FRN.

Ryman, N. 1983. Patterns of distribution of biochemical genetic variation in salmonids: Differences between species. *Aquaculture* 33:1–21.

Ryman, N., F. W. Allendorf, and G. Ståhl. 1979. Reproductive isolation with little genetic divergence in sympatric populations of brown trout. *Genetics* 92:247–62.

Ryman, N. and L. Laikre. 1991. Effects of supportive breeding on the genetically effective population size. *Conservation Biology* 5:325–29.

Sale, J. B. 1986. Reintroduction in Indian wildlife management. *Indian Forester* 112:867–73.

Schuck, H. A. 1948. Survival of hatchery trout in streams and possible methods of improving the quality of hatchery trout. *Progressive Fish-Culturist* 10:3–14.

Slatkin, M. 1987. Gene flow and the geographic structure of natural populations. *Science* 236:787–92.

Soulé, M., M. Gilpin, W. Conway, and T. Foose. 1986. The millennium ark: How long a voyage, how many staterooms, how many passengers? *Zoo Biology* 5:101–13.

Stromberg, M. R. and M. S. Boyce. 1986. Systematic and conservation of the swift fox, *Vulpes velox,* in North America. *Biological Conservation* 35:97–110.

Taggart, J. B. and A. Ferguson. 1986. Electrophoretic evaluation of a supplemental stocking programme for brown trout, *Salmo trutta* L. *Aquaculture and Fisheries Management* 17:155–62.

Templeton, A. R. 1986. Coadaptation and outbreeding depression. In M. E. Soulé, ed., *Conservation Biology*, pp. 105–16. Sunderland, Mass.: Sinauer.

Templeton, A. R., H. Hemmer, G. Mace, U. S. Seal, W. M. Shields, and D. S. Woodruff. 1986. Local adaptation, coadaptation, and population boundaries. *Zoo Biology* 5:115–26.

Utter, F., P. Aebersold, and G. Winans. 1987. Interpreting genetic variation detected by electrophoresis. In N. Ryman and F. Utter, eds., *Population Genetics and Fishery Management*, pp. 21–45. Seattle: University of Washington Press.

Utter, F. M., G. Milner, G. Ståhl, and D. Teel. 1989. Genetic population structure of chinook salmon in the Pacific Northwest. *Fisheries Bulletin* (USA) 87:239–64.

Vincent, R. E. 1960. Some influences of domestication upon three stocks of brook trout (*Salvelinus fontinalis* Mitchill). *Transactions of the American Fisheries Society* 89:35–52.

Vuorinen, J. and O. K. Berg. 1989. Genetic divergence of anadromous and non-anadromous Atlantic salmon (*Salmo salar*) in the River Namsen, Norway. *Canadian Journal of Fisheries and Aquatic Sciences* 46:406–9.

Waples, R. S. 1987. A multispecies approach to the analysis of gene flow in marine shore fishes. *Evolution* 41:385–400.

Wishard, L. N., J. E. Seeb, F. M. Utter, and D. Stefan. 1984. A genetic investigation of suspected redband trout populations. *Copeia* 1984:120–32.

Wohlfarth, G. W. 1986. Decline in natural fisheries: A genetic analysis and suggestion for recovery. *Canadian Journal of Fisheries and Aquatic Sciences* 43:1298–1306.

Wright, S. 1931. Evolution in Mendelian populations. *Genetics* 16:97–159.

Wright, S. 1943. Isolation by distance. *Genetics* 28:114–38.

Wright, S. 1969. *The Theory of Gene Frequencies: Evolution and the Genetics of Populations*. Vol. 2. Chicago: Chicago University Press.

Index

Abedares National Park, xvii
Acinonyx jubatus (cheetah), 205,
296, 319; genetic variation in, 205
Actitis macularia (spotted sandpiper), 197
adaptation, to captive environment,
77, 303–13, 327, 346, 355
additive relationship matrix, 60
Allee effects, 318
Amazona villata (Puerto Rican parrot), 1
American Association of Zoological
Parks and Aquariums, 83, 115,
183, 284
Ammodramus maritimus nigrescens
(dusky seaside sparrow); population differentiation, 208
animal welfare, in zoos, 125
Anser caerulescens (lesser snow
geese); parentage determination in,
201
Anthias squamipinnis (coral reef
fish); genetic relationships in larvae
of, 202

artificial insemination, 281
Asian Rhino Action Plan, 281
Australasian Regional Association of
Zoological Parks and Aquariums,
284

bottlenecks, 117, 205, 296, 312, 359
British Federation of Zoos' Joint
Management of Species Group, 284

Canis rufus (red wolf), xix, 1
captive breeding. objectives of, 77;
for supporting wild populations,
355–59
captive breeding programs; Europäisches Erhaltungszucht Programm, 284; genetic management,
see genetic management; global,
289; international cooperation
among, 76, 284, 285; masterplans,
285; minimizing artificial selection
in, 303–13; objectives of, 283–84,
331–32; regional programs, 284;
role of, in conservation strategies,